Kinesiology 169 Diversity, Stress, and Health

Department of Kinesiology
San Jose State University

JONES & BARTLETT
LEARNING

World Headquarters
Jones & Bartlett Learning
5 Wall Street
Burlington, MA 01803
978-443-5000
info@jblearning.com
www.jblearning.com

Jones & Bartlett Learning books and products are available through most bookstores and online booksellers. To contact Jones & Bartlett Learning directly, call 800-832-0034, fax 978-443-8000, or visit our website, www.jblearning.com.

This book is produced through PUBLISH – a custom publishing service offered by Jones & Bartlett Learning. For more information on PUBLISH, contact us at 800-832-0034 or visit our website at www.jblearning.com.

Disclaimer

This publication is sold with the understanding that the publisher is not engaged in rendering medical, legal, accounting, or other professional services. If medical, legal, accounting, or other professional service advice is required, the service of a competent professional should be sought. The authors, editor, and publisher have designed this publication to provide accurate information with regard to the subject matter covered. However, they are not responsible for errors, omissions, or for any outcomes related to the use of the contents of this publication and make no guarantee and assume no responsibility or liability for the use of the products and procedures described, or the correctness, sufficiency, or completeness of stated information, opinions, or recommendations. Treatments and side effects described in this publication are not applicable to all people; required dosages and experienced side effects will vary among individuals. Drugs and medical devices discussed herein are controlled by the Food and Drug Administration (FDA) and may have limited availability for use only in research studies or clinical trials. Research, clinical practice, and government regulations often change accepted standards. When consideration is being given to the use of any drug in the clinical setting, the health care provider or reader is responsible for determining FDA status of the drug, reading the package insert, and reviewing prescribing information for the most current recommendations on dose, precautions, and contraindications and for determining the appropriate usage for the product. This is especially important in the case of drugs that are new or seldom used. Any references in this publication to procedures to be employed when rendering emergency care to the sick and injured are provided solely as a general guide; other or additional safety measures might be required under particular circumstances. This publication is not intended as a statement of the standards of care required in any particular situation; circumstances and the physical conditions of patients can vary widely from one emergency to another. This publication is not intended in any way to advise emergency personnel concerning their legal authority to perform the activities or procedures discussed. Such local determination should be made only with the aid of legal counsel. Some images in this publication feature models; these models do not necessarily endorse, represent, or participate in the activities represented in the images.

Cover Image: © Ivan Mikhaylov/Dreamstime.com

6048
Printed in the United States of America
18 17 16 15 14   10 9 8 7 6

Contents

The Nature of Stress

"Tension is who you think you should be. Relaxation is who you are."
— Ancient Chinese proverb

Are you stressed? If the answer is yes, then consider yourself to be in good company. Several recent Harris and Gallup polls have noted an alarming trend in the psyche of the American public and beyond—to nearly all citizens of the global village. Across the board, without exception, people admit to having an increasing sense of anxiety, frustration, unease, and discontent in nearly every aspect of their lives. From the events of September 11th and the 2007 Virginia Tech massacre to economic woes and global warming (e.g., Hurricane Katrina, heat-breaking records in the summer of 2007), the face of **stress** can be found everywhere. Sadly, episodes of suicides, road rage, school shootings, and personal bankruptcies are so common that they no longer are headline news. Ironically, in a country where the standard of living is considered to be the highest anywhere in the world, the Centers for Disease Control and Prevention estimates that nearly one-quarter of the American population is reported to be on antidepressants. Moreover, it is estimated that the average person has accrued between $5,000–8,000 in credit card debt (Gilson, 2007), and current estimates suggest that one in three people suffer from a chronic disease, ranging from cancer and coronary heart disease to rheumatoid arthritis, diabetes, and lupus. For a country with the highest standard of living, something is very wrong with this picture!

Furthermore, since the terrorism events of September 11, 2001, a blanket of fear has covered much of the country, if not the world, keeping people in a perpetual, albeit low, state of anxiety. Global problems only seem to intensify our personal stressors. It doesn't make a difference if you're a college student or a CEO of a multinational corporation, where you live, or how much money is in your checking account; stress is the equal opportunity destroyer! But it doesn't have to be this way. Even as personal issues collide with social and planetary problems creating a "perfect storm" of stress, we all have choices—in both our attitude and behaviors. This textbook will help you connect the dots between mind, body, and spirit to create positive choices that empower you to navigate your life through the turbulent waters of the human journey in the twenty-first century.

Times of Change and Uncertainty

Today the words stress and change have become synonymous and the winds of change are in the air. Changes in the economy, technology, communications, information retrieval, health care, and dramatic changes in the weather are just some of the gale forces blowing in our collective faces. By and large, the average person doesn't like change because change tends to disrupt one's comfort zones. It appears that the "known," no matter how bad, is a safer bet than the unknown. Change, it should be noted, has always been part of the human landscape. However, today the rate of change has become so fast and furious, without an adequate reference point to anchor oneself, that stress holds the potential to create a perpetual sense of uneasiness in the hearts and minds of nearly everyone. Yet it doesn't have to be this way. Where there is change, there is opportunity.

At one time, getting married, changing jobs, buying a house, raising children, going back to school, dealing with the death of a friend or close relative, and suffering from a chronic illness were all considered to be major life events that might shake the foundations of anyone's life. Although these major life events can and do play a significant role in personal upheaval, a new crop of social stressors has added to the critical mass of an already volatile existence, throwing things further out of balance. Consider how these factors directly influence your life: the rapid acceleration of technology (from software upgrades to Internet downloads), the use of (if not addiction to) the World Wide Web (e.g., Facebook.com), the proliferation of cell phone and WiFi use, an accessible 24/7 society, global economic woes (e.g., gasoline prices, subprime loan foreclosures, rent, food prices), global terrorism, carbon footprints, and public health issues from AIDS and West Nile virus to the latest outbreak of contagious staphylococcus infections. Times of change and uncertainty tend to magnify our personal stress. Perhaps the biggest looming concern facing people today is the issue of personal boundaries or lack thereof. The advances of high technology combined with a rapidly changing social structure have eroded personal boundaries. These boundaries include, but are not limited to, home and work, finances, nutritional habits, relationships, and many, many more, all of which add to the critical mass of one's personal stress. Even the ongoing war on terrorism appears to have no boundaries! Ironically, the lack of boundaries combined with factors that promote a fractured society, where people feel a lack of community and belonging, leads to a greater sense of isolation and this also intensifies our personal stress levels. Believe it or not, life wasn't always like this.

The stress phenomenon, as it is referred to today, is quite new with regard to the history of humanity. Barely a household expression when your parents were your age, use of the word *stress* is now as common as the terms *global warming* and *cell phones*. In fact, however, stress in terms of physical arousal can be traced back to the Stone Age as a "survival mechanism." But what was once designed as a means of survival is now associated with the development of disease and illness that claims the lives of millions of people worldwide. The American Institute of Stress (www.stress.org) cites the following statistics:

- 43 percent of all adults suffer adverse health effects due to stress.

- 75 to 90 percent of all visits to primary care physicians are for stress-related complaints or disorders.

Stress has been linked to all the leading causes of death, including heart disease, cancer, lung ailments, accidents, cirrhosis, and suicide. Some health experts now speculate that perhaps as much as 70 to 85 percent of all diseases and illnesses are stress-related.

Government figures compiled by the National Center for Health Statistics in 2004 provide a host of indicators suggesting that human stress is indeed a health factor to be reckoned with. Prior to 1955, the leading causes of death were the sudden onset of illness by infectious diseases (e.g., polio, rubella, tuberculosis, typhoid, and encephalitis) that in most cases have since been eradicated or brought under control by vaccines and medications. The post–World War II era ushered in the age of high technology, which considerably altered the lifestyles of nearly all peoples of every industrialized nation. The start of the twenty-first century has seen the influence of high technology dramatically alter our lifestyles. The introduction of consumer products, such as the washer, dryer, microwave oven, television, DVD player, laptop computer, and cell phone, were cited as luxuries to add more leisure time to the workweek. But as mass production of high-technology items increased, so too did the competitive drive to increase human effort and productivity, which in turn actually decreased leisure time, and thus created a plethora of unhealthy lifestyles, most notably obesity.

Currently, the leading causes of death are dominated by what are referred to as lifestyle diseases—those diseases whose pathology develops over a period of several years, and perhaps even decades. Whereas infectious diseases are treatable by medication, lifestyle diseases are, for the most part, preventable or correctable by altering the habits and behaviors that contribute to their etiology. Previously, it was suggested that an association existed between stress and disease. Current research, however, suggests that there may, indeed, be a causal factor involved with several types of diseases, particularly **auto-immune diseases** (Segerstrom and Miller, 2004). Regardless, it is well understood that the influence of stress weakens the body's physiological systems, thereby rapidly advancing the disease process. The most notorious lifestyle disease, coronary heart disease (CHD), continues to be one of the leading causes of death in the United States, far exceeding all other causes. The American Heart Association states that one person dies from heart disease every 34 seconds. Although the incidence of CHD has decreased over the past decade, cancer—in all its many types—continues to climb the statistical charts as the second leading cause of death. According to 2007 statistics from the American Cancer Society (www.cancer.org), cancer claims the lives of one out of every four people in the United States. Alarming increases in suicides, child and spouse abuse, self-mutilation, homicides, alcoholism, and drug addiction are only additional symptoms of a nation under stress. Today, research shows that people still maintain poor coping skills in the face of the personal, social, and even global changes occurring over the course of their lives.

Originally, the word *stress* was a term used in physics, primarily to describe enough tension or force placed on an object to bend or break it. Relaxation, on the other hand, was defined as any nonwork activity done during the evenings or on Sunday afternoons when all the stores were closed. On rare occasions, if one could afford it, relaxation meant a vacation or holiday at some faraway place. Conceptually, relaxation was a value, influenced by several religions and represented as a day of rest. The word stress as applied to the human condition was first made popular by noted physiologist Hans Selye in his book *The Stress of Life* (1976), where he described his research: to understand the physiological responses to chronic stress and its relationship to disease (dis-ease). Today, the word *stress* is frequently used to describe the level of tension people feel is placed on their minds and souls by the demands of their jobs, relationships, and responsibilities in their personal lives. Oddly, for some, stress seems to be a status symbol tied to self-esteem. Relaxation, meanwhile, has been transformed from an

American value into a luxury many people find they just don't have enough time for. With the current economic situation, some interesting insights have been observed regarding work and leisure. The average workweek has expanded from 40 to 60 hours. The U.S. Department of Labor and Statistics reports that, with more service-related jobs being created, more overtime is needed to meet the demands of the customers. Not only do more people spend more time at work, they spend more time driving to and from work (which is not considered work time). Moreover, leisure time at home is often related to work activities, resulting in less time for rest and relaxation. Downtime is also compromised. In a *New York Times* article (Egan, 2006) on the topic of the American vacation, Mike Pina, a spokesperson for the American Automobile Association (AAA), states: "The idea of somebody going away for two weeks is really becoming a thing of the past. It's kind of sad, really, that people can't seem to leave their jobs anymore." When they do, they take their BlackBerry devices and laptops (Quintos, 2007). Staying plugged in does not give the mind a chance to unwind or the body a chance to relax. Moreover, 40 percent of Americans canceled or postponed vacations because of work, with 574 million unused hours of vacation days being returned to employers (Lawlor, 2006). The "dividend" of high technology has proven to be an illusion that has resulted in a stressed lifestyle, which in turn creates a significant health deficit.

Definitions of Stress

In contemporary times, the word *stress* has many connotations and definitions based on various perspectives of the human condition. In Eastern philosophies, stress is considered to be an absence of inner peace. In Western culture, stress can be described as a loss of emotional control. Noted healer Serge Kahili King has defined stress as any change experienced by the individual. This definition may be rather general, but it is quite correct. Psychologically speaking, stress as defined by noted researcher Richard Lazarus is a state of anxiety produced when events and responsibilities exceed one's coping abilities. Physiologically speaking, stress is defined as the rate of wear and tear on the body. Selye added to his definition that stress is the nonspecific response of the body to any demand placed upon it to adapt, whether that demand produces pleasure or pain. Selye observed that whether a situation was perceived as good (e.g., a job promotion) or bad (e.g., the loss of a job), the physiological response or arousal was

very similar. The body, according to Selye, doesn't know the difference between good and bad stress.

However, with new psychoneuroimmunological data available showing that there are indeed some physiological differences between good and bad stress (e.g., the release of different **neuropeptides**), specialists in the field of **holistic medicine** have expanded Lazarus's and Selye's definitions as follows: Stress is the inability to cope with a perceived (real or imagined) threat to one's mental, physical, emotional, and spiritual well-being, which results in a series of physiological responses and adaptations (Chopra, 2000; Dossey, 2004). The important word to emphasize here is *perceived* (the interpretation), for what might seem to be a threat to one person may not even merit a second thought to another individual. For example, not long ago a raffle was held, with the winning prize being an all-expenses-paid one-week trip for two to a beach resort in Bermuda. Kelly, who won the prize, was ecstatic and already had her bags packed. Her husband, John, was mortified because he hated to fly and he couldn't swim. In his mind this would not be a fun time. In fact, he really wished they hadn't won. Each perceived the same situation in two entirely different ways. Moreover, with the wisdom of hindsight, our perceptions often change. Many episodes that at the time seemed catastrophic later appear insignificant, as humorously stated by Mark Twain when he commented, "I'm an old man and I have known a great many troubles, but most of them never happened." The holistic definition of stress points out that it is a very complex phenomenon affecting the whole person, not just the physical body, and that it involves a host of factors, some of which may not yet even be recognized by scholars and researchers. As more research is completed, it becomes increasingly evident that the responses to stress add up to more than just physical arousal; yet it is ultimately the body that remains the battlefield for the war games of the mind.

The Stress Response

In 1914 Harvard physiologist **Walter Cannon** first coined the term **fight-or-flight response** to describe the dynamics involved in the body's physiological arousal to survive a threat. In a series of animal studies, Cannon noted that the body prepares itself for one of two modes of immediate action: to attack or fight and defend oneself from the pursuing threat, or to run and escape the ensuing danger. What Cannon observed was the body's reaction to acute stress, what is now commonly called the **stress reaction**. Additional observations suggested that the fight response was triggered by anger or aggression and was usually employed to defend territorial boundaries or attack aggressors equal to or smaller in size. The fight response required physiological preparations that would recruit power and strength for a short duration, or what is now described as short but intense anaerobic work. Conversely, the flight response, he thought, was induced by fear. It was designed to fuel the body to endure prolonged movement such as running away from lions and bears. In many cases, however, it included not only fleeing but also hiding or withdrawal. (A variation on the flight response is the **freeze response**, often noted with post-traumatic stress disorder, where a person simply freezes, like a deer staring into a car's headlights.) The human body, in all its metabolic splendor, actually prepares itself to do both (fight and flight) at the same time. In terms of evolution, it appears that this dynamic was so advantageous to survival that it developed in nearly all mammalian species, including us (some experts now suggest, however, that our bodies have not adapted to the stress-induced lifestyles of the twenty-first century).

In simple terms, there are four stages of the fight-or-flight response:

Stage 1. Stimuli from one or more of the five senses are sent to the brain (e.g., a scream, the smell of fire, the taste of poison, a passing truck in *your* lane).

Stage 2. The brain deciphers the stimulus as either a threat or a nonthreat. If the stimulus is not regarded as a threat, this is the end of the response (e.g., the scream came from the television). If, however, the response is decoded as a real threat, the brain then activates the nervous and endocrine systems to quickly prepare for defense and/or escape.

Stage 3. The body stays activated, aroused, or "keyed-up" until the threat is over.

Stage 4. The body returns to **homeostasis**, a state of physiological calmness, once the threat is gone.

It is hypothesized that the fight-or-flight response developed primarily against threats of a physical nature, those that jeopardized the survival of the individual. Although clear physical threats still exist in today's culture, including possible terrorism, they are nowhere near as prevalent as those threats perceived by the mind and, more specifically, the ego. In a theory put forward by a disciple of Selye's, Simeons (1961), and repeated by Sapolsky (1998), it is suggested that, in effect, the fight-or-flight response is an antiquated mechanism that has not kept evolutionary pace with the development of the human mind. Consequently, the **stress response** becomes activated in all types of threats, not just physical intimidations. The physiological repercussions can, and do, prove fatal. The body enters a state of physical readiness when you are about to receive your final exam grades or walk into an important meeting late, just as it does when you sense someone is following you late at night in an unlit parking lot. Moreover, this same stress response kicks in, to the same degree and intensity, even when the threat is wholly imaginary, in reaction to everything from monsters hiding under your bed when you were 4 years old, to the unsubstantiated idea that your boss doesn't like you anymore and is out to get you.

Cannon noted the activation of several physiological mechanisms in this fight-or-flight response, affecting nearly every physiological system in the body, for the preparation of movement and energy production. These are just a few of the reactions:

1. Increased heart rate to pump oxygenated blood to working muscles
2. Increased blood pressure to deliver blood to working muscles
3. Increased ventilation to supply working muscles with oxygen for energy metabolism
4. Vasodilation of arteries to the body's periphery (arms and legs) with the greatest muscle mass
5. Increased serum glucose for metabolic processes during muscle contractions
6. Increased free fatty acid mobilization as an energy source for prolonged activity (e.g., running)
7. Increased blood coagulation and decreased clotting time in the event of bleeding
8. Increased muscular strength
9. Decreased gastric movement and abdominal blood flow to allow blood to go to working muscles
10. Increased perspiration to cool body-core temperature

Unfortunately, the metabolic and physiological changes that are deemed essential for human movement in the event of attack, pursuit, or challenge are quite *ineffective* when dealing with events or situations that threaten the ego, such as receiving a parking ticket or standing in a long line at the grocery store, yet the body responds identically to all types of perceived threats.

Tend and Befriend

Do women respond differently to stress than men? The answer may seem obvious.

Generally speaking, men are prone to act more hostile while women have a proclivity to be more nurturing. Yet until recently every source on stress addressed the fight-or-flight response as if it were the only human default response. It was the work of Shelley Taylor and colleagues that filled in the missing piece with regard to the female response to stress. Curious about why only men were studied to formulate the basis for the fight-or-flight response, Taylor hypothesized that the stress response needed to be reexamined, this time including astute observations of the female gender. In 2000 Taylor and colleagues proposed a new theory for the female stress response that they termed **tend and befriend**. Although both men and women have a built-in dynamic for the survival of physical danger, women also have an inherent nurturing response for their offspring as well as a means to befriend others. This in turn creates a strong social support system, an invaluable coping technique. Taylor suggests that the female response to stress is hardwired into the DNA and revealed through a combination of brain chemistry and hormones. The tend-and-befriend behavior is built on connectedness—a caregiving process, possibly triggered by a release of oxytocin in conjunction with female reproductive hormones, that may actually override the flood of stress hormones so pronounced in women's male counterparts. Generational social factors may support the tend-and-befriend behavior pattern as well.

Not only do men and women have differences in their stress physiology, but there appears to be gender-specific behaviors for discussing and solving problems as well. Whereas men tend to think their way through by looking for solutions to problems, women like to talk about problems. Women bond quickly by sharing confidences. However, although talking may be beneficial, researchers note that merely talking about stressors tends to perpetuate rather than solve one's stressors. Researchers refer to stress-based conversations as "corumination." Although talking may strengthen female friendships, it is also known to increase anxiety and depression if solutions aren't introduced quickly. Experts warn against "unhealthy rumination" and the emotional contagion that results from it (Stepp, 2007).

It is fair to say that the concepts of survival are complex and perhaps not so neatly packaged by hormones or gender. Women are known to back-stab their "friends" and regrettably, on occasion, ditch their newborn babies in dumpsters and run away. Conversely, some men choose peace over violence (Gandhi and Martin Luther King, Jr., come to mind) and, when times get tough, men are known to bond together over a beer or game of golf.

Types of Stress

To the disbelief of some, not all stress is bad for you. In fact, there are many who believe that humans need some degree of stress to stay healthy. The human body craves homeostasis, or physiological calm, yet it also requires physiological arousal to ensure the optimal functioning of several organs, including the heart and musculoskeletal system. How can stress be good? When stress serves as a positive motivation, it is considered beneficial. Beyond this optimal point, stress of any kind does more harm than good.

Actually, there are three kinds of stress: **eustress, neustress**, and **distress**. Eustress is good stress and arises in any situation or circumstance that a person finds motivating or inspiring. Falling in love might be an example of eustress; meeting a movie star or professional athlete may also be a type of eustress. Usually, situations that are classified as eustress are enjoyable and for this reason are not considered to be a threat. Neustress describes sensory stimuli that have no consequential effect; it is considered neither good nor bad. News of an earthquake in a remote corner of the world might fall into this category. The third type of stress, distress, is considered bad and often is abbreviated simply as stress. There are two kinds of distress: **acute stress**, or that which surfaces, is quite intense, and disappears quickly, and **chronic stress**, or that which may not appear quite so intense, yet seems to linger for prolonged periods of time (e.g., hours, days, weeks, or months). An example of acute stress is the following: You are casually driving down the highway, the wind from the open sunroof is blowing through your hair, and you feel pretty good about life. With a quick glance in your rearview mirror you see flashing blue lights. Yikes! So you slow down and pull over. The police car pulls up behind you. Your heart is racing, your voice becomes scratchy, and your palms are sweating as you try to retrieve license and registration from your wallet while rolling your window down at the same time. When the officer asks you why you were speeding you can barely speak; your voice is three octaves higher than usual. After the officer runs a check on your car and license, he only gives you a warning for speeding. Whew! He gets back in his car and leaves. You give him time to get out of sight, start your engine, and signal to get back onto the highway. Within minutes your heart is calm, your palms dry, and you start singing to the song on the radio. The threat is over. The intensity of the acute stress may seem cataclysmic, but it is very short-lived.

Chronic stressors, on the other hand, are not as intense but their duration is unbearably long. Examples might include the following: being stuck for a whole semester with "the roommate from hell," a credit card bill that only seems to grow despite monthly payments, a boss who makes your job seem worse than that of a galley slave, living in a city you cannot tolerate, or maintaining a relationship with a girlfriend, boyfriend, husband, or wife that seems bad to stay in but worse to leave. For this reason, chronic stressors are thought to be the real villains. According to the American Institute of Stress (AIS), it is this type of stress that is associated with disease because the body is perpetually aroused for danger.

A concept called the **Yerkes-Dodson principle**, which is applied to athletic performance, lends itself quite nicely to explaining the relationship among eustress, distress, and health. As can be seen in **Fig. 1 ▶**, when stress increases, moving from eustress to distress, performance or health decreases and there is greater risk of disease and illness. The optimal stress level is the midpoint, prior to where eustress turns into distress. Studies indicate that stress-related hormones in optimal doses actually improve physical performance and mental-processing skills like concentration, making you more alert. Beyond that optimal level, though, all aspects of performance begin to decrease in efficiency. Physiologically speaking, your health is at serious risk. It would be simple if this optimal level was the same for all people, but it's not. Hence, the focus of any effective stress-management program is twofold: (1) to find out where this optimal level of stress is for you so that it can be used to your advantage rather than becoming a detriment to your health status, and (2) to reduce phys-

ical arousal levels using both coping skills and relaxation techniques so that you can stay out of the danger zone created by too much stress.

Types of Stressors

Any situation, circumstance, or stimulus that is perceived to be a threat is referred to as a **stressor**, or that which causes or promotes stress. As you might imagine, the list of stressors is not only endless but varies considerably from person to person. Acute stress is often the result of rapid-onset stressors—those that pop up unexpectedly—like a phone call in the middle of the night or the discovery that you have lost your car keys. Usually the body begins to react before a full analysis of the situation is made, but a return to a state of calm is also imminent. Chronic stressors—those that may give some advance warning yet manage to cause physical arousal anyway, often merit more attention because their prolonged influence on the body appears to be more significant. Much research has been conducted to determine the nature of stressors, and they are currently divided into three categories: bioecological, psychointrapersonal, and social (Giradano, Everly, and Dusek, 2000).

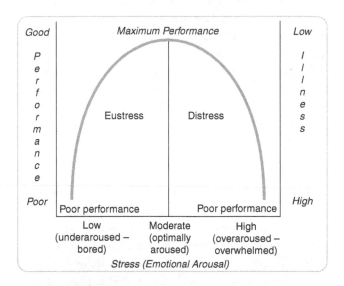

FIGURE 1 The Yerkes-Dodson curve illustrates that, to a point, stress or arousal can actually increase performance. Stress to the left of the midpoint is considered to be eustress. Stress beyond the midpoint, however, is believed to detract from performance and/or health status and is therefore labeled distress.

Bioecological Influences

There are several biological and ecological factors that may trigger the stress response in varying degrees, some of which are outside our awareness. These are external influences, including sunlight, gravitational pull, solar flares, and electromagnetic fields, that affect our biological rhythms. From the field of chronobiology we learn that these factors affect three categories of biological rhythms: (1) circadian rhythms, fluctuations in physiological functions over the course of a 24-hour period (e.g., body temperature); (2) **ultradian rhythms**, fluctuations that occur over less than a 24-hour period (such as stomach contractions and cell divisions); and (3) infradian rhythms, changes that occur in periods longer than 24 hours (e.g., the menses). These biological changes are influenced by such natural phenomena as the earth's orbit and axis rotation, which give us periods of light and darkness as well as seasonal differences. A prime example of a bioecological influence is **seasonal affective disorder (SAD)**, a condition affecting many people who live at or near the Arctic Circle. Many of these people become depressed when they are deprived of sunlight for prolonged periods of time. But technological changes are also included in this category, an example being jet lag as a result of airplane travel through several time zones. Electrical pollution, environmental toxins, solar radiation, and noise pollution are other potential bioecological influences. Genetically modified organisms (GMOs), petrochemicals, synthetic chemicals, and some types of nanotechnology are considered new bioecological threats. In addition, some synthetic food additives may trigger the release of various stress hormones throughout the body. Note that there is a growing opinion among some health practitioners that increased stress levels in the twenty-first century may be a direct result of our being out of touch with the *natural* elements that so strongly influence our body's physiological systems. In any case, some of these bioecological factors can be positively influenced by lifestyle changes, including dietary habits, exercise, and the regular practice of relaxation techniques, which bring a sense of balance back into our lives.

Psychointrapersonal Influences

Our current understanding is that psychointrapersonal influences make up the greatest percentage of stressors. These are the perceptions of stimuli that we create through our own mental processes. Psychointrapersonal stressors involve those thoughts, values, beliefs, attitudes, opinions, and perceptions that we use to defend our identity or ego. When any of these is challenged, violated, or even changed, the ego is often threatened and the stress response is the outcome. Psychointrapersonal stressors reflect the unique constructs of our personality, and in the words of stress researcher Kenneth Pelletier, represent "the chasm between the perceived self and the ideal self-image." Because these influences are the most likely to cause stress, they are a major focus of this book and great emphasis is placed on helping you manage your stress through learning and practicing effective cognitive coping techniques that aim to resolve stress-related issues. For this reason it becomes imperative to intercept the stress response in the mind before it cascades down as a rush of stress hormones into the body to cause potential damage.

Social Influences

Social influences have long been the subject of research to explain the plight of individuals who are unable to cope with their given environment. Most notable is the issue of overcrowding and urban sprawl. Studies conducted on several species have shown that when their numbers exceed the territorial boundary of each animal, despite an abundance of food and water, several seemingly healthy animals die off (Allen, 1983). This need for personal space appears to be universal in the animal kingdom. This includes humans, who likewise begin to show signs of frustration in crowded urban areas, traffic jams, long lines at checkout stands, or whenever their personal space is "invaded." The origin of this particular social influence may be instinctual in nature. Additional social causes of stress include financial insecurity, the effects of relocation, some technological advances, violation of human rights, and low socioeconomic status, to name but a few. New to the list of social influences are global warming concerns and water resource issues as the global population increases, taxing our very lifestyles with regard to scarcity issues.

Social influences related to stress also include major life changes. Two researchers who made significant gains in understanding the relationship between stress and disease through life changes were Thomas Holmes and Richard Rahe. Based on the Life Chart theory of Adolph Meyer, Holmes and Rahe set out to determine what events in people's lives were most stressful. Surveying thousands of individuals, they created a list of circumstances that represent typical life stressors, or events that require some adaptation or readjustment to a situation. Their list, with a total of 43 events, included several life events that, on the surface, appear to be positive, such as vacations, weddings, and outstanding personal achievements, as well as traumatic ordeals such as the death of a child. Then they devised a system to weigh each event according to its stress potential. All events were assigned numerical values based on their degree of disruption of one's life and readjustment following the event. These values were called **life-change units**, or LCUs.

The result of their efforts was an inventory called the **Social Readjustment Rating Scale (SRRS)**, which ranked the 43 life events from most stressful to least stressful. In further research using this assessment tool, Holmes and Rahe gave this inventory to several physicians and then compared their results with major health changes reported by the physicians. There was a significant correlation between life-event scores and personal health histories, with an LCU score of 150 being the point of demarcation between the exposure to major life stressors and health-related problems. With further analysis, they created categories based on LCU scores: 150–199 points suggested a mild life crisis, 200–299 points suggested a moderate life crisis, and any score over 300 points indicated a major life crisis. Based on the work by Holmes and Rahe, this survey and similar ones designed for special populations (e.g., college students) are now used to predict the likelihood of disease and illness following exposure to stressful life events. It is important to note that a high LCU score does not predict illness for all people, and this fact has led to criticism of research. It also shows the complexity of quantifying the stress phenomenon. Evidence indicates that in the face of repeated disasters, some people, by nature of their personalities, appear immune to stress.

Although major life events like getting married or relocating for a new job may be chronic stressors to some, renowned stress researcher **Richard Lazarus** hypothesized in 1984 that the accumulation of acute stressors or **daily life hassles**, such as locking your keys in your car, playing telephone tag, or driving to work every day in traffic, is just as likely to adversely affect one's health as the death of a spouse. These hassles are often based on unmet expectations that trigger an anger response of some type, whereas stressors of a chronic nature more often than not appear to have a greater association with fear and anxiety. Lazarus defined hassles as "daily interactions with the environment that were essentially negative." He also hypothesized that a balance of emotional experiences—positive emotions as well as negative ones—is necessary, and that people who have no exposure to life's "highs" or emotional uplifts are also susceptible to disease and illness. Further research by Lazarus (1983, 1984), Ornstein and Sobel (1989), and others has proved that his hypothesis has significant merit regarding stress and disease. As might be expected, the issue of lifestyle habits, changes, and hassles as social influences has come under attack by those who argue that perception or cognition plays an important role in the impact of stressors. Suffice it to say that all stressors, regardless of classification, are connected to human well-being in a very profound way.

The General Adaptation Syndrome

Following Cannon's lead early in the twentieth century, Hans Selye, a young endocrinologist who created a name for himself as a leading researcher in this field, studied the fight-or-flight response, specifically the physiological effects of chronic stress, using rats as subjects. In experiments designed to stress the rats, Selye noted that several physiological adaptations occurred as a result of repeated exposures to stress, adaptations that had pathological repercussions. Examples of these stress-induced changes included the following:

1. Enlargement of the adrenal cortex (a gland that produces stress hormones)

2. Constant release of stress hormones; corticosteroids released from the adrenal cortex

3. Atrophy or shrinkage of lymphatic glands (thymus gland, spleen, and lymph nodes)

4. Significant decrease in the white blood cell count

5. Bleeding ulcerations of the stomach and colon

6. Death of the organism

Many of these changes were very subtle and often went unnoticed until permanent damage had occurred. Selye referred to these collective changes as the **general adaptation syndrome (GAS)**, a process in which the body tries to accommodate stress by adapting to it.

From his research, Selye identified three stages of the general adaptation syndrome:

Stage one: **Alarm reaction.** The alarm reaction describes Cannon's original fight-or-flight response. In this stage several body systems are activated, primarily the nervous system and the endocrine system, followed by the cardiovascular, pulmonary, and musculoskeletal systems. Like a smoke detector alarm buzzing late at night, all senses are put on alert until the danger is over.

Stage two: **Stage of resistance.** In the resistance stage, the body tries to revert back to a state of physiological calmness, or homeostasis, by resisting the alarm. Because the perception of a threat still exists, however, complete homeostasis is never reached. Instead, the body stays activated or aroused, usually at a lesser intensity than during the alarm stage but enough to cause a higher metabolic rate in some organ tissues. One or more organs may in effect be working overtime and, as a result, enter the third and final stage.

Stage three: **Stage of exhaustion.** Exhaustion occurs when one (or more) of the organs targeted by specific metabolic processes can no longer meet the demands placed upon it and fails to function properly. This can result in death to the organ and, depending on which organ becomes dysfunctional (e.g., the heart), possibly the death of the organism as a whole.

Selye's general adaptation syndrome outlined the parameters of the physiological dangers of stress. His research opened the doors to understanding the strong relationship between stress and disease and the mind-body-spirit equation. In addition, his work laid the foundation for the utilization of relaxation techniques that have the ability to intercept the stress response, thereby decreasing susceptibility to illness and disease. Congruent with standard medical practice of his day (and even today), initial stress management programs were geared toward reducing or eliminating the *symptoms* of stress. Unfortunately, this approach has not always proved successful.

Stress and Insomnia

Muscle tension may be the number one symptom of stress, but in our ever-present, demanding 24/7 society, insomnia runs a close second. **Insomnia** is best defined as poor-quality sleep, abnormal wakefulness, or the inability to sleep, and it can affect anyone. Overall, Americans get 20 percent less sleep than their nineteenth-century counterparts. According to a recent survey by the National Sleep Foundation, more than 60 percent of Americans suffer from poor sleep quality, resulting in everything from falling asleep on the job and marital problems to car accidents and lost work productivity. Does your stress level affect your sleep quality? Even if you sleep well, it is hard these days not to notice the proliferation of advertisements for sleep prescriptions, suggesting a serious public health concern.

Numerous studies have concluded that a regular good night's sleep is essential for optimal health, whereas chronic insomnia is often associated with several kinds of psychiatric problems (MAAS, 2001). Emotional stress (the preoccupation with daily stressors) is thought to be a primary cause of insomnia. The result: an anxious state of mind where thoughts race around, ricocheting from brain cell to brain cell, never allowing a pause in the thought processes, let alone allowing the person to nod off.

Many other factors (sleep stealers) detract from one's **sleep hygiene** that can affect the quality of sleep, including hormonal changes (e.g., premenstrual syndrome, menopause), excessive caffeine intake, little or no exercise, frequent urination, circadian rhythm disturbances (e.g., jet lag), shift work, medication side effects, and a host of lifestyle behaviors (e.g., prolonged television watching, alcohol consumption, cell phone use) that infringe on a good night's sleep.

How much sleep is enough to feel recharged? Generally speaking, 8 hours of sleep is the norm, although some people can get as few as 6 hours of sleep and feel fully rested. Others may need as many as 10 hours. New findings suggest that adolescents, including all people up to age 22, need more than 8 hours of sleep (Dawson, 2008).

Not only can stress (mental, emotional, physical, or spiritual) affect quality and quantity of sleep, but the rebound effect of poor sleep can, in turn, affect stress levels, making the poor sleeper become more irritable, apathetic, or cynical. Left unresolved, it can become an unbroken cycle (negative feedback loop). Although many people seek medical help for insomnia and are often given a prescription, drugs should be considered as a last resort. Many (if not all) techniques for stress management have proven to be effective in promoting a good night's sleep, ranging from cardiovascular exercise to meditation.

The field of sleep research began in earnest more than 60 years ago. Yet, despite numerous studies, the reason why we spend approximately one-third of our lives in slumber still baffles scientists. From all appearances, sleep promotes physical restoration. However, when researchers observe sleep-deprived subjects, it's the mind—not the body—that is most affected, with symptoms of poor concentration, poor retention, and poor problem-solving skills.

Insomnia is categorized in three ways: transient (short term with one or two weeks affected), intermittent (occurs on and off over a prolonged period), and chronic (the inability to achieve a restful night of sleep over many, many months). Although each of these categories is problematic, chronic insomnia is considered the worst.

All-nighters, exam crams, late-night parties, and midnight movies are common in the lives of college undergraduates, but the cost of these behaviors often proves unproductive. Unfortunately, the population of people who seem to need the most sleep, but often gets the least amount, are adolescents younger than age 20.

Although sleep may be relaxing, it is important to remember that sleeping is not a relaxation technique. Studies show that heart rate, blood pressure, and muscle tension can rise significantly during the dream state of sleep. What we do know is that effective coping and relaxation techniques greatly enhance one's quality of sleep. (Throughout the course of this book, the topic of sleep will be addressed.)

Stress in a Changing World

All you need do is glance at the covers of *Time, Newsweek, U.S. News and World Report,* or the home page of your Internet browser (e.g., MSNBC.com) to see and read what we already know: These are stressful times! But the stress we are encountering as a nation is not specific to being a world power. The problem seems to have reached every corner of the planet, permeating the borders of every country, province, and locale. In fact, after conducting several surveys on the topic of stress and illness, the World Health Organization came to the conclusion that stress is hitting a fever pitch in every nation. So alarmed were they by the results of their study that the WHO researchers cited stress as "a global epidemic."

On the home front it appears that stress, like a virus, has infected the American population, and the symptoms are everywhere: Radio talk shows and blogs have become national forums for complaining; political pundits repeatedly describe voter anger; headlines are filled with stories of people who have gone berserk with hostility, most notably road rage, sports rage, phone rage, and air rage; television talk shows are reduced to airing personal catharses; workplace violence has escalated to several incidences per month in which co-workers are shot and killed; the American dream is out of reach for many; and psychologists describe a spiritual malaise that has swept the country. In 2001, a small but prophetic article titled "Bowling Alone," by Harvard political scientist Robert Putnam, sent ripples throughout the nation. Years of research led Putnam to discover that communities are disintegrating, as are the civic institutions on which communities are based. And in the landmark book *Emotional Intelligence,* author Daniel Goleman (1995) provides a dismal forecast with regard to the emotional state of this nation's children, a generation of youngsters raised on television violence. Yet where there is despair, there is also compassion. The devastating earthquake in China and the cyclone in Myanmar (Burma) in May 2008 and the devastation of Hurricane Katrina in 2005 brought out the best in some, as countless people came to the aid of their fellow human beings across the globe.

The sociology of stress can prove to be a fascinating study of interrelated factors that form a confluence of several recognizable stressors. Indeed, we encounter many social triggers daily, yet, at a closer look, the finger often points to our relationship with technology and our dependence on it. Whether it be BlackBerry devices, downloads, email, iPhones, teleconferences, beepers, YouTube.com, cell phones, or laptops, there is a growing dependence on the convenience of high technology and concerns of privacy. Current estimates reveal that we spend more time at work, leaving less time to be at home with the family, and we are now accessible 24 hours a day. What's more, with several years of corporate downsizing and restructuring, Americans are realizing for the first time that there really is no such thing as job security as many jobs become outsourced overseas.

Stress, it seems, knows no age, race, gender, religion, nationality, or socioeconomic class. For this reason, it is called "the equal opportunity destroyer," for when left unresolved, stress can undermine all aspects of your life. Although it may seem that stress becomes a critical mass in your life once you leave home and go to college, the truth is that the episodes and behaviors associated with stress start much earlier than the college years. Pressures in high school, even grade school, as evidenced by school shootings, cases of self-mutilations, MySpace.com issues, and insomnia are well documented. Combined with the stress of high technology, the effects are exponential. First let's take a look at high-tech stress and then focus on stress in the college setting, occupational stress, racial and gender stress, and finally stress and the retired population.

Technostress

As we begin a new century and millennium, a new term has taken hold in the American vernacular: **technostress**. It means to cope (or not cope) with the rapid pace of technology. The boom in the telecommunications industry and computer industry, pillars of the information age, have led to an overnight lifestyle change in American (and global) society. In their book *Technostress*, authors Weil and Rosen (1998) suggest that the rapid pace of technology will only continue with greater speed in the coming years, giving a whole new meaning to the expression "a remote-controlled 24/7 society." They predict, as do others, that the major-

ity of people, feeling overwhelmed, will not deal well with this change. The result will be more stress, more illness and disease, more addictions, more dysfunction, and a greater imbalance in life. There is a general consensus that the rate of change with technology has far outpaced the level of responsibility and moral codes that typically accompany the creative process. Change is happening so fast that the result has left many people without a reference point to stay grounded. The following are some aspects of technostress as they currently affect one's life and will continue to do so:

- *Information overload:* Among a flood of emails, text messages, satellite radio, Internet advertisements, pop-ups, instant messages, blogs, and voice mail, it is easy to become overwhelmed with the inundation of information, particularly emails. The time spent reviewing and responding to a slew of emails and voice mails, not to mention deleting spam and pop-up ads, can set one back several hours.

- *Boundaries:* Less than 20 years ago, there were clear-cut boundaries between one's personal and professional lives. Today the boundaries have dissolved to a point where it's hard to tell where one ends and the next begins. With cell phones, BlackBerries, and handheld computers, a person can be accessed every minute of the day. People feel compelled to take these devices to movie theaters, restaurants, and even on vacations. Although the expression "24/7" was first coined to refer to retail shopping, it now conveys non-stop accessibility.

- *Privacy:* With constant accessibility one forfeits privacy. However, with many purchases made on the Web, each person develops a consumer profile, which then is sold to a host of other vendors. From "cookies" to electronic/digital markers, privacy has become a real issue in the information age. With advances in reducing the microchip to the size of a molecule, information storage will go from the smart card to biotech implants.

- *Ethics:* With the completion of the Human Genome Project, scientists may be able to identify persons likely to inherit genetic-based diseases. Fear arises when this information falls into the hands of insurance companies that can revoke policies based on genetic profiling.

Although gene treatment therapy is currently in the experimental stages, another scientific breakthrough is genetic cloning, which carries with it many moral and ethical concerns, as does genetic research. Genetically modified foods (GMOs), where genes of herbicides, flounder, and nuts, for example, are placed in tomatoes, corn, and soybeans, are raising ethical issues as well. What are your thoughts on genetically modified or cloned foods? What ethical issues, if any, do you see with this technology? Would you eat cloned beef?

- *Less family time:* A recent study at Stanford University revealed that unlike television watching, which can be done as a family, surfing the Internet is a singular activity. Thus, people are spending more time on their home computers and less time with each other.

- *Computer dating:* As people spend more and more time plugged into their computers, they find less time for social activities. Many people turn to chat rooms to enter the realm of cyber dating. To this list we can add dating through MySpace.com, Facebook.com, E-harmony.com, and Match.com. Although many are happy to have this new venue to meet people and they have great luck with it, some find their expectations are left unfulfilled by people who falsely represent themselves.

- *Outdated technology:* What was once considered science fiction (cell phones on *Star Trek*) is now becoming a reality. It is suggested that with file formats like MP3, music CDs will soon become obsolete. VCRs have given way to DVDs, which in turn are giving way to Blu-ray discs. The money spent on these "toys" often goes down the drain in a short time.

- *Technology and the generational divide:* Are you constantly being asked by your parents to assist them with all things digital, such as helping to program their iPods and digital cameras, download music, install software packages, upgrade operating systems, or set up WiFi in the house? It's not an uncommon hassle among the younger generation, who feel like they are constantly on call for at-home/parental tech support.

Obviously, technology has tremendous benefits. The real key is to strike a balance. Are you frustrated by operating system upgrades, memory space issues, Facebook friends, or a daily flurry of emails or do you handle technology with great ease? Do you find your email and cell phone addictive at times or are you glad to have 24/7 accessibility? How do you strike a balance with the technology you use?

College Stress

What makes the college experience a significant departure from the first 18 years of life is the realization that with the freedom of lifestyle choices come the responsibilities that go with it. Unless you live at home while attending school, the college experience is one in which you transition from a period of dependence (on your parents) to independence. As you move from the known into the unknown, the list of stressors a college student experiences is rather startling. Here is a sample of some of the more common stressors that college students encounter:

- *Roommate dynamics:* Finding someone who is compatible is not always easy, especially if you had your own room in your parents' house. As we all know or will quickly learn, best friends do not make the best roommates, yet roommates can become good friends over time. Through it all, roommate dynamics involve the skills of compromise and diplomacy under the best and worst conditions. And should you find yourself in an untenable situation, remember, campus housing does its best to accommodate students and resolve problems. However, their time schedule and yours may not always be the same. For those college students who don't leave home, living as an adult in a home in which your parents and siblings are now roommates can become its own form of stress.

- *Professional pursuits:* What major should I choose? Perhaps one of the most common soul-searching questions to be asked in the college years is, What do I want to do the rest of my life? It is a well-known fact that college students can change majors several times in their college careers and many do. The problem is compounded when there is parental pressure to move toward a specific career path (e.g., law or medicine) or the desire to please your parents by picking a major that they like but you don't.

- *Academic deadlines (exams, papers, and projects):* Academics means taking midterms and finals, writing research papers, and completing projects. This is, after all, the hallmark of measuring what you have learned. With a typical semester load of fifteen to twenty credits, many course deadlines can fall on the same day, and there is the ever-present danger that not meeting expectations can result in poor grades or academic probation.

- *Financial aid and school loans:* If you have ever stood in the financial aid office during the first week of school, you could write a book on the topic of stress. The cost of a college education is skyrocketing, and the pressure to pay off school loans after graduation can make you feel like an indentured servant. Assuming you qualify for financial aid, you should know that receiving the money in time to pay your bills is rare. Problems are compounded when your course schedule gets expunged from computer records because your financial aid check was 2 weeks late. These are just some of the problems associated with financial aid.

- *Budgeting your money:* It's one thing to ask your parents to buy you some new clothes or have them pick up the check at a restaurant. It's quite another when you start paying all your own bills. Learning to budget your money is a skill that takes practice. And learning not to overextend yourself is not only a skill, but also an art. Most Americans owe an average of $5,000–8,000 on their credit cards (Gilson, 2007). At some time or other, everyone bounces a check. The trick to avoid doing it is not to spend money you do not have and to live within your means.

- *Lifestyle behaviors:* The freedom to stay up until 2 A.M. on a weekday, skip a class, eat nothing but junk food, or take an impromptu road trip carries with it the responsibilities of these actions. Independence from parental control means balancing freedom with responsibility. Stress enters your life with a vengeance when freedom and responsibility are not balanced.

- *Peer groups and peer pressure (drugs and alcohol):* There is a great need to feel accepted by new acquaintances in college, and this need often leads to succumbing to peer pressure—and in new environments with new acquaintances, peer pressure can be very strong. Stress arises when the actions of the group are incongruent with your own philosophies and values. The desire to conform to the group is often stronger than your willpower to hold your own ground.

- *Exploring sexuality:* Although high school is the time when some people explore their sexuality, this behavior occurs with greater frequency during the college years, when you are away from the confines of parental control and more assertive with your self-expression. With the issue of sexual exploration come questions of values, contraception, pregnancy, homosexuality, bisexuality, AIDS, abortion, acceptance, and impotence, all of which can be very stressful.

- *Friendships:* The friendships made in college take on a special quality. As you grow, mature, and redefine your values, your friends, like you, will change, and so will the quality of each friendship. Cultivating a quality relationship takes time, meaning you cannot be good friends with everyone you like. In addition, tensions can quickly mount as the dynamics between you and those in your close circle of friends come under pressure from all the other college stressors.

- *Intimate relationships:* Spending time with one special person with whom you can grow in love is special indeed. But the demands of an intimate relationship are strong, and in the presence of a college environment, intimate relationships are under a lot of pressure. If and when the relationship ends, the aftershock can be traumatic for one or both parties, leaving little desire for one's academic pursuits.

- *Starting a professional career path:* It's a myth that you can start a job making the same salary that your parents make, but many college students believe this to be true. With this myth comes the pressure to equal the lifestyle of one's parents the day after graduation. (This may explain why so many college graduates return home to live after graduation.) The perceived pressures of the real world can become so overwhelming that seniors procrastinate on drafting a resume or initiating the job search until the week of graduation.

For the nontraditional college student, the problem can be summarized in one word: balance! Trying to balance a job, family, and schoolwork becomes a juggling act extraordinaire. In attempting to satisfy the needs of your supervisor, colleagues, friends, spouse, children, and parents (and perhaps even pets), what usually is squeezed out is time for yourself. In the end everything seems to suffer. Often schoolwork is given a lower priority when addressing survival needs, and typically this leads to feelings of frustration over the inadequacy of time and effort available for assignments or exams. Of course, there are other stressors that cross the boundaries between work, home, and school, all of which tend to throw things off balance as well.

Race and Gender Stress

America has often been described as a melting pot, but recently another metaphor has been used to describe the makeup of her citizens: a tossed salad, where assimilation meets head-on with cultural diversity. Race and ethnic issues currently make headline news due to illegal immigration issues nationwide, disenfranchised black voters in Florida, poverty in New Orleans, and Muslim Americans facing episodes of discrimination. Ethnic and gender tensions, however, are not new. It could be argued that they are as old as humanity itself: the repeated persecution of Jews, the killing fields of Cambodia, ethnic cleansing in Kosovo, ethnic genocide in Rwanda, and now the war in Darfur (located in Sudan). Throughout history, it seems some people felt threatened by other people because of different skin color, ethnicity, gender, or sexual preference. Stress, you will remember, is defined as a "perceived threat," a threat generated by the ego. These threats manifest in a variety of ways including stereotyping, prejudice, discrimination, harassment, and even death. It starts early in life, too, as many children can attest to regarding school bullies, and it continues with middle school and high school cliques and social outcasts. The emotional stress associated with this type of angst includes low self-esteem, alienation, anxiety, and frustration. Everybody wants to feel accepted.

The 2008 presidential primaries drove home the point about race and gender issues with the top two Democratic contenders, Barack Obama and Hillary Clinton, vying for their party's single nomination. Although it started a national discussion, it did not resolve the issues of intolerance. Even television shows have tried to better reflect the demographics of American society, with such shows as *Lost* and *Heroes* containing a cast representing a variety of ethnicities. Although this is a step in the right direction, neither television shows nor presidential candidates can change the world overnight. Remember that when people demonstrate a bias toward race, gender, ethnic background, or anything related, they are projecting their fears on you. A common reaction is to meet stress with stress, but the best answer is to rise above it and take the high road.

Occupational Stress

Stress doesn't end with college exams and research papers. It seems to continue and perhaps increase as one continues on a career path. Paul Rosch, MD, director of the American Institute of Stress, notes that in U.S. society today, job stress is at an all-time high. He defines job stress as "occupational duties in which the individual perceives having a great deal of responsibility, yet little or no authority or decision making latitude" (1991).

In the first decade of the twenty-first century, more companies are merging, meaning more corporate restructuring. Companies looking to appease stockholders will look for ways to trim budgets, especially by letting go of senior employees and replacing them with a young and eager workforce, and outsourcing the rest of the jobs to India or China. According to the 2007 Stress and Anxiety Disorders Study, 73 percent of those questioned indicated significant stress from work. Few of these people take advantage of employee assistance programs offered at their worksites (Scott, 2007). The American Institute on Stress reports that job stress remains a concern, citing data from the 2001 Attitudes in the Workplace VII document where 80 percent of workers reported feeling on-the-job stress. One of the first signs of stress at the workplace is burnout, followed by absenteeism. For those who go to work but are unproductive and unmotivated, the term *presenteeism* was coined to describe this problem (www.wordspy.com).

The cost of stress is not insignificant in terms of work productivity or the bottom line of corporate profits. Rosch (1991) noted that the fiscal consequences of occupational stress cost an average of $200 billion each year. Moreover, between 60 and 80 percent of all industrial accidents are stress induced, as are more than 80 percent of all office visits to primary care physicians. Perhaps most striking is that workers' compensation claims associated with stress are skyrocketing, with 90 percent of claims being awarded in settlements.

What are some reasons for job stress? Although perceptions will vary from person to person, the following is a list compiled by the National Safety Council:

- Too much responsibility with little or no authority
- Unrealistic expectations, deadlines, and quotas
- Corporate downsizing, restructuring, or job relocation
- Inadequate training
- Lack of appreciation
- Inadequate time to complete job responsibilities
- Inability to voice concerns
- Lack of creativity and autonomy
- Too much to do with too few resources
- Lack of clear job descriptions
- Commuting and traffic difficulties
- Keeping pace with technology
- Inadequate child care
- Poor working conditions (lighting, noise, ventilation)
- Sexual harassment and racial discrimination
- Workplace violence

Rosch (1991) noted that in a recent study, the Public Health Service placed stress-management courses as its top priority in an effort to improve health standards at the worksite. However, Rosch, who surveyed several hundred existing stress-management programs in cooperation with the Office of Occupational Safety and Health, came to the conclusion that few stress-management programs currently taught in the corporate or industrial setting offer enough substance to make a positive influential change in lifestyle behaviors because they are too narrow in focus or too brief in duration. Those programs he did find to be effective showed reduced illness and absenteeism, higher morale, and increased productivity.

Stress and the Retired Population

A gold watch at age 65 was once a coveted prize as one transitioned from the career path to the vacation path of retirement, but not anymore. Loss of corporate pensions and benefits, decreased Social Security funds, ris-

ing health care costs, and jeopardized Medicare benefits leave one quite vulnerable. Several polls by the American Federation of Senior Citizens reveal that the biggest concerns seniors have today include health care and the economy, making ends meet financially, and maintaining a quality of life comparable to what they had prior to retirement. Seniors do not take their retirement lightly. Any lawmaker will tell you that one of the biggest and most powerful lobbying groups on Capitol Hill today is the AARP, a strong voice for people who intend to make sure their voice is heard well after they retire from the workforce.

As the baby boomer generation (which could include your parents or grandparents) starts to collect their first Social Security checks, many are realizing that retirement at age 65 may be a bit premature because of lost pensions or insufficient retirement funds. Those who do retire in financial comfort are not devoid of stress either. Studies of seniors reveal that those who place all their self-worth in their jobs, without any outside interests (e.g., hobbies), leave their job structures and quickly fall prey to disease and illness. Added to the stress of financial insecurity are the ever-changing dynamics of increased health problems, the deaths of close friends, the death of a spouse, changes in living environments, and the realization of one's own mortality. As the first wave of baby boomers begins to retire and becomes eligible for government-subsidized health benefits, the threat of these programs collapsing holds the potential to become a major life stressor.

Post-Traumatic Stress Disorder 101

There is stress and then there is STRESS! Although most people claim (even brag) to live stressful lives, the truth of the matter is that few people encounter truly horrific events of death and carnage. The repeated horrors of war, however, have notoriously ranked at the top of every list as the most unbearable of all stressors that anyone can endure psychologically—and for good reason. To quote Civil War General William T. Sherman, "War is hell." Exposure to these types of events typically include those that threaten one's life, result in serious physical injury, expose one to horrific carnage, or create intense psychological shock, all of which are so strongly influenced by the intensity and duration of the devastation either experienced or observed first hand. The result is an emotional wound embedded in the unconscious mind that is very hard to heal.

Every war seems to have its own name for this type of anxiety disorder. Somber Civil War soldiers were described as having "soldier's heart." Affected military personnel returning from World War I were described as being "shell-shocked," whereas soldiers and veterans from World War II exhibiting neurotic anxiety were described as having severe "battle fatigue" or "combat fatigue." The term post-traumatic stress disorder—more commonly known as PTSD—emerged during the treatment of returning soldiers from Vietnam who seemed to lack industrial-strength coping skills to deal with the hellacious memories that haunted them both day and night. This emotional disorder was first registered in the *Diagnostic and Statistical Manual of Mental Disorders* (*DSM*) in 1980 and has been the topic of intense investigation ever since. Sadly, the wars in Iraq and Afghanistan have provided countless case studies for this anxiety disorder today.

Although mortal combat ranks at the top of the list of hellacious experiences, one doesn't have to survive a suicide bomber in the streets of Baghdad to suffer from PTSD. Survivors and rescue workers of the World Trade Center and Pentagon catastrophes are known to still be dealing with this trauma, as are several thousands of people still displaced from the wrath of Hurricanes Katrina and Rita. Violent crime victims, airplane crash survivors, sexual/physical assault victims, and occasionally first responders (e.g., police officers, fire fighters, emergency medical technicians) are also prone to this condition. Given the nature of global warming and climate change and terrorism, it is suggested that PTSD may become a common diagnosis among world citizens, with the ripple effect affecting legions of friends, colleagues, and family members alike. Secondary PTSD is a term given to family members, friends, and colleagues who are negatively affected by the ripples of strife from loved ones (even patients) who have had direct exposure to severe trauma.

The symptoms of PTSD include the following: chronic anxiety, nightmares, flashbacks, insomnia, loss of appetite, memory loss, hyper vigilance, emotional detachment, clinical depression, helplessness, restlessness, suicidal tendencies, and substance addictions (MayoClinic.com). Typically a person suffering from PTSD has several of these symptoms at one time. Whereas the symptoms for some individuals may last months, for others PTSD becomes a lifelong ordeal, particularly if treatment is avoided, neglected, or shunned. The key to working with PTSD patients is to access the power of the unconscious mind by identifying deep-seated memories so that they may be acknowledged and released in a healthy manner rather than repressed and pushed deeper in the personal unconscious mind.

Specialists who treat patients with PTSD recommend that treatment begin as soon as possible to prevent a worsening effect. Initial treatment (intervention) is referred to as critical incidence stress management (CISM). The purpose of CISM is to (1) significantly reduce the traumatic effects of the incident and (2) prevent further deep-seated PTSD occurrences. Specific treatment modalities include eye movement desensitization and reprocessing (EMDR), counseling, and group therapy as a means to promote emotional catharsis. The Trauma Recovery Institute also cites art therapy, journal writing, and hypnosis as complementary coping skills for emotional catharsis. Many patients are also prescribed medications. Although medications may help reduce anxiety, it should be noted they do not heal emotional wounds. Whereas the nature of this book is not specifically directed toward those who suffer from PTSD, the breadth and depth of this book's content are found in all types of counseling and therapeutic modalities.

The Premise of Holistic Stress Management

Honoring the premise of this ageless wisdom, holistic stress management promotes the integration, balance, and harmony of one's mind, body, spirit, and emotions for optimal health and well-being. Stress affects all aspects of the wellness paradigm. To appreciate the dynamics of the whole, sometimes it's best to understand the pieces that make up the whole. What follows is a definition of each of the four aspects that constitute the human entity, and the effect that unresolved stress plays on each.

Emotional well-being: The ability to feel and express the entire range of human emotions, and to control them, not be controlled by them. Unresolved stress tends to perpetuate a preponderance of negative emotions (anger and fear), thus compromising emotional balance and causing the inability to experience and enjoy moments of joy, happiness, and bliss.

Physical well-being: The optimal functioning of the body's physiological systems (e.g., cardiovascular, endocrine, reproductive, immune). Not only does unresolved stress create wear and tear on the body, but the association between stress and disease is approximately 80–85 percent. Ultimately, stress can kill.

Mental well-being: The ability of the mind to gather, process, recall, and communicate information. Stress certainly compromises the ability to gather, process, recall, and communicate information.

Spiritual well-being: The maturation of higher consciousness as represented through the dynamic integration of three facets: relationships, values, and a meaningful purpose in life. Most, if not all, stressors involve some aspect of relationships, values (or value conflicts), and the absence, search, or fulfillment of a meaningful purpose in one's life.

The Nature of Holistic Stress Management

With the appreciation that the whole is always greater than the sum of its parts, here are some insights that collectively shine light on this timeless wisdom of the nature of holistic stress management:

- Holistic stress management conveys the essence of uniting the powers of the conscious and unconscious minds to work in unison (rather than in opposition) for one's highest potential. Additionally, a holistic approach to coping effectively with stress unites the functions of both the right and left hemispheres of the brain.

- Holistic stress management suggests a dynamic approach to one's personal energy where one lives consciously in the present moment, rather than feeling guilty about things done in the past or worrying about things that may occur in the future.

- Holistic stress management underlies the premise of using a combination of **effective coping skills** to resolve issues that can cause perceptions of stress to linger and sound relaxation techniques to reduce or eliminate the symptoms of stress and return the body to homeostasis. This is different from the standard practice of merely focusing on symptomatic relief.

- Holistic stress management is achieving a balance between the role of the ego to protect and the purpose of the soul to observe and learn life's lessons. More often than not, the ego perpetuates personal stress through control and manipulation.

- Holistic stress management is often described as moving from a motivation of fear to a place of unconditional love.

When all of these aspects are taken into consideration, the process of integrating, balancing, and bringing harmony to mind, body, spirit, and emotions becomes much easier, and arriving at the place of inner peace is easier to achieve. This book integrates all four components of the wellness paradigm, mind, body, spirit, and emotions. First, because it is so visible, we will look at stress from the physical point of view, including both the dynamics involved in fight-or-flight and the most current theories attempting to explain the relationship between stress and disease. We then focus on mental and emotional factors, outlining pertinent theoretical concepts of psychology: the stress emotions, anger, and fear, as well as specific personality types that are thought to be either prone or resistant to stressful perceptions. The much-neglected component of spiritual well-being will round out the first part of the book, showcasing selected theories of this important human dimension and its significant relationship to stress. The remainder of the book will focus on a host of coping strategies and relaxation techniques, and come full circle to the physical realm of wellness again, with positive adaptations to stress promoted through the use of physical exercise. As you will surely find, true to the wellness paradigm, where all components are balanced and tightly integrated, there will be much overlap between the physical, mental, emotional, and spiritual factors in these chapters because these factors are virtually inseparable. And just as the word *stress* was adopted from the discipline of physics, you will see that some other concepts and theories from this field are equally important to your ability to relax (e.g., entrainment). To understand the stress phenomenon accurately, it is important to see the human condition as one collective living system. Once this is understood, it becomes easier to manage stress effectively. It is my hope that the strategies in this book will enable you to access and enhance your inner resources, which in turn will enable you to design your own holistic stress management program. As Selye stated in his popular book, *Stress without Distress*, "I cannot and should not be cured of my stress but merely taught to enjoy it." The enjoyment comes from the ability to manage stress effectively.

The Power of Adaptation

One of the greatest attributes of the human species is the ability to adapt to change. Adaptation is the number one skill with which to cope with the stress of life. Adaptation involves a great many human attributes, from resiliency and creativity to forgiveness, patience, and many, many more. Given the rapid rate of change in the world today, combined with the typical changes one goes through in a lifetime, the ability to adapt is essential. Those who incorporate a strategy to adapt positively not only will be healthier, but also, in the long run, will be much happier. Adaptation to stress means to make small changes in your personal lifestyle so that you can move in the flow with the winds of change taking place in the world and not feel personally violated or victimized. Sometimes, adaptation to change means merely fine-tuning a perception or attitude. In the best stress management program reduced to 27 words, the following quote attributed to Reinhold Niebuhr speaks to this process: "God, grant me the serenity to accept the things I cannot change, the courage to change the things I can and the wisdom to know the difference." The skills introduced in this text are designed to help you gracefully adapt to the winds of change.

The Focus of This Text

The purpose of this text is to help you address the issues of stress from a holistic perspective: mind, body, spirit, and emotions. The aim is to assist you to resolve the causes of your stress, as well as help you relieve and minimize the physical symptoms that accompany the general wear and tear of everyday life. The goal of this text is for you to live your life from a place of balance, rather than feeling as if you are teetering on the brink of disaster. Restoring and maintaining a sense of personal balance are the underlying themes of this text.

The next four chapters highlight the unique relationship between stress and one's physical, mental, emotional, and spiritual well-being, respectively. In Chapter 5, a special emphasis has been placed on the most neglected component of the wellness paradigm, spiritual well-being.   addresses the topic of effective coping skills to initiate the resolution process, while   provides insights on a host of relaxation techniques to restore personal homeostasis.   invites you to design your own personal relaxation program.

Reading and learning the time-tested theories of stress management is one thing, but putting this wisdom to use is quite another. As the adage states, "To know and not to do, is not to know." Therefore, at the end of each chapter you will find one or several exercises to assist you in the process of moving from theory to the direct application of this knowledge, so you can begin to integrate these concepts fully into your life (see the exercises as the end of this chapter to get started). If you get one thing out of this book to make your life a little easier and help you adapt to one or more of the many life changes you are going through, then it's well worth it.

Chapter Summary

- The advancement of technology, which promised more leisure time, has actually increased the pace of life so that many people feel stressed to keep up with this pace.

- Lifestyles based on new technological conveniences are now thought to be associated with several diseases, including coronary heart disease and cancer.

- *Stress* is a term from the field of physics, meaning physical force or tension placed on an object. It was adopted after World War II to signify psychological tension.

- There are many definitions of stress from both Eastern and Western philosophies as well as several academic disciplines, including psychology and physiology. The mind-body separation is now giving way to a holistic philosophy involving the mental, physical, emotional, and spiritual components of well-being.

- Cannon coined the term *fight-or-flight response* to describe the immediate effects of physical stress. This response is now considered by many to be inappropriate for nonphysical stressors.

- There are three types of stress: eustress (good), neustress (neutral), and distress (bad). There are two types of distress: acute (short-term) and chronic (long-term), the latter of which is thought to be the more detrimental because the body does not return to a state of complete homeostasis.

- Stressors have been categorized into three groups: (1) bioecological influences, (2) psychointrapersonal influences, and (3) social influences.

- Holmes and Rahe created the Social Readjustment Rating Scale to identify major life stressors. They found that the incidence of stressors correlated with health status.

- Selye coined the term *general adaptation syndrome* to explain the body's ability to adapt negatively to chronic stress.

- Females are not only wired for fight-or-flight but also have a survival dynamic called "tend and befriend," a specific nurturing aspect that promotes social support in stressful times.

- The association between stress and insomnia is undeniable. The United States is said to be a sleep-deprived society, but techniques for stress management, including physical exercise, biofeedback, yoga, and diaphragmatic breathing, are proven effective to help promote a good night's sleep.

- Stress can appear at any time in our lives, but the college years offer their own types of stressors because it is at this time that one assumes more (if not complete) responsibility for one's lifestyle behaviors. Stress continues through retirement with a whole new set of stressors in the senior years.

- The rapid pace of technology may appear to make life simpler, but experts agree that the fallout, called technostress, will take its toll by increasing demands on both time and money, and decreasing personal time.

- Previous approaches to stress management have been based on the mechanistic model, which divided the mind and body into two separate entities. The paradigm on which this model was based is now shifting toward a holistic paradigm, where the whole is greater than the sum of the parts, and the whole person must be treated by working on the causes as well as the symptoms of stress.

- Effective stress-management programming must address issues related to mental (intellectual), physical, emotional, and spiritual well-being.

Additional Resources

American Heart Association. www.american heart.org.

Beckford, M. Working nine to five is becoming a thing of the past. *The Daily Telegraph*. May 4, 2007.

Brown, L. *Plan B: Rescuing a Planet Under Stress and a Civilization in Trouble*. New York: Norton; 2004.

Business Management Daily. U.S. workers using less vacation time, survey says. May 10, 2009. http://www.businessmanagementdaily.com/articles/18810/1/US-workers-using-less-vacation-time-survey-says/Page1.html#

Carlson, R. *Don't Sweat the Small Stuff*. New York: Hyperion Books; 1997.

Eisenberg, D., et al. Unconventional Medicine in the United States. *New England Journal of Medicine* 328 (1993): 246–252.

Eisenberg, D., et al. Trends in Alternative Medicine Use in the United States, 1990–1997: Results of a Follow-up National Survey. *JAMA* 280 (1998): 1569–1575.

Gallwey, W.I. *The Inner Game of Stress*. New York: Random House; 2009.

Gilson, D. House of Cards: Gambling with Credit Card Debt. *Mother Jones*. August 28, 2007. www.motherjones.com/news/exhibit/2007/09/exhibit.html

Hetler, W. *The Six Dimensional Wellness Model*. The National Wellness Institute. www.nationalwellness.org/index.php?id=391&id_tier=381. Accessed February 26, 2008.

Krugman, M. *The Insomnia Solution*. New York: Grand Central Publishing; 2005.

Lawlor, M. Take Your Time . . . Vacation Time, that is. *Signal Connections*. July 17, 2006. http://www.imakenews.com/signal/e_article000617059.cfm?x=b11,0,w

Levy, S. Facebook grows up. *Newsweek*. August 20, 2007, p. 41–46.

Luskin, F., & Pelletier, K. *Stress Free For Good: 10 Scientifically Proven Life Skills for Health and Happiness*. New York: HarperOne; 2005.

Maas, J. *Power Sleep*. New York: Quill Books; 2001.

Mayo Clinic. *Post-traumatic Stress Disorder*. www.mayoclinic.com/health/post-traumatic-stress-disorder/DS00246. Accessed February 26, 2008.

McEwen, B. *The End of Stress as We Know It*. Washington, DC: Joseph Henry Press; 2002.

Mitchum Report on Stress in the 90's. New York: Research and Forecast Inc.; 1990.

Moyers, B. *Healing and the Mind*. Public Broadcasting System; 1993.

Moyers, B. *Healing and the Mind*. New York: Doubleday; 1993.

Overworked Americans Can't Use Up Their Vacation. May 13, 2003. www.hrmguide.net/usa/worklife/unusedvacation.htm

Quintos, N. Vacation-deficit disorder. *National Geographic Traveler*. November/December. p. 22–27; 2007.

Rosch, P., president of the American Stress Institute, as quoted in 2003 Reuters Limited, www.msnbc.com/news/950045.asp

Salposky, R. M. *Why Zebras Don't Get Ulcers*. New York: W. H. Freeman; 1998.

Seaward, B. L. *Stressed Is Desserts Spelled Backward*. Berkeley, CA: Conari Press; 1999.

Selye, H. *The Stress of Life*. New York: McGraw-Hill; 1978.

Taylor, S. *The Tending Instinct*. New York: Owl Books; 2003.

Weil, M., & Rosen, L. *Technostress: Coping with Technology @ Work, @ Home and @ Play*. New York: John Wiley & Sons; 1998.

Wong, M. Vacationing Americans Have Given New Meaning to the Advertising Slogan, Don't Leave Home without It. *Associated Press*. September 1, 2000.

World Health Organization (WHO). 525 23rd Street N.W., Washington, DC 20037.

EXERCISE   1: Are You Stressed?

Although there is no definitive survey composed of 20 questions to determine if you are stressed or burnt out or just exactly how stressed you really are, questionnaires do help increase awareness that, indeed, there may be a problem in one or more areas of your life. The following is an example of a simple stress inventory to help you determine the level of stress in your life. Read each statement, and then circle either the word Agree or Disagree. Then count the number of "Agree" points (one per question) and use the Stress Level Key to determine your personal stress level.

Statement	*Agree*	*Disagree*
1. I have a hard time falling asleep at night.	Agree	Disagree
2. I tend to suffer from tension and/or migraine headaches.	Agree	Disagree
3. I find myself thinking about finances and making ends meet.	Agree	Disagree
4. I wish I could find more to laugh and smile about each day.	Agree	Disagree
5. More often than not, I skip breakfast or lunch to get things done.	Agree	Disagree
6. If I could change my job situation, I would.	Agree	Disagree
7. I wish I had more personal time for leisure pursuits.	Agree	Disagree
8. I have lost a good friend or family member recently.	Agree	Disagree
9. I am unhappy in my relationship or am recently divorced.	Agree	Disagree
10. I haven't had a quality vacation in a long time.	Agree	Disagree
11. I wish that my life had a clear meaning and purpose.	Agree	Disagree
12. I tend to eat more than three meals a week outside the home.	Agree	Disagree
13. I tend to suffer from chronic pain.	Agree	Disagree
14. I don't have a strong group of friends to whom I can turn.	Agree	Disagree
15. I don't exercise regularly (more than three times per week).	Agree	Disagree
16. I am on prescribed medication for depression.	Agree	Disagree
17. My sex life is not very satisfying.	Agree	Disagree
18. My family relationships are less than desirable.	Agree	Disagree
19. Overall, my self-esteem can be rather low.	Agree	Disagree
20. I spend no time each day dedicated to meditation or centering.	Agree	Disagree

Stress Level Key

Less than 5 points	You have a low level of stress and maintain good coping skills.
More than 5 points	You have a moderate level of personal stress.
More than 10 points	You have a high level of personal stress.
More than 15 points	You have an exceptionally high level of stress.

EXERCISE 2: Personal Stress Inventory: Top 10 Stressors

It's time to take a personal inventory of your current stressors—those issues, concerns, situations, or challenges that trigger the fight-or-flight response in your body. The first step to resolving any problem is learning to identify exactly what the problem is. Take a moment to list the top 10 issues that you are facing at the present moment. Then place a check mark in the columns to signify whether this stressor directly affects one or more aspects of your health (mind, body, spirit, emotions). Then, next to each stressor, chronicle how long it has been a problem. Finally, record whether this stressor is one that elicits some level of anger, fear, or both.

Stressor	Mental	Emotional	Spiritual	Physical	Duration of Problem
1.					
2.					
3.					
4.					
5.					
6.					
7.					
8.					
9.					
10.					

EXERCISE 3: Self-Assessment: Poor Sleep Habits Questionnaire

Please take a moment to answer these questions based on your typical behavior. If you feel your sleep quality is compromised, consider that one or more of these factors may contribute to patterns of insomnia by affecting your physiology, circadian rhythms, or emotional thought processing. Although there is no key to determine your degree of insomnia, each question is based on specific factors associated with either a good night's sleep or the lack of it. Use each question to help you fine-tune your sleep hygiene.

1. Do you go to bed at about the same time every night?   YES   NO

2. Does it take you more than 30 minutes to fall asleep once in bed?   YES   NO

3. Do you wake up at about the same time every day?   YES   NO

4. Do you drink coffee, tea, or caffeinated soda after 6 p.m.?   YES   NO

5. Do you watch television from your bed?   YES   NO

6. Do you perform cardiovascular exercise 3–5 times per week?   YES   NO

7. Do you use your bed as your office (e.g., homework, balance checkbook, write letters)?   YES   NO

8. Do you take a hot shower or bath before you go to sleep?   YES   NO

9. Do you have one or more drinks of alcohol before bedtime?   YES   NO

10. Are you engaged in intense mental activity before bed (e.g., term papers, exams, projects, reports, finances, taxes)?   YES   NO

11. Is your bedroom typically warm or even hot before you go to bed?   YES   NO

12. Does your sleep partner snore, become restless, etc., in the night?   YES   NO

13. Is the size and comfort level of your bed satisfactory?   YES   NO

14. Do you suffer from chronic pain while laying down?   YES   NO

15. Is your sleep environment compromised by noise, light, or pets?   YES   NO

16. Do you frequently take naps during the course of a day?   YES   NO

17. Do you take medications (e.g., decongestants, steroids, antihypertensives, asthma medications, for depression)?   YES   NO

18. Do you tend to suffer from depression?   YES   NO

19. Do you eat a large heavy meal right before you go to bed?   YES   NO

20. Do you use a cell phone regularly, particularly in the evening?   YES   NO

Photo Credits

Unless otherwise indicated, all photographs and illustrations are under copyright of Jones and Bartlett Publishers, LLC, or have been provided by the author.

Brian Luke Seaward, Essentials of Managing Stress, Second Edition, 2011

The Body: The Battlefield for the Mind's War Games

"The immune system does not reside solely in the body."

— Patricia Norris, PhD

Here is a startling statistic: More than 80 percent of patients' visits to physicians' offices are associated with stress (unresolved issues of anger and fear). Moreover, 80 percent of worker's compensation claims are directly related to stress. Here is another statistic: Researchers in the field of psychoneuroimmunology (PNI) and energy healing not only suggest that as much as 85 percent of illness and disease is associated with stress, but also note a direct causal link, giving a new perspective on the word *dis-ease*. Anyone who has ever suffered a tension headache knows intuitively how strong the mind-body connection really is.

Today, it is well documented that stress aggravates several health conditions, particularly Type II diabetes and rheumatoid arthritis. Furthermore, many diseases, such as lupus, fibromyalgia, Epstein-Barr, rheumatoid arthritis, and Type I diabetes, are now thought to have an autoimmune component to them. The list of stress-related illnesses continues to grow, from herpes and hemorrhoids to the common cold, cancer, and practically everything in between. Pharmaceuticals and surgery are the two tools of the trade used in Western (allopathic) medicine, yet the trade-offs can include severe side effects. This is one reason why so many people are turning to complementary forms of alternative healing for chronic health problems.

Prior to the discovery of vaccinations and antibiotics, the leading cause of death was infectious diseases. Today the leading causes of death are lifestyle diseases (e.g., most cancers, diabetes, obesity, strokes, coronary heart disease), all of which have a strong stress component to them. Moreover, an increasing number of people suffer from chronic pain that ranges from bothersome discomfort to complete immobility. The Western model of health care (which some people label as "sick care") places a strong focus on symptomatic relief rather than prevention and healing restoration. As we are now learning, the most advantageous approach appears to combine the best of allopathic and holistic healing to address both the causes and symptoms of stress that will return one back to homeostasis, turning the battleground into a peaceful landscape. Exercise 1 is a personal stress inventory to help you determine any association between stress and symptoms of stress in your body.

Stress and Chronic Pain

In addition to issues related to chronic disease, an increasing number of Americans suffer from debilitating chronic pain. Muscular pain associated with the lower back, hips, shoulders, and neck is a constant nightmare, so much so that it steals your attention from practically everything else. The connection between stress and chronic pain cannot be ignored. Neither can the connection between stress and obesity. All of these factors are tightly integrated. It may come as no surprise that many of the coping and relaxation techniques in the cadre of holistic stress management used to maintain health and well-being are well-documented as a means to help restore a sense of homeostasis as well.

Your Human Space Suit

Renowned inventor and philosopher Buckminster Fuller once said that the human body is our one and only space suit in which to inhabit the planet Earth. It comes with its own oxygen tank, a metabolic waste removal system, a sensory detector system to enjoy all the pleasures of planetary exploration, and an immune defense system to ensure the health of the space suit in the occasionally harsh global environment. This specially designed space suit also is equipped with a unique program for self-healing. Factors associated with this self-healing process include the basic common health behaviors associated with longevity: regular physical exercise, proper nutrition, adequate sleep, the avoidance of drugs, and a supportive community of friends and family. Unfortunately, most people don't take good care of their space suits and many have forgotten the means to activate the program for self-healing.

Fight-or-Flight with a Bite

The fight-or-flight response may begin with a perception in the mind, but this thought process quickly becomes a series of neurological and chemical reactions in the body. In the blink of an eye, the nervous system releases epinephrine and norepinephrine throughout the body for immediate blood redistribution and muscle contraction. At the same time, a flood of hormones prepares the body for immediate and long-term metabolic survival. Similar to the cascade of a waterfall, hormones are secreted from the brain's pituitary and hypothalamus glands as messengers moving quickly downstream to the adrenal gland (cone-shaped organs that sit atop each kidney). Upon command, cortisol, aldosterone, and other glucocorticoids infiltrate the bloodstream to do their jobs, all in the name of physical survival.

What works well for acute stress can cause serious problems with chronic stress. Repeated synthesis and release of these stress hormones day after day (the consequence of prolonged bouts of unresolved stress issues) can literally wreak havoc on the physical body. In essence, the body becomes the battlefield for the war games of the mind.

Gross Anatomy and Physiology

Your body is composed of a network of several amazing systems that work together as an alliance for the necessary functions of all daily life activities. For centuries, these aspects were identified as nine separate systems living under the anatomical structure of the human body. Now most health experts agree (through the wisdom of PNI) that this is truly one system, with the whole always being greater than the sum of the parts. The parts are the musculoskeletal system, nervous system, cardiovascular system, pulmonary system, endocrine system, reproductive system, renal system, digestive system, and immune system. If you have a health problem with one of these systems initially, eventually all other systems become directly affected. In union with this "one system" are the many anatomical organs responsible for the integrity of its work, including, but not limited to, the heart, lungs, kidneys, liver, stomach, pancreas, brain, and lymph nodes. Physical well-being is often described as the optimal functioning of all of these physiological systems. What comes to mind when you hear the expression "the picture of health"? For most people this conjures up an image of a physically fit person enjoying some rigorous outdoor activity well into their later years. Sadly, this has now become an image few can relate to. Stress not only can affect the optimal functioning of all of these physiological systems to destroy the picture of health, but also can literally shut down the entire body. Simply stated: Left unresolved, stress kills! Exercise 2 is a questionnaire that brings to your attention the health habits that make a composite of your current health picture.

Subtle Anatomy and Physiology

Equally important, yet often less obvious than gross anatomy, are three other systems critical to the operations of the human space suit. These are more commonly known as **subtle anatomy** and physiology, and they are the human energy field, the meridian system, and the chakra system. A holistic perspective of health would be incomplete without mentioning this aspect of health. The following sections provide a more detailed look at the aspects of our subtle anatomy and physiology.

The Human Energy Field

Western science has recently discovered that the human body has a unique field of electromagnetic energy that not only surrounds, but also permeates the entire body. Often called the "human aura" by mystics, it is the basis of Kirlian photography and the diagnosis of disease through magnetic resonance imaging (MRI). Ageless wisdom notes that there are many layers of the **human energy field**, with each layer associated with some aspect of consciousness (e.g., instinct, intellect, intuition, emotions). This and other findings support the timeless premise that our mind isn't located in our body. Instead, our body is located in our mind!

Each layer of consciousness in the human energy field is considered a harmonic vibration. Like keys on a piano keyboard, the frequency of the body's vibrations, and that of the emotional, mental, and spiritual fields, are set at different octaves, yet are within the harmonic range of each other. If a thought coupled with an emotion is left unresolved, it can cause dissonance or imbalance within the layers of energy in the aura. Distortion first appears in the aura outside the physical body. When left unresolved, these emotional frequencies cascade through the layers of energy (which include the chakras and meridians) to pool within various cell tissues. The end result is dysfunction in the corresponding area in the physical body. Dissonance (the opposite of resonance) eventually appears at the cellular level, and the once harmonic vibration is no longer tuned to homeostasis, hence, setting the stage for disease and illness. Medical intuitives including Mona Lisa Schulz, MD; Judith Orloff, MD; Caroline Myss; Donna Eden; Mietek Wirkus; and others describe the initial stage of illness and disease as unresolved emotions (e.g., anger or fear). Through this model of well-being, disease develops outside the body and filters down through the layers of energy. Ironically, physical symptoms in the body are not the first signs of illness, but the last. The body indeed becomes the battlefield for the war games of the mind.

The Meridian System

First brought to the world's attention through the ancient Chinese culture, the physical body holds 12 rivers (**meridians**) of energy or *chi*. Each meridian connects to one or more vital organs (e.g., heart, lungs, liver, kidneys). When energy is blocked or congested in any meridian, the health of the associated organ will suffer. Acupuncture is the primary modality used to ensure the free flow of energy through these meridians, by placing tiny bulblike needles at various gates (acupuncture points) along the meridian pathways to unblock energy congestion. Acupressure (also known as shiatsu) is another method used for energy regulation. Although Western medicine doesn't quite acknowledge the concept of chi or meridians, it does recognize many remarkable outcomes of acupuncture (without side effects) in the treatment of chronic illnesses, in which Western medicine itself has proven less than effective.

The Chakra Energy System

The human body is said to have seven major energy portals. The ancient Sanskrit word for these energy portals is *chakra*, which translates to mean "spinning wheel," and looks like a small tornado attached to the body. Like the meridian energy system, each **chakra** is associated with the health of vital organs specific to the region to which it's attached. When the chakra shows signs of congestion or distortion, then the life force of energy through the chakra cannot be maintained in its specific region, and the health of those organs is compromised. Each chakra is associated with not only a body region, but also a layer of consciousness in the human energy field, directly linking mind, body, and spirit. Exercise 3 explores the concept of chakras and your health status.

The science behind subtle energy provides valuable insight into a problem that has vexed Western health experts who study the area of stress and disease: Why is it that two people who go through a similar stressful experience can contract different chronic illnesses? The answer may appear to be strongly associated with the dynamics of the chakra energy system. The following is a brief summary of the seven primary chakras.

First Chakra. The first chakra is commonly known as the root chakra and is located at the base of the spine. The root chakra is associated with issues of safety and security. There is also a relationship with our connectedness to the earth and feelings of groundedness. The root chakra is tied energetically to some organs of the reproductive system, as well as the hip joints, lower back, and pelvic area. Health problems in these areas, including lower-back pain, sciatica, rectal difficulties, and some cancers (e.g., prostate), are thought to correspond to disturbances with the root chakra. The root chakra is also known as the seat of the Kundalini energy, a spiritually based concept yet to be understood in Western culture.

Second Chakra. The second chakra, also known as the sacral chakra, is recognized as being associated with the sex organs, as well as personal power in terms of business and social relationships. The second chakra deals with emotional feelings associated with issues of sexuality and self-worth. When self-worth is viewed through external means such as money, job, or sexuality, this causes an energy distortion in this region. Obsessiveness with material gain is thought to be a means to compensate for low self-worth, hence a distortion to this chakra. Common symptoms associated with this chakra region may include menstrual difficulties, infertility, vaginal infections, ovarian cysts, impotency, lower-back pain, prostate problems, sexual dysfunction, slipped disks, and bladder and urinary infections.

Third Chakra. Located in the upper stomach region, the third chakra is also known as the solar plexus chakra. Energetically, this chakra feeds into the organs of the GI tract, including the abdomen, small intestine, colon, gallbladder, kidneys, liver, pancreas, adrenal glands, and spleen. Not to be confused with self-worth, the region of the third chakra is associated with self-confidence, self-respect, and empowerment. The wisdom of the solar plexus chakra is more commonly known as a gut feeling, an intuitive sense closely tied to our level of personal power, as exemplified in the expression, "This doesn't feel right." Blockages to this chakra are thought to be related to ulcers, cancerous tumors, diabetes, hepatitis, anorexia, bulimia, and all stomach-related problems. Issues of unresolved anger and fear are deeply connected to organic dysfunction in this body region.

Fourth Chakra. The fourth chakra is affectionately known as the heart chakra, and it is considered to be one of the most important energy centers of the body. The heart chakra represents the ability to express love. Like a symbolic heart placed over the organic heart, feelings of unresolved anger or expressions of conditional love work to congest the heart chakra, which in turn has a corresponding effect on the anatomical heart, as noted by renowned cardiologist Dean Ornish. The heart, however, is not the only organ closely tied to the heart chakra. Other organs include the lungs, breasts, and esophagus. Symptoms of a blocked heart chakra can include heart attacks, enlarged heart, asthma, allergies, lung cancer, bronchial difficulties, circulation problems, breast cancer, and problems associated with the upper back and shoulders. Also, an important association exists between the heart chakra and the thymus gland. The thymus gland, so instrumental in the making of T cells, shrinks with age.

Fifth Chakra. The fifth chakra lies above and is connected to the throat. Organs associated with the throat chakra are the thyroid and parathyroid glands, mouth, vocal cords, and trachea. As a symbol of communication, the throat chakra represents the development of personal expression, creativity, purpose in life, and willpower. The inability to express oneself in feelings or creativity or to exercise one's will freely inevitably distorts the flow of energy to the throat chakra and is thought to result in chronic sore throat problems, temporomandibular joint dysfunction (TMJD), mouth sores, stiffness in the neck area, thyroid dysfunction, migraines, and even cancerous tumors in this region.

Sixth Chakra. The sixth chakra is more commonly known as the brow chakra or the third eye. This chakra is associated with intuition and the ability to access the ageless wisdom or bank of knowledge in the depths of universal consciousness. As energy moves through the dimension of universal wisdom into this chakra it promotes the development of intelligence and reasoning skills. Directly tied to the pituitary and pineal glands, this chakra feeds energy to the brain for information processing. Unlike the solar plexus chakra, which is responsible for a gut level of intuition with personal matters, the wisdom channeled through the brow chakra is more universal in nature with implications for the spiritual aspect of life. Diseases caused by dysfunction of the brow chakra (e.g., brain tumors, hemorrhages, blood clots, blindness, comas, depression, schizophrenia) may be caused by an individual's not wanting to see something that is extremely important to his or her soul growth.

Seventh Chakra. If the concept of chakras is foreign to the Western mind, then the seventh chakra may hold promise to bridge East and West. Featured most predominantly in the Judeo-Christian culture through paintings and sculptures as the halo over saintly beings, the seventh chakra, also known as the crown chakra, is associated with matters of the soul and the spiritual quest. When the crown chakra is open and fully functioning, it is known to access the highest level of consciousness. Although no specific disease or illness may be associated with the crown chakra, in truth, every disease has a spiritual significance.

Although not everyone can see or sense the human energy field, meridians, or the chakras, you can be trained to do so. Exercise 4, "Energy Ball Exercise," is an introductory session to the perceptions of the human energy field. Exercise 5 includes several ideas for maintaining a healthy flow of personal energy or chi.

Stress and the Immune System

It's no surprise to learn that under chronic stress, the immune system is greatly compromised, beginning with the immunoglobulins in the saliva down to the natural killer cells that scan the body for unwanted pathogens and mutant cancer cells. Chances are if you were to look back to the most recent time you became ill, right before it (days, even weeks) you'll find a stressful experience that triggered a cascade of unresolved stress emotions, in turn washing a flood of stress hormones through your body.

What physiological factors are responsible for a suppressed immune system? At first, the finger was pointed at the central nervous system (e.g., epinephrine, norepinephrine). Then attention soon turned to **cortisol**, the stress hormone secreted by the adrenal glands responsible for a host of metabolic survival activities. Apparently, when cortisol gets done with its fight-or-flight duties, for some unknown reason, it has a nasty habit of attacking and destroying white blood cells, the front-line defense of the immune system. Research suggests that cortisol is not the only culprit when it comes to an immune system compromised by stress. Landmark research by Candace Pert (1997) and others determined that various neuropeptides, secreted by the brain and other cells in the body, are triggered by emotional responses. Pert calls these "molecules of emotion," and they can either enhance or detract from the efficacy of the immune system. In essence, thoughts are energy—they can kill or heal.

Through the lens of holistic wellness, it is important to realize that the immune system does not reside solely in the body. The aspects that comprise your subtle anatomy also constitute your immune system.

The Stress and Disease Connection

Through the eyes of Western science, which views each human being as a machine, stress is often described as "wear and tear" on the physical body. Like a car that has more than 200,000 miles, the body has parts that typically break down and need to be fixed or replaced. In this paradigm, these parts are often called "target organs," because they seem to be specifically targeted by neurochemical pathways produced by chronic stress. Any organ can be a target organ: hair, skin, blood vessels, joints, muscles, stomach, colon, and many others. In some people one organ may be targeted, whereas in others many organs can be affected.

First, we'll take a look at disease and illness from a Western perspective and then conclude with a holistic view of the healing system. Western science has categorized stress-related disorders into two classifications: **nervous system–related disorders** and **immune system–related disorders**. The following is a brief listing of chronic diseases from each of these two categories.

Nervous System–Related Disorders

- *Tension headaches:* Tension headaches are produced by contractions of the muscles of the forehead, eyes, neck, and jaw. Increased pain results from increased contraction of these muscles. Lower back pain can also result from the same process. Although pain relievers such as aspirin are the most common source of relief, tension headaches have also been shown to dissipate with the use of meditation, mental imagery, and biofeedback.

- *Migraine headaches:* A migraine headache is a vascular headache. Symptoms can include a flash of light followed by intense throbbing, dizziness, and nausea. Migraines are thought to be related to the inability to express anger and frustration. Although several medications are prescribed for migraines, biofeedback, mental imagery, and the herb feverfew can be equally effective and used with fewer side effects.

- *Temporomandibular joint dysfunction:* Excessive contraction of the jaw muscles can lead to a phenomenon called temporomandibular joint dysfunction (TMJD). In many cases, people are unaware that they have this illness because the behavioral damage (grinding one's teeth) occurs during sleep. Like migraines, TMJD is often associated with the inability to express feelings of anger. Relaxation techniques, including biofeedback and progressive muscular relaxation, have been shown to be effective in decreasing the muscular tension associated with TMJD.

- *Bronchial asthma:* This is an illness in which a pronounced secretion of bronchial fluids causes a swelling of the smooth-muscle tissue of the large air passageways (bronchi). The onset of asthmatic attacks is often associated with anxiety. Currently drugs (e.g., prednisone) are the first method of treatment. However, relaxation techniques, including mental imagery, autogenic training, and meditation, may be just as effective in both delaying the onset and reducing the severity of these attacks.

- *Irritable bowel syndrome (IBS):* IBS is characterized by repeated bouts of abdominal pain or tenderness, cramps, diarrhea, nausea, constipation, and excessive flatulence. One reason IBS is considered so directly related to stress is that the hypothalamus, which controls appetite regulation (hunger and satiety), is closely associated with emotional regulation as well. Relaxation skills, including thermal biofeedback, progressive muscular relaxation, mental imagery, and reframing, can help to reduce existing levels of anxiety with promising results.

- *Coronary heart disease (CHD):* Elevated blood pressure (hypertension) is a significant risk factor for CHD. Stress hormones are often responsible for increasing blood pressure. When pressure is increased in a closed system, the risk of damage to vascular tissue due to increased turbulence is significantly increased. This damage to the vessel walls appears as small microtears, particularly in the intima lining of the coronary heart vessels, which supply the heart muscle (myocardium) itself with oxygen. As a way of healing these tears, several constituents floating in the blood bind with the damaged vascular cell tissue. Paradoxically, the primary "healing" agent is a sticky substance found floating in the blood serum called cholesterol, resulting in atherosclerosis, which can eventually lead to a heart attack.

Immune System–Related Disorders

- *The common cold and influenza:* Stress hormones (specifically cortisol) tend to destroy members of the white blood cell family, suppressing the immune system, hence leaving one susceptible to cold and flu.

- *Allergies:* An allergic reaction is initiated when a foreign substance (e.g., pollen, dust spores) enters the body. However, in some people, allergic reactions can occur just by thinking about a stimulus that provoked a previous attack. Allergic reactions are also more prevalent and severe in people who are prone to anxiety. Over-the-counter medications containing antihistamines and allergy shots are the most common approaches to dealing with allergies. Relaxation techniques also help minimize the effects of allergy-promoting substances.

- *Rheumatoid arthritis:* Rheumatoid arthritis, a joint and connective tissue disease, occurs when synovial membrane tissue swells, causing the joint to become inflamed. In time, synovial fluid may enter cartilage and bone tissue, causing further deterioration of the affected joint(s). The severity of arthritic pain is often related to episodes of stress, particularly suppressed anger. The treatment for this disease varies from pain relievers (e.g., aspirin) to steroid injections (e.g., cortisone), depending on the severity of pain and rate of joint deterioration. Relaxation techniques offer a complementary modality to help reduce these symptoms.

- *Ulcers and colitis:* More than 75 percent of ulcers are caused by the bacteria known as *Helicobacter,* creating an open wound that stomach acids only worsen. Treatment with antibiotics is now shown to be highly effective for a large percentage of people who have ulcers, yet two questions remain: What makes some people more vulnerable to *Helicobacter* than others? Why are antibiotics effective in only 75 percent of the cases of people with ulcers? Stress is thought to be the answer.

- *Cancer:* Cancer has proved to be one of the most perplexing diseases of our time, affecting one out of every three Americans. The body typically produces an abnormal cell once every 6 hours, but the natural killer cells of the immune system roam the body to search for and destroy these mutant cells. Stress hormones tend to suppress the immune system, allowing some mutant cells to become cancerous tumors. The treatments for cancer include chemotherapy, radiation, and surgery. However, coping skills involving cognitive restructuring, art therapy, and relaxation techniques including mental imagery and meditation are being used as complementary healing methods. Although these methods are not a cure for cancer in themselves, in some cases they seem to have a pronounced effect when used in combination with traditional medicine.

The Dynamics of Self-Healing

All things being equal, the body craves homeostasis and will do all it can to maintain a sense of balance. The body has a remarkable ability to heal itself, when given the chance to do so. Exercise and nutrition play an essential role in the healing process, but so do our thoughts and feelings. Ultimately, disease, in all its many forms, is a sign that something is clearly out of balance. Chronic illness suggests that the body's attempt to regain that inner balance is compromised, most likely by lifestyle behaviors that don't support the healing process.

In his book *Spontaneous Healing*, Dr. Andrew Weil documents the unique **self-healing** process of the human body, from the body's wisdom to kill germs by raising the body's core temperature clear down to the role of a specific enzyme to repair DNA. Deepak Chopra approaches the topic in a similar way in his book, *Quantum Healing*. For instance, Chopra explains that every cell in the body regenerates itself; some regenerate within a matter of days, others take years. The life span of red blood cells, for instance, is approximately 37 days. Nerve cells, it seems, take the longest. We know now that even brain cells have the capacity to regenerate. Consequently, within a 7-year time period, you have a completely new body of cells.

Most cancerous tumors take years, even decades, to grow. So why is it, then, that with a new body we have old tumors? Perhaps the answer resides in the vibrations of consciousness that surround and permeate each and every cell and that get passed on from generation to generation of cells through a process called entrainment. Entrainment is a physics term used to describe sympathetic resonance between two objects. It's commonly known in physics circles as the law of conservation of energy. The classic example of human entrainment is observed when women who live or work together begin to see a synchronization of their menstrual periods. Where there are neighboring energies, there is entrainment as well. Every cell vibrates with energy, as do tumors.

Unlike conventional wisdom that states that only brain cells hold some level of consciousness, it now appears that every cell in the body contains a vibration of consciousness. It is suggested that this imprint of conscious frequency is then transferred via entrainment from cell to cell, thus allowing a tumor to develop and keep growing, long after the original aberrant cells have died off. Can changes in one's thoughts change the vibration of cells? The answer appears to be yes, in a critical mass of people—those who demonstrate "spontaneous remission."

Which emotions are prone to compromise the integrity of the immune system? In simplest terms, any lingering unresolved emotion associated with the fight-or-flight response. It would be too hard to single out anger and fear as the only culprits; however, both of these serve as umbrella emotions for literally hundreds of other emotions, which along with joy, love, and happiness constitute the full spectrum of feelings. As was mentioned earlier, when used properly, none of these emotions are bad, not even anger or fear. However, when left unresolved, anger or fear and all the many ways in which these two survival emotions manifest, over time, will suppress the immune system. In doing so, they open the door wide to a multitude of health-related problems.

Just as a preponderance of unhealthy emotions can suppress the immune system, so can positive thoughts and feelings enhance it. Although all aspects of the inherent self-healing program are not fully understood, one thing is clear: Effective coping skills that help to resolve the causes of stress in tandem with effective relaxation skills that strive to return the body to homeostasis offer the best opportunity to engage the healing process to its fullest potential.

Chapter Summary

- An extended stress response beyond "physical survival" creates wear and tear on many physiological systems of the human body including the cardiovascular, digestive, and endocrine systems.

- Just as there is gross anatomy, there is also subtle anatomy, specifically the human energy field and the meridian and chakra systems, all of which are connected to the mind-body-spirit continuum.

- Prolonged (chronic) stress definitely has an impact on the immune system—in essence, suppressing it—thus making one more vulnerable to disease and illness.

- The stress and disease connection is very real. Chronic stress is now related to a number of health-related problems from the common cold to cancer.

- The body actually needs some stress (e.g., exercise), but also craves homeostasis. Many, if not all, stress management techniques promote self-healing dynamics by helping the body return to homeostasis.

Additional Resources

Anodea, J. *Eastern Body, Western Mind*. Berkeley, CA: Celestial Arts; 2004.

APA Online. Stress Affects Immunity in Ways Related to Stress Type and Duration, As Shown by Nearly 300 Studies. Media Information. July 4, 2004. http://www.apa.org/releases/stress_immune.html.

Arntz, W., Chasse, B., & Vicente, M. *What the Bleep Do We Know!?* Deerfield Beach, FL: Health Communications, Inc.; 2005.

Chopra, D. *Quantum Healing*. New York: Bantam Books; 1989.

Dale, C. *The Subtle Body: An Encyclopedia of Your Energetic Body*. Boulder, CO: Sounds True; 2009.

Dispenza, J. *Evolve Your Brain: The Science of Changing Your Mind*. Deerfield Beach, FL: Health Communications, Inc.; 2007.

Eden, D. *Energy Medicine*. New York: Tarcher/Putnam; 2008.

Gerber, R. *Vibrational Medicine* (3rd ed.). Rochester, VT: Bear & Co.; 2001.

Lipton, B. *The Biology of Belief: Unleashing the Power of Consciousness, Matter, and Miracles*. Santa Rosa, CA: Mountain of Love/Elite Books; 2005.

McTaggart, L. *The Field*. New York: Harper Collins; 2002.

Ornish, D. *Love and Survival*. New York: Harper Collins; 1998.

Pert, C. *Everything You Need to Know to Feel Go(o)d*. Carlsbad, CA: Hay House Books; 2007.

Pert, C. *Molecules of Emotion*. New York: Scribner Books; 1997.

Powell, D., & Institute of Noetic Sciences. *The 2007 Shift Report: Evidence of a World Transforming*. Petaluma, CA: Institute of Noetic Sciences; 2007, pp. 28–36.

Sarno, J. *Mindbody Prescription*. New York: Warner Books; 1998.

Segerstrom, S. C., & Miller, G. E. Psychological stress and the human immune system: A meta-analytical study of 30 years of inquiry. *Psychological Bulletin* 130(4):601–630; 2004.

Weil, A. *Spontaneous Healing*. New York: Knopf Books; 1997.

EXERCISE   1: Physical Symptoms Questionnaire

Please look over this list of stress-related symptoms and circle how often they have occurred in the past week, how severe they seemed to you, and how long they lasted. Then reflect on the past week's workload and see if you notice any connection.

	How Often? (number of days in the past week)	How Severe? (1 = mild, 5 = severe)	How Long? (1 = 1 hour, 5 = all day)
1. Tension headache	0 1 2 3 4 5 6 7	1 2 3 4 5	1 2 3 4 5
2. Migraine headache	0 1 2 3 4 5 6 7	1 2 3 4 5	1 2 3 4 5
3. Muscle tension (neck and/or shoulders)	0 1 2 3 4 5 6 7	1 2 3 4 5	1 2 3 4 5
4. Muscle tension (lower back)	0 1 2 3 4 5 6 7	1 2 3 4 5	1 2 3 4 5
5. Joint pain	0 1 2 3 4 5 6 7	1 2 3 4 5	1 2 3 4 5
6. Cold	0 1 2 3 4 5 6 7	1 2 3 4 5	1 2 3 4 5
7. Flu	0 1 2 3 4 5 6 7	1 2 3 4 5	1 2 3 4 5
8. Stomachache	0 1 2 3 4 5 6 7	1 2 3 4 5	1 2 3 4 5
9. Stomach/abdominal bloating/distention/gas	0 1 2 3 4 5 6 7	1 2 3 4 5	1 2 3 4 5
10. Diarrhea	0 1 2 3 4 5 6 7	1 2 3 4 5	1 2 3 4 5
11. Constipation	0 1 2 3 4 5 6 7	1 2 3 4 5	1 2 3 4 5
12. Ulcer flare-up	0 1 2 3 4 5 6 7	1 2 3 4 5	1 2 3 4 5
13. Asthma attack	0 1 2 3 4 5 6 7	1 2 3 4 5	1 2 3 4 5
14. Allergies	0 1 2 3 4 5 6 7	1 2 3 4 5	1 2 3 4 5
15. Canker/cold sores	0 1 2 3 4 5 6 7	1 2 3 4 5	1 2 3 4 5
16. Dizzy spells	0 1 2 3 4 5 6 7	1 2 3 4 5	1 2 3 4 5
17. Heart palpitations (racing heart)	0 1 2 3 4 5 6 7	1 2 3 4 5	1 2 3 4 5
18. TMJD	0 1 2 3 4 5 6 7	1 2 3 4 5	1 2 3 4 5
19. Insomnia	0 1 2 3 4 5 6 7	1 2 3 4 5	1 2 3 4 5
20. Nightmares	0 1 2 3 4 5 6 7	1 2 3 4 5	1 2 3 4 5
21. Fatigue	0 1 2 3 4 5 6 7	1 2 3 4 5	1 2 3 4 5
22. Hemorrhoids	0 1 2 3 4 5 6 7	1 2 3 4 5	1 2 3 4 5
23. Pimples/acne	0 1 2 3 4 5 6 7	1 2 3 4 5	1 2 3 4 5
24. Cramps	0 1 2 3 4 5 6 7	1 2 3 4 5	1 2 3 4 5
25. Frequent accidents	0 1 2 3 4 5 6 7	1 2 3 4 5	1 2 3 4 5
26. Other (please specify) _____	0 1 2 3 4 5 6 7	1 2 3 4 5	1 2 3 4 5

Score: Look over this entire list. Do you observe any patterns or relationships between your stress levels and your physical health? A value over 30 points may indicate a stress-related health problem. If it seems to you that these symptoms are related to undue stress, they probably are. Although medical treatment is advocated when necessary, the regular use of relaxation techniques may lessen the intensity, frequency, and duration of these episodes.

EXERCISE 2: Your Picture of Health

We all have an idea of what ideal health is. Many of us take our health for granted until something goes wrong to remind us that our picture of health is compromised and less than ideal. Although health may seem to be objective, it will certainly vary from person to person over the entire aging process. The following statements are based on characteristics associated with longevity and a healthy quality of life (none of which considers any genetic factors). Rather than answering the questions to see how long you may live, please complete this inventory to determine your current picture of health.

3 = Often	2 = Sometimes	1 = Rarely	0 = Never

	3	2	1	0
1. With rare exception, I sleep an average of 7 to 8 hours each night.	3	2	1	0
2. I tend to eat my meals at the same time each day.	3	2	1	0
3. I keep my bedtime consistent every night.	3	2	1	0
4. I do cardiovascular exercise at least three times per week.	3	2	1	0
5. My weight is considered ideal for my height.	3	2	1	0
6. Without exception, my alcohol consumption is in moderation.	3	2	1	0
7. I consider my nutritional habits to be exceptional.	3	2	1	0
8. My health status is considered excellent, with no pre-existing conditions.	3	2	1	0
9. I neither smoke, nor participate in the use of recreational drugs.	3	2	1	0
10. I have a solid group of friends with whom I socialize regularly.	3	2	1	0
TOTAL SCORE				

Score: 26–30 points = Excellent health habits
20–25 points = Moderate health habits
14–19 points = Questionable health habits
0–13 points = Poor health habits

EXERCISE   3: Subtle Anatomy Energy Map

The following is an outline of the human body highlighted with the seven primary chakras. Note the body region associated with each chakra and then take a moment to identify any health issues or concerns associated within this specific region of your body. Write your observations on the following pages. Once you have done this, refer back to   and ask yourself honestly if you happen to recognize any connection between the important aspects of the chakra(s) associated with the region(s) in which you have indicated a specific health concern.

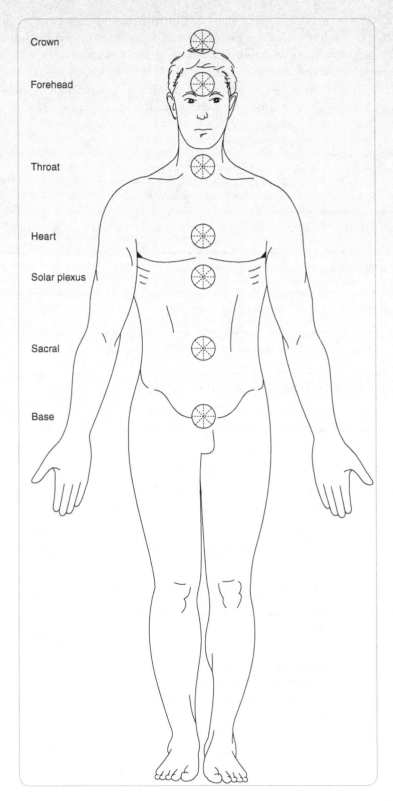

Crown

Forehead

Throat

Heart

Solar plexus

Sacral

Base

EXERCISE   3: Subtle Anatomy Energy Map cont....

	Chakras	Body Region	Related Health Issue
1.			
2.			
3.			
4.			
5.			
6.			
7.			

EXERCISE 4: Energy Ball Exercise

This is a relaxation technique taught to me by the renowned bioenergy healers Mietek and Margaret Wirkus. I have adapted and taught this technique many times in classes and workshops throughout the country with great success. Although it was introduced to me as the first of many healing techniques in bioenergy healing, first and foremost, this is a relaxation exercise. This technique is done through the following steps.

1. Begin by sitting comfortably with your legs crossed and your back straight. You may wish to sit up against a wall. In this exercise, it really helps to keep your back straight. Close your eyes and focus your attention on your breathing. Take a moment to clear your mind of distracting thoughts and feelings. Place your attention on your breathing. If it helps to have some soft instrumental music in the background, then try this as well. Sometimes, to set the tone, it helps to think of a happy moment in your life, when you were filled with utter joy. Allow this feeling to resonate within every cell in your body. Then take a couple of comfortably slow deep breaths to let it be absorbed.

2. Unlike belly breathing, which is typically taught in relaxation workshops, this particular exercise requires that you focus your attention on the upper lobes of your lungs. Take a moment to place your hands on your upper chest to become fully conscious of your upper lungs. Then take five breaths, breathing comfortably slow and deep into your upper lungs.

3. Once you have completed this, then place your hands on your knees and repeat this breathing style by taking five slow deep breaths. As you exhale, repeat this phrase to yourself, *"My body is calm and relaxed."* As you say this, feel a deep sense of relaxation throughout your body with each exhalation.

4. Next, being fully conscious of your hands resting on your knees or thighs, take five more deep breaths, but this time as you exhale, repeat this phrase to yourself, *"I am my hands."* With each breath, place all of your concentration, all of your attention, on your hands. Sense what your hands feel like. Are they warm? If so, where? On the palms, fingertips, or backs of your hands? Where? Again, remind yourself of the phrase, *"I am my hands."*

5. Using your imagination, picture a small window in the center of each palm, about the size of a dime. Imagine now that as you breathe, air comes not only into your nose or mouth, but also into your hands. If you prefer, you may use the image of light coming into your palms. Imagine that as you inhale, air or light enters your palms and moves up your arms, to the center (heart space) of your upper chest. As you exhale, feel the energy return from where it entered through your hands. Try repeating this several times, again taking several slow deep breaths and again repeating to yourself, *"I am my hands."*

6. Next, slowly lift your hands off your knees or thighs so that they rest comfortably in the air, suspended in front of your chest, with the palms facing up, toward the ceiling.

EXERCISE   4: Energy Ball Exercise cont....

7. Next, fully conscious of your hands, take five more deep breaths. As you exhale each breath, repeat the phrase, *"I am my hands."* With each breath, place all of your concentration, all of your attention, on your hands. Again sense what your hands feel like. Are they warm? If so, where? On the palms, the fingertips, the backs of your hands? Do your hands feel heavy? If so, how heavy? What other sensations do you feel? Again, remind yourself as you exhale, *"I am my hands."* As you do this, notice if you see any colors.

8. Now, keeping your hands about 10–12 inches apart, allow the palms of each hand to face each other. Again using your imagination, picture or sense that between your hands is a large sponge ball. As you hold this ball, slowly press in and then release. What do you feel as you do this? Again, bring your hands closer together without touching, then begin to separate them farther apart. Ask yourself, what do you feel? At what distance is the sensation the strongest?

9. Now, placing the palms of your hands about 6–12 inches apart, imagine that there is a beam of light from palm to palm, window to window. Take a slow deep breath and as you exhale, slowly compress the beam by slowly bringing your palms together without touching. Then, during the next inhalation, allow your hands to separate again slowly. What do you feel as you do this? Is the sensation between your hands stronger when you inhale or exhale?

10. Again, return to the sensation between your hands. Between your hands is a ball of energy, the healing energy ball. Take this ball of energy and place it into a region of your body that feels stressed or desires healing. If you are completely relaxed, try placing this energy in your heart. Take five slow deep breaths and repeat the phrase, *"My body is calm and relaxed."* Feel a sense of relaxation throughout your entire body. Take one final slow deep breath and enjoy this sensation again.

11. When you are done, slowly place your hands back on your knees or thighs. Recognize that although you feel relaxed, you feel energized. When you are ready, open your eyes to a soft gaze in front of you. Then make yourself aware of your surroundings so that you may continue on with your daily activities.

EXERCISE   5: Subtle Energy System "Vitamins"

Donna Eden is a renowned energy healer with a gift for not only observing subtle energies, but also teaching others how to regulate their subtle energy for enhanced health and well-being. Integrating the flow of energy through the human aura, chakras, and meridians, Donna combines a variety of self-help techniques so that, in her words, "You keep your energies humming and vibrant." The following are ideas and suggestions that Donna teaches in her energy medicine workshops, exercises that she calls energy system vitamins. She recommends that you do this short routine daily.

Three Body Taps: There are various acupuncture/acupressure points that, when stimulated, will help direct the flow of energy, and thus increase your vitality and help boost your immune system.

1. *Chest bone tap:* Known to acupuncturists as KD-27 (from points on the kidney meridian), gently tap on the top of your chest bone just below the medial ends of the two clavicles for about 15–20 seconds. This should open your breathing, relax the chest, and tonify the immune system.

2. *Thymus gland tap:* Your thymus gland (an important gland of the immune system) resides between your throat and your heart, but the point to tap is in the center of your chest bone about 2 inches below KD-27. Once you have found this point, tap on it with your fingertips for about 15–20 seconds.

3. *Spleen points tap:* The spleen is also an essential organ to your immune system. The spleen points are located on the rib cage, directly below your nipples. Once you have found these two points, tap vigorously with your fingers for about 15–20 seconds.

Cross Crawl Movements: To do the cross crawl, first you must understand that the left side of the brain controls the right side of the body, and vice versa. Many people's energies are not vibrant or harmonized due to stagnation from the lack of neural energy from the right to left or left to right sides of the brain. Poor energy movement is referred to as a homolateral pattern, and this will affect thought processes, coordination, and vitality. Sitting or standing, raise your right knee and your left arm (you can touch knee to elbow if you'd like). Follow this by raising your left knee and your right arm. Twist your torso so that your arms cross the midpoint of your body. Try this movement pattern for about 30–60 seconds.

The Crown Pull: Placing your hands on top of your forehead and crown of the head, imagine that your fingers are pulling from the center down to your ears, in a motion starting from the front of your head and working to the back of your skull. The purpose of this exercise is to move stagnant energy from the top of your head, and it helps to open the crown chakra. This exercise can be helpful in relieving headaches, too.

Zip Up: The central meridian (in the front of your body), also known as the conception vessel, can easily become congested, open, or exposed to others' energy. This technique invites you to close your auric field as a means of health and protection. Start by tapping the KD-27 point again and then reach down to the top of your thighs with your right (or left) hand, take a deep breath, and pull up as if you were pulling up a zipper, clear up to your chin. Repeat this three times. By pulling up, you trace the directional flow of the central meridian and strengthen the flow of energy. This technique is recommended before making speeches or dealing with someone who is very angry.

Photo Credits

Unless otherwise indicated, all photographs and illustrations are under copyright of Jones and Bartlett Publishers, LLC, or have been provided by the author.

Brian Luke Seaward, Essentials of Managing Stress, Second Edition, 2011

The Emotions: From a Motivation of Fear to a Motivation of Love

"Until you extend the circle of compassion to all living things, you will not find inner peace."

— Albert Schweitzer, MD

Love. Anger. Grief. Happiness. Anxiety. Bliss. Sorrow. Guilt. Mirth. Compassion. Despair. Joy. Emotional well-being can best be described as the ability to feel and express the entire range of human emotions, and to control them, not be controlled by them. This may sound like a tall order, but it's not impossible. The spectrum of human emotions spans the continuum from anger to love, and everything in between. Humans are thought to be unique among all the earth's creatures in our capacity to exhibit such an array of emotions. This gift comes with a price. We also seem to be the only species on the planet that can become a slave to our emotions and spiritually immobilized in the process.

Healthy Emotions

Given this definition of emotional well-being, all emotions are considered part of the spectrum, yet the question begs to be asked: "What constitutes a **healthy emotion?**" From a holistic perspective, the expression of all emotions is considered healthy, because to deny the ability to feel and express any emotion suggests a serious emotional imbalance. Each sensation in the spectrum of human emotions is included in the software of the human mind for a reason—to feel and express ourselves in every possible way. The expression of each emotion also allows a release of feelings, or what is more commonly known as a "catharsis."

Many people consider joy, bliss, euphoria, and love to be the healthy emotions, whereas anger and fear are labeled as unhealthy. In truth, anger and fear are also considered to be healthy emotions, when they are used specifically for their intended purpose. Both anger and fear are considered to be survival emotions and therefore essential for human life. Each is only meant to last long enough to get out of harm's way. Healthy emotions quickly become unhealthy when they last longer than the intended purpose for which they serve. Unhealthy emotions appear like a black cloud hanging over our heads. Left unresolved, they can cause serious problems in the mind-body-spirit dynamics of optimal health.

Unhealthy Emotions

Ideally, anger, fear, and all the many ways in which they manifest in the spectrum of human emotions serve to protect you. Upon the slightest inkling of danger, they summon an alarm to move rapidly into a state of physical survival. Both anger and fear are only meant to last long enough to get us out of danger, which typically takes seconds, perhaps minutes, but not much longer. When feelings of anger and/or fear linger longer than the amount of time needed to reach a place of safety, then we do not control our emotions, they control us! As such, our emotional well-being is greatly compromised.

When we hang on to feelings of anger or fear, rather than letting them go, we literally give our power away. To feel "emotionally drained" is the hallmark of when a healthy emotion becomes unhealthy. Prolonged anger, fear, grief, and depression are not only classic, but also all too common examples of unhealthy emotions reflected on the faces of Americans everywhere today.

The Stress Emotions: Anger and Fear

Stated simply, anger and fear are the two primary stress emotions. Anger is the fight response. Fear is the flight response. Anger is exhibited in a great many ways, including impatience, guilt, envy, indignation, intimidation, intolerance, frustration, rage, prejudice, and hostility. Like anger, the color of fear also comes in many hues, including doubt, embarrassment, anxiety, apprehension, insecurity, and paranoia, to name a few. A quick glance at the headlines on any given day reveals the extreme level of stress in the world, with anger and fear underscoring nearly every news story. From school shootings and suicides to road rage and acts of international terrorism, anger has increasingly become part of the human landscape. For this reason it merits attention.

Mismanaged Anger Styles

Every episode of anger is the result of an unmet expectation. On average, the typical person gets angry about 15 to 20 times per day. When one realizes how anger can manifest, from impatience to rage, this number begins to make more sense. Given the number of expectations one has in the course of a day, this number may appear quite low. Although anger can be felt and expressed in a great many ways, there are four specific patterns in which people from all global cultures tend to mismanage their anger. Typically, we tend to exhibit all of these, but it has been noted that one mismanaged anger style seems to dominate our personality. Please read through this list and note any signs of familiarity.

- *The somatizer:* The **somatizer** is best described as a person who doesn't express his or her anger; instead, the person suppresses it. Unexpressed emotions carry a price, and in this case the body (soma) pays this price with serious physical problems, including migraine headaches, temporomandibular joint dysfunction (TMJD), ulcers, liver problems, hypertension, and rheumatoid arthritis. Women, more than men, tend to be somatizers.

- *The self-punisher:* **Self-punishers** feel guilty about feeling angry; hence, they tend to substitute feelings of anger for some obsessive behavior including excess eating, drinking, exercise, shopping, and sex. Sadly, self-mutilators (cutters) also fall into this category.

- *The exploder:* The **exploder**'s main outlet of anger is intimidation. Like a volcano, exploders erupt, spewing their hot lava in the direction of the perceived threat. Road rage, foul language, acts of violence, and hostility top the list of this mismanaged anger style. Explosive behavior is more common in men, but women can exhibit it as well.

- *The underhander:* Revenge is a motive for **underhanders** in what they perceive to be considered socially acceptable behavior, particularly at the worksite. Sarcasm is the most common form of underhanded behavior, but there are other passive–aggressive behaviors in this style of mismanaged anger as well.

In each of these **mismanaged anger styles**, prolonged anger results in the person trying to control him- or herself (somatizer and self-punisher) or others (exploder and underhander). Instead, they are being controlled by their anger and giving their power away. We now know that if we wish to change our behavior, we first have to identify what we are doing so we can then learn to behave differently. These mismanaged anger styles are merely labels to help you identify undesirable behaviors associated with unresolved issues. Exercises 1 and 2 are inventories to help you identify which mismanaged anger style dominates your personality. Exercise 3 invites you to think up ways to creatively manage your anger, so that you can begin to control it, and not have it control you. Grieving also is a part of anger. Exercise 5 invites you to explore any unresolved issues through the Mandala of Healthy Grieving exercise.

Depression: The Black Cloud of Stress

It's no secret that **depression** is a huge problem in U.S. culture. Some estimates suggest that as much as one quarter of the population takes prescribed antidepressants. Although many factors are involved with depression, including an imbalance of the neurochemicals seratonin and dopamine, a holistic approach to stress suggests that there is a strong relationship between an emotional imbalance and a chemical imbalance. Is there a connection between depression and anger? Most holistic practitioners believe so. As the joke goes, "Depression is anger without the enthusiasm." Although pharmaceuticals may assist in bringing balance to one's brain chemistry, medications don't heal emotional wounds. As the Food and Drug Administration (FDA) announced, in some cases, medications may actually make things worse, including increasing suicidal urges.

Facing Your Fear

Simply stated, fear is a response to physical danger. Rarely in this day and age, however, do we encounter physical danger that requires us to run away and hide. However, the emotion of fear is there in case we do. Self-promoted feelings of fear and worry are extremely prevalent in today's society, and the reasons have more to do with a perceived sense of failure, rejection, and the unknown than any real physical danger. Credit card debt, struggling relationships, loss of a job, and terminal illnesses tend to top a long list of common chronic stressors associated with fear and anxiety.

If rational fears are triggered by physical danger, then one might assume that fear under any other prolonged circumstance is irrational. In truth, any fear that is not quickly resolved is often referred to as unwarranted or **irrational fear**, and this type of fear can certainly become emotionally draining. Unlike anger, which is a very energizing emotion, fear is energy-depleting. However, like unresolved anger, over time, fear can be very toxic to the body.

For fear to be fully resolved, it must be confronted diplomatically. This means that each circumstance where fear surfaces must be faced, without a loss of self-esteem. As the expression goes, "Face your fear and it will disappear." If other people are involved, then the confrontation must not make them defensive or angry, beccause this will only perpetuate the problem. Diplomacy is essential with each confrontation. Exercise 4, "Confrontation of a Stressor," addresses this issue of making peace with fear.

From a Motivation of Fear Toward a Motivation of Love

One of the primary areas of study in the field of psychology is the aspect of motivational behavior—why we do the things we do. A conclusion by many is that, by and large, most of our behaviors are fear-based thoughts and actions (anger being considered an aspect of fear). This perspective suggests that humans operate from a fight-or-flight response the majority of time. Although this may sound preposterous, a quick glance through the annals of human history supports this theory. From a personal perspective, consider making a habit of observing your thoughts and behaviors to determine the source of motivation behind these actions. You may be surprised at the outcome.

Moving from fear to love means responding rather than reacting to stress. It means showing tolerance rather than anger, patience rather than hostility, forgiveness rather than resentment, and humor rather than arrogance. Ultimately, it means not placing yourself first all the time and viewing the bigger picture with an open heart rather than a closed mind. All humans are capable of this endeavor!

Joy and Happiness: The Other (Eustress) Emotions

As was discussed in Chapter 1, not all stress is bad. Good stress is a necessary part of life, as are all the emotions associated with it. Joy, happiness, love, compassion, and all the feelings that hearty laughter brings are essential to optimal health. These emotions generate a whole pharmacopia of beneficial neuropeptides that enhance the immune system. Emotional well-being is truly a balance of emotional experiences. By not seeking a balance to the full emotional spectrum with frequent exposure to the emotions associated with good stress, all aspects of our personal wellness paradigm are affected. Therefore, it's in our best interest to seek out the peak experiences, the joyful moments, and the comic relief that give balance to our lives. Moreover, as you will see in later chapters, it is these emotions that, when combined with a host of coping skills and relaxation techniques, create very powerful results. Exercise 6 offers you a chance to explore the emotions of love and compassion.

Chapter Summary

- The emotional spectrum ranges from fear to love. All emotions are thought to have a reason. They are considered healthy emotions when they are used for their intended purpose. They are consider unhealthy when they last longer than needed for their purpose.

- There are two stress emotions, anger (fight) and fear (flight). They are considered to be survival emotions for physical threats.

- Prolonged anger is considered a negative emotion. There are four mismanaged anger styles in which people hang on to anger: the somatizer, exploder, self-punisher, and underhander.

- Depression and anger are deeply entwined. Some suggest that depression is rooted in unresolved anger issues (depression is anger turned inward).

- Holistic stress management can be described as moving from a motivation of fear to a motivation of love and compassion.

- Two emotions associated with good stress (eustress) are joy and happiness.

Additional Resources

Britten, R. *Fearless Living*. Berkeley, CA: Perigee Books; 2001.

Cox, D., Bruckner, K., & Stabb, S. *The Anger Advantage*. New York: Broadway Books; 2003.

Emmons, R. *Thanks: How the Science of Gratitude Can Make You Happier*. New York: Houghton Mifflin; 2007.

Fleeman, W. *Pathways to Peace: Anger Management Workbook*. Alameda, CA: Hunter House; 2003.

Lerner, H. *The Dance of Anger*. New York: Harper & Row; 1985.

Seligman, M. *Authentic Happiness: Using the New Positive Psychology to Realize Your Potential for Lasting Fulfillment*. New York: Free Press; 2002.

Seligman, M. *What You Can Change and What You Can't: The Complete Guide to Successful Self-Improvement*. New York: Ballantine Books; 1995.

Skog, S. *Depression: What Your Body Is Trying to Tell You*. New York: Wholecare; 1999.

Tavris, C. *Anger: The Misunderstood Emotion*. New York: Touchstone; 1989.

Warren, N. C. *Make Anger Your Ally*. New York: Simon & Schuster; 1983.

Williams, R. *Anger Kills*. New York: Harper Collins; 1994.

EXERCISE 1: Anger Recognition Checklist

"He who angers you, conquers you."— Elizabeth Kenny

The following is a quick exercise to understand how anger can surface in the course of a normal working day and how you *may* mismanage it. Please place a check mark in front of any of the following that apply to you when you "get angry" or "feel frustrated or upset." After completing this section, please refer to the bottom right-hand corner and estimate the number of anger episodes, on average, you experience per day.

When I feel angry, my anger tends to surface in the following ways:

_____ anxious	_____ threaten others
_____ depressed	_____ buy things
_____ overeat	_____ frequent lateness
_____ start dieting	_____ never feel angry
_____ trouble sleeping	_____ clenched jaw muscles, TMJD
_____ excessive sleeping	_____ bored
_____ careless driving	_____ nausea, vomiting
_____ chronic fatigue	_____ skin problems
_____ abuse alcohol/drugs	_____ easily irritable
_____ explode in rage	_____ sexual difficulty
_____ cold withdrawal	_____ sexual apathy
_____ tension headaches	_____ busy work (clean, straighten)
_____ migraine headaches	_____ sulk
_____ use sarcasm	_____ hit, throw things
_____ hostile joking	_____ complain, whine
_____ accident prone	_____ cut/mutilate myself
_____ guilty and self-blaming	_____ insomnia
_____ smoke or drink	_____ promiscuity
_____ high blood pressure	_____ help others
_____ frequent nightmares	
_____ tendency to harp or nag	_____ Other? _____
_____ intellectualize	
_____ upset stomach (e.g., gas, cramps, IBS)	
_____ muscle tension (neck, lower back)	
_____ swear and/or name call	* My average number of anger episodes
_____ cry	per day is _____.

46

EXERCISE   2: Mismanaged Anger Style Indicator

Part I: Check the statements that are true for you the majority of the time.

_____ 1. Even though I may wish to complain, I usually don't.

_____ 2. When upset, I have a habit of slamming, punching, or breaking things.

_____ 3. When I feel guilty, I have been known to contemplate self-destructive behaviors.

_____ 4. I can be really nice to people, but then back-stab them when they're not around.

_____ 5. I have a habit of grinding my teeth at night.

_____ 6. When I am really irritated or frustrated by others, I tend to intimidate them.

_____ 7. When I am frustrated, I feel like going shopping and spending money.

_____ 8. I can manipulate people without them even knowing it.

_____ 9. It's fair to say that I rarely, if ever, get angry or mad.

_____ 10. I have been known to talk back to people of authority.

_____ 11. Sleeping in is a good way to forget about my problems and frustrations.

_____ 12. Watching TV or playing video games offers a good escape from my frustrations.

_____ 13. If I complain, I feel people won't like me as much, so I usually don't.

_____ 14. When driving at times, I feel like I want to run over people with my car.

_____ 15. When I get mad or frustrated, I have been known to eat to calm my nerves.

_____ 16. I plan a script or rehearse what I am going to say to win a conflict.

_____ 17. It's hard/uncomfortable for me to say the words "I am angry."

_____ 18. I usually try to get the final say in situations with others.

_____ 19. I have been known to use alcohol and/or drugs to deal with my anger feelings.

_____ 20. By and large, I tend to agree with the statement, "Don't get mad, get even."

_____ 21. I tend to keep my feelings to myself.

_____ 22. When I get angry, I have been known to swear a lot.

_____ 23. I usually feel guilty about feeling angry, frustrated, or annoyed.

_____ 24. It's OK to use sarcasm to make a point.

_____ 25. I am the kind of person who calms the waters when tempers flare at home or work.

_____ 26. It's easy to say the words "I am angry" or "I am pissed" and really mean it.

_____ 27. On more than one occasion, I have imagined taking my own life.

_____ 28. I think of various ways to put people down.

_____ 29. Typically, I place the needs of others before myself.

_____ 30. I suffer from migraine headaches, TMJD, rheumatoid arthritis, or lupus.

EXERCISE 2: Mismanaged Anger Style Indicator cont....

Part II: Score Sheet

Write down the numbers of the statements that you have checked off:

_____

As a rule, we tend to engage in all of these behaviors at some time; however, some behaviors are very common whereas others are more occasional, suggesting that when certain predominant behaviors are grouped together they reveal a specific style of mismanaged anger. Mismanaged anger leads to a host of serious problems for both ourselves and others. By learning to recognize series of behaviors that fall into one or perhaps two categories, we can more easily identify this behavior and then make a strategy to change or modify it so that stress is reduced rather than perpetuated. Labels are good to identify behaviors, but they are not meant to serve as a mismanaged scarlet letter.

- If you have four or more answers from these choices—1, 5, 9, 13, 17, 21, 25, 29, 30—your mismanaged anger style suggests you might be a somatizer.

- If you have four or more answers from these choices—3, 7, 11, 12, 15, 19, 23, 27—your mismanaged anger style suggests you might be a self-punisher.

- If you have four or more answers from these choices—2, 6, 10, 14, 18, 22, 26—your mismanaged anger style suggests you might be an exploder.

- If you have four or more answers from these choices—4, 8, 16, 20, 24, 28—your mismanaged anger style suggests you might be an underhander.

EXERCISE 3: Creative Anger Management Skills Action Plan

Dealing with anger effectively means working to resolve the issues and expectations that surfaced from the anger episode. There are many ways to creatively resolve anger so that you reclaim your emotional sovereignty. The following is a synthesis of suggestions from a variety of sources. Read through each suggestion and below it write a description of what steps you can implement to creatively manage your anger and keep each episode of anger within a healthy time period.

1. Know your anger style: What is your most predominant mismanaged anger style?

_____

2. Learn to self-monitor your anger: Reflect on the past day's events (including listening to the news) and estimate the number of times you felt anger.

_____

3. Learn to de-escalate your anger: List three ways to let off steam (e.g., leave the room, take a big sigh, count to 10, etc.).

a. _____ b. _____ c. _____

4. Learn to out-think your anger: Many times anger results from insufficient information. Identify an anger situation and reprocess the information to neutralize your anger feelings.

_____

5. Get comfortable with all your feelings: Some people have a hard time saying the phrase "I am angry" or "I feel angry." Are you one of them? Please explain.

_____

6. Plan in advance: Although avoidance is not advocated, making plans to work around a problem is known as the path of least resistance. Identify a current frustration and then list three things you can do as an action plan to rise above the occasion.

a. _____ b. _____ c. _____

7. Develop a strong support system: List three people whom you can turn to vent your frustrations as well as provide an objective voice about your stressful situation.

_____

8. Develop realistic expectations for yourself and others: Pick one anger situation you have had today (or yesterday), identify the expectation that wasn't met, and then refine the expectation.

Unmet expectation: _____

Refined expectation: _____

9. Turn complaints into requests: As the expression goes, you catch more flies with honey than vinegar. Script a phrase that you can use to incorporate the magic of request.

_____

10. Make past anger pass: Letting go of anger begins with forgiveness. List three people you feel have violated you in some way, with whom the steps of forgiveness need to be taken.

a. _____ b. _____ c. _____

EXERCISE 4: Confrontation of a Stressor

It happens to us all the time. Someone or something gets us frustrated, and we literally or figuratively head for the hills, either avoiding the person or thing altogether or ignoring the situation in the hope that it will go away. But when we ignore situations like this, they typically come back to haunt us. In the short run, avoidance looks appealing, even safe. But in the long run, it is bad policy. Really bad policy! We avoid confrontation because we want to avoid the emotional pain associated with it, the pain our ego suffers. Handled creatively, diplomatically, and rationally, the pain is minimal, and it often helps our spirits grow. After all, this is what life is all about: achieving our full human potential.

The art of peaceful confrontation involves a strategy of creativity, diplomacy, and grace to ensure that you come out the victor, not the victim. In this sense, confrontation doesn't mean a physical battle but rather a mental, emotional, or spiritual battle. Unlike a physical battle where knights wear armor, this confrontation requires that you set aside the shield of your ego long enough to resolve the fear or anger associated with the stressor. The weapons of this confrontation are self-assertiveness, self-reliance, and faith. There is no malice, spite, or deceit involved. Coping mechanisms that aid the confrontation process include, but are not limited to, the following strategies: communication, information seeking, cognitive reappraisal, social engineering, and values assessment and clarification.

We all encounter stressors that we tend to run away from. Now it is time to gather your internal resources and make a plan to successfully confront your stressor. When you initiate this confrontation plan, you will come out the victor with a positive resolution and a feeling of accomplishment. First, reexamine the list of your top 10 stressors. Then, select a major stressor to confront and resolve. Prepare a plan of action, and then carry it out. When you return, write about it: what the stressor was, what your strategy was, how it worked, how you felt about the outcome, and perhaps most important, what you learned from this experience.

EXERCISE 4: Confrontation of a Stressor cont....

The Stressor: (State the stressor you plan to confront here.)

_____
_____
_____
_____
_____
_____
_____
_____

Action Plan: (State your plan of diplomatic confrontation here.)

_____
_____
_____
_____
_____
_____
_____
_____
_____
_____

Emotional Processing: (After you have faced your fear, describe here what happened and how you now feel having done this. Also, what did you learn from this experience?)

_____
_____
_____
_____
_____
_____
_____
_____
_____

EXERCISE 5: Mandala of Healthy Grieving

"I felt sorry for myself because I had no shoes, till I met a man who had no feet." — Anonymous

Description: Grieving is a natural part of the human condition; however, new insights suggest that loss (big or small) is a metaphor of our own personal death—something most people tend to avoid. Everyone grieves in their own way, yet the most important aspect of grieving is not to get stuck in a prolonged (unhealthy) grieving process.

First consider an experience of loss. Using the template of the circle (mandala or medicine wheel; see page 79), draw in four quadrants (north, south, east, and west). Take a moment to reflect on and then write answers to these questions. Start with the quadrant of the east and move through to the south, followed by the west, and conclude with the north.

East (Past):

- What are your best memories of this loss experience?
- What issues, if any, are left unresolved?
- What emotions do you associate with this loss?
- What regrets, if any, do you have about this loss?

South (Lessons):

- What lesson did you learn from this experience?
- What do you feel you can share with others about this experience?
- What fears hold you back from similar experiences?
- What frustrations misdirect your next leg of the human journey?

West (Future):

- List three things you would like to do that you have never done before.
- List two personal goals you wish to accomplish in the next 6 months.
- List one new activity that you can do to meet/make a new friend.
- List three lifetime wishes or dreams.

North (Inspiration):

- What is your gift(s) to the world?
- How can you best offer this gift to the world?
- List three way to volunteer (provide service) to your community.
- What is the best way to pay tribute to your loss?

EXERCISE 6: Creative Altruism: The Power of Unconditional Love

Love, it is said, is the glue that holds the universe together. The expression of love can be made manifest in a great many ways. The following questions encourage you to explore the concept of unconditional love as an alternative to the motivation of fear.

1. Write your best definition of love:

_____

_____

2. If love is the energy that moves the human spirit, then fear is the metaphorical brake that stops love in its tracks. How does fear impede your ability to express love?

_____

_____

3. The slogan "random acts of kindness" was coined by a woman who was searching for a way to make the world a better place in which to live. She created this catchphrase as a means to express heartfelt altruism. The idea of performing a random act of kindness means to give anonymously without the expectation of receiving anything back. Compose a list of five ways to "give" altruistically and identify at least three ways that don't involve money.

a. _____

b. _____

c. _____

d. _____

e. _____

4. Service! One cannot speak on the topic of altruism without speaking of the concept of service. Although there are more stories in the news about acts of service (e.g., Habitat for Humanity), examples are not as common as one might expect. It's hard to feel sorry for yourself when you are helping others who are less fortunate. For more than a decade, the Institute of Noetic Sciences has given the Temple Awards for Creative Altruism to those unique individuals who demonstrate the spirit of selfless service. If you could create an altruistic nonprofit organization to help others, what would you do? Explain it here:

_____

_____

_____

_____

_____

_____

_____

Photo Credits

Unless otherwise indicated, all photographs and illustrations are under copyright of Jones and Bartlett Publishers, LLC, or have been provided by the author.

The Mind: The Psychology of Stress

"And yet the mind seems to act independently of the brain in the same sense that the programmer acts independently of the computer."

— Wilder Penfield,
The Mystery of the Mind

For eons, philosophers, scientists, theologians, psychologists, as well as countless planetary citizens have all wondered, hypothesized, and speculated on the topic of the human mind. What is it? Where is it? How does it work? Why do identical twins have different minds? Where does the mind go when we die? What is a premonition? Can the mind be trained? What is intelligence? What is conscience? How fast can the mind travel? What is a thought?

As we begin the dawn of the 21st century, scientists are now beginning to confirm what the mystics stated long ago: The mind is a reservoir of conscious energy that surrounds and permeates the human body. From a holistic perspective, the mind and the brain are not the same thing. The mind, the quintessential seat of consciousness, merely uses the brain as its primary organ of choice. With new revelations from organ transplant recipients, apparently the mind uses other organs as well. In fact, new research suggests that every cell has consciousness, giving rise to a new term, *cell memory*.

The study of the mind (and the brain) has led to a deeper understanding of human consciousness, yet it's fair to say that through this vast exploration of dreams, cognitive inventories, hypnosis, meditation, DNA, EEGs, and MRIs, our knowledge, at best, is still embryonic. Current research in the field of consciousness reveals interesting insights about a phenomenon that only grows more fascinating with further study. For example, distant healing, remote viewing, premonitions, synchronicities, near-death experiences, out-of-body experiences, spontaneous healings, and much more only begin to substantiate that mind, as consciousness, is certainly not a simple consequence of brain chemistry, though there are many who still believe this.

This much we do know: Much like a laptop computer, mental well-being is the ability to gather, process, recall, and communicate information. We also know that stress compromises the mind's ability to do all of these functions. Information is constantly gathered and processed through the portals of the five senses for a variety of reasons (from threats to simple curiosity). Yet it's no secret that information comes into the conscious mind in other ways, including intuition, meditation, and what can only be explained as extrasensory perception. Just as we know that the mind can generate stress without any outside stimulus, the power of the mind to heal the body is also well documented.

Although no one book can begin to elaborate on the psychology of stress or the secrets to mental well-being, the following offers some keen insights into the psychology of stress, as observed by renowned leaders in the field who have shared the greatest wisdom to date on the mysteries of the mind.

The Anatomy of Ego

When it comes to the mind, one cannot look at stress without first examining the role of the **ego**. Many claim that the ego is the cause of both personal and worldly problems, and although this may not be far from the truth, it must also be recognized that the ego is not always bad either. A healthy ego generates high self-esteem. As **Freud** accurately pointed out, the ego serves a role of protection. It also constitutes one's identity (or as Freud stated, Id-entity). Perhaps more accurately, the ego is the mind's bodyguard and censor. In an effort to protect one from harm, the ego sounds the alarm of imminent danger for mental, emotional, and physical threats. Sometimes the ego goes overboard in its role as the mind's bodyguard and tends to make mountains out of molehills. Experts in the field of psychology call this **cognitive distortion**.

The ego has many tricks up its sleeve for protection. Freud called these **defense mechanisms**—thoughts and behaviors that act to decrease pain and perhaps even increase pleasure to the mind and body. He said that, by and large, we use more than one at a time, and for the most part we are not even aware of it. Here is a quick overview of some of the more common defenses of the ego:

- *Denial:* I didn't do it!
- *Repression:* I don't remember doing it!
- *Projection:* He did it!
- *Displacement:* He made me do it!
- *Rationalization:* Everyone does it!
- *Humor:* I did it and a year from now maybe I'll laugh about this!

At its best, the ego serves as the bodyguard for the soul. At its worst, the ego tries to control and manipulate everything (and perhaps everybody). When ruled by fear and anger, the ego transitions from a place of power to control, or what some people refer to as the unhealthy ego. Freud might have been the first person in the West to study this aspect of the mind, but he certainly wasn't the first to acknowledge it. Philosophers as far back as ancient Greece, India, China, and Tibet often spoke of the mind's shadow side. In Eastern culture, the ego is called the small mind (also called the false self), and ancient traditions suggest that the best means for mental well-being is to domesticate the small mind so that it can work in harmony with the larger mind of the universe. Psychologist Carl Jung described this process as "embracing the shadow." Ultimately, this means moving beyond a motivation of fear toward a motivation of love and compassion, a process that is not impossible but requires much discipline.

In terms of coping with the perceptions of stress rather than using a defense mechanism to avoid it, the holistic approach to stress management suggests following advice from the Eastern tradition by learning to domesticate the ego. Meditation is the premier skill to accomplish this goal. Exercise 1 can also help you start with this process.

The Power of Two Minds

Metaphorically speaking, you have not one, but two minds: the conscious mind and the unconscious mind. The conscious mind is best described as an awareness, like that which appears on your computer screen, and it receives nearly all of the attention of the ego. The unconscious mind is analogous to not only that which appears on your hard drive, but also some would say the entire Internet as well. Like an iceberg with nearly 90 percent of its entirety below water, the total mind is vast. It contains a wealth of information that often is never realized, yet is the model for today's typical computer. Unlike the conscious mind, which shuts down when you sleep, the unconscious mind works 24 hours a day, every day of your life. It, too, offers a sense of awareness. It is a reservoir of endless wisdom as well as a container of all your personal memories **Fig. 1 ▶**.

It would be simple if these two minds spoke the same language, but unfortunately this is not the case. Whereas the conscious mind is fluent in verbal skills, linear thinking, rational thinking, and many, many other cognitive functions that are now associated with the left hemisphere of the brain, the unconscious mind is fluent in intuition, imagination, and acceptance, cognitive skills associated with the right brain. Like a

virus scanner on your computer, the ego serves the role of censor and gatekeeper, making sure nothing bubbles up to the surface of the conscious mind that might prove to be a threat. Unfortunately, much of this wisdom never passes through the gates of the ego. In no uncertain terms, stress can be defined as the conflict between the conscious and unconscious minds.

It was **Carl Jung**, one-time protégé of Sigmund Freud, who began, in earnest, to study the workings of the unconscious mind, particularly through dream analysis, but also through artwork and other nonverbal means of communication. Jung was of the opinion that if people took the time to learn the language of the unconscious mind, often expressed in archetypal symbols, and, in turn, gathered the wisdom that is there for the asking, then as a whole we would have a lot less stress in our lives.

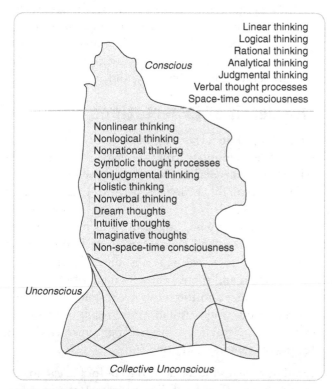

FIGURE 1 The metaphor of an iceberg is often used to describe the complexities of the mind, with the conscious mind (10 percent) above the water and the unconscious mind (90 percent) below; each aspect of the mind employs different thought processes.

Jung was also of the belief that the mind was a gateway to the soul. Anxiety, he suggested, was not merely a consequence of physical survival but the evolution of the human spirit. In other words, when we take the time to learn from our life experiences, then stress offers an opportunity for spiritual growth. The mind and the soul share a common space in the landscape of the human spirit. The word *psyche*, from which the word *psychology* is derived, means soul, and it goes without saying that there is tremendous overlap between the quadrants of mental well-being and spiritual well-being. Carl Jung was quick to note this association when he stated that every crisis over the age of 30 is a spiritual crisis. It was Jung who also noted that although we each have a personal unconscious composed of personal thoughts and memories, we are each connected to a larger reservoir of wisdom that he called the "collective unconscious," where time and space play by different rules. In fact, it was a conversation with Albert Einstein about the theory of relativity that seeded the idea of the collective unconscious in Jung's mind. Much of Jung's work can be found in the roots of many stress management therapies, including dream therapy, mental imagery, and art therapy.

The Death of Expectations

Anger (fight) and fear (flight) make up the two primary stress emotions from which all other stress-related emotions derive. Over the past century, anxiety stole the spotlight, primarily because Freud thought this was the easier of the two instinctual emotions to work with. Meanwhile anger, in all its many manifestations, began to boil over on the back burner on the world stage, from road rage and the Columbine massacre to child and spouse abuse to international acts of terrorism. First and foremost, every episode of anger, no matter how big or small, is the result of an unmet expectation. Behind every episode of anger awaits the feelings of remorse and grief.

Death is perhaps the hardest concept for the ego to reconcile. In an effort to maintain control, the ego does everything in its power to keep the upper hand. The work of Elisabeth Kübler-Ross, who observed the progression of thoughts and behaviors one experiences through one's own personal death and dying process, has now become such common knowledge that it can be found everywhere from greeting cards to cereal boxes. The stages are the following: denial, anger, bargaining, withdrawal, and acceptance. Grieving is a natural part of the human experience. All of these stages constitute the fine art of grieving. (It should be noted that the stage after acceptance is adaptation.) Prolonged grieving, however, is not healthy and serves only to perpetuate chronic stress, yet many people never move beyond anger to acceptance, a crucial step in the resolution of all stressors.

You don't have to come down with terminal cancer to experience this progression of thought processes. Most likely you experience this same linear process with the death of each expectation, no matter how big or small, whether it's a dent in your new car or the breakup of your marriage. The next time you find yourself angry, ask yourself what expectation wasn't met, and therein may lie the answer to your problem.

Finding the Meaning of Life

There is a wise proverb that states: "Pain is inevitable, suffering is optional." *Suffering* is another word for stress, and chronic stress proves to be quite common with those who find themselves in an existential vacuum—a life that seems to have no purpose or meaning. Angst is a common plight among those who find themselves retired from a lifelong career, roaming an empty house made vacant by the last teenager leaving home, experiencing the sudden loss of a loved one, or even among Olympic athletes who walk off the podium with a bronze medal. Angst is also common among people who dislike their jobs. Interestingly, more heart attacks occur on Monday mornings than at any other time of the week, suggesting a link between the meaning of life and one's health. Depression, the hallmark cry of the soul, is a common malady in our stress-filled world. Despite the magic bullet of modern medicine, a chemical cure through prescribed pharmaceuticals does nothing to treat the trauma of emotional wounds. In some cases, it only masks these wounds and makes them worse by doing so.

How can suffering be optional? The voice of ageless wisdom, as echoed by Nazi concentration camp survivor Viktor Frankl in his classic book *Man's Search for Meaning*, suggests that to ease the angst of suffering, one must create a new meaning in one's life. To do this, one must find a new passion, make a new goal or goals, and make a commitment in deciding how to spend one's life energy, rather than letting it drain away. The voice of ageless wisdom advises the weary traveler to acknowledge the past, but not dwell on it. Rather, one must set one's eyes on the future, one day at a time, one step at a time, till one regains balance and can move forward on the human journey.

Energy Psychology

Perhaps because the field of psychology has worked so hard to establish credibility as a science, it has stayed clear of all things metaphysical, including all things categorized as paranormal. However, a handful of maverick scientists and luminaries in the field of psychology has taken the initiative to integrate various aspects of ageless wisdom with many theoretical principles of modern psychology. The result forges a path to different offshoots of this discipline, starting with humanistic psychology, health psychology, and transpersonal psychology and moving on to the emerging field of **energy psychology**: a field of study that honors the mind-body-spirit dynamics and techniques to help counsel patients and clients through a wide range of psychological conditions. The premise of energy psychology is based on the ageless wisdom of the human energy matrix of subtle anatomy, including the auric field (layers of consciousness), chakras, and meridians. By using the human energy grid to detect congestion and distortions associated with mental and emotional disturbances, great gains can be made at the spiritual, mental, emotional, and physical levels to restore one back to optimal health.

In the field of energy psychology, just as each layer of the auric field is associated with a specific layer of consciousness, each of the primary chakras is associated with one or more aspects of one's personality. By recognizing the various aspects of each chakra, one can begin to process and resolve issues that tend to manifest as physical symptoms. (Consider reading the section on chakras in Chapter 2.)

Stress-Prone and Stress-Resistant Personalities

No topic of mental well-being would be complete without some discussion of personality types that make up the collective persona of the human species. It's fair to say that the topic of personalities is as complex as it is popular to discuss and demystify. Personality is composed of attitudes, behaviors, values, philosophies, opinions, belief systems, and perhaps much, much more. Character, a component of one's personality, is often said to be how you behave when no one else is looking. The Myers-Briggs personality type inventory (based on the work of Carl Jung) is one of many personality profiles used to determine and predict how people will get along with each other. The Enneagram personality type inventory is another. Perhaps because there are so many variables, personality assessments still remain more of an art than a science. Nonetheless, they offer keen insight into the complexities of the mind and how we deal with stress.

Whereas hard science points to genetic aspects (nature) that comprise aspects of one's personality, the softer sciences suggest a host of environmental factors (nurture) associated with the make-up of one's thoughts, attitudes, behaviors, and beliefs. Still others add a third dimension, ranging from astrological aspects to spiritual (karmic) considerations—all of which, to some extent, play a part in the complexities of the personality of each individual.

Although using a questionnaire to determine one's personality may be limiting, observations of character traits under stressful conditions can be quite revealing. Based on several decades of work, the following personality types have been assessed as being either stress-prone or stress-resistant.

Stress-Prone Personalities

These personality types not only do poorly in stressful situations, but with low self-esteem, they also actually tend to attract more stress into their lives. Exercise 2 offers an assessment of possible **stress-prone personality** traits.

- *Type A:* Once labeled as the impatient personality, the **Type A personality** is now regarded as someone with latent anger issues that manifest in explosive, competitive, and impetuous behaviors.

- *Type D:* New research reveals that symptoms of chronic depression (suppressed anger) may also play a primary role in coronary heart disease, and perhaps other chronic illnesses. As such, Type D, like Type A, is now considered a stress personality in the category of stress-prone personalities.

- *Co-dependent:* This personality is composed of many traits that coalesce as a collective defense mechanism to cope with problems such as alcoholic parents or loved ones. The co-dependent personality is also known in rehab circles as the enabler. Approval seeking, being a super overachiever with poor boundaries, and living with a constant level of fear (primarily the fear of rejection) are common traits of this personality. Exercise 2 is an example of a survey to help identify traits associated with this stress-prone personality.

- *Helpless-hopeless:* This personality style best describes someone who, for whatever reason, has met failure at every turn (e.g., child abuse, sexual abuse). Self-esteem is at rock bottom and the individual feels a lack of personal resources to help cope with problems, both big and small. Depression and feelings of helplessness and hopelessness are often associated with each other, in what sometimes can be described as a downward spiral.

Stress-Resistant Personalities

These people tend to let small things roll off their back and deal with big problems in a very positive way. Exercise 3 offers an assessment of your **stress-resistant personality** traits.

- *Hardy personality:* Marked by three distinct characteristics, people who exhibit the hardy personality demonstrate commitment to see a problem through to resolution, challenge themselves to accomplish a goal or resolve a crisis with honor, and control their emotions in a balanced way.

- *Survivor personality:* These people are true heroes who exhibit a balance of right and left brain skills so that problems can be approached creatively and solutions executed with confidence. Lance Armstrong (cancer survivor and seven-time winner of the Tour de France) and Aron Ralston (celebrated rock climber) are two examples of the survivor personality.

- *Calculated risk taker:* This person approaches life with courage rather than fear. The calculated risk taker sees danger and may even thrive on it, but only after surveying all options and choosing the most level-headed approach. People who do extreme sports would fall in this category.

The evidence is quite clear that changing one's personality is impossible, yet we can begin to change our thoughts, attitudes, beliefs, and perceptions that either influence or negate various personality traits. Although you may demonstrate traits associated with the Type A or the co-dependent personality, it doesn't mean that you cannot change your thinking patterns to stop those behaviors and begin to adopt stress-resistant traits instead.

The Power of the Mind

Holistic stress management honors the ageless wisdom of the power of the mind—the collective spirit of both conscious and unconscious minds to work in unison, as partners rather than rivals. History is punctuated with unfathomable stories of men and women who have harnessed the power of their minds to perform truly remarkable human feats. Lance Armstrong, seven-time winner of the Tour de France; Ernest Shackleton, the captain of the *Endurance*; Rosa Parks, civil rights leader; and Aron Ralston, mountain climber, are but a few examples of people who have harnessed the power of their minds to overcome adversity. Their secret of success is no secret. You, too, have the means within you to harness the power of your mind. Meditation, music therapy, visualization, mental imagery, humor therapy, and positive affirmations are just a few of the many ways that the power of the mind can be disciplined and utilized to not only cope with the stress of life, but also rise to our highest human potential. Exercise 4 offers you a unique opportunity to begin to cultivate the powers of your mind.

Chapter Summary

- According to Freud, the ego includes several defense mechanisms: denial, repression, projection, displacement, rationalization, and even humor.

- The power of two minds includes the unconscious mind, often forgotten in stress management courses. It is said that the unconscious mind controls many of our behaviors.

- Many unresolved anger issues result in prolonged grieving (the death of expectations), as explained by Elisabeth Kübler-Ross in her death and dying model, which has five stages: denial, anger, bargaining, withdrawal, and acceptance.

- The psychology of stress includes a meaningful purpose in life, as described by Viktor Frankl. When meaning is missing, stress ensues.

- Energy psychology combines the concepts of the human energy system (e.g., chakras) with states of consciousness and the resolution of stress.

- Some people seem prone to stress whereas others seem to be immune from it. The concept of stress-prone and stress-resistant personalities invites us to examine our personality and change behaviors that promote stress while enhancing factors that resist it.

Additional Resources

Beattie, M. *Codependent No More*. Center City, MN: Hazelden Books; 1992.

Eden, D. *Energy Medicine*. New York: Tarcher/Putnam Books; 2008.

Frankl, V. *Man's Search For Meaning*. Boston, MA: Beacon Press; 1959, 1992.

Kübler-Ross, E. *On Death and Dying* (Revised). Berkeley, CA: Celestial Arts; 2008.

Miller, M.C. The dangers of chronic distress. *Newsweek*. pp. 58–59. October 3, 2005.

Seligman, M. *Authentic Happiness*. New York: Free Press; 2002.

Shackleton, E. *South: The Last Antarctic Expedition of Shackleton and the Endurance*. New York: Lyons Press; 1919, 2008.

Siebert, A. *The Survivor Personality*. New York: Perigee Books; 1996.

EXERCISE   1: Domestication of the Ego

Renowned psychologist Carl Jung once said, "The conscious mind rejects that which it does not understand." What he meant by that statement is that the ego acts as a powerful censor to the wealth of information residing just below the surface of conscious thought. The ego not only makes no attempt to understand the unconscious mind, but also reacts to all unfamiliar ideas as enemies at the gate, ready to be shot down on a whim. Like an overactive security system that twitches at the hint of a threat, the ego defends us not only against real danger, but also against illusionary dangers that it creates itself. The net result is that we lose out on a lot in life by having an overprotective ego, always trying to maintain control, rather than empowering us to new heights.

In Eastern culture, there is an expression that reminds us to beware of an overprotective ego. It is said that we need to learn to "domesticate our ego," or else run the risk of having "poop" all over the place. What can one do to start this domestication process? First, you have to admit that, indeed, your ego can be the source of problems, if nothing else, holding you back and limiting your human potential. To do this, you have to observe your thought processes on a regular basis, repeatedly catch yourself in the act, and stop this limiting ego process in mid-air enough times so that this new behavior takes root, becomes second nature, and replaces the old and useless thought processes of an overreactive and self-defeating ego.

Carl Jung often used the term "embracing the shadow," an expression he is credited with coining to represent the dark side of the ego. But before you embrace (vs. exploit) your dark side, you must first tame it by being conscious of thoughts that are fear-based.

Domesticating the ego requires more than easing up on the suppressing role of the censor. It also means not seeing people, things, and opportunities as a threat to one's existence. Furthermore, it means engaging in acts of forgiveness, tolerance, patience, and compassion.

The following are some questions to ponder about things that might push buttons, but with a little bit of thought, might also allow you to house-train your ego.

1. What types of people do you feel a sense of prejudice toward/against? List them here, and next to each answer write a short reason why you harbor these feelings.

a. _____

b. _____

c. _____

2. What stereotypes do you find yourself labeling people with? What is the basis for these thoughts?

_____

_____

_____

_____

_____

3. Name three people you find yourself trying to control or manipulate.

a. _____

b. _____

c. _____

EXERCISE   1: Domestication of the Ego cont....

4. If you had to list three insecurities you have, what would you identify?

a. _____

b. _____

c. _____

5. Describe in a few words your most common recurring dream.

_____

_____

_____

_____

_____

6. List three of the deepest fears that you can identify.

a. _____

b. _____

c. _____

7. What three people are you holding grudges against? Next to each name write the duration of time you have been holding this sense of resentment, and why the grudge still exists.

a. _____

b. _____

c. _____

Additional Thoughts: _____

_____

_____

_____

_____

_____

EXERCISE 2: Stress-Prone Personality Survey

The following is a survey based on the traits of the co-dependent personality. Please answer the following questions with the most appropriate number.

3 = Often   2 = Sometimes   1 = Rarely   0 = Never

1. I tend to seek approval (acceptance) from others (e.g., friends, colleagues, family members).	3	2	1	0
2. I have very strong perfection tendencies.	3	2	1	0
3. I am usually involved in many projects at one time.	3	2	1	0
4. I rise to the occasion in times of crisis.	3	2	1	0
5. Despite problems with my family, I will always defend them.	3	2	1	0
6. I have a tendency to put others before myself.	3	2	1	0
7. I don't feel appreciated for all the things I do.	3	2	1	0
8. I tend to tell a lot of white lies.	3	2	1	0
9. I will help most anyone in need.	3	2	1	0
10. I tend to trust others' perceptions rather than my own.	3	2	1	0
11. I have a habit of overreacting to situations.	3	2	1	0
12. Despite great achievements, my self-esteem usually suffers.	3	2	1	0
13. My family background is better described as victim than victor.	3	2	1	0
14. I have been known to manipulate others with acts of generosity and favors.	3	2	1	0
15. I am really good at empathizing with my friends and family.	3	2	1	0
16. I usually try to make the best impression possible with people.	3	2	1	0
17. I like to validate my feelings with others' perceptions.	3	2	1	0
18. I am an extremely well-organized individual.	3	2	1	0
19. It's easier for me to give love and much more difficult to receive it.	3	2	1	0
20. I tend to hide my feelings if I know they will upset others.	3	2	1	0
TOTAL SCORE				

Score: A score of more than 30 points indicates that you most likely have traits associated with the co-dependent personality, a personality style known to be stress-prone.

EXERCISE 3: Stress-Resistant Personality Survey

The following survey is composed of statements based on the hardy, survivor, and risk-taking personality traits—all of which share common aspects that resist rather than attract or promote stress in one's life. Please answer the following questions with the most appropriate number.

4 = Always   3 = Often   2 = Sometimes   1 = Rarely   0 = Never

	4	3	2	1	0
1. I wake up each morning ready to face a new day.	4	3	2	1	0
2. I tend not to let fear run my life.	4	3	2	1	0
3. I would consider myself to be an optimist.	4	3	2	1	0
4. I tend to see "problems" as opportunities for personal growth and success.	4	3	2	1	0
5. Although I like to be in control of my fate, I know when to go with the flow when things are out of my control.	4	3	2	1	0
6. Curiosity is one of my stronger attributes.	4	3	2	1	0
7. Life isn't always fair, but I still manage to enjoy myself.	4	3	2	1	0
8. When things knock me off balance, I am resilient and get back on my feet quickly.	4	3	2	1	0
9. My friends would say that I have the ability to turn misfortune into luck.	4	3	2	1	0
10. I believe that if you don't take risks, you live a boring life and won't get far.	4	3	2	1	0
11. I like to think of myself as being a creative person.	4	3	2	1	0
12. I believe in the philosophy that "one person truly can make a difference."	4	3	2	1	0
13. I am both organized and flexible with my life's day-to-day schedule.	4	3	2	1	0
14. Sometimes having nothing to do is the best way to spend a day.	4	3	2	1	0
15. I trust that I am part of a greater force of life in the universe.	4	3	2	1	0
16. I believe in the philosophy that "you make your own breaks."	4	3	2	1	0
17. I approach new situations with the idea that I will learn something valuable, regardless of the outcome.	4	3	2	1	0
18. When I start a project, I see it through to its successful completion.	4	3	2	1	0
19. I am strong willed, which I see as a positive characteristic to accomplish hard tasks.	4	3	2	1	0
20. I am committed to doing my best in most everything in life.	4	3	2	1	0
TOTAL SCORE					

Score: A score of more than 30 points indicates that you most likely have traits associated with the hardy, survivor, and calculated risk-taker personalities—personality types known to be stress-resistant.

EXERCISE   4: Mind over Matter: Harnessing the Power of Your Mind

Spoon bending may seem to be in a different league than the spontaneous remission of a cancerous tumor, but in reality, the premise of each is the same. Most likely you've heard the expression "mind over matter," yet few people actually put this philosophy into play. Mind over matter simply means using the power of your mind (both conscious and unconscious minds) to accomplish a task. Mind over matter isn't a means to control others. It's a means of becoming empowered rather than giving your power away. Those who teach mind power often use the spoon-bending exercise as the first stepping stone toward the goal of other, seemingly larger but no less challenging goals. Mind over matter isn't magic, an illusion, or a cute parlor trick. It's merely the manifestation of an inherent power that we each hold in the center of our own minds. The process of mind over matter involves the following three distinct steps.

Step One: Focus Your Mind. The first step of mind over matter requires your mind to be focused completely and entirely on the task at hand. A wandering mind is analogous to irritating static on your favorite radio station making the transmission inaudible.

Step Two: Believe. Once the mind is clear of distracting thoughts and is completely focused on the task at hand, the heart and mind (conscious and unconscious minds) must be aligned. This means that all doubt must be cast aside and faith must galvanize you with a sense of absolutely knowing that you will, indeed, accomplish the deed (whatever it happens to be). To reinforce the belief process, use the power of your imagination to picture the event as having already occurred. Feel the exhilaration of completing this task.

Step Three: State the Command. State the command to complete the desired action. To bend a spoon, you might simply state, "Bend!" To dissolve a tumor, state the command, "Dissolve away!"

Spoon Bending 101

Locate an old spoon (or fork) from the silverware drawer (one that you don't intend to use again). Hold the base of the utensil in one hand and with a slight effort with the free hand apply a little pressure simply to test the strength of the metal. Follow steps 1–3 above. After stating the command "Bend!" once again hold the top of the utensil and bend it at the neck. If possible, bend the neck of the spoon or fork into a loop. Sometimes it helps to visualize the neck of the spoon as molten red, right before you apply pressure to bend the spoon. Once the utensil is transformed, consider keeping it in a place where you can see it often as a symbol to remind you of the power of your mind.

Spoon bending is really nothing more than a simple metaphor of the power of mind over matter. Once you have mastered this task, consider trying this technique in other areas of your life.

Photo Credits

Reframing: Creating a Positive Mind-Set

"Attitude is the paintbrush with which we color the world."
— Ancient proverb

The Ageless Wisdom of Positive Thinking

There are those who say the world is composed of two kinds of people: optimists and pessimists. Ageless wisdom reveals that within the mind of each person there are at least two voices, a positive and a negative influence, suggesting that each of us contains the potential for both mind-sets. Since the days of Plato and perhaps much earlier, it has been observed that the direction of one's life, by and large, is a product of one's thoughts and attitudes. To be sure, we cannot avoid life's problems; however, our attitude about each situation tends to reveal the outcome. Changing one's attitude provides the impetus to change the direction of one's life. As the old adage goes, "Attitude is the paintbrush with which we paint the world."

In his critically acclaimed book, *Man's Search for Meaning*, Viktor Frankl credited his survival in the most notorious Nazi concentration camp, Auschwitz, to his ability to find meaning in his suffering, a meaning that strengthened his willpower and choice of attitude. Frankl noted that despite the fact that prisoners were stripped of all their possessions and many essential human rights, the one thing concentration camp officials could not take away was their ability to choose the perceptions of their circumstances. To quote another adage, "Each situation has a good side and a bad side. Each moment, you decide."

If you listen to the news much these days you might notice several references to the Great Depression with regard to the economy. As it turns out, the period of the Great Depression was a study not only in the economy, but also in psychology. Although many people struggled day by day, several people thrived in the face of adversity. We are already seeing that same dichotomy emerge once again in these troubled economic times.

The phrase *self-fulfilling prophecy* was used long before Freud coined the word *ego*. Ageless wisdom confirms the idea that negative thoughts tend to create and often perpetuate negative circumstances. Likewise, positive thoughts do the same. Current research regarding the power of intention upholds this timeless wisdom. Our thoughts, attitudes, perceptions, and beliefs unite as a powerful source of conscious energy. Therefore, it makes sense to use this energy for the best means possible.

The Influence of the Media

Current estimates suggest that the average person is bombarded with more than 3,000 advertisements a day from television, radio, T-shirts, billboards, and the Internet—all of which constantly inundate us with messages that strike at our insecurities. In marketing circles it is known as aggressive, in-your-face tactics. The desired result leaves one with an underlying sense of inadequacy if not an inferiority complex. There is no doubt this method works, otherwise marketers would move on to a different strategy.

Corporate marketing is only part of the fear-based media equation. As was so poignantly illustrated in the 2002 Academy Award–winning documentary *Bowling for Columbine*, both local and national news broadcasts have discovered that the addictive nature of fear sells. Even the Weather Channel has changed its focus recently to broadcast weather-related disasters between forecast updates just to keep viewers' attention. Moreover, the federal government was accused of using the media to fan the flames of anxiety with hyper-vigilant color-coded terrorism alerts. One of the best ways to increase your tolerance to negative media is to reduce your exposure to it, limiting the time you spend watching television, if not getting rid of it altogether.

An Attitude of Gratitude

Although it's true that it is difficult, if not impossible, to give sincere thanks for a crisis the moment it appears (that's called denial), continuously dwelling on a problem only tends to make things worse. A shift in consciousness toward those things that are blessings tends to balance the negative thoughts that persist from personal stressors. In doing so, an attitude of gratitude provides a perspective that helps resolve the problem at hand. In the midst of stress, regardless of the size of the problem, it is easy to take things for granted.

The preferred option is to count your blessings by seeing even the smallest things as gifts. One aspect of **reframing** suggests to do just that—adopt an attitude of gratitude for all things in life that are going right, rather than curse all the things that seem to be going wrong. In a society where only 1 day out of 365 is dedicated to giving thanks, the regular practice of an attitude of gratitude may not seem to be encouraged, but remember, this is the same society that promotes fear-based television programming. Buck the tide and make a habit of giving thanks regularly.

In hindsight, what appears to be a curse may actually be looked upon as a blessing. Many people caught in the midst of a crisis utter the words, "This is the worst thing that ever happened to me," only to reframe this perspective later to say, "This was the best thing that ever happened to me."

The Art of Acceptance

Clearly, there are some things in life we cannot change, nor can we change the people involved with these situations. Attempting to do so becomes a series of control dramas that only perpetuate the cycles of stress. The ability to accept a situation for what it is, rather than exerting (and wasting) your energy to alter what you cannot change, is a unique human resource, and a valuable component of reframing. Acceptance isn't a sense of resignation or defeat. Rather, it is a sense of liberation that allows you to release any emotional baggage and move on with your life. Acceptance may be an overnight epiphany for some, but for most people it's an attitude that takes several days, weeks, or months to adopt.

The Power of Positive Affirmations

If you were to eavesdrop on the continuous stream of your conscious thoughts, you might be surprised to hear whispers of sabotage. The overbearing voice of the ego is constantly striving to dominate the passionate voice of the soul. By the time most people reach their late teens, the ego has practically declared victory! Sometimes the voice of the ego sounds like background static. Other times it sounds like blaring headline news. The ego best communicates throughout the landscape of the mind by providing a steady stream of negative or fear-based thoughts, attitudes, beliefs, and perceptions that, over time, begin to cloud almost everything you see.

Renowned psychologist Carl Jung referred to the constant mental chatter of the ego as "psychic tension." Many people suffer from this type of stress; however, there is a way to break this cycle and redirect your thoughts toward a positive direction. Jung called this "psychic equilibrium," and the balance of this mind-set is within the grasp of each individual—including you!

Using an apt metaphor, the negative voice of the ego that feeds subliminal (and perhaps obvious) messages of fear is similar to the broadcast of a local radio station. The good news is that there is a better choice of quality programming to listen to, primarily the optimistic voice that provides a clear message of your highest qualities, your inner resources (e.g., humor, creativity, faith), to reach your highest human potential.

If you were to talk to those people who have groomed themselves for success, from Olympic athletes and Grammy-winning musicians to the countless untold heroes of every age, you would find that they have learned to switch the mind's radio dial from the nagging voice of the ego to the passionate, grounded voice of the soul. In doing so, they have become the master of their destiny on the voyage of their highest human potential. You can do this too! People like Lance Armstrong, Rosa Parks, and Google.com creator Sergey Brin have learned that confidence is not the same thing as arrogance. **Positive affirmations** become the mind's compass, leading the way toward humble success.

Developing Your Mastery of Reframing and Optimism

Grooming your mind's thoughts is a skill that takes practice, but it's not impossible. A quick study of elite athletes and Broadway actors reveals that they didn't get to the top by listening to the negative voice in their head. They redirected their thoughts toward an optimistic belief system.

1. The first step of reframing a situation is to gain an awareness of your thoughts and feelings. When you encounter a difficult situation, get in the habit of asking yourself how you feel, and why you feel this way. If you need validation of your perceptions, consider asking a friend for his or her honest opinions.

2. Once you have become familiar with the recurring pattern of your thoughts and feelings, the next step is to match each negative thought with a positive thought. In essence, find something positive in the negative situation—and there is always something positive in every bad situation. Every situation, good, bad, and ugly, offers a valuable life lesson, and when this is acknowledged, something good can be gleaned from it.

3. Negative thoughts about a situation act like a mirror image to our own thoughts about ourselves, and they can have an immense negative

impact on our self-esteem. Another step in the reframing process is to take an inventory of your personal strengths. By doing so, you begin to focus on your positive attributes rather than aspects that contribute to low self-esteem.

4. The last suggestion for adopting a positive mind-set is to include the ageless wisdom of counting your blessings. Rather than focusing on what's not right, shift your attention to all that *is* right. There is a concept known as the self-fulfilling prophecy. Others call it the law of universal attraction. It states that the more you think about negative things, the more negative things come into your life to think about. The same is true for positive things. In essence, to a large extent, you attract into your life that which you think most about.

Remember, negativity and the repeated thought processes that produce it can become a downward spiral of consciousness.

Tips to Incorporate the Practice of Reframing

There are many ways to shift the focus of your attention from a negative mind-set to a neutral or positive frame of mind. Remember that reframing isn't a denial of the situation; rather, it is a positive twist that acts to first recognize, and then neutralize the sting of a potentially bad situation. Try these suggestions:

1. When you find a situation to be stressful, ask yourself what can be learned from the situation.

2. When you find yourself in a stressful circumstance, take a moment to grieve for the situation and then try to come up with between three and five things for which you are grateful.

3. When things don't go as planned (unmet expectations), rather than focusing on your negative attributes, come up with three positive aspects about yourself that you know are your personal strengths. Then pick one and start to use it. Examples might include creativity, humor, and faith.

4. To cultivate a positive mind-set in nonstressful times so that you have it to use during stressful times, place a short list of positive affirmations on your bathroom mirror or computer monitor.

Exercise 1 invites you to try your hand at the reframing process.

Tips to Incorporate the Practice of Positive Affirmation Statements

Effective positive affirmation statements have a few things in common:

1. The use of the words "I am" to begin each statement (e.g., "I am a wonderful human being," or "I am confident of my abilities to succeed in this endeavor")

2. Scripting the phrase in the affirmative (e.g., "I am going to make it" vs. "I am not going to make it")

3. Scripting the phrase in the present tense (e.g., "I am succeeding in this endeavor" vs. "I am going to succeed in this endeavor")

The following are empowering affirmations to awaken the often slumbering human spirit; suggestions offered for *your* internal radio station. The purpose is for you to consciously reprogram and incorporate these thoughts into the perpetually running tapes of your conscious and unconscious minds, so that you may achieve what Carl Jung called psychic equilibrium, or mental homeostasis—the foundation for all success.

The ultimate goal in this process is to reclaim your mental and spiritual sovereignty, which in turn allows you to transition from inertia to inspiration, from victim to victor on the path of what Joseph Campbell called "the hero's journey."

Please feel free to embellish, edit, and adapt any or all of these affirmations to best suit your needs. Keep in mind that, as with any new skill, listening to these might seem awkward at first, yet after a few sessions, it will begin to feel quite normal, in fact, second nature. Soon you will notice that these thoughts, these affirmations, will become integrated into your normal thinking process, particularly in times of personal challenge, and brightly color everything you do with confidence and grace.

1. I am calm and relaxed. (or, My body is calm and relaxed.)

2. I am grateful for all the many blessings in my life, even those that appear to be less than desirable.

3. I seek a balance in my life by bringing an optimistic perspective to everyday challenges, big and small.

71

Exercise 2 asks you to think of all that is going "right" in your life.

Best Benefits of Reframing

The benefits of reframing and positive affirmations are amazing. With a new focus on life through an optimistic lens, your world will transform from black and white to full color. This is not to say that you are fooling yourself into thinking that life is a continual vacation at Disney World or in denial with a Pollyanna perspective. Rather, reframing and positive affirmations become one of many resources to strengthen your resiliency during stressful times.

Chapter Summary

- Positive thinking, one form of reframing, isn't a denial of reality; rather, it is an approach to balance the ego's constant running commentary of negativity.

- The ego can generate negative thoughts, but it has been suggested that it is influenced by the media in very subtle ways to chip away at one's self-esteem.

- One aspect of reframing suggests focusing on what we have rather than what we don't have: an attitude of gratitude, because it's hard to be stressed when you are grateful.

- Reframing invites us to look at the big picture and not see ourselves as victims. Some things we cannot change. Acceptance is a coping technique that empowers us to deal with that which we cannot change and move on with our lives.

- The power of positive affirmations suggests that unless we employ both the conscious and the unconscious minds, no amount of positive self-talk will change anything.

- To master the art of reframing and optimism one needs to cultivate the skills of the mind.

Additional Resources

There are many great books on the topic of positive affirmations and reframing, a selection of which is listed here. There also are many wonderful guided mental imagery CDs with tracks that include positive affirmations.

Books

Armstrong, L. *It's Not About the Bike*. New York: Putnam; 2000.

Dyer, W. *The Power of Intention*. Carlsbad, CA: Hayhouse; 2004.

Frankl, V. *Man's Search for Meaning*. New York: Pocket Books; 1974.

Frederickson, B. *Positivity*. New York: Crown Books; 2009.

Ornstein, R., & Sobel, D. *Healthy Pleasures*. Reading, MA: Addison-Wesley; 1989.

Peale, N. V. *The Power of Positive Thinking*. New York: Fawcett Columbine; 1996.

Ryan, M. J. *Attitude of Gratitude*. Berkeley, CA: Conari Press; 2000.

Seligman, M. *Learned Optimism*. New York: Knopf; 1991.

CDs

Naparstek, B. *General Wellness*. Time Warner Audiobooks; 1993. 800.800.8661

Seaward, B. L. *Sweet Surrender*. Boulder, CO: Inspiration Unlimited; 2003. 303.678.9962

Shamir, I. *A Thousand Things Went Right Today*. www.yourtruenature.com

EXERCISE 1: Reframing: Seeing from a Bigger, Clearer Perspective

Anger and fear that arise from encountering a stressful situation can narrow our focus of the bigger picture. Although the initial aspects of dealing with these situations involve some degree of grieving, the secret to coping with stress is to change the threatening perception to a nonthreatening perception. This exercise invites you to identify one to three stressors and, if necessary, draft a new "reframed" perspective (not a rationalization) that allows you to get out of the rut of a myopic view and start moving on with your life.

1. Situation: _____
_____
_____
_____

Reframed Perspective: _____
_____
_____
_____

2. Situation: _____
_____
_____
_____

Reframed Perspective: _____
_____
_____
_____

3. Situation: _____
_____
_____
_____

Reframed Perspective: _____
_____
_____
_____

EXERCISE   2: 1,000 Things Went Right Today!

In a stress-filled world, it becomes easy to start focusing on the negative things in life. Pretty soon you begin to attract more negative things into your life. Breaking free from this thought process isn't easy, but neither is it impossible. There is an expression, coined by Ilan Shamir, that states, "A thousand things went right today."® The concept behind this expression suggests that by beginning to look for the positive things in life, you will start attracting these as well, and let's face it, we can all use more positive things in our lives.

Rather than taxing your mind to come up with 1,000 things, or even 100, try starting with 10 things that went right today, and then see if you can begin to include this frame of mind at the midpoint of each day to keep you on course. Remember, in a world of negativity, it takes just a little more effort to be happy!

1. _____

2. _____

3. _____

4. _____

5. _____

6. _____

7. _____

8. _____

9. _____

10. _____

After having written these things, is there any lesson that you can learn from completing this exercise?

_____

_____

_____

_____

Photo Credits

Unless otherwise indicated, all photographs and illustrations are under copyright of Jones and Bartlett Publishers, LLC, or have been provided by the author.

The Art of Breathing

"There are over 40 different ways to breathe."
— Ancient Chinese proverb

The Ageless Wisdom of Breathing

There is an ancient proverb that is often cited to students learning the art of self-discipline. It states, "There are over 40 ways to breathe." If you are like most people, you might laugh or perhaps even smirk at this notion. After all, most people think there is only one way to breathe—a combination of inhaling and exhaling. The ageless wisdom of this proverb, however, suggests that the art of breathing opens the mind and body to a profound sense of relaxation. Although there is no one-size-fits-all relaxation technique that works for everyone, there is one that comes close. If you look closely at the plethora of relaxation techniques, from hatha yoga to tai chi to autogenics and meditation, you will see that **diaphragmatic breathing** is used in all of these. Indeed, of the many ways to breathe that promote relaxation, most if not all place the emphasis of the breath on the lower abdomen. The beauty of this technique is that it can be done anywhere and anytime.

By and large, Americans are thoracic breathers, meaning that we tend to breathe with our upper chest. Diaphragmatic breathing, also known as belly breathing, places the emphasis of each breath on the lower abdominal area. If you were to watch anyone breathing while they sleep, you would notice that this is the only way they breathe; this is the way that you breathe when you sleep, because in a resting state, the body tries to maintain the greatest level of homeostasis.

The Breath Cycle

There are four specific phases of each breath cycle. They include:

- *Phase 1:* The inhalation of air, also called the "in-breath"

- *Phase 2:* A very slight pause before you exhale

- *Phase 3:* The exhalation of air, also called the "out-breath"

- *Phase 4:* A very slight pause before you inhale again

You should remember not to hold your breath during phases 2 and 4 but to merely acknowledge that indeed there is a pause between the in-breath and the out-breath. In a normal resting state, the average person has between 14–16 breath cycles per minute. Under situations of stress this number can double, as breathing becomes more rapid and shallow. There are, however, those who tend to hold their breath when under stress (being stuck in phase 2 or phase 4). Holding one's breath tends to increase heart rate and blood pressure, thus being counterproductive to relaxation. When people are VERY relaxed, they may breath as few as 3–6 breath cycles per minute.

How to Incorporate the Art of Conscious Breathing into Your Life

Exercises 1 ("Breathing Clouds Meditation") and 2 ("Dolphin Breath Meditation") guide you through the steps of diaphragmatic breathing. The best way to incorporate breathing as a relaxation technique is to practice belly breathing every day, even if it's only for 5 minutes each day—and we all have 5 minutes. Here are some suggestions:

- When you wake up in the morning, before you get out of bed, take five comfortably slow, deep breaths.

- While in the shower, with your hands at your side, take five comfortably deep breaths.

- On the way to work or class, turn off the radio or iPod for 5 minutes and consciously breathe.

- Close the door for 5 minutes and sit quietly and simply breathe.

- Take five deep sighs on the way home from work or class.

- Take five deep sighs waiting in line at the campus center, grocery store, post office, or bank.

- As you close your eyes to fall asleep, take five comfortably slow, deep breaths.

Developing Your Mastery of Diaphragmatic Breathing

Believe it or not, this is one technique you have already mastered. At this point all you need to do is practice what you already know. Simply place the emphasis of each breath on your lower abdomen. This sensation may feel awkward at first, but soon it will feel quite comfortable and normal. Exercises 1 and 2 are just two of the "40" techniques available that can help you develop your mastery of diaphragmatic breathing.

Another breathing technique in Exercise 3 invites you to relax the whole body in this manner.

Stress Relief and Chronic Pain

Breathing can become quite short and shallow during high-pressure situations, which is why body wisdom generates a long, deep sigh every now and then. Long, deep breaths begin to reverse the physical effects of a stressful moment. Many pain centers incorporate breathing techniques as a complementary modality for chronic pain. One technique specifically invites the individual to imagine breathing into the area where there is pain as a means to reduce the tension in this area, often with great results.

Best Benefits of Diaphragmatic Breathing

If you were to sit in the presence of a meditating yogi and count the number of his breath cycles per minute, you might find that he can comfortably breathe one breath cycle (inhaling and exhaling) per minute. If you were to count the number of breaths you take per minute in the course of any given day, most likely you would count between 14 and 16 breath cycles per minute. When people get stressed they tend to breathe more frequently per minute, with each breath being more shallow. The benefits of breathing may seem simple, but they have a profound influence on other aspects of human physiology, including decreasing resting heart rate, resting blood pressure, and muscle tension.

Stop reading for a moment and take a long, deep sigh. Notice how you feel when you exhale. Relief! The breathing cycle is actually a cycle of slight tension or expansion (inhalation) followed by a phase of complete relaxation (exhalation). This is why the exhalation phase is considered to be the most relaxing phase of the breathing cycle. Diaphragmatic breathing works the same way as a deep sigh.

Chapter Summary

- Diaphragmatic breathing is the most relaxed way to breathe (as opposed to thoracic breathing).

- There are four phases of each breath cycle: 1) inhalation, 2) very slight pause, 3) exhalation, 4) very slight pause.

- In a normal resting state, we tend to breathe about 14–16 breath cycles per minute. When stressed, this number can double. When relaxed, this number can be as low as 3–6 breaths.

- The exhalation phase (phase 3) is believed to be the most relaxing phase of breathing.

- Diaphragmatic breathing is known to help relieve chronic pain.

Additional Resources

Farhi, D. *The Breathing Book*. New York: Owl Books; 1996.

Hendricks, G. *Conscious Breathing*. New York: Bantam Books; 1995.

Iyengar, B. K. *Light on Pranayama*. New York: Crossroad; 1981.

Rosen, R. *The Yoga of Breathing: A Step by Step Guide to Pranayama*. Boston: Shambhala Books; 2002.

EXERCISE   1: Breathing Clouds Meditation

The words *spirit* and *breath* are synonymous in virtually all cultures and languages. So important is the breath as a means to achieve inner peace that it is *the* hallmark of nearly every meditation practice. Breath is the life force of energy. If you have ever been aware of your own normal breathing style, you may have noticed that when under stress, your breathing becomes more shallow. You may also come to realize *just how good* a deep sigh really feels. *This* is the underlying message of the breathing clouds meditation: to instill a wonderful sense of inspiration with each inhalation, and total relaxation with each exhalation.

Ancient mystics have said that there are more than 40 different ways to breathe. What they mean by this is that the breath serves as a powerful metaphor for releasing thoughts and feelings and cleansing the mind, thus promoting a deeper level of contemplation, as well as achieving a profound sense of inner wisdom. Although there are many ways to achieve this goal, conscious breathing—that which unites mind, body, and spirit—offers a direct *and* unencumbered path toward inner peace.

This meditation/visualization exercise is deeply rooted in the Eastern culture, a world rich in metaphor. The implied message here is to release, detach, and let go of any and all thoughts and feelings that no longer serve your highest good. This powerful image of breathing clouds is a vehicle to do just that.

As with any type of visualization exercise, please feel free to augment, edit, and embellish the suggestions given in this exercise, to make them vivid *and* the most empowering for you.

Primarily with this meditation, there are two images: The first is of white clouds, which represent the inhalation phase of the breathing cycle. The second is of dark clouds, which symbolize the exhalation phase. The white clouds symbolize clean, fresh air. The dark clouds represent stressful thoughts, lingering anxieties, nagging problems, issues, or concerns that trouble you or simply add weight to an already busy mind.

The goal of this meditation is to clear any and all pressing issues, those unresolved feelings, those negative thoughts, or perhaps even excess energy, so that your mind becomes clear of thought and your body becomes completely relaxed.

This breathing exercise includes 12 breathing cycles, with each cycle composed of one inhalation (breathing in through your nose) and one exhalation phase (breathing out through your mouth). As we come to the 11th and 12th cycles—with your mind cleared of mental chatter—you may notice that the air you exhale has become as clean and clear as the air you inhale. This is the goal: homeostasis!

Once again, remember that as you follow the suggestions of this meditation please follow a breathing cycle that is most comfortable for you.

Instructions

- To begin, find a comfortable place to sit or lie down where there are no interruptions; a time and place for you, and for you alone. Take a moment to adjust any clothing to enhance your own comfort level.

- Then close your eyes and take a comfortably slow, deep breath. Breathe in slowly, and as you exhale, feel a sense of calm throughout your *entire* body. Please repeat this casual normal breathing cycle about four more times, making each breath comfortably slow and comfortably deep. Should your mind wander, know that this is OK, but gently guide your attention back to your breath.

As you do this, feel your abdominal area expand as you inhale, and then contract as you exhale.

EXERCISE   1: Breathing Clouds Meditation cont....

1. After several comfortable breath cycles, when you feel ready, imagine that the next breath that you take in (inhaling through your nose) is drawn from a beautiful cloud of pure white air—clean, fresh air! As you slowly breathe in this cloud of clean air through your nose, feel it circulate up to the top of your head and down the back of your spine, to where it resides at the *base* of your spine. Then, when you are ready to exhale, feel the air move up from your stomach area, into your lungs, and out through your mouth. As you *slowly* exhale, visualize that the air you breathe out is a dark cloud of dirty air—this symbolizes any stress and tension you may be feeling. As you begin to exhale, call to mind a problem or issue that has occupied your thoughts for the past several days. Then, allow this thought or feeling to leave as you exhale through your mouth.

2. Once again, using your mind's eye to focus on a beautiful white cloud, breathe in clean, fresh air through your nose, and feel it circulate throughout your body.

When you are ready to exhale, breathe slowly out through your mouth; as you do, once again visualize a cloud of dark air leaving your body, symbolic of any thoughts and feelings that at one time may have served you, but now no longer do. To hang on to these thoughts and feelings only weighs you down and holds back your highest potential.

3. On the next inhalation, slowly breathe in a white cloud of clean, fresh air through your nose, and again feel it circulate throughout your body and, this time, cleanse every cell in your body.

When you are ready to exhale, breathe slowly out through your mouth, and once again as you do, visualize a cloud of dark air leaving your body. Again, this represents any frustrations, anxieties, or anything that needs to be released.

4. Slowly now, inhale clean, fresh air through your nose. When you're ready, slowly exhale dark, dirty air through your mouth.

5. Inhale.   Exhale.

6. Inhale.   Exhale.

7. Inhale.   Exhale.

8. Inhale.   Exhale.

9. Inhale.   Exhale.

10. Inhale.   Exhale.

11. Slowly inhale clean, fresh air though your nose, and as you do, feel the air slowly circulate up to the top of your head. As it begins to move down the back of your spine, feel this clean, pristine air move into every cell in your body, to cleanse and invigorate the entire cell, clear down to the structure of your DNA.

As you begin to exhale, once again, breathe out slowly through your mouth, and as you do this, notice that the air you breathe out is nowhere near as dark as the air you first exhaled moments ago. Continue exhaling through your mouth, and observe the air you exhale.

12. Inhale clean, fresh air through your nose once more, and as you do, feel the air slowly circulate up to the top of your head. As it begins to move down the back of your spine, feel this clean, pristine air move into every cell in your body. Allow it to cleanse and invigorate the entire cell, including the strands of your DNA.

As you slowly begin to exhale, breathe out, once again through your mouth, and notice that the air you breathe out has become as clear as the air you have been breathing in. This symbolizes a deep sense of inner peace. Continue to exhale through your mouth and observe the air you breathe out.

EXERCISE   1: Breathing Clouds Meditation cont....

13. Now begin to notice that as you become more and more relaxed, more calm, and more energized by the clean, fresh air circulating through your body, your body is completely relaxed, and your mind is wonderfully calm and clear.

As you return to normal breathing, think to yourself this phrase as you begin to exhale: "I AM calm and relaxed." (Repeat!)

14. Now, with your next breath, slowly bring yourself back to the awareness of the room you are in. Become aware of the time of day, the day of the week, and what you have planned after you have completed this relaxation session.

15. When you feel ready, slowly open your eyes to a soft gaze in front of you. If you'd like, go ahead and stretch your arms and shoulders. Notice that although you feel very relaxed, you don't feel tired or sleepy. You feel fully energized and ready to accomplish whatever goals you have planned, fully realizing that now you are renewed and refreshed to once again feel the power of relaxation, as it energizes your whole being.

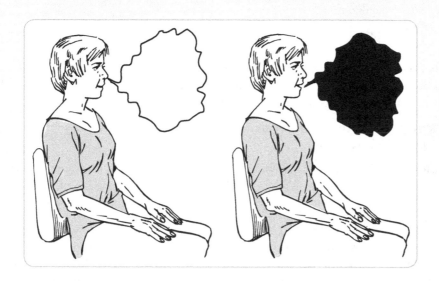

EXERCISE   2: Dolphin Breath Meditation

Breathing is, perhaps, the most common way to promote relaxation. Taking a few moments to focus on your breathing, to the exclusion of all other thoughts, helps to calm mind, body, and spirit. By focusing solely on your breathing, you allow distracting thoughts to leave the conscious mind. In essence, clearing the mind of thoughts is very similar to deleting unwanted emails, thus allowing more room to concentrate on what is really important in your life: that which really deserves attention.

In a normal resting state, the average person breathes about 14–16 breath cycles per minute. Under stress, this can increase to nearly 30 breath cycles per minute. Yet in a deep relaxed state, it is not uncommon to have as few as 3–6 breath cycles in this same time period. The breathing style that produces the greatest relaxation response is that which allows the stomach to expand, rather than the upper chest. (This is actually how you breathe when you are comfortably asleep.) Take a few moments to breathe, specifically focusing your attention on your abdominal area. If any distracting thoughts come to your attention, simply allow these to fade away as you exhale.

Sometimes, combining visualization with breathing can augment the relaxation response. The dolphin breath meditation is one such visualization.

Instructions

Imagine, if you will, that like a dolphin, you have a hole in the crown of your head with which to breathe. Although you will still breathe through your nose or mouth, imagine that you are now taking in slow, deep breaths through the opening at the top of your head.

As you do this, feel the air, or energy, come in through the top of your head, down past your neck and shoulders to reside momentarily at the base of your spine.

Then, when you feel ready, very slowly exhale, allowing the air to move back out through the dolphin spout, the opening situated at the top of your head. As you slowly exhale, feel a deep sense of inner peace reside throughout your body.

Once again, using all your concentration, focus your attention on the opening at the top of your head. Now, slowly breathe air in through this opening—comfortably slow, comfortably deep. As you inhale, feel the air move down into your lungs, yet allow it to continue farther down, deep into your abdominal region. When you feel ready, slowly exhale, allowing the air to move comfortably from your abdominal region up through the top of your head.

Now, take three slow, deep dolphin breaths; each time you exhale, feel a deep sense of relaxation all throughout your body.

1. Pause . . . Inhale . . . Exhale.

2. Pause . . . Inhale . . . Exhale.

3. Pause . . . Inhale . . . Exhale.

Just as you imagined a hole in the top of your head, now imagine that in the sole of each foot, there is also a hole through which you can breathe. As you create this image, take a slow, deep breath and through your mind's eye visualize air coming in through the soles of each foot. Visualize the air moving in from your feet, up through your legs, past your knees and waist, to where it resides in your abdominal region. When you feel ready, begin to exhale slowly, and allow the air to move back out the way it came, out through the soles of your feet.

EXERCISE   2: Dolphin Breath Meditation cont....

Using all your concentration, again focus your attention on the openings at the bottom of your feet and once again breathe in air through these openings, comfortably slow, comfortably deep. As before, feel the air move up your legs and into your abdominal region as your lungs fill with air. Then, when you feel ready, exhale, allowing the air to move slowly from your abdominal region, back through your legs, and out the soles of your feet.

Once again, please take three slow, deep breaths, this time through the soles of your feet; each time you exhale, feel a deep sense of relaxation all throughout your body.

4. Pause . . . Inhale . . . Exhale.

5. Pause . . . Inhale . . . Exhale.

6. Pause . . . Inhale . . . Exhale.

Now, with your concentration skills fully attentive, with your mind focused on the openings in *both* the top of your head and the soles of your feet, use your imagination to inhale air through both head and feet.

As you do this, slowly allow the passage of air entering from both head and feet to move toward the center of your body, where it resides in the abdominal region, until you exhale. Then, when you feel ready, slowly exhale and direct the air that came in through the top of your head to exit through the dolphin hole, while at the same time, directing the air that entered through the soles of your feet to leave from this point of entry as well. Once you have tried this, repeat this combined breath again three times, and with each exhalation, notice how relaxed your body feels.

7. Pause . . . Inhale . . . Exhale.

8. Pause . . . Inhale . . . Exhale.

9. Pause . . . Inhale . . . Exhale.

When you're done, allow this image to fade from your mind, but retain the sense of deep relaxation this experience has instilled throughout your mind, body, and spirit.

Then take one final slow, deep breath, feeling the air come into your nose or mouth, down into your lungs, and allow your stomach to extend out and then deflate as you begin to exhale. Again, feel a deep sense of calm as you exhale.

When you feel ready, allow your eyes to open slowly to a soft gaze in front of you, and bring your awareness back to the room where you now find yourself. As you bring yourself back to the awareness of the room you are now in, you feel fully energized, recharged, revitalized, and ready to accomplish whatever tasks await you.

EXERCISE   3: The Circle Breath

According to many Asian wisdom keepers, there are over 40 different ways to breathe. This breathing exercise is practiced in many parts of the world, including Tibet, Hawaii, and Peru, and goes by many names and variations. Some call it the "protection breath"; others call it the "healing breath." We will simply call it the circle breath. Please read the instructions and then follow the five easy steps several times each day to relax and keep yourself grounded in the course of living in a busy and fast-paced world. Although throughout the entire exercise you will be breathing in through your nose or mouth, this exercise invites you to use your imagination and begin the exercise by feeling yourself breathe air in through your heart space (the center of your upper chest).

1. Take a long, slow, deep breath in through your heart space and draw this air (or energy) up to the crown of your head as you inhale.

2. As you slowly exhale, allow the air (energy) to gently cascade down from the top of your head, down the back of your spine to where it resides at the base of your spine.

3. Slowly inhale. As you do, draw this air (energy) from the base of your spine up to your heart space. As you lift the air from the base of your spine through your stomach area, become aware of a sense of balance in your mind, body, and spirit.

4. Slowly exhale out through your heart space in the direction of the sun (some people exhale to the sea, others to the mountains—whatever works for you). As you exhale, direct any distracting thoughts, nervous energy, or wandering thoughts from your heart space outward.

5. Repeat steps one through four 5 times.

Photo Credits

Unless otherwise indicated, all photographs and illustrations are under copyright of Jones and Bartlett Publishers, LLC, or have been provided by the author.

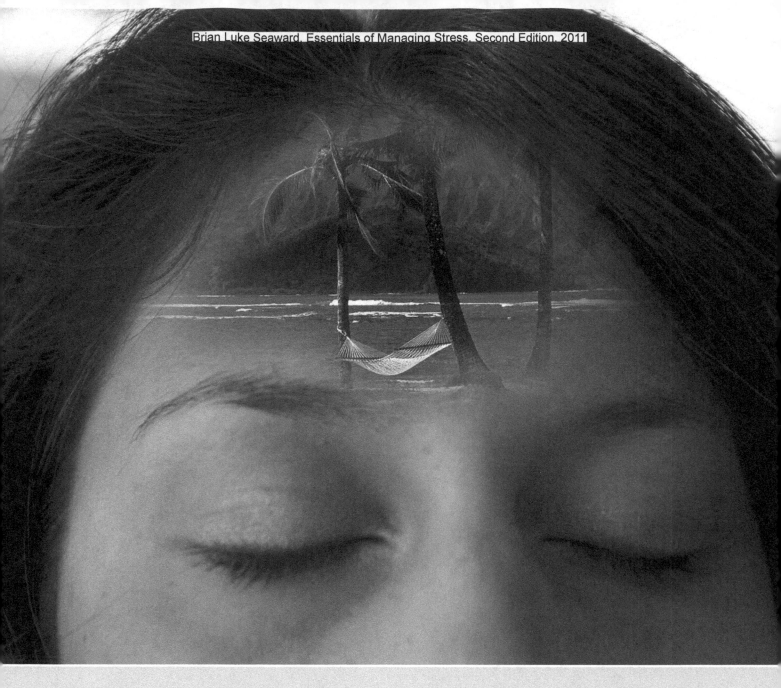

Brian Luke Seaward. Essentials of Managing Stress. Second Edition. 2011

The Power of Mental Imagery and Visualization

"All this or something better now manifests for me in totally satisfying and harmonious ways, for the highest good of all concerned."
— Shakti Gawain

The Ageless Wisdom of Imagery and Visualization

Plato once said that no thought exists without an image to accompany it. This insight is as true today as it was at the time he first said it over two millennia ago. The power of the mind is nothing less than phenomenal. When combined with the power of the human spirit, nothing, it seems, is impossible. Take, for example, Joe Simpson, who after falling several hundred feet only to shatter his right leg, descended single-handedly down Siula Grande in the Peruvian Andes and lived to tell about it in his book and subsequent movie, *Touching the Void*. By imagining himself moving painstakingly slowly from point to point, he did the impossible and survived. Simpson is not alone in his efforts to harness the power of visualization, but his story is certainly one of the most dramatic ever told.

Just as the mind can create positive images to accomplish the impossible, it can also manufacture images to immobilize our human potential. Perhaps with the proliferation of television and visual media to be found everywhere, visual images abound, thus accentuating each person's ability to create images (real or imagined) in his or her mind. The power of the mind to create images that can either heal or hurt is well founded throughout the history of humanity. Perhaps as no surprise, people unknowingly practice the art of visualization all the time, particularly imagining a series of worst-case scenarios with the anticipation of a stressful event. In the words of Albert Einstein, "No problem can be solved from the same consciousness that created it." Visualization and mental imagery require a different mind-set than the typical frenetic consciousness so prevalent today.

Visualization and Imagery

Although the terms **visualization** and **mental imagery** may seem like the same concept (and to many they are), those who specialize in the area of mind-body-spirit healing note a distinct difference, based on both the study of the mind and personal experience with scores of clients.

Visualization is the conscious direction of images on the screen of the mind's eye. Conscious intention is the hallmark of creative visualization. In the process of visualization, you are the writer, director, producer, and audience, all in one, which can become a very empowering experience. Conversely, mental imagery is best described as a series of images that bubble up from the unconscious mind without the ego's censorship. Mental imagery is often described as a spontaneous flow of thoughts originating from the unconscious mind. Uncensored spontaneity is the hallmark of mental imagery. Keeping in mind the wealth of wisdom contained in the depths of the unconscious mind, mental imagery can often prove to be far more effective than the work of the conscious mind alone.

The Art of Guided Visualization

Many people who find it hard to hold their concentration for prolonged periods of time find it easier to listen to someone else direct them through a visualization process. Focusing the mind for an intended period of time certainly requires discipline. Keeping your mind focused with the help of guided visualization CDs is one way to achieve the intended goal of relaxation or healing. Continued exposure to guided visualization CDs may also help you to augment your own imagination and creative abilities. As with any exposure to experiences that cultivate the powers of your mind, embellish all suggestions to your liking from the selected tracks and ignore any and all suggestions that you do not have a strong comfort level with.

Types of Visualization

Your imagination can take you wherever you wish to go, yet it seems that visualizations tend to fall into one of three categories.

- *Tranquil scenes:* The epitome of a tranquil scene is a sublime beach with waves of aqua blue water slowly edging toward the shore. Tranquil scenes range from primeval forests to thick snowflakes falling from the sky. And the sky is the limit when it comes to tranquil scenes. When looking to relax using this technique, imagine a scene that provides you with the deepest sense of relaxation. Exercise 1 is an example of using a tranquil image as a metaphor to promote relaxation.

- *Behavioral changes:* Mental imagery and visualization became mainstream several decades ago when coaches started using these techniques to enhance sports performance with their star athletes. Under the name of mental training, athletes would rehearse their events again and again in their mind to gain an edge over their competition. Since then, and perhaps even before, visualization has been used as a core technique in the area of behavior modification, including smoking cessation and changes in eating behaviors.

- *Internal healing body images:* Perhaps nowhere else has the use of visualization been more dramatic than in the efforts to improve one's health status, from the repair of broken bones to the evaporation of tumors (both benign and malignant). Patients use both visualization and mental imagery to not only understand the illness, but also make peace with it. Exercises 2 and 3 are examples of employing visualization and mental imagery to promote physical healing.

The Essential Components of Visualization

Both visualization and mental imagery employ the faculties of both the conscious and unconscious minds, though visualization has a greater hand in the direction of the script. To gain the greatest benefit from guided visualization, it's best to understand how to coordinate the efforts of both the conscious and unconscious minds. The following are some aspects to consider to enhance this experience.

- *Present tense:* To the unconscious mind there is only one time zone: the present moment. Past memories and events as well as future events and aspects are all considered to be included in the present moment. Simply stated, the unconscious mind appears not to understand events as anything other than now! Therefore, as you craft your image, think in terms of bringing the image into the present moment as if you are experiencing it now.

- *Incorporate all five senses:* The stronger the image, the more real it becomes. Where appropriate, call to mind not only the power of your sense of sight, but also that of your sense of smell, touch, sound, and taste, if possible. Make the image as real as you possibly know how.

- *Positive thoughts and intentions:* Just as the unconscious mind understands only one time zone, it also understands only positive thoughts. Words expressed negatively are translated into a positive framework. Therefore, to coordinate both the conscious and unconscious minds toward a unified goal, construct your healing intention in a positive mind frame.

- *Emotional vibration:* New research on visualization and prayer indicates that thoughts alone produce no lasting effect. What really galvanizes the power of visualization is the emotion behind the thought. So as you begin to create the desired image, whether it be for a sense of tranquility, a positive behavior change, or the restoration of healing, generate a feeling of compassion with the image or series of images.

- *Detached outcomes:* Placing an expected outcome on the desired intention of each visualization is analogous to throwing down an anchor on a boat that is about to set sail. It halts any progress. Although it's human to have expectations, this too becomes an emotional vibration that negates the intended outcome. The ego projects strong expectations. For visualization to have the greatest effect one must detach the ego from the outcome and simply let what happens, happen.

- *Attitude of gratitude:* Upon the completion of the visualization, offer an expression of gratitude for the experience. An honest expression of gratitude fills the sails of every visualization with wind to transport it to the intended destination, wherever that may be.

How to Incorporate Imagery and Visualization into Your Life Routine

Although the practice of visualization can be as varied as the person doing it, here are some suggestions to get the most out of this process, in addition to the template previously mentioned that includes using the present tense, positive thoughts, detached outcomes, and the expression of an attitude of gratitude. If you intend to use this relaxation skill, you will find that like any other skill, the more you practice it, the better it will serve you. The beauty of visualization is that the practice can be done practically anywhere you can sit or lay quietly with your eyes closed for several minutes.

The following are some time-honored aspects of the creative visualization process that can help augment your experience to the fullest extent.

Step 1: Relaxation: The brain's right hemisphere is at its strongest in the presence of total relaxation. This means to create a desirable image, the mind must be clear of mental chit-chat and ego-based distractions. Loosen any tight-fitting clothing and find a comfortable place to unwind. Once you have minimized or eliminated all distractions, begin by taking a slow, deep breath and let all random thoughts leave your mind as you exhale.

Step 2: Concentration: A focused mind is a clear mind. Using your powers of concentration, focus your attention toward your breathing as a means to ensure a clear mind. If your mind wanders with distractions, acknowledge these thoughts and feelings and then focus your attention entirely back to your breathing.

Step 3: Visualization: Next, combine a desired image with an intention and focus on this for several minutes. If you find your mind wandering (and this will happen from time to time), merely redirect your attention back to the desired image with a comfortable, slow, deep breath.

Step 4: Affirmation: Metaphorically speaking, a positive affirmation used in tandem with visualization is the postage needed to properly deliver the intended message. Combining an image with a word or phrase unites the energies of both the right and left brain hemispheres for the best desired result.

Stress Relief and Chronic Pain

Visualization holds the potential to offer immediate satisfaction for stress relief, by simply closing your eyes to the outside world. For this reason and many others, both mental imagery and visualization have been used extensively to help treat chronic pain. With the understanding that chronic pain is more than a physical ailment, mental imagery helps translate the language of the unconscious mind to provide insights for healing and restoration in areas such as the lower back, neck, shoulders, or even cancer. Visualization empowers the conscious energy to create a new vibration of healing for whatever area of the body seeks it.

Best Benefits of Imagery and Visualization

In its simplest sense, visualization is like taking a mini vacation, leaving all your cares and worries behind to get to a place of inner peace. The effects of visualization and mental imagery range from being mildly relaxing to profoundly enlightening, depending on the particular image used, the frequency employed, and the conditions under which the visualization was experienced. Everyone can gain significant benefits from a single experience of guided visualization.

Chapter Summary

- Visualization is the conscious direction of images on the screen of the mind's eye. Mental imagery describes specific images that bubble up from the unconscious mind.

- The three most common types of visualization for relaxation and healing are 1) tranquil scenes, 2) behavioral changes, and 3) internal healing body image.

- To get the most out of visualization one should 1) use the present tense, 2) use all five senses, 3) use positive thoughts and intentions, 4) use positive emotions, 5) have no expectations of the outcome, and 6) include an attitude of gratitude.

- Both mental imagery and visualization have been used to help decrease chronic pain.

Additional Resources

Dyer, W. *Getting into the Gap*. Carlsbad, CA: Hay House; 2003.

Gawain, S. *Creative Visualization*. New York: Bantam Books; 1978.

Katra, J., & Targ, R. *The Heart of the Mind*. Navato, CA: New World Library; 1999.

Locke, S. *The Healer Within*. New York: Mentor Books; 1986.

Roman, S. *Spiritual Growth: Being Your Higher Self*. Tiburon, CA: H. J. Kramer; 1989.

Simonton, O. C. *Getting Well Again*. New York: Bantam Books; 1978.

Targ, R., & Katra, J. *Miracles of Mind*. Navato, CA: New World Library; 1998.

Thondup, T. *The Healing Power of Mind*. Boston: Shambhala Books; 1996.

EXERCISE   1: Solitude of a Mountain Lake

Imagine yourself walking alone in the early morning, along a path of a primeval forest, through a gauntlet of towering pine trees. Each step you take is softly cushioned by a bed of golden-brown needles. Quietness consumes these surroundings and then is broken by the melody of a songbird. As you stroll along at a leisurely pace, you focus on the sweet, clean scent of the pines and evergreens, the coolness of the air, the warmth of the sun as it peeks through the trees, and the gentle breeze as it passes through the boughs of the pines and whispers past your ears.

Off in the distance, you hear the rush of water cascading over weathered rocks, babbling as it moves along. Yards ahead, a chipmunk perches on an old decaying birch stump along the side of the path, frozen momentarily to determine its next direction, then in the blink of an eye, it disappears under the ground cover and all is silent again. As you continue to walk along this path you see a clearing up ahead, and you notice your pace picks up just a little to see what is there. First boulders appear ahead, then behind them, a deep blue mountain lake emerges from beyond the rocks. You climb up on a boulder to secure a better view, and you find a comfortable spot carved out of the weathered stone to sit and quietly observe all the elements around you.

The shore of the lake is surrounded by a carpet of tall green grass and guarded by a host of trees: spruce, evergreen, pine, aspen, and birch. On top of one of the spruce trees, an eagle leaves his perch and spreads his wings to catch the remains of a thermal current, and gracefully glides over the lake. On the far side of the lake, off in the distance, dwarfing the tree line, is a rugged stone mountain. The first snows of autumn have dusted the fissures and crevasses, adding contrast to the rock's features. The color of the snow matches the one or two puffy white clouds and morning crescent moon that interrupt an otherwise cloudless day. A slight warm breeze begins to caress your cheeks and the backs of your hands as you direct your attention to the surface of the mountain lake.

The slight breeze sends tiny ripples across the surface of the lake. As you look at the water's surface, you realize that this body of water, this mountain lake, is just like your body—somewhat calm, yet yearning to be completely relaxed, completely calm. Focus your attention on the surface of the water. These ripples that you observe represent or symbolize any tensions, frustrations, or wandering thoughts that keep you from being completely relaxed. As you look at the surface of this mountain lake, slowly allow the ripples to dissipate, fade away, and disappear. To enhance this process take a very slow, deep breath and feel the relaxation this brings to your body as you exhale. And as you exhale, slowly allow the ripples to fade away, giving way to a calm surface of water. As you continue to focus on this image, you see the surface of the lake becoming more and more calm, in fact very placid, reflecting all that surrounds it.

Feel how relaxed you feel as you see the surface of the lake remain perfectly still, reflecting all that is around it. The water's surface reflects a mirror image of the green grass, the trees, the mountain face, even the clouds and crescent moon. Your body is as relaxed as this body of water, this mountain lake. Try to lock in this feeling of calmness and etch this feeling into your memory bank so that you can call it up to your conscious mind when you get stressed or frustrated. Remember this scene so that you can recall the serenity of this image that you have created to promote a deep sense of relaxation, and feel your body relax just by thinking of the solitude of this mountain lake.

EXERCISE 2: The Body Flame

Imagine, if you will, that the energy that you burn all day long is not just physical energy (such as calories), it's mental and emotional energy, as well. Imagine that this source of energy, which invigorates *every* cell, resides in the center of your body. The Japanese call this reservoir of energy the *hara*. The Chinese refer to it as the *dan tien*. Although it cannot be measured by Western science at this time, this energy is essential to *your* well-being.

Take a moment now to locate the center of your body, and feel where this is, your center of gravity, the center of your entire body. As you begin to focus on this area, realize that this is about an inch or two below your belly button.

It is believed that when this energy is too excessive (perhaps from a flurry of thoughts or unresolved emotions) you begin to feel frantic and overwhelmed, sometimes just plain exhausted.

The body flame meditation, like the breathing clouds exercise in Chapter 14, is a way to help clear your mind of excess thoughts and excess energy and return your mind–body to a profound sense of inner peace. As you do this meditation, as with all meditations, call to mind the power of your five senses, and the power of your imagination and memory, to draw forth the power of this visualization.

To begin this meditation, the best position is to lie comfortably flat on your back, keeping your spine aligned from your head straight down to your hips. If you choose to sit, this will work as well.

Next, concentrate on your breathing by making each breath comfortably slow and comfortably deep. If your mind should happen to wander, gently guide it back to the focus of your breathing.

If your eyes are not already closed, go ahead and close your eyes and once again, locate the center of your body; then, using your mind's eye, call to mind an image of a flame hovering over this part of your body.

Metaphorically speaking, this flame is a symbol of your state of relaxation. It feeds off your body's energy. When your body has an abundance of energy—perhaps nervous thoughts or negative feelings—this flame will be quite tall. Perhaps even like a blow torch.

When you are completely relaxed, your flame will be quite small. This small flame is called the "maintenance flame." It's like that which you would see as a pilot light in a gas stove. This is the desired size for complete relaxation.

So now, focus with your mind's eye, and take a look at the size of your body's flame. See its size relative to your body's level of energy. So, what does your flame look like? How big or small does it seem to you right now?

As you place all of your attention on the flame of your body, look at its color. Your body flame may be an intense, brilliant yellow/white color. As you look at this image, what color does your flame hold?

Once again with your mind's eye, take a look at the *shape* of your body's flame. Direct your attention to the base of the flame and notice, is the bottom round or oval? How does it appear to you?

Then, as you focus your eyes toward the tip of the flame, notice that it comes to a jagged point.

You may even notice that your flame dances around a bit or perhaps it remains still. As you look at this flame, *feel* it feed off the excess energy in your body, and let it burn off any excess energy that you wish to release to return to a complete sense of relaxation.

EXERCISE   2: The Body Flame cont....

Take a deep breath and let your flame burn off any excess energy you feel detracts from your ability to relax.

Once again, if you find your mind is distracted by wandering thoughts that pull your attention away from the image of the flame, gently redirect your attention back to this image, and then allow your mind to send these thoughts and feelings from your head to your body's center and up through the flame.

As you continue to watch this image of the flame, feel your body slowly become more calm and relaxed. And to help this out, take a nice, slow, comfortable, deep breath. As you exhale, feel a greater sense of calm throughout your body.

Now look once again at the image of your flame; as your body becomes more tranquil, notice the flame decrease in height. Soon you will notice that your flame decreases in size, to about a quarter to one-half inch tall.

As you focus on the image of your body flame, once again notice the color, shape, and size. And as you see the flame decrease in size, feel your body relax, as you draw your attention to the relaxation effect of the maintenance flame.

There are times when this flame can be used to aid in the healing process of your physical body. Place the flame over a specific part of your body, an area that is sore or experiencing pain, and allow the flame to feed off the excess energy of this area and restore a sense of peace to the organ or physiological system that is yearning for wholeness.

Now, take several slow, deep breaths, and as you exhale, allow your body flame to return a sense of peace to this area. As you do this, feel peace reside here. When you feel ready, slowly return the image of the flame back to the center of your body.

Now, continue to focus your mind's eye on your body flame. When you feel completely relaxed, with your flame very small, notice how still it is. Then, when you feel you are at a point of complete relaxation, slowly allow this image to fade from your mind, but retain this feeling of relaxation, knowing that your mind is now clear with fewer and fewer distractions.

To augment this relaxation process, please take one more slow, deep breath and then slowly bring yourself back to the awareness of the room you are in. Become aware of the time of day, the day of the week, and what you have planned after you have completed this relaxation session. When you feel ready, very slowly open your eyes to a soft gaze in front of you. If you would like, go ahead and stretch your arms and shoulders. Notice that although you feel relaxed, you don't feel tired or sleepy. You feel fully energized and revitalized, ready to do whatever you have planned for the rest of the day.

EXERCISE 3: Body Colors and the Healing Light

The human body craves wholeness, and given the chance, the body will do all it can to return to a place of optimal health. In all its splendor, the body's innate ability to return to wholeness is a wonder to behold.

The word *health* comes from the root word *hal*, which means to be whole or holy. When we call upon the strength of the human spirit to work in unison with our mind and body, wholeness, expressed through inner peace, is achieved.

This meditation/visualization exercise calls upon the unconscious mind to awaken the innate healing powers of mind, body, and spirit so that you may return to that place of wholeness, that place of inner peace, wherever you may be.

As you do this meditation, as with all meditations, call to mind the power of your five senses and the power of your imagination and memory, to draw forth the power of this visualization.

As with any type of visualization exercise, please feel free to augment, edit, and embellish the suggestions in this exercise, to make them vivid *and* the most empowering for you.

Imagine yourself lying in a warm, shallow pool of clear blue water. Visualize, through your mind's eye, that as you float effortlessly, your internal body reflects just one color—a brilliant white, as if you are observing a white silhouette in a pool of turquoise blue water. As you visualize this image, clearly picture a complete outline of your body, the contents of which are illuminated by the color white.

Now, focusing on this white silhouette, take a moment to carefully examine all parts and regions of your body, from your head down to your toes. As you do this, search for any specific locations or regions of your body that feel tense, active, or perhaps express a sensation of pain. This can include any muscles, joints, organs, physiological systems (like the immune system or cardiovascular system), or any part of your body that seems less than whole, yet *craves* wholeness. For some, this might even include your mind, if by chance you find that a multitude of thoughts are constantly racing through your mind, with each thought competing for your attention.

Through this systematic scanning process, please locate one or perhaps several areas that are under stress and strain and have not been allowed to fully relax to the same capacity as the rest of your body.

For the moment, let's refer to these "active" areas as "hot spots," because typically they *are* more metabolically active than all other areas that are more relaxed. As you locate a specific area of tension, allow yourself to envision that this area is symbolized by a strong, pulsating red light. Symbolically, the color red indicates a higher metabolic level of arousal or energy state, and here the same meaning can be quite literal.

Invite yourself to take a slow, deep breath, and as you do, imagine that you are slowly inhaling *and* exhaling through an opening in this area. Follow this breath with one more, even slower, even deeper breath. As you breathe once more through this area, feel the flow of energy move through this region, as if a logjam floating on a river has been set free.

As you envision your body represented by these two colors—a mass of white, with one, two, or perhaps several red pulsating areas—take a moment to specifically focus on the red pulsating lights. As you do this, through your conscious intention, invite these areas to become calm, as calm as the rest of your body.

With your mind's eye, imagine that this hot spot *slowly* begins to change color, transforming from a bright, pulsating red light to a bright, but less intense orange color. Then take a nice, slow, deep breath, and as you exhale watch the color change to orange. As you observe the color transform from red to orange, so, too, does the intensity of pulsation change to a slower rate—symbolizing that indeed, the area *is* becoming more calm.

EXERCISE   3: Body Colors and the Healing Light cont....

Once again, take a slow, deep breath, and as you do, imagine that you are once again inhaling and exhaling through the region of your body acknowledged with a small pulsating orange light. Please follow this breath with one more, even slower, even deeper breath. Once again, as you breathe once more through this area, feel the flow of energy move through this region like a slow, yet strong flowing river of water.

Observe closely: As you look at and feel this area of tension or pain, once again become aware of the color orange and feel a deeper sense of calming beginning to occur in this region. The color orange is symbolic of change. The intention of this meditation *is* change, changing any areas of tension to a calm, tranquil sense of homeostasis, from stress to inner peace.

Now, with this calming sensation taking hold, begin to see the orange-colored light transform from bright orange to the color yellow. Once again take a slow, deep breath, and note the change as you exhale. The color yellow is symbolic of energy. In this case, a healing energy that enables the area in question to slowly return to homeostasis. As you observe the yellow color, note that the yellow light pulsates very infrequently, if at all. This means that this focus of your attention really is becoming more relaxed.

At your leisure, take a slow, deep breath, and as you do, imagine that you are inhaling and exhaling *through* this area. Follow this with one more even slower, even deeper breath. As you breathe once more through this area, feel the flow of energy move effortlessly through this region of your body.

Now, as you observe the area, symbolized by a yellow light, you sense and feel that this area you have focused your attention on is much more relaxed, more calm. Notice, as you observe the white silhouette of your body, that now all areas begin to match the sensation of calmness that you feel in the rest of your body.

As you look at this image of your entire body, you notice a beautiful reflection of white light. Once again, take a slow, deep breath, and as you exhale, observe that the yellow area is now blending to become white with the brilliant white color that your internal body reflects. As you continue to look at this image you have created, you now see that your entire internal body image is one color—a brilliant white, radiating a calm light all around it. This color is symbolic of your level of complete relaxation and optimal health, and this image is one that you can recall to your consciousness at any time to invoke a sense of personal tranquility.

Take a slow, deep breath, and as you exhale, think to yourself this phrase, "I am calm and relaxed. I am whole!"

Now, once again, imagine your body lying comfortably and effortlessly in a shallow pool of warm water. Directly overhead, suspended about 4–5 feet above you, is a crystal bowl, filled with beautiful rays of light. These rays cascade down, like a fountain of water, over you. This crystal bowl contains an unending supply of golden-white light, a source of dynamic life force and energy. As this light pours over your body, it has the ability to stimulate and augment the healing process that *you* have initiated with your own ability to heal—through the color transformations from red to orange to yellow.

Using the power of your mind, slowly move this waterfall of luminescent energy over a specific part of your body that you feel needs the reinforcement of deep healing. With the power of intention, allow the crystal bowl to tip its contents over this specific region of your body. Feel the warmth of this healing light as it continually pours into your body. More and more, allow the warmth of the healing light to move to the desired location and feel your body absorbing the light where it needs it the most.

As you do this, see the image of golden-white light within you and all around you. Take a moment to sense what this really feels like. Then, take a slow, deep breath and feel a deep sense of relaxation throughout your entire body. Once again, repeat to yourself the phrase, "I am calm and relaxed. I am whole."

EXERCISE 3: Body Colors and the Healing Light cont....

Notice now that you feel calm and relaxed, yet at the same time you feel wonderfully energized.

Take one final slow, deep breath, and as you exhale, feel the sensation of relaxation envelop your whole body.

At your leisure, when you feel ready, slowly open your eyes to a soft gaze in front of you. Take a moment to familiarize yourself with your surroundings, by thinking about what you have planned once you finish this meditation. Realize that although you feel relaxed, you don't feel tired or sleepy; you feel fully energized and revitalized and ready to accomplish whatever task awaits you today.

Photo Credits

Unless otherwise indicated, all photographs and illustrations are under copyright of Jones and Bartlett Publishers, LLC, or have been provided by the author.

Self-Hypnosis and Autogenics

"Open your mind to the power of self-suggestion."
— Johannes Schultz

The Ageless Wisdom of Self-Hypnosis

For decades, if not centuries, Western science held the belief that the mind, as powerful as it is, could not control the autonomic nervous system. Aspects of human physiology including heart rate, blood pressure, breathing, blood distribution, and other parameters were thought to be totally under the influence of brain regions that were not influenced by conscious thought. All of this changed dramatically in the early 20th century when Western scientists traveled to the Himalayan region of India to observe yogis who appeared to display mystical powers of human physiology. The ability to sit comfortably on a bed of nails paled in comparison to the ability to control one's breathing, heart rate, and blood flow.

The average person breathes 14–16 times per minute. When completely relaxed, the average person can take as few as 6 breaths per minute. These yogis could comfortably breathe less than once per minute. Moreover, they could decrease their heart rates to less than 20 beats per minute. For all intents and purposes they appeared dead. These feats were thought to be humanly impossible. Perhaps even more amazing was the demonstration of certain yogis to redistribute the flow of blood entirely to the right side of the body, leaving the left side stone cold. Punctures to the skin produced no bleeding.

In the 1960s, Elmer and Alyce Green, from the Menninger Clinic, traveled to India to conduct scientific investigations of these talented yogis. They even convinced one yogi, Swami Rama, to come back and be studied under laboratory conditions. Results revealed that these changes were neither magic nor the ploy of some adept conjurer. These yogis, who had cultivated a wealth of mental discipline, were indeed able to defy the autonomic nervous system and consciously influence a host of physiological parameters. They not only redefined the word *homeostasis,* but also opened the door to a view of consciousness that had only been hinted at as an illusion before, and sowed the seeds for a new field of study: psychoneuroimmunology.

It's well known that in a relaxed state, the mind is more receptive to suggestions—either those one gives to oneself or those one hears from someone else. The receptivity to the power of suggestion is more commonly known as hypnosis. Most likely, everyone has seen or heard of people volunteering to be hypnotized on stage by an entertainer. Through the use of hypnosis, participants perform ludicrous acts that appear to defy reality. However, centuries before some magician thought to use hypnosis as part of his Las Vegas act, the power of suggestion through the use of guided hypnosis was used. In the late 1700s, Anton Mesmer combined the use of hypnotic suggestion with magnets as a means to heal people of a host of serious diseases. Today the word *mesmerized* is used to suggest a trance-like state of bewilderment.

In 1939 two German physicians, Johannes Schultz and Wolfgang Luthe, combined the use of hypnosis and relaxation to create what is commonly known today as **autogenic training** or self-regulation: the ability to follow a series of self-suggestions to promote a deep sense of relaxation. The technique of autogenics did not go unnoticed by magicians either. Houdini, and many others who followed in his footsteps, was known for using the power of self-suggestion and self-regulation to perform many of his escape tricks and illusions. It goes without saying that you would have to be very relaxed to be handcuffed in a straightjacket and submerged under water and escape unscathed!

The Power of Suggestion

Some people shudder at the mention of hypnosis, and for that matter **self-hypnosis**, but in truth, people give themselves suggestions all the time. Usually it's the ego doing the suggesting, directing people to watch out for this or avoid that. The ego is a master at the power of suggestion and becomes even more so during times of stress. The real power of human potential comes not from the ego, however, but a deeper source of strength hidden in the unconscious mind often censored by the ego. In a relaxed state, the ego is disarmed. Self-guided suggestions (or even those provided by others such as a therapist on a guided imagery CD) allow you to unite the power of the conscious and unconscious minds to achieve states of physiological homeostasis that are not possible when the ego is standing guard. As a rule, people are most open to the power of suggestion when they are relaxed. This is the promise of self-regulation.

The Art of Self-Regulation

The secret to autogenic training is to make your arms, hands, legs, and/or feet feel comfortably warm and heavy. The warmth and heaviness come from the flow of blood that you consciously direct to whatever region you focus your awareness on. In a resting state, the majority (80 percent) of your body's blood resides in your gastrointestinal (GI) tract. The other 20 percent circulates throughout the body to provide oxygen and a host of nutrients for metabolic functions. By consciously directing the flow of blood from your body's core to your arms and hands or your legs and feet, you begin to send a message to the autonomic nervous system to constrict the blood vessels in your stomach area and dilate the blood vessels in either the arms or the legs, thus allowing the movement of blood to these areas.

Because muscles are not normally saturated with blood in a resting state, the autogenic effect is very relaxing (similar to the feelings when sitting in a Jacuzzi). To initiate this technique, all you need do is give yourself a series of suggestions to have either your arms and hand, or legs and feet (some even suggest trying the back of your head) feel warm and heavy. If you wish, you can add to this suggestion a visualization of blood flowing to the desired areas. Turn to Exercise   1 to begin the process of this new mind-set.

How to Incorporate Autogenics into Your Life Routine

Lie on your back in a comfortable position, with your arms by your side. Take a moment to focus your awareness on your breathing, following the flow of air in through your nostrils and down deep into your lungs. As you exhale, simply relax. This is the first stage of autogenics. Exercise   2 guides you through an entire autogenics session.

Many people who use autogenics feel that it is a great technique to use to fall asleep at night. For this reason, autogenics is a technique to use late at night, or perhaps on weekend mornings when there is no rush to get out of bed. When done properly, this technique takes about 15–30 minutes, and like most skills, the more you practice it, the easier it becomes. It is an easy technique to use for muscle soreness. It has also been used by patients (with the help of their physicians) who are undergoing surgery. They experience fewer complications with healing.

Developing Your Mastery of Autogenic Training

To begin the practice of autogenic training, please consider following these guidelines:

1. Be sure to minimize all distractions such as blaring radios, televisions, and cell phones.

2. Find a quiet place to lie down. (It's best to try this technique lying down, but it can be done sitting.)

3. Get comfortable, loosening any tight-fitting clothing. Begin to focus on your breathing. Pay close attention to your body's physiology and your heart rate.

4. Follow the directions in Exercise   2. You can read through these directions first and then call to mind the progression of steps with either the arms, legs, or head.

Stress Relief and Chronic Pain

When people take the time to learn the premise of autogenic training, they find it to be one of the most powerful means of relieving the symptoms of physical stress. It also is a favorite for people with insomnia and people suffering from Raynaud's disease. Autogenics is often used in tandem with clinical biofeedback (see Chapter 23) and is found to be very useful as a means to control not only sensations of pain, but also, in some cases, the causes of it as well.

Best Benefits of Autogenics

The immediate effects of autogenics are similar, in some ways, to a muscle massage. Like a dry sponge, tight muscles have very poor blood flow due to constricted blood vessels and capillaries. The practice of autogenics allows for a greater distribution of blood flow to the intended area, helping to saturate the muscles with blood, and in a sense, massaging them from the inside. Metaphorically speaking, the dry sponge becomes saturated, making the tissue more pliable and relaxed. The neural endings in the muscles decrease their firing, which, in turn, sends a message to the brain to relax. The long-term effects of autogenic training give one a sense of profound relaxation through autosuggestion. It also provides a sense of empowerment knowing that there are some things you truly have control over, and this tends to carry over into other areas of your life.

Chapter Summary

- Autogenic training means self-regulation, referring to the ability to self-regulate your body's physiological systems.

- In simple terms, autogenic training teaches one to relax by making various body parts (e.g., hands, arms, legs) feel warm and heavy (like an internal muscle massage).

- Autogenic training is based on the concept of self-hypnosis, the ability to talk yourself into a relaxed state.

- Many people swear by the effects of autogenic training for deep relaxation and easing chronic pain.

Additional Resources

Alman, B., & Lambrou, P. *Self-Hypnosis: The Complete Manual for Health and Self-Change*, 2nd ed. New York: Brunner/Mazel; 1991.

Blair, F. R. *Instant Self-Hypnosis*. New York: Sourcebooks; 2004.

Green, E., & Green, A. *Beyond Biofeedback*. New York: Delacorte Press; 1977.

EXERCISE   1: The Power of Self-Suggestion

The following is a brief exercise to assist you in uniting the powers of your conscious and unconscious minds by giving yourself your own suggestions to follow as a means to promote a deeper sense of relaxation. Please first create and then read through your own suggestions so that you have a strong comfort level with them. Then assume a comfortable position and talk yourself through each of these suggestions. Remember that in a relaxed state you are open to the power of suggestions, particularly those that you give yourself. After giving some thought to one or more of these behaviors you might wish to change, write these down as well, so they can be used in a relaxed state.

Suggestions for Relaxation

Example: "My body is calm and relaxed."

1. _____
2. _____
3. _____
4. _____

Suggestions for Self-Improvement and Confidence

Example: "I can do anything!"

1. _____
2. _____
3. _____
4. _____

EXERCISE 2: The Direct Approach of Autogenics

Autogenic training has both a direct and an indirect approach to relaxation. The direct approach is a more detailed visual interpretation than simple general instructions to feel warm and heavy. In this exercise, a slight variation on the original technique offers added instructions for those who need more understanding of how the physiological changes occur. In the direct approach, the specific mechanisms involved in warmth and heaviness are focused on to initiate a stronger sense of relaxation. Here, you start out with diaphragmatic breathing to induce relaxation. When mind and body become relaxed through this technique, the mind becomes more receptive to additional thoughts (warmth and heaviness), and thus the selected awareness process is enhanced.

The length of time required for this approach will vary. To begin, you may want to work on only one body region, such as the arms and hands. With proficiency, you can add to the duration of each session. The following instructions can be read prior to your session, or they can be read to you by a friend while you are performing this technique. Assume a comfortable position and become as relaxed as possible.

Instructions

1. First, concentrate on your breathing. Feel the air come in through your nose or mouth, down into your lungs, and feel your stomach rise and then fall as you exhale the air through your mouth.

2. Take a comfortably slow, deep breath, feeling the air enter the lower chambers of your lungs. Feel your stomach rise slowly with the intake of air, and then slowly descend as the air leaves your lungs. Repeat this, making the breath even slower and deeper. With each exhalation, feel how relaxed your body has become.

3. Focus on your heartbeat. Listen to and feel your heart beating in your chest. As you concentrate on this, allow a longer pause after each heartbeat. Just by allowing the thought of your heart relaxing, you can make it do so. Allow a longer pause after each beat. Now, to help relax the heart muscle, take one more slow, deep breath, and as you exhale feel how relaxed your heart has become. Again, consciously choose to place a longer pause after each heartbeat.

4. Take a moment to realize that in the resting state you are now in, your body's core receives the greatest percentage (80 percent) of blood, most of it going to the gastrointestinal tract. While the body's core is receiving a great supply of blood, the periphery—arms and legs—receive only a maintenance supply.

5. Be aware that when your muscles are saturated with blood, they become very relaxed and pliable, like a wet sponge. Now, think to yourself that you would like to re-create the feeling of relaxation in the muscles of your arms and hands.

EXERCISE   2: The Direct Approach of Autogenics cont....

6. Allow the blood to move from the body's core up to your shoulders and down toward your arms and hands. As you think and desire this, you will begin to constrict the blood vessels of your stomach area while at the same time dilating those of your arms and hands.

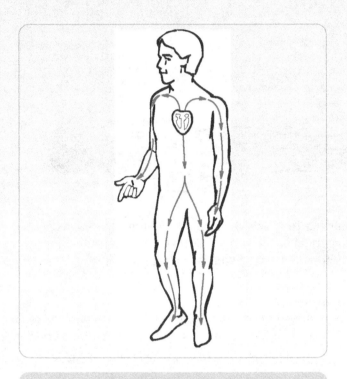

Visualizing the flow of blood to the extremities.

7. With each breath you take, with each beat of your heart, allow the flow of blood to move from your stomach area to your arms and hands.

8. You will begin to notice that as you allow this movement of blood from your core to your arms and hands, they begin to feel slightly heavy. They feel heavy because they are not quite used to the sensation of additional blood flow to this region. You will also notice that your arms and particularly your hands feel warm, especially your palms and fingers, because they have the greatest number of temperature receptors.

9. With each breath and each beat of your heart, allow the blood to continue to move from your stomach area toward your arms and hands. Feel how comfortable your arms and hands have become. They feel warm and heavy, and very relaxed. As the muscles become saturated with blood, stiffness dissipates and relaxation ensues.

10. Soon you will notice that your arms feel increasingly heavy, so much so that should you want to move them you couldn't because they feel immobilized. You feel as if they are making indentations in the floor or chair frame. Your arms and hands feel so relaxed they just don't want to move.

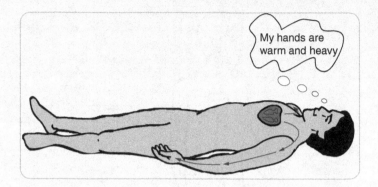

My hands are warm and heavy

Visualizing the flow of blood to the arms and hands, the breath even slower and deeper. With each exhalation, feel how relaxed your body has become.

11. With each breath and each beat of your heart, continue to send the flow of blood to your arms and hands. Feel the warmth spread from your arms all the way down to your palms and fingers.

12. Take a long, slow, deep breath and gauge how relaxed your whole body feels as you exhale. Sense how relaxed your arms and hands feel.

13. Now, take one more slow, deep breath, and as you exhale allow the flow of blood to return to your stomach area. Reverse the flow of blood from your arms and hands back to your body's core. By thinking this, you now allow the blood vessels of the arms and hands to constrict, shunting the blood back to the GI tract. At the same time, you allow the blood vessels of the stomach area to dilate and receive the flow of blood you have sent to it.

14. As the blood returns, you may notice that your arms begin to feel a little lighter, but the sensation of warmth still lingers.

15. With each breath you take, with each beat of your heart, allow the flow of blood to return to where it came from.

16. Again, concentrate on your breathing. Feel the air come in through your nose or mouth, down into your lungs, and feel your stomach rise and then descend as you exhale the air through your mouth.

17. Now, take a comfortably slow, deep breath and feel the air enter the lower chambers of your lungs. Feel your stomach rise slowly with the intake of air, and slowly descend as the air leaves your lungs. Do this again, making the breath even slower and deeper. With each exhalation, become more aware of how relaxed your body has become.

EXERCISE   2: The Direct Approach of Autogenics cont....

18. Next, focus again on the beat of your heart. Listen to and feel your heart beating in your chest. As you concentrate on this, allow a longer pause between heartbeats. Just by allowing the thought of your heart relaxing you can make it do so. Think to allow a longer pause between beats. To help relax the heart muscle, take one more slow, deep breath, and feel how relaxed your heart has become as you exhale. Again, place a longer pause after each heartbeat.

19. Again, take a moment to realize that in the resting state you are now in, your body's core contains the greatest percentage of your blood supply, roughly 80 percent.

20. Think to yourself that when your muscles are saturated with blood, they become very relaxed and pliable like a wet sponge. Now become consciously aware that you desire to re-create that feeling of relaxation in the muscles of your legs and feet.

21. Allow the blood from your stomach area to move down toward your legs and feet. As you think and desire this, the blood vessels of your stomach area will begin to constrict, while at the same time those of your legs and feet will begin to dilate. This constriction process in your body's core will begin to shunt blood to your thighs, hamstrings, calves, and feet, where the dilating vessels will be able to receive more blood.

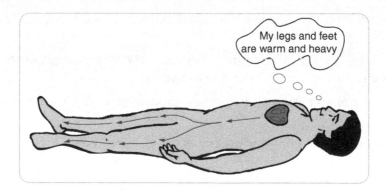

Visualizing the flow of blood to the legs and feet.

22. With each breath you take, with each beat of your heart, allow the flow of blood to move from your stomach area down toward your legs and feet.

23. You will begin to notice that as you allow this movement of blood from your body's core to your legs and feet, both your legs and feet begin to feel slightly heavy. This heaviness increases with each breath and each heartbeat. They feel very heavy because muscles in this region are not used to the sensation of additional blood flow. You will also notice that your legs and particularly your feet feel warm, especially the heels of your feet and your toes, because they have the greatest number of temperature receptors.

EXERCISE 2: The Direct Approach of Autogenics cont....

24. With each breath and each beat of your heart, allow the blood to continue to move from your stomach area to your legs and feet. Feel how comfortable your thighs and calves are. They feel warm, comfortably heavy, and very relaxed. As the muscles become saturated with blood, stiffness dissipates and relaxation ensues.

25. Be aware that your legs now feel increasingly heavy, so much so that you want to move them but they feel immobilized. You feel as if each leg has sunk under its weight into the floor. Your legs and feet feel so relaxed they don't want to move.

26. With each breath and each beat of your heart, continue to send the flow of blood to legs and feet. Feel the warmth spread from your stomach area all the way down to your toes.

27. Take a long, slow, deep breath and gauge how relaxed your whole body feels as you exhale. Feel how relaxed your legs and feet feel.

28. Now, take one more slow, deep breath, and as you exhale allow the flow of blood to return to your stomach area. Reverse the flow of blood from your legs and feet back to your body's core. By thinking this, you allow the blood vessels of the legs and feet to constrict, shunting the blood back to the GI tract. At the same time, you allow the blood vessels of the stomach area to dilate and receive the flow of blood you are sending to it.

29. As the blood returns, you will notice that your legs are beginning to feel a little lighter, but the sensations of warmth linger, especially in your feet and toes.

30. With each breath you take, with each beat of your heart, allow the flow of blood to return to where it came from.

31. As your body returns to a resting state, feel the sensation of relaxation throughout. Although you feel relaxed, you don't feel tired or sleepy. You feel alert and energized.

32. When you feel ready, open your eyes and stretch the muscles of your arms, shoulders, and legs.

Photo Credits

Unless otherwise indicated, all photographs and illustrations are under copyright of Jones and Bartlett Publishers, LLC, or have been provided by the author.

Brian Luke Seaward, Essentials of Managing Stress, Second Edition, 2011

Additional Relaxation Techniques

"That the birds fly overhead, this you cannot stop. That the birds make a nest in your hair, this you can prevent."

— Ancient Chinese proverb

Tai Chi

There is a life force of subtle energy that surrounds and permeates us all. This energy goes by many names; the Chinese call it *chi*. To move in unison with this energy is to move as freely as running water. A congestion or distortion of one's life energy ultimately leads to disease and illness. Therefore, the goal in life is to be in harmony with the flow of chi, because this promotes tranquility and a sense of being one with the universe. This is the essence of tai chi, a moving meditation that dates back to ancient China and provides a means to create and maintain this harmony and balance with the vital life force of universal energy and the natural world of which we are very much a part.

The words *tai chi* can best be translated to mean the "supreme ultimate," a symbolic representation of balance, power, and enlightenment. Although it is often called the softest of the martial arts, those who study this art form know that above all else, it is a discipline that unites mind, body, and spirit. The art of self-defense comes much later, if at all. Mental, emotional, and spiritual stress can block the flow of chi through the body. It is the progression of moves consciously executed with precision and finesse in the practice of tai chi that works to unblock and regulate the life force of universal energy, hence restoring health. To see tai chi practiced by a master is nothing less than poetry in motion, which is why it is often called a moving meditation. The majority of people who practice tai chi perform it not as a means of self-defense, but rather as an exercise to promote health and vitality.

The underlying premise of tai chi is to learn to move with the flow of energy rather than fight or resist it. In everyday life this philosophy translates to the concept of going with the flow of things you cannot control, rather than wasting or depleting your personal energy. The philosophy of tai chi is based on the Taoist concept of yin/yang, where opposites come together to form a whole (e.g., soft/hard, masculine/feminine, hot/cold). Exercise   2 leads you through a pattern of opposites to understand the concept of balance. However, any good tai chi instructor will tell you that the Taoist path is not one of extremes, but rather the middle road where one strives to live in balance and harmony with all aspects of one's life.

To learn this relaxation technique correctly, it is best to find a teacher whose philosophy of tai chi matches yours (e.g., self-defense vs. healthy vitality). Books or videos may serve as a good supplement, but they rarely provide a sound method of quality instruction. As any good tai chi instructor will tell you, once you have learned the sequence of steps, it will take years, if not decades, to fully master them. If you have an interest in or curiosity about this technique, consider checking your yellow page directory, newspaper community listings, or the Internet for classes in your area. When you find a course, ask if you can observe or participate in one class to get a feel for the instructor and decide from there if you wish to continue.

Progressive Muscular Relaxation

Nearly all relaxation techniques, from massage and meditation to yoga and tai chi, trace their origins back to the ancient cultures of Asia. One exception is the technique known as progressive muscular relaxation (PMR), which was created by an American physician several decades ago. As a physician, Edmund Jacobson noted that virtually all his patients who were sick appeared to have one common symptom: muscle tension. So concerned was he about this phenomenon that he decided to create a muscle relaxation technique that would help alleviate tense muscles and possibly restore people to health.

Jacobson designed a systematic approach to reducing muscle tension whereby a person begins at the top of his or her head and isolates a specific muscle group. He or she then begins a process of tensing and relaxing each muscle group, moving from head to toe, so that the individual can recognize the difference between tension and relaxation. By doing so, the desired effect is to be aware of muscle tension that may exist and work to release it through progressive relaxation. Progressive muscular relaxation has proven to be a beneficial technique for people with insomnia, TMJD, and even those who wish to quit smoking. Exercise   1 is a modified example of this technique.

Clinical Biofeedback

As we have seen throughout this book, the mind holds an incredible power to influence the body—in both positive and negative ways. Clinical biofeedback is a technique that enhances the mind's power of healing with the assistance of technology that simply amplifies one or more of the body's physiological parameters so the mind can get a better picture of what is going on inside. Through the wonderful complexities of biochemistry the human body gives off a number of vibrations of electrical impulses. Monitoring various physiological indices such as heart rate, blood pressure, muscle tension, brain waves, body temperature, and blood flow allows technology to mirror specific aspects of human physiology. In doing so, the mind can intercept these stress-prone areas (e.g., muscle tension) and help the body return to a deeper state of homeostasis.

Through the use of electrodes, transducers, a television monitor, and a certified biofeedback specialist, an individual is taught to observe an aspect or area of his or her body and then, through self-regulation, consciously decrease activity in this area with the help of the television monitor (or stereo speakers).

Clinical biofeedback has been very instrumental in helping people treat and heal a range of physical problems caused by stress, such as tension headaches, migraine headaches, lower back pain, TMJD, hypertension, Raynaud's disease, and many, many others. For this reason it is regarded as one of the premier modalities of complementary medicine. If this is something you wish to explore, consider locating a certified biofeedback specialist in your area.

Chapter Summary

- Tai chi is known as a moving meditation, a simple exercise to help regulate the flow of chi through your body. The practice of tai chi is a metaphor to "go with the flow."

- Progressive muscular relaxation is a technique to help reduce muscular tension by learning (and practicing) the regulation of muscle tension throughout the body.

- Clinical biofeedback is a relaxation technique in which a person uses a machine to amplify one or more body functions (e.g., heart rate, temperature, muscle tension) and learns to control these for optimal relaxation.

Additional Resources

Chen, T. *Step-by-Step Tai Chi with Tiffany Chen* (DVD). 2008.

Freeze-Frames (a biofeedback program). The HeartMath Institute. www.heartmath.org.

Huang, A. *Complete Tai Chi*. Boston: Tuttle Publishing; 1993.

The Journey to the Wild Divine: The Passage (a biofeedback video game). The Wild Divine Project. 1.866.594.WILD, www.wilddivine.com.

EXERCISE   1: Progressive Muscular Relaxation

The following is a slight variation of Jacobson's original technique, which divides muscle contractions into three intensities—100, 50, and 5 percent—for 5 seconds' duration, followed by the relaxation phase of 5–10 seconds' duration after each contraction. By sensing the differences between muscle contraction intensities, you become more aware of your muscle-tension levels over the course of a day. The instructions below were written to be read yourself before you perform the technique, or to be read out loud by a friend or colleague. Included here are three muscle groups (the face, neck and shoulders, and hands); however, you can expand this to include your abdominal area, upper legs, buttocks, calf muscles, and feet as well. Before you begin, find a comfortable position (preferably on your back on a carpeted floor); loosen any restrictive clothing; kick off your shoes; take several slow, comfortable, deep breaths; and simply begin to unwind in the starting position.

Starting position.

1. *Face.* Tense the muscles of the forehead and eyes, as if you were pulling all your facial muscles to the center of your nose. Pull really tight, as tight as you can, and hold it. Feel the tension you create in these muscles, especially the forehead and eyes. Now relax and exhale. Feel the absence of tension in these muscles, how loose and calm they feel. Try to compare this feeling of relaxation with the tension just produced. Now, contract the same muscles, but this time at 50 percent of the intensity, and hold it. Then relax and exhale. Feel how relaxed those muscles are. Compare this feeling to that during the last contraction. This comparison should make the muscles even more relaxed. Finally, contract the same facial muscles slightly, at only 5 percent intensity. This is like feeling a slight warm breeze on your forehead and cheeks. Hold it. And relax. Take a comfortably slow and deep breath and, as you exhale, feel how relaxed the muscles are.

EXERCISE 1: Progressive Muscular Relaxation cont....

2. *Shoulders.* Concentrate on the muscles of your shoulders and isolate these from surrounding neck and upper arm muscles. Take a moment to sense the muscles of the deltoid region. Notice any degree of residual tension. (The shoulder muscles can also harbor a lot of undetected muscle tension, resulting in stiffness. Quite literally, your shoulders carry the weight of all your thoughts, the weight of your world.) Now consciously tense the muscles of your shoulders really tight, as tight as you can, and hold it, even tighter, and hold it. Now relax these muscles and feel the tension disappear completely. Sense the difference between how these muscles feel now and how they felt during contraction. Once again, contract these same muscles, but this time at half the intensity. Hold the tension, keep holding; and now completely relax these muscles. Sense how relaxed your shoulder muscles are. Compare this feeling with what you felt at 100 percent intensity. Finally, contract these same muscles at only 5 percent, only just sensing clothing touching your shoulder muscles. Hold it, keep holding, and relax. Release any remaining tension so that these muscles are completely loose and relaxed. Feel just how relaxed these muscles are. To enhance this feeling of relaxation, take a comfortably slow, deep breath and sense how relaxed your shoulder muscles have become.

3. *Hands and forearms.* Concentrate on the muscles of your hands and forearms. Take a moment to feel these muscles, including your fingers, palms, and wrists. Notice the slightest bit of tension. Now consciously tense the muscles of each hand and forearm really tight by making a fist, as tight as you can, and hold it as if you were hanging on for dear life. Make it even tighter, and hold it. Now release the tension and relax these muscles. Feel the tension disappear completely. Open the palm of each hand slowly, extend your fingers, and let them recoil just a bit. Sense the difference between how relaxed these muscles feel now compared with what you just experienced at 100 percent contraction. They should feel very relaxed. Now contract these same muscles at a 50 percent contraction. Hold the tension, keep holding, and relax again. Sense how relaxed these muscles are. Compare this feeling of relaxation with what you just felt. Now, contract these same muscles at only 5 percent, like holding an empty eggshell in the palm of your hand. Now hold it, keep holding, and relax. Release any remaining tension so that these muscles are completely relaxed. Feel just how relaxed these muscles have become. To enhance this feeling of relaxation, take a comfortably slow, deep breath and sense how relaxed your forearm and hand muscles have become.

When you are done, lie comfortably for several moments and sense how your body feels. Take several slow, deep breaths and begin to retain this feeling of deep relaxation all throughout your body. When you feel ready, slowly make yourself aware of your surroundings. Then open your eyes to a soft gaze in front of you. If you wish you can begin to stretch your arms and hands. When you feel ready, sit up and bring yourself back to the full awareness of the room where you find yourself.

EXERCISE   2: The Yin/Yang of Life

Tai chi is based on the Taoist concept of seeking balance and going with the flow. The yin/yang symbol represents the balance of life where two opposite aspects come together, not in opposition but in union of the totality of the whole. The yin/yang symbol represents the balance of life.

1. Take a moment to fill in the blanks of the table below

Yin	Yang
_____	heaven
moon	_____
autumn, winter	_____
_____	masculine aspects
cold, coolness	_____
_____	brightness
inside, interior	_____
_____	things large and powerful
_____	the upper part
water, rain	_____
_____	movement
night	_____
_____	the left side
the west and north	_____
_____	the back of the body
exhaustion	_____
_____	clarity
development	_____
conservation	_____
_____	aggressiveness
contraction	_____

EXERCISE   2: The Yin/Yang of Life cont....

2. Assuming you have tried or currently practice the art of tai chi, please describe your impressions of this type of exercise as a means to promote relaxation.

_____

3. How do you see the effects (philosophy) of tai chi carrying over into other aspects of your life?

_____

_____

_____

4. The concept of balance is crucial to life, yet in this 24/7 society, balance seems to be a rare commodity. List five things you can do to bring balance to your life.

a. _____

b. _____

c. _____

d. _____

e. _____

5. Please share any other comments regarding tai chi here:

_____

_____

_____

Photo Credits

Unless otherwise indicated, all photographs and illustrations are under copyright of Jones and Bartlett Publishers, LLC, or have been provided by the author.

Introduction to Multicultural Health

We have become not a melting pot but a beautiful mosaic. Different people, different beliefs, different yearnings, different hopes, different dreams.

—Author unknown

One day our descendants will think it incredible that we paid so much attention to things like the amount of melanin in our skin or the shape of our eyes or our gender instead of the unique identities of each of us as complex human beings.

—Author unknown

KEY CONCEPTS

- Multicultural health
- Culture
- Cultural competency
- Race
- Acculturation
- Ethnicity
- Ethnocentricity
- Cultural relativism
- Racism

- Discrimination
- Minority
- Cultural adaptation
- Dominant culture
- Assimilation
- Heritage consistency
- Health disparities
- *Healthy People 2010*

CHAPTER OBJECTIVES

1. Explain why cultural considerations are important in health care.
2. Describe the processes of acculturation and assimilation.
3. Define race, culture, ethnicity, ethnocentricity, and cultural relativism.
4. Explain what cultural adaptation is and why it is important in health care.
5. Explain what health disparities are and their related causes.
6. List the five elements of the determinants of health and describe how they relate to health disparities.

Why do we need to study **multicultural health**? Why is **culture** important if we all have the same basic biological make-up? Isn't health all about science? Shouldn't people from different cultural backgrounds just adapt to the way that we provide health care in the United States if they are in this country?

For decades, the role that culture plays in health was virtually ignored, but the links have now become more apparent. As a result, the focus on the need to educate health care professionals about the important role that culture plays in health has escalated. Health is influenced by factors such as genetics, the environment, and socioeconomic status, as well as cultural and social forces. Culture impacts people's perception of health and illness, how they pursue and adhere to treatment, their health behaviors, beliefs about why people become ill, how symptoms and concerns about the problem are expressed, what is considered to be a health problem, and ways to maintain and restore health. This is why recognizing cultural similarities and differences is an essential component to delivering effective health care services. To provide quality care, health care professionals need to provide services within a cultural context, which is the focus of multicultural health.

Multicultural health is the phrase used to reflect the need to provide health care services in a sensitive, knowledgeable, and nonjudgmental manner with respect for people's health beliefs and practices when they are different than your own. It entails challenging your own assumptions, asking the right questions, and working with the patient and/or community in a manner that takes into consideration their lifestyle and approach to maintaining health and treating illness. Multicultural health integrates different approaches to care and incorporates the culture and belief system of the health care recipient while providing care within the legal, ethical, and medically sound practices of the practitioner's medical system.

Knowing the health practices and cultures of all groups is not possible, but becoming familiar with various groups' general health beliefs and variances can be very beneficial and improve the effectiveness of health care services. In this book, we make generalizations about cultural groups, but it is important to realize that many sub-cultures exist within those cultures, and people vary in the degree to which they identify with the beliefs and practices of their culture of origin. Awareness of general differences can help health care professionals provide services within a cultural context, but it is important to distinguish between stereotyping (the mistaken assumption that everyone in a given culture is alike) and generalizations (awareness of cultural norms) (Juckett, 2005). Generalizations can serve as a starting point and do not preclude factoring in individual characteristics, such as education, nationality, faith, and level of cultural adaptation. Stereotypes and assumptions can be problematic and can lead to errors and ineffective care. Remember, every person is unique, but understanding the generalizations can be beneficial, because it moves people in the direction of becoming culturally competent.

Cultural competency refers to possessing knowledge, awareness, and respect for other cultures (Juckett, 2005). Cultural competence occurs on a continuum, and this is the first chapter of a book that is geared to help you progress along the cultural competency scale. There are many key terms used that are related to multicultural health, such as **race** and **acculturation**, that need to be clarified, so we begin this chapter by defining and describing these terms. Then we move into a discussion about types and degrees of cultural adaptation, how the demographic landscape of the population in the United States is changing, and why it is important to take those demographic changes into consideration when delivering health care services.

KEY CONCEPTS AND TERMS

Some of the terminology related to multicultural health can be confusing, because the differences are difficult to distinguish. This section is designed to clarify the terminology. The terms described here are culture, race, **ethnicity**, **ethnocentricity**, and **cultural relativism**.

Culture

There are countless definitions of culture. The short explanation is that culture is everything that makes us who we are. E. B. Tylor, who is considered to be the founder of cultural anthropology, provided the classical definition of culture. Tylor stated in 1871, "Culture, or civilization, taken in its broad, ethnographic sense, is that complex whole which includes knowledge, belief, art, morals, law, custom, and any other capabilities and habits acquired by man as a member of society" (Tylor, 1924/1871, p. 1). Tylor's definition is still widely cited today. A more current definition is, "The thoughts, communications, actions, customs, beliefs, values, and institutions of racial, ethnic, religious, or social groups" (Office of Minority Health, 2001, p. 131).

Culture is learned, changes over time, and is passed on from generation to generation. It is a very complex system, and many subcultures exist within the dominant culture. For example, universities, businesses, neighborhoods, age groups, homosexuals, athletic teams, and musicians are sub-cultures of the American dominant culture. People simultaneously belong to numerous sub-cultures, because we can be students at a university, fathers or mothers, and employees at the same time.

Race and Ethnicity

Race refers to a person's physical characteristics and/or genetic or biological makeup, but the reality is that race is not a scientific construct; it is a social construct. Race was developed so that people can be categorized, and it is based on the notion that some races are superior to others. Many professionals in the fields of biology, sociology, and anthropology have determined that race is a social construct and not a biological one because not one characteristic, trait, or gene distinguishes all the members of one so-called race from all the members of another so-called race. "There is more genetic variation within races than between them, and racial categories do not capture biological distinctiveness" (Williams, Lavizzo-Mourey, & Warren, 1994). So why is race important if it does not really exist? Race is important because society makes it important. Race shapes social, cultural, political, ideological, and legal functions in society. The result is that race is an institutionalized concept that has had devastating consequences. Race has been the basis for deaths from wars and murders and suffering caused by discrimination, violence, torture, and hate crimes. The ideology of race has been the root of suffering and death for centuries even though it has no scientific merit.

In the 2000 U.S. census, the question of race was asked differently than in previous years. Respondents were given the option of selecting one or more race categories to indicate their racial identities. The race categories and their related definitions were:

White: a person having origins in any of the original peoples of Europe, the Middle East, or North Africa

Black or African American: a person having origins in any of the black racial groups of Africa

American Indian or Alaska Native: a person having origins in any of the originals peoples of North and South America (including Central America) and who maintain tribal affiliation or community attachment

Asian: a person having origins in any of the original peoples of the Far East, Southeast Asia, or the Indian subcontinent, including, for example, China, India, and the Philippine Islands

Native Hawaiian or other Pacific Islander: a person having origins in any of the original peoples of Hawaii, Guam, Samoa, or other Pacific Islands

The United States government declared that Hispanics and Latinos are an ethnicity and not a race, which is correct, and the rationale is explained in Chapter 7. The government defines Hispanic or Latino as a person of Cuban, Mexican, Puerto Rican, South or Central American, or other Spanish culture or origin regardless of race.

United States Census 2000

U.S. Department of Commerce • Bureau of the Census

This is the official form for all the people at this address. It is quick and easy, and your answers are protected by law. Complete the Census and help your community get what it needs — today and in the future!

Start Here

Please use a black or blue pen.

1. How many people were living or staying in this house, apartment, or mobile home on April 1, 2000?

[   ] Number of people

INCLUDE in this number:
- foster children, roomers, or housemates
- people staying here on April 1, 2000 who have no other permanent place to stay
- people living here most of the time while working, even if they have another place to live

DO NOT INCLUDE in this number:
- college students living away while attending college
- people in a correctional facility, nursing home, or mental hospital on April 1, 2000
- Armed Forces personnel living somewhere else
- people who live or stay at another place most of the time

2. Is this house, apartment, or mobile home — *Mark* ☒ *ONE box.*
- ☐ Owned by you or someone in this household with a mortgage or loan?
- ☐ Owned by you or someone in this household free and clear (without a mortgage or loan)?
- ☐ Rented for cash rent?
- ☐ Occupied without payment of cash rent?

3. Please answer the following questions for each person living in this house, apartment, or mobile home. Start with the name of one of the people living here who owns, is buying, or rents this house, apartment, or mobile home. If there is no such person, start with any adult living or staying here. We will refer to this person as Person 1.

What is this person's name? *Print name below.*

Last Name
[| | | | | | | | | | | | |]

First Name   MI
[| | | | | | | | | | | | |] [ ]

OMB No. 0607-0856: Approval Expires 12/31/2000

Form **D-61A**

4. What is Person 1's telephone number? *We may call this person if we don't understand an answer.*

Area Code + Number
[| |] – [| |] – [| | |]

5. What is Person 1's sex? *Mark* ☒ *ONE box.*
- ☐ Male   ☐ Female

6. What is Person 1's age and what is Person 1's date of birth?

Age on April 1, 2000
[|]

Print numbers in boxes.
Month   Day   Year of birth
[|]   [|]   [| | |]

→ **NOTE: Please answer BOTH Questions 7 and 8.**

7. Is Person 1 Spanish/Hispanic/Latino? *Mark* ☒ *the* **"No"** *box if* **not** *Spanish/Hispanic/Latino.*
- ☐ **No,** not Spanish/Hispanic/Latino   ☐ Yes, Puerto Rican
- ☐ Yes, Mexican, Mexican Am., Chicano   ☐ Yes, Cuban
- ☐ Yes, other Spanish/Hispanic/Latino — *Print group.* ↙

[| | | | | | | | | | | | | | |]

8. What is Person 1's race? *Mark* ☒ *one or more races* to indicate what this person considers himself/herself to be.
- ☐ White
- ☐ Black, African Am., or Negro
- ☐ American Indian or Alaska Native — *Print name of enrolled or principal tribe.* ↙

[| | | | | | | | | | | | | | |]

- ☐ Asian Indian   ☐ Japanese   ☐ Native Hawaiian
- ☐ Chinese   ☐ Korean   ☐ Guamanian or Chamorro
- ☐ Filipino   ☐ Vietnamese   ☐ Samoan
- ☐ Other Asian — *Print race.* ↙   ☐ Other Pacific Islander — *Print race.* ↙

[| | | | | | | | | | | | | | |]

- ☐ Some other race — *Print race.* ↙

[| | | | | | | | | | | | | | |]

→ **If more people live here, continue with Person 2.**

Source: U.S. Census Bureau, Public Information Office, http://www.census.gov/dmd/www/2000quest.html.

It is important to note that there is great variation within each of the government's racial and ethnic categories, and in this book we address the basic foundation of each group. It is rare to identify all of the themes in any individual due to differences in the level of their acculturation. Also, within each racial and ethnic category is great variation. For example, the Asian category includes Chinese and Indians, who have variations between them. Therefore, it is essential to be aware of the differences that occur within these groups and to not stereotype people.

Stereotyping people by their race and ethnicity may lead to **racism**. Racism is the belief that some races are superior to others by nature and can result in discrimination. **Discrimination** occurs when people act on a belief, and differences in treatment transpire as a result. Discrimination can occur because of beliefs related to factors such as race, sexual orientation, dialect, religion, or gender.

Ethnicity is "the characteristic of a group of people who share a common and distinctive racial, national, religious, linguistic, or cultural heritage" (Office of Minority Health, 2001, p. 131). Ethnicity is made up of the following characteristics:

- Geographic origins
- Family patterns
- Language
- Values and symbols
- Cultural norms
- Religion
- Literature
- Music
- Dietary patterns
- Gender roles
- Employment patterns

So how is ethnicity different from culture? One can belong to a culture without having ancestral roots to that culture. For example, a person can belong to the hip–hop culture, but he or she is not born into the culture.

Cultural Ethnocentricity and Cultural Relativism

Cultural ethnocentricity refers to when a person believes that his or her culture is superior to another one. This can cause problems in the health care field if a professional believes that his or her way is the better way to prevent or treat a health problem and disrespects or ignores the patient's or client's cultural beliefs and values. The health care professional may not take into consideration that the listener may have different views than the provider. This can lead to ineffective communication and treatment and leave the listener feeling unimportant, frustrated, disrespected, or confused about how to prevent or treat the health issue, and he or she might view the professional as uneducated, uncooperative, unapproachable, or closed-minded. To be effective, one needs to see and appreciate the value of different cultures; this is referred to as cultural relativism.

Cultural relativism came about in an attempt to refute the idea of cultural ethnocentricity. The phrase was derived in the field of anthropology, and it is an approach that posits that all cultures are of equal value and need to be studied from a neutral point of view. It rejects value judgments on cultures and holds the belief that no culture is superior. Cultural relativism takes an objective view of cultures and incorporates the idea that if a society's moral code believes that something is right (or wrong), then it is right (or wrong) for members of that society.

DIVERSITY WITHIN THE UNITED STATES

A great strength of the United States is the diversity of the people. Historically, waves of immigrants have come to the United States to start their lives in the land of opportunity in pursuit of a better quality of life. The immigrants brought with them their traditions, languages, and cultures to create a country with a very diverse landscape. Some of the diverse landscape occurred for other reasons, such as Africans being forced to come to the United States and the American Indians who originated here. An unfortunate outcome of this diversity is that it has contributed to the history of racial and cultural clashes along with imbalances in equality and opportunities that continue today. These positive and adverse consequences of diversity must be considered in our health care approaches, particularly because the demographics are continuing to change and the inequalities persist. The delivery of health care to individuals, families, and communities must meet the needs of the wide variety of people who reside in and visit the United States.

The percentage of the United States population characterized as white is decreasing (see Figure   1). The term **minority** is becoming outdated because the minority population grew 11 times as rapidly as the white, non-Hispanic population between 1980 and 2000 (Hobbs & Stoops, 2002), and it is projected that by 2050 nearly one-half of the United States population will be composed of non-whites (McKenzie, Pinger, & Kotecki, 2005). This is an important consideration for health care providers, because ethnic minorities experience poorer health status. These disparities in health are discussed later in this chapter.

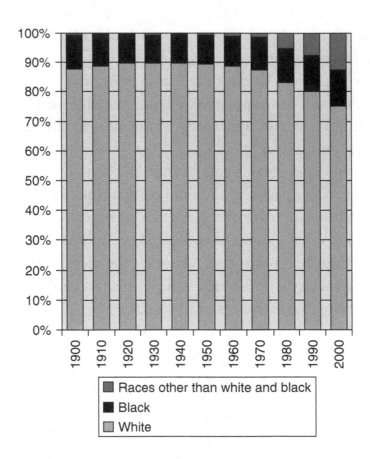

FIGURE 1 Distribution of population by race: 1900 to 2000.
Source: Adapted from Hobbs and Stoops. (2002).

CULTURAL ADAPTATION

With this changing landscape in the United States, professionals are encouraged to consider the degree of cultural adaptation that the person has experienced. **Cultural adaptation** refers to the degree to which a person or community has adapted to the **dominant culture** and retained their traditional practices. Generally, a first-generation individual will identify more with his or her culture of origin than a third-generation person. Therefore, when working with the first-generation person, the health care professional will need to be more sensitive to issues such as language barriers, distrust, lack of understanding of the American medical system, and the person's ties to his or her traditional beliefs. Acculturation and **assimilation** are terms that relate to the degree of adaptation that has taken place.

Acculturation refers to a process in which members of one cultural group adopt the beliefs and behaviors of another group. Essentially, members of one cultural

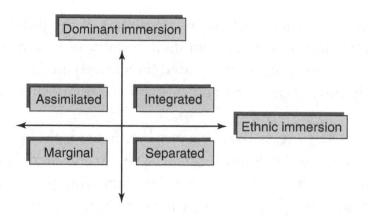

FIGURE 2 Acculturation framework.

group acquire a second culture. Usually the minority culture takes up many of the dominant culture's traits. People can experience different levels of acculturation as illustrated in Berry and colleagues' acculturation framework, which is illustrated in Figure 2.

An assimilated individual demonstrates high dominant and low ethnic society immersion. This entails moving away from one's ethnic society and immersing fully in the dominant society (Stephenson, 2000). An individual who rejects his or her country of origin would fall into this category. An integrated person has high dominant and ethnic immersion. Integration entails immersion in both ethnic and dominant societies (Stephenson, 2000). An example of an integrated person is a French American who socializes with the dominant group but chooses to speak French at home and marries a person who is French. Separated individuals have low dominant immersion and high ethnic immersion. A separated individual withdraws from the dominant society and completely immerges in the ethnic society (Stephenson, 2000). An example is a person who lives in ethnic communities such as Little Italy or Chinatown. A marginalized individual has low dominant and ethnic immersion and does not identify with any particular culture or belief system.

The marginalized people tend to have the most psychological problems and highest stress levels. These individuals often lack social support systems and are not accepted by the dominant society or their culture of origin. A person in the separated mode is accepted in his or her ethnic society but may not be accepted by the dominant culture, leaving the person feeling alienated. The integrated and assimilated modes are considered to be the most psychologically healthy adaptation styles, although some individuals benefit more from one than from the other. Western Europeans and individuals whose families have been in the United States for a number of generations (and are not discriminated against) are most likely to adopt an assimilated mode because they have many beliefs and attributes of the dominant society. Individuals who retain value structures from their country of origin and encounter discrimination benefit more from an integrated (bicultural) mode. To be bicultural one must be knowledgeable about both cultures and see the positive attributes of both of them.

Assimilation is the process that occurs when individuals or groups of different cultures are absorbed into the dominant society. As a result there is a disappearance of a minority group through the loss of particular identifying physical or socio-cultural characteristics. This usually occurs when people immigrate into a new geographic region, and through their contact with the dominant groups and their desire to be a part of the mainstream they give up most of their culture traits of origin and take on a new cultural identity, which is the one of the dominant culture. The reality is that many people do not fully assimilate because they tend to keep some of their cultural beliefs from the origin.

The degree to which people identify with their culture of origin is sometimes referred to as **heritage consistency**. Some indicators that can help professionals assess the level of cultural adaptation are inquiring about how long the person has been in the country, how often the person returns to his or her culture of origin, what holidays the person celebrates, what language the person speaks at home, and how much knowledge the person has of his or her culture of origin.

Are people who have higher levels of cultural adaptation healthier? Despite increasing research on the relationships between acculturation and health, the answer is not clearly defined. The influence of acculturation on health in the literature indicates contradictory results because the variables are complex. The answer also is dependent upon what health habits are incorporated into one's lifestyle and what ones are lost. For example, acculturation can have detrimental effects on one's dietary patterns if a person is from a culture where eating fruits and vegetables is common and the person incorporates the habit of eating at fast food restaurants, which is common in the United States. On the other hand, if someone moves from a culture where smoking is common to a culture where it is frowned upon, the person may stop smoking.

As noted, acculturation can have both negative and positive affects on health. Zambrana, Scrimshaw, Collins, and Dunkel-Schetter (1997) found that Mexican American women who are undergoing the process of immersion in the mainstream culture "experience a decrease in culture-specific protective factors that are integrally related to the quality of the community environment in which they live" (Zambrana, et al., 1997, p. 1025). In the study conducted by Zambrana and colleagues (1997), risky health behaviors, stress levels, and medical risks all seemed to increase with greater acculturation and decrease in protective factors, such as social support, in the Hispanic community. Lack of fluency in English may adversely affect health as the prevalence of risks for chronic disease and injury among certain racial and ethnic groups increases. Some immigrants are highly educated and have high incomes (Council of Economic Advisors for the President's Initiative on Race, 1998), but their lack of familiarity with the United States public and private health care systems, different cultural attitudes about the use of traditional and United States conventional medicine (Centers for Disease Control and Prevention [CDC], 1991), and lack of fluency in English may pose barriers to obtaining appropriate health care (CDC, 1997). Poverty also is associated with lower levels of acculturation, which affects immigrants' health as well.

On the contrary, acculturation can have a favorable impact on immigrants' health. For example, people with higher acculturation levels learn how to navigate the health care system in the United States and may have language skills that enable them to communicate more effectively. Tran, Fitzpatrick, Berg, and Wright (1996) wrote that the level of acculturation has a significant affect upon health status. Less acculturated respondents experienced higher rates of self-reported health problems than people with higher levels of acculturation. Fewer language skills and less education are factors that are related to the avoidance of obtaining health-care services (Tran, et al., 1996).

HEALTH DISPARITIES

Health disparities are differences in the incidence, prevalence, mortality, burden of diseases, and other adverse health conditions or outcomes that exist among specific population groups in the United States. The specific population groups can be based on gender, age, ethnicity, socioeconomic status, geography, sexual orientation, disability, or special health care needs. Health disparities occur among groups who have persistently experienced historic trauma, social disadvantage, or discrimination. They are widespread in the United States as demonstrated by the fact that many minority groups in the United States have a higher incidence of chronic diseases, higher mortality, and poorer health outcomes when compared to whites (Goldberg, Hayes, & Huntley, 2004).

Eliminating health disparities is an important goal for our nation as indicated by the fact that it is the second major goal of *Healthy People 2010*. Some ways to eliminate health inequalities include changing policy, increasing access to care, and creating a culturally competent health-care system. Examples of health disparities are addressed throughout this book, but the following sections describe a few revealing statistics.

African Americans

In 2003, the death rate for African Americans was higher than that for whites for heart diseases, stroke, cancer, asthma, influenza and pneumonia, diabetes, human immunodeficiency virus (HIV)–acquired immunodeficiency syndrome (AIDS), and homicide.

The following statistics were compiled by the Office of Minority Health (n.d.):

- In 2003, African American men were 1.4 times as likely to have new cases of lung and prostate cancer compared to non-Hispanic white men.
- African American men were twice as likely to have new cases of stomach cancer as non-Hispanic white men.
- In 2003, diabetic African Americans were 1.8 times as likely as diabetic whites to be hospitalized.
- In 2004, African Americans were 2.2 times as likely as non-Hispanic whites to die from diabetes.
- In 2004, African American men were 30% more likely to die from heart disease compared to non-Hispanic white men.
- African Americans were 1.5 times as likely as non-Hispanic whites to have high blood pressure.
- African American women were 1.7 times as likely as non-Hispanic white women to be obese.
- Although African Americans make up only 13% of the total United States population, they accounted for 47% of HIV–AIDS cases in 2005.
- African American males had more than eight times the AIDS rate of non-Hispanic white males.
- African American females had more than 23 times the AIDS rate of non-Hispanic white females.
- In 2005, African Americans aged 65 years and older were 40% less likely to have received an influenza (flu) shot in the past 12 months compared to non-Hispanic whites of the same age group.
- In 2005, African American adults aged 65 years and older were 30% less likely to have ever received a pneumonia shot compared to non-Hispanic white adults of the same age group.
- African American infants were almost four times as likely to die from causes related to low birth-weight compared to non-Hispanic white infants.
- African Americans had 2.1 times the sudden infant death syndrome mortality rate as non-Hispanic whites.

- African American mothers were 2.6 times as likely as non-Hispanic white mothers to begin prenatal care in the third trimester or not receive prenatal care at all.
- African American adults were 50% more likely than their white adult counterparts to have a stroke.

American Indians and Alaska Natives

Some of the leading diseases and causes of death among American Indians and Alaska Natives are heart disease, cancer, unintentional injuries (accidents), diabetes, and stroke (Office of Minority Health, n.d.). American Indians and Alaska Natives also have a high prevalence and greater risk factors for mental health problems and suicide, obesity, substance abuse, sudden infant death syndrome (SIDS), teenage pregnancy, and liver disease. American Indians and Alaska Natives have an infant death rate almost double the rate for Caucasians and are twice as likely to have diabetes as Caucasians. American Indians and Alaska Natives also have disproportionately high death rates from unintentional injuries and suicide.

The following statistics were compiled by the Office of Minority Health (n.d.):

- American Indian and Alaska Native men were twice as likely to be diagnosed with stomach and liver cancers as white men.
- American Indian women were 20% more likely to die from cervical cancer compared to white women.
- American Indian and Alaska Native adults were 2.3 times as likely as white adults to be diagnosed with diabetes.
- American Indian and Alaska Natives were twice as likely as non-Hispanic whites to die from diabetes in 2003.
- American Indian and Alaska Native adults were 1.3 times as likely as white adults to have high blood pressure.
- American Indian and Alaska Native adults were 1.2 times as likely as white adults to have heart disease.
- American Indian and Alaska Native adults were 1.4 times as likely as white adults to be current cigarette smokers.
- American Indian and Alaska Native adults were 1.6 times as likely as white adults to be obese.
- American Indian and Alaska Native adults were 1.3 times as likely as white adults to have high blood pressure.

- American Indians and Alaska Natives had a 40% higher AIDS rate than their non-Hispanic white counterparts.
- American Indian and Alaska Native babies were 2.2 times as likely as non-Hispanic white babies to die from sudden infant death syndrome (SIDS).
- American Indian and Alaska Native infants were 3.6 times as likely as non-Hispanic white infants to have mothers who began prenatal care in the third trimester or did not receive prenatal care at all.
- American Indian and Alaska Native adults were 60% more likely to have a stroke than their white adult counterparts.

Asian Americans

Asian American women have the highest life expectancy (85.8 years) of any other ethnic group in the United States (Office of Minority Health, n.d.). Life expectancy varies among Asian subgroups: Filipino (81.5 years), Japanese (84.5 years), and Chinese women (86.1 years). However, Asian Americans contend with numerous factors that may threaten their health. Some negative factors are infrequent medical visits due to issues such as the fear of deportation, language and cultural barriers, and the lack of health insurance. Asian Americans are most at risk for cancer, heart disease, stroke, unintentional injuries (accidents), and diabetes. Asian Americans also have a high prevalence of chronic obstructive pulmonary disease, hepatitis B, HIV–AIDS, smoking, tuberculosis, and liver disease.

The following statistics were compiled by the Office of Minority Health (n.d.):

- In 2006, tuberculosis was 10 times more common among Asian Americans and five times more common among Native Hawaiians and Pacific Islanders compared to the white population.
- In 2003, Asian American and Pacific Islander women were 1.2 times as likely to have cervical cancer compared to non-Hispanic white women.
- Asian American and Pacific Islander men and women had higher incidence and mortality rates for stomach and liver cancer.
- Asian Americans were 20% less likely than non-Hispanic whites to die from diabetes.
- Overall, Asian American and Pacific Islander adults were less likely than white adults to have heart disease, and they were less likely to die from heart disease.
- Asian Americans and Pacific Islanders were 40% less likely to die from heart disease compared to non-Hispanic whites.

- Asian Americans and Pacific Islanders had lower AIDS rates than non-Hispanic white counterparts, and they were less likely to die of HIV–AIDS.
- One Asian American–Pacific Islander child was diagnosed with AIDS in 2006.
- In 2005, Asian American and Pacific Islander adults aged 65 years and older were 40% less likely to have ever received a pneumonia shot compared to non-Hispanic white adults of the same age group.
- Asian American and Pacific Islander adults were less likely to die from a stroke.
- Asian American and Pacific Islander adults had lower rates of being overweight or obese, lower rates of hypertension, and they were less likely to be current cigarette smokers compared to white adults.

Hispanics and Latin Americans

Hispanics' health is often shaped by factors such as language and cultural barriers, lack of access to preventive care, and the lack of health insurance. The Centers for Disease Control and Prevention has cited some of the leading causes of illness and death among Hispanics, which include heart disease, cancer, unintentional injuries (accidents), stroke, and diabetes. Some other health conditions and risk factors that significantly affect Hispanics are asthma, chronic obstructive pulmonary disease, HIV–AIDS, obesity, suicide, and liver disease. Hispanics have higher rates of obesity than non-Hispanic Caucasians. There also are disparities among Hispanic subgroups. For example, although the rate of low birth-weight infants is lower for the total Hispanic population in comparison to non-Hispanic Caucasians, Puerto Ricans have a low birth-weight rate that is 50% higher than the rate for non-Hispanic Caucasians (Office of Minority Health, n.d.). Puerto Ricans also suffer disproportionately from asthma, HIV–AIDS, and infant mortality. Mexican-Americans suffer disproportionately from diabetes.

The following statistics were compiled by the Office of Minority Health (n.d.):

- Mexican American adults were two times more likely than non-Hispanic white adults to have been diagnosed with diabetes by a physician.
- In 2002, Hispanics were 1.5 times as likely to start treatment for end-stage renal disease related to diabetes compared to non-Hispanic white men.
- In 2004, Hispanics were 1.5 times as likely as non-Hispanic whites to die from diabetes.
- Mexican American women were 1.3 times more likely than non-Hispanic white women to be obese.
- Hispanic males had over three times the AIDS rate as non-Hispanic white males.

- Hispanic females had over five times the AIDS rate as non-Hispanic white females.
- In 2005, Hispanic adults aged 65 years and older were 50% less likely to have ever received a pneumonia shot compared to non-Hispanic white adults of the same age group.
- In 2004, infant mortality rates for Hispanic subpopulations ranged from 4.6 per 1,000 live births to 7.8 per 1,000 live births compared to the non-Hispanic white infant mortality rate of 5.7 per 1,000 live births.
- Puerto Rican infants were twice as likely to die from causes related to low birth-weight compared to non-Hispanic white infants.
- Mexican American mothers were 2.5 times as likely as non-Hispanic white mothers to begin prenatal care in the third trimester or not receive prenatal care at all.

Gays, Lesbians, and Bisexuals

Gays, lesbians, and bisexuals also encounter disparate health concerns. For example, major health issues for gay men are HIV–AIDS and other sexually transmitted diseases, substance abuse, depression, and suicide. Some evidence suggests that lesbians have higher rates of smoking, being overweight, alcohol abuse, and stress than heterosexual women (CDC, 2007a). The issues surrounding personal, family, and social acceptance of sexual orientation can place a significant burden on mental health and personal safety (CDC, 2007a).

CAUSES OF HEALTH DISPARITIES

The causes of health disparities are due to both voluntary and involuntary factors. Voluntary factors are related to health behaviors, such as smoking and diet, and can be avoided. Factors such as genetics, living and working in unhealthy conditions, limited or no access to health care, language barriers, limited financial resources, and low health literacy skills are often viewed as being involuntary and unfair, because they are not within that person's control.

The Lalonde report was produced in Canada in 1974 and was titled *A New Perspective on the Health of Canadians*. This report probably was the first acknowledgment by a major industrialized country that health is determined by more than biological factors. The report led to the development of the health field concept, which identified four health fields that were interdependently responsible for individual health.

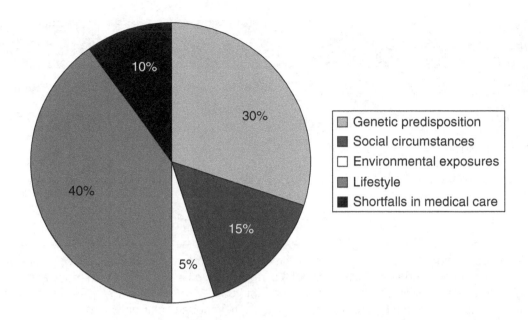

FIGURE 3 Domains and their percentage of contributions to early death.
Source: Data from: McGinnis, Williams-Russo, and Knickman. (2002).

1. *Environment.* All matters related to health external to the human body and over which the individual has little or no control. Includes the physical and social environment.
2. *Human biology.* All aspects of health, physical and mental, developed within the human body as a result of organic make-up.
3. *Lifestyle.* The aggregation of personal decisions over which the individual has control. Self-imposed risks created by unhealthy lifestyle choices can be said to contribute to, or cause, illness or death.
4. *Health care organization.* The quantity, quality, arrangement, nature, and relationships of people and resources in the provision of health care.

These four domains were later changed to five intersecting domains, which are environmental exposures, genetics, behavior (lifestyle) choices, social circumstances, and medical care (Institute of Medicine [IOM], 2001). A rough estimate of the impact of each domain on early deaths is illustrated in Figure 3.

We discuss each one of the five domains in more detail, but it is important to note that all of the domains are integrated and affected by one another. For example, people who have more education usually have higher incomes, are more likely to have healthcare coverage, and live in neighborhoods with fewer environmental health risks.

TABLE 1

TABLE 1	Segregation of Ethnic Minorities Compared with Whites, United States, 1980 to 2000		
	1980	**1990**	**2000**
American Indians	37.3	36.8	33.3
African Americans	72.7	67.8	64.0
Asian Americans and Pacific Islanders	40.5	41.2	41.1
Hispanics	50.2	50.0	50.9

Segregation was determined using the index of dissimilarity, which measures the evenness of groups over space and can be interpreted as the percentage of a particular group who would have to move to integrate the two groups over the region as a whole. For example, in 2000, 64% of all African Americans (or whites) would have to move to another census tract to integrate all metropolitan areas nationwide.

Data source: Gee and Payne-Sturges. (2004).

Environmental Exposures

Environmental conditions are believed to play an important role in producing and maintaining health disparities (Lee, 2002; Yen & Syme, 1999). The environment influences our health in many ways, including through exposures to physical, chemical, and biological risk factors and through related changes in our behavior in response to those factors. In general, whites and minorities do not have the same exposure to environmental health threats, because they live in different neighborhoods. Residential segregation still exists.

Segregation, the spatial separation of the residences of racial groups from one another, has persisted for many decades (Iceland, Weinberg, & Steinmetz, 2002; Massey, 2001; Massey & Denton, 1993). Table 1 shows the segregation of African Americans, Hispanics, American Indians, and Asian Americans–Pacific Islanders compared with whites from 1980 to 2000 for metropolitan areas, as measured with the index of dissimilarity (Logan, 2003; US Census Bureau, 2003). Scored from 0 to 100, a given value of the index indicates the percentage of that group who would have to move to integrate the metropolitan area. Segregation from whites is highest for African Americans, followed by Hispanics, Asian Americans and Pacific Islanders, and American Indians.

Although a common argument is that segregation is harmful to the health of minorities, there is some indication that segregation may have a counterbalancing effect by concentrating social resources, such as black political power (LaVeist, 1993). Others have reported that the clustering of ethnic groups may build a sense of collective identity that helps mitigate trauma (Mazumdar, Mazumdar, Docuyanan, & McLaughlin, 2000). Thus, supportive social relationships within minority communities may help promote health and ameliorate the effects of community risks. Segregation concentrates both risks and resources.

Minority Neighborhoods

Ethnicity is highly correlated with residential location, and minority neighborhoods experience greater exposure to environmental health risks. These two links lead to the idea that health disparities are, in part, caused by the difference in exposure levels to environmental hazards. Minority neighborhoods tend to have higher rates of mortality, morbidity, and health risk factors compared with white neighborhoods, even after accounting for economic and other characteristics (Cubbin, Hadden, & Winkleby, 2001; Deaton & Lubotsky, 2003; Geronimus, Bound, Waidmann, Colen, & Steffick, 2001).

A contributing factor is greater exposure to environmental toxicants, such as air pollution, pesticides, and lead, which can lead to health problems such as asthma, cancer, and chemical poisoning. Low socioeconomic neighborhoods are more likely than middle or higher socioeconomic neighborhoods to be situated near toxic waste sites and other potential environmental hazards (Mohai & Bryant, 1992).

People who live in poor neighborhoods might not have access to nutritious foods, safe places to exercise, and other resources that improve health. Poor and minority neighborhoods tend to have fewer grocery stores with healthy foods (Morland, Wing, Diez-Roux, & Poole, 2002) and fewer pharmacies with needed medications (Morrison, Wallenstein, Natale, Senzel, & Huang, 2000). Other research indicates that healthy foods are not only less abundant, they also are more costly in low-income neighborhoods. Poor nutrition can increase susceptibility to environmental pollutants by compromising immune function (Beck & Weinstock 1988; Rios, Poje, & Detels, 1993). Additionally, disadvantaged neighborhoods also are exposed to greater health hazards, including tobacco and alcohol advertisements, toxic waste incinerators, and air pollution (Morello-Frosch, Pastor, Porras, & Sadd, 2002). Finally, economic stress within a community may exacerbate tensions between social groups, magnify workplace stressors, induce maladaptive coping behaviors, such as smoking and alcohol use (Brenner, 1995), and translate into individual stress, which makes individuals more vulnerable to illness when they are exposed to environmental hazards. Tobacco and alcohol use can increase susceptibility to environmental toxicants that are normally metabolized by impairing host defense (Rios, et al., 1993).

Neighborhood physical conditions also may contribute to health disparities (Cohen, et al., 2003). Minorities are more likely to live in areas with building code violations and neighborhoods with deteriorated housing (Perera, et al., 2002). In 1999, 3.4% of blacks, 3.8% of Hispanics, and 1.7% of Asian Americans and Pacific Islanders reported living in housing units with severe problems with heating, plumbing, electricity, public areas, or maintenance, compared with 1.5% of whites (US Census Bureau, 2000). Substandard housing may contribute to a variety of problems, including exposure to toxicants, increased risk of injuries from falls and fires, and illness due to ineffective waste disposal and presence of disease vectors (Bashir, 2002; Jacobs, et al., 2002; Northridge, Stover, Rosenthal, & Sherard, 2003).

Factors associated with living in poor neighborhoods, such as crime and physical deterioration, can cause stress, which can lead to health problems. Stress is a state of activation of physical and psychological readiness to act, which helps an organism survive external threats. Stressors are the factors that produce stress and include such phenomena as crime, domestic violence, and noise (Babisch, Fromme, Beyer, & Ising, 2001; Ouis, 2001), traffic (Gee & Takeuchi, 2004), litter, density, and residential crowding (Fleming, Baum, & Weiss, 1987; Evans & Lepore, 1993). Stress has effects on the physical and psychological state of humans and as a result can lead to health problems such as high blood pressure or depression (Gee & Payne-Sturges, 2004).

Genetics

Genetics have been linked to many diseases, including diabetes, cancer, sickle-cell anemia, obesity, cystic fibrosis, hemophilia, Tay-Sachs disease, schizophrenia, and Down syndrome. Currently, about 4,000 genetic disorders are known. Some genetic disorders are a result of a single mutated gene, and other disorders are complex, multifactorial or polygenic mutations. Multifactorial means that the disease or disorder is likely to be associated with the effects of multiple genes in combination with lifestyle and environmental factors. Examples of multifactorial disorders are cancer, heart disease, and diabetes. Although there have been numerous studies that link genetics to health, social and cultural factors play a role as well. For example, smoking may trigger a genetic predisposition to lung cancer, but that gene may not have been expressed if the person did not smoke.

There are concerns about relating genetics and health disparities because race is not truly biologically determined, so the relationship between genetics and race is not clear cut. There are more genetic differences within races than among them, and racial categories do not capture biological distinctiveness (Williams, et al., 1994). Another problem with linking genetics to race is that many people have a mixed gene pool due to inter-racial marriages and partnerships. Also, it is difficult at times to determine which diseases are related to genetics and which are related to other factors, such as lifestyle and the environment. Sometimes disease is caused by a combination of factors. For example, African-Americans have been shown to have higher rates of hypertension than whites (Williams, et al., 1994), but is that difference due to genetics? African-Americans tend to consume less potassium than whites and have stress related to discrimination, which, instead of genetics, could be the cause of their higher rates of hypertension. Health disparities also can be related to the level of exposure to environmental hazards, such as toxins and carcinogens, that exist among racial groups. Therefore, it is difficult to link health disparities to genetics, because they could be a result of a variety of factors, but that does not mean that genetics do not play a role in health because some clear links have been made.

Lifestyle

Behavior patterns are factors that the individual has more control over. Many of the diseases of the twenty-first century are caused by personal modifiable factors, such as smoking, poor diet, and physical inactivity. So how does lifestyle relate to ethnicity?

Studies reveal that differences in health behaviors exist among racial and ethnic groups. Bolen and colleagues (1997) summarized findings from the 1997 Behavioral Risk Factor Surveillance System (BRFSS) of the distribution of access to health care, health-status indicators, health-risk behaviors, and use of clinical preventive services across five racial and ethnic groups (i.e., whites, blacks, Hispanics, American Indians or Alaska Natives, and Asian Americans or Pacific Islanders) and by state. BRFSS is an ongoing state-specific surveillance system about modifiable risk factors for chronic diseases and other leading causes of death among adults that are collected annually (Bolen, Rhodes, Powell-Griner, Bland, & Holtzman, 1997). The results of Bolen and colleagues' (1997) research showed that variations in risk for chronic disease and injury among racial and ethnic groups exist both within states and across states (see Table   2).

Social Circumstances

Social circumstances include factors such as socioeconomic status (SES), income, stress, discrimination, marriage and partnerships, and family roles. SES is made up of a combination of variables including occupation, education, income, wealth, place of residence, and poverty. These variables do not have a direct affect on health, but they do have an indirect effect. For example, low SES does not cause disease, but poor

TABLE 2   Medians and Ranges of Values for Health-Status Indicators, Health-Risk Behaviors, and Clinical Preventive Services, by Race or Ethnicity— Behavioral Risk Factor Surveillance System, 1997*

	Total %	White %	Black %	Hispanic %	American Indian or Alaska Native %	Asian American or Pacific Islander %
Cost as a barrier to obtaining health care	9.9	9.4	13.2	16.2	12.6	11.6
No routine physical examination	16.8	18.0	8.7	18.2	14.5	17.1
Obesity	16.6	15.6	26.4	18.2	30.1	4.8
No leisure-time physical activity	28.0	25.1	38.2	34.2	37.2	28.9
Alcohol Consumption						
Current drinking	53.5	55.4	40.4	50.8	50.5	38.2
Binge drinking	14.4	14.3	8.7	16.2	18.9	6.7
Cigarette smoking	23.3	23.6	22.8	23.1	41.3	10.7
Lack of safety belt use	30.7	30.0	37.6	30.3	40.9	18.6
Clinical Preventive Services						
Blood cholesterol checked	69.2	71.2	67.4	59.3	54.7	67.8
Papanicolaou test	84.8	84.7	91.1	80.9	†	†
Breast Cancer Screening						
Mammogram	73.7	73.7	76.1	63.5	†	†
Clinical breast examination	77.0	77.5	78.2	75.5	†	†
Mammogram plus clinical breast examination	66.4	67.6	67.8	57.8	†	†
Colorectal Cancer Screening						
Home-kit blood stool test	18.1	18.2	20.3	14.2	†	†
Sigmoidoscopy	30.1	30.4	28.2	22.4	†	†

* Lowest and highest state estimates.

† Median is not considered meaningful for the three or fewer states that had ≤50 respondents in this racial or ethnic category and is not shown.

Data source: Bolen, Rhodes, Powell-Griner, Bland, and Holtzman. (1997).

nutrition, limited access to health care, and substandard housing certainly do, and these are just a few of the many indirect effects. Discrimination does not cause poor health directly either, but it can lead to depression and high blood pressure.

One variable of social circumstances, poverty, can be measured in many ways. One approach is to measure the number of people who are recipients of federal aid programs, such as food stamps, public housing, and Head Start. Another method is through labor statistics, but the most common way is through the federal government's measure of poverty based on income. The federal government's definition of poverty is based on a threshold defined by income, and it is updated annually. In 2003, a person in the 48 contiguous states and the District of Columbia whose income was $8,980 or less was considered to be living in poverty, and a family of four with earnings of $18,400 or less was considered to be below the poverty level. For each additional person, the threshold increased by $3,140 (Federal Register, 2003). So how is poverty related to ethnicity?

The official poverty rate in 2003 was 12.5%, which equates to 35.9 million people (Denavas-Walt, Proctor, & Mills, 2004). The two-year average for 2002 and 2003 by race can be found in Table 3. Poverty is higher among certain racial and ethnic groups, and hence, it is a contributing factor to health disparities because poverty impacts many factors, such as where people live and their access to health care.

TABLE 3 Poverty Rates by Race and Hispanic Origin Using 2002 and 2003 Averages	
Race and Hispanic Origin	**Percentage in Poverty**
Black alone	24.3%
American Indian and Alaska Native alone	23.9%
Hispanic origin	22.1%
Asian American alone	10.9%
White alone, not Hispanic	8.1%

When the race or origin is followed by the word "alone," it indicates that the person did not indicate any other race category.

Source: Denavas-Walt, Proctor, and Mills. (2004).

Education is an important indicator of health status. Higher education appears to lead to better health because it increases knowledge about health, helps to assert health-promoting behaviors to prevent disease and maintain health, and increases income, which helps determine where someone lives and other important factors related to health (McKenzie, et al., 2005). Education is related to higher social position, and there is a clear association between socioeconomic position and health. Further, the relationship between socioeconomic position and health holds not only at the individual level but also at the community level. That is, persons living in poor neighborhoods, even after accounting for their individual socioeconomic characteristics, tend to have worse health outcomes.

Racism is a factor of social circumstances, and there is an association between racism and health. One of the most prominent stressors may be racial discrimination. "Stress resulting from institutionalized racism and discrimination, be it real or perceived, blatant or muted, is an 'added pathogenic factor' that contributes to well-above average levels of hypertension, respiratory illness, anxiety, depression, and other ills in minority populations" (Williams, 2007). Because racial discrimination has profoundly shaped the experiences of racial groups, discrimination may be among the factors that shape health disparities. Evidence suggests that racial discrimination still occurs in the present day, especially in structurally important domains such as housing, education, and employment. Audit studies that send a white and a minority prospective tester with identical portfolios (e.g., similar income and job titles) to assess a given housing market have consistently found that whites are favored over minorities. Hispanics, for example, are more likely to be quoted a higher rent for a given unit than are their white counterparts. Other studies have shown that minorities are more likely to face discrimination in applying for a job or shopping.

Stress from discrimination may lead to illness. Kessler and colleagues (1999) suggested that discrimination is among the most important of all the stressful experiences that have been implicated as causes of mental health problems. Studies have reported that stress due to racial discrimination is associated with high blood pressure, mental health problems (Gee, 2002; Kessler, Mickelson, & Williams, 1999), and alcohol consumption (Yen & Syme, 1999).

Psychosocial conditions, including crowding, social disorganization, racial discrimination, fear, and economic deprivation, also may be sources of stress. One stressor that has received extensive attention is fear of crime, and minority neighborhoods tend to have higher crime rates. Perceptions of crime and disorder within an individual's community has been associated with numerous health outcomes, including anxiety, depression, posttraumatic stress disorder, and substance use.

Medical Care

The shortfalls for minorities in the health-care system in the United States can be categorized into three general areas: (1) lack of access to care, (2) lower quality of care, and (3) limited providers with the same ethnic background.

Lack of Access to Medical Care

Research has shown that without access to timely and effective preventive care, people may be at risk for potentially avoidable conditions, such as asthma, diabetes, and immunizable conditions (National Center for Health Statistics, 2006). It also is important for prompt treatment and follow-up to illness and injury. Access to health care is a problem for many Americans as the number of people who are uninsured continues to climb. According to the National Health Interview Survey, in the first half of 2007, 42.5 million Americans (14.3%) were uninsured (Cohen & Martinez, 2007). Access to health care is particularly problematic for minorities, because they have higher rates of being uninsured than whites. Indicators to access to care include having a regular place to go for medical care, whether a person receives his or her care in the right place (for example, whether care for a non-urgent condition is sought at a physician's office or in an emergency department), and the ability to pay for care (which includes having health insurance).

Access to care is unequal among ethnicities. Non-whites are more likely to lack insurance coverage. Approximately 31% of Hispanic or Latino persons were uninsured in the first part of 2007 compared to 10.2% of non-Hispanic whites, 14.4% of blacks, 13% of Asian Americans, and 23.6% of other and multiple races (Cohen & Martinez, 2007). According to the 2005 National Health Interview Survey, 77.1% of Hispanics have a usual place to go for health care compared to 85.7% of non-Hispanic blacks and 89.4% of non-Hispanic whites (National Center for Health Statistics, 2006 as cited in Cohen & Martinez, 2007). In 2004, the emergency department utilization rate for blacks was significantly higher than for whites (68.9 versus 35.2 per 100 persons) (National Center for Health Statistics, 2006 as cited in Cohen & Martinez, 2007).

Lower Quality of Care

When minorities do have access to care, research shows that unequal treatment exists, and minorities receive a lower quality of care even when social determinants and insurance status are controlled (Betancourt & Maina, 2004). A review by the

Institute of Medicine (2001) concluded that racial and ethnic minorities tend to receive lower quality health-care services than non-minorities, even when access-related factors, such as patients' insurance status and income, are controlled. The study committee found evidence that stereotyping, biases, and uncertainty on the part of health-care providers can contribute to unequal treatment. For example, minorities appear to have longer waiting times for kidney transplants and liver transplants and report less satisfaction with their medical visits. African-Americans and other minorities have been shown to be less likely to receive expensive and high-tech procedures and kidney dialysis and transplants (Williams, 2007). These same groups were more likely to receive lower-limb amputations for diabetes (Williams, 2007).

Limited Providers with the Same Ethnic Background

Ethnic minorities are poorly represented among physicians and other health care professionals. Although Hispanics, African Americans, and American Indians represent more than 25% of the United States population, they comprise fewer than 6% of doctors and 9% of nurses (Cooper & Powe, 2004). As a result, minority patients are frequently treated by professionals from a different racial or ethnic background. Many programs, funding agencies, and research studies suggest that more diversity is needed among health care professionals to improve quality of care and reduce health disparities, but is there evidence that racial concordance (patients being treated by people in the same ethnic group) accomplishes these goals?

Cooper and Powe (2004) conducted an extensive literature review about patient–provider concordance with regard to race and ethnicity, and they compared and contrasted these findings to the literature on patient–provider language concordance. They found that race-concordant visits were longer and had greater positive effects for patients than race-discordant visits. Patients in race-concordant visits reported higher levels of satisfaction, perceived their physicians as more participatory, regardless of the communication that occurred during the visit, and was associated with longer visits and measurably better communication. Few studies have focused on the utilization and health outcomes of race-concordant relationships. Regardless of whether race concordance is linked to health outcomes, there is support for the notion that increasing racial and ethnic diversity among physicians will provide ethnic minority patients with more choices and better experiences with care processes, including positive effects, longer visit durations, higher patient satisfaction, and better participation in care.

Cooper and Powe (2004) researched the under-representation of certain ethnic groups in health care professions and focused on four hypotheses:

1. *The service patterns hypothesis.* Health care professionals from racial and ethnic minority and socioeconomically disadvantaged backgrounds are more likely than others to serve racial and ethnic minority and socioeconomically disadvantaged populations, thereby improving access to care for vulnerable populations and, in turn, improving health outcomes.

2. *The concordance hypothesis.* Increasing the number of racial and ethnic minority health care professionals—by providing greater opportunity for minority patients to see a practitioner from their own racial or ethnic group or, for patients with limited English proficiency, to see a practitioner who speaks their primary language—will improve the quality of communication, comfort level, trust, partnership, and decision making in patient–practitioner relationships, thereby increasing use of appropriate health care services and adherence to effective programs, ultimately resulting in improved health outcomes.

3. *The trust in health care hypothesis.* Greater diversity in the health care workforce will increase trust in the health care delivery system among minority and socioeconomically disadvantaged populations and will thereby increase their propensity to use health services that lead to improved health outcomes.

4. *The professional advocacy hypothesis.* Health care professionals from racial and ethnic minority and socioeconomically disadvantaged backgrounds will be more likely than others to provide leadership and advocacy for policies and programs aimed at improving health care for vulnerable populations, thereby increasing health care access and quality, and ultimately health outcomes, for those populations.

The research generated the following findings (Cooper & Powe, 2004):

- Under-represented health professionals, particularly physicians, disproportionately serve minority and other medically underserved populations.
- Minority patients tend to receive better interpersonal care from practitioners of their own race or ethnicity, particularly in primary care and mental health settings.
- Non-English-speaking patients experience better interpersonal care, greater medical comprehension, and have a greater likelihood of keeping follow-up appointments when they see a language-concordant practitioner, particularly in mental health care.
- Insufficient evidence exists as to whether greater diversity in health care professionals leads to greater trust in health care or greater advocacy for disadvantaged populations.

CHAPTER SUMMARY

One of the great attributes of the United States is the diverse landscape. Known by some as a melting pot, immigrants (voluntary and forced) who have come to the United States and natives of this country have experienced different levels of cultural adaptation to blend into the dominant society. Some have retained their strong cultural ties to create a society of rich and diverse cultures filled with various beliefs, traditions, languages, and societal norms. Understanding and respecting this diverse landscape is a goal for the nation, specifically for the health care industry. Health care providers need to be knowledgeable about and sensitive to cultural differences to provide effective care and education.

The goal of this chapter is to provide an understanding of the foundations of multicultural health and the key terms and concepts associated with it, such as culture, race, assimilation, and cultural relativism. We want readers to have a general appreciation of how culture impacts health, the breadth and depth of health disparities, and their related causes. In the next chapter, we go further into the topic of culture and health by building upon these foundations.

REVIEW

1. What is the focus of multicultural health, and why is it important?
2. Is race a biological or social construct? Why is race important?
3. What is the difference between ethnicity and culture? What is the difference between race and ethnicity?
4. Explain cultural ethnocentricity and relativism.
5. Explain the difference between acculturation, assimilation, and bicultural.
6. Does the level of acculturation have a positive or negative affect on health? Explain.
7. What are health disparities and their causes?

CASE STUDY

The book titled *The Spirit Catches You and You Fall Down*, by Anne Fadiman, tells the story of Lia Lee, a Hmong child, with epilepsy, who lived in Merced, California. When 3-month-old Lia Lee arrived at the county hospital emergency room in Merced, a chain of events was set in motion from which Lia, her parents, and her doctors would never recover. Lia's parents, Foua and Nao Kao, were part of a large Hmong community in

Merced, refugees from the "Quiet War" in Laos. Her parents and doctors both wanted the best for Lia, but their ideas about the causes of her illness and its treatment were very different. The Hmong see illness and healing as spiritual matters that are linked to virtually everything in the universe, but the medical community marks a division between body and soul and concerns itself almost exclusively with the former. Lia's doctors attributed her seizures to the misfiring of her cerebral neurons; her parents called her illness "qaug dab peg"—the spirit catches you and you fall down—and ascribed it to the wandering of her soul. The doctors prescribed anticonvulsants; her parents preferred animal sacrifices. *The Spirit Catches You and You Fall Down* moves from hospital corridors to healing ceremonies, and from the hill country of Laos to the living rooms of Merced, uncovering in its path the complex sources and implications of two dramatically clashing worldviews.

Lia's doctors prescribed a complex regimen of medication designed to control her seizures. However, her parents believed that the epilepsy was a result of Lia "losing her soul" and did not give her the medication as indicated because of the complexity of the drug therapy and the adverse side effects. Instead, they did everything logical in terms of their Hmong beliefs to help her. They took her to a clan leader and shaman, sacrificed animals, and bought expensive amulets to guide her soul's return. Lia's doctors believed that her parents were endangering her life by not giving her the medication, so they called child protective services, and Lia was placed in foster care. Lia was a victim of a misunderstanding between these two cultures that were both intent on saving her. The results were disastrous: A close family was separated, and Hmong community faith in Western doctors was shaken.

Lia was surrounded by people who wanted the best for her and her health. Unfortunately, the involved parties disagreed on the best treatment because they understood her epilepsy differently. The separate cultures of Lia's caretakers had different concepts of health and illness.

This example illustrates how culture and health impact each other and at times clash. To help ensure good care for diverse patients, health-care providers must address cultural issues and respect the cultural values of each patient.

There are several issues to consider about this case:

- How can health care providers prepare for situations like Lia's?
- Should child protective services have been contacted?
- Were Lia's parents irresponsible?
- How did the parents' belief system impact Lia's health care?
- Were the parents' decisions morally and legally wrong?

GLOSSARY TERMS

multicultural health

culture

cultural competency

race

acculturation

ethnicity

ethnocentricity

cultural relativism

racism

discrimination

minority

cultural adaptation

dominant culture

assimilation

heritage consistency

health disparities

Healthy People 2010

REFERENCES

Babisch, W., Fromme, H., Beyer, A., & Ising, H. (2001). Increased catecholamine levels in urine in subjects exposed to road traffic noise: The role of stress hormones in noise research. *Environment International, 26,* 475–481.

Bashir, S. A. (2002). Home is where the harm is: Inadequate housing as a public health crisis. *American Journal of Public Health, 92,* 733–738.

Beck, B. D., & Weinstock, S. (1988). Age and nutrition. In: J. D. Brian (Ed.), *Variations in susceptibility to inhaled pollutants: Identification, mechanisms, and policy implications* (pp. 104–126). Baltimore: Johns Hopkins University Press.

Betancourt, J. R., & Maina, A. W. (2004, October). The Institute of Medicine Report: "Unequal Treatment": Implications for academic health centers. *The Mount Sinai Journal of Medicine, 71*(5).

Berry J., Trimble J., & Olmedo E. (1986). Assessment of acculturation. In: W. J. Lonner & J. W. Berry (Eds), *Field Methods in Cross-cultural Research* (pp. 291–324). Thousand Oaks, CA: Sage Publications.

Bolen, J. C., Rhodes, L., Powell-Griner, E. E., Bland, S. D., & Holtzman, D. (1997). National Center for Chronic Disease Prevention and Health Promotion. *State-specific prevalence of selected health behaviors, by race and ethnicity—Behavioral Risk Factor Surveillance System, 1997.* Retrieved March 24, 2008, from http://www.cdc.gov/mmwr/preview/mmwrhtml/ss4902a1.htm

Brenner, M. H. (1995). Political economy and health. In: B. C. Amick, S. Levine, A. R. Tarlov, & D. Chapman Walsh (Eds.), *Society and health* (pp. 211–246). New York: Oxford University Press.

Burt, C. W., McCaig, L. R., & Rechtsteiner, E. A. (2007). *Ambulatory medical care utilization estimates for 2005.* Retrieved December 26, 2007, from http://www.cdc.gov/nchs/data/ad/ad388.pdf

Campinha-Bacote, J. (1994). Cultural competence in psychiatric mental health nursing: A conceptual model. *Nursing Clinics in North America, 29*(1), 1–8.

Carter-Porras, O., & Baquest, C. (2002, September–October). Association of Schools of Public Health. What is a "health disparity"? *Public Health Reports, 117.*

Centers for Disease Control and Prevention. (1991). Behavioral risk factor survey of Vietnamese—California.

Centers for Disease Control and Prevention. (1997). Behavioral risk factor survey of Korean Americans—Alameda County, California, 1994. MMWR.

Centers for Disease Control and Prevention. (2004). *Fact sheet. Racial/ethnic health disparities.* Retrieved December 20, 2007, from http://www.cdc.gov./od/oc/media/pressrel/fs040402.htm

Centers for Disease Control and Prevention. (2007a). *Lesbian, gay, bisexual and transgender health.* Retrieved January 19, 2008, from http://www.cdc.gov/lgbthealth/index.htm

Centers for Disease Control and Prevention. Office of Minority Health and Health Disparities. (2007b). *Eliminating racial and ethnic health disparities.* Retrieved October 21, 2007, from http://www.cdc.gov/omhd/About/disparities.htm

Cohen, D. A., Mason, K., Bedimo, A., Scribner, R., Basolo, V., & Farley, T. A. (2003). Neighborhood physical conditions and health. *American Journal of Public Health, 93,* 467–471.

Cohen, R. A., & Martinez, M. E. (2007). Centers for Disease Control and Prevention. *Health insurance coverage: Early release of estimates from National Health Interview Survey, January–June 2007.* Retrieved December 26, 2007, from http://www.cdc.gov/nchs/data/nhis/earlyrelease/insur 200712.pdf

Cooper, L. A., & Powe, N. R. (2004). *Disparities in patient experiences, health care processes, and outcomes: The role of patient–provider racial, ethnic, and language concordance.* Retrieved January 19, 2008, from http://www.commonwealthfund.org/publications/publications_show.htm?doc_id=231670

Council of Economic Advisors For the President's Initiative on Race. (1998). Changing America: Indicators of Social and Economic Well-being by Race and Hispanic Origin. Retrieved January 19, 2008, from http://www.gpoaccess.gov/eop/ca/pdfs/toc.pdf.

Cubbin, C., Hadden, W. C., & Winkleby, M. A. (2001). Neighborhood context and cardiovascular disease risk factors: The contribution of material deprivation. *Ethnicity and Disease, 11,* 687–700.

Deaton, A., & Lubotsky, D. (2003). Mortality, inequality and race in American cities and states. *Social Science and Medicine, 56,* 1139–1153.

Denavas-Walt, C., Proctor, B. D., & Mills, R. J. (2004). US Census Bureau. Income, poverty, and health insurance: Coverage in the United States: 2003.

Evans, G. W., & Lepore, S. J. (1993). Household crowding and social support: A quasiexperimental analysis. *Journal of Personality and Social Psychology, 65,* 308–316.

Federal Register, No. 26, Vol. 68 pp. 6456–6458 (2003, February 7).

Fleming, I., Baum, A., & Weiss, L. (1987). Social density and perceived control as mediators of crowding stress in high-density residential neighborhoods. *Journal of Personality and Social Psychology, 52,* 899–906.

Gee, G. C., & Payne-Sturges, D. C. (2004, December). Environmental health disparities: A framework integrating psychosocial and environmental concepts. *Environmental Health Perspectives, 112*(17), 1645–1653. Retrieved November 11, 2007, from http://www.pubmedcentral.nih.gov/articlerender.fcgi?artid=1253653#b125-ehp0112-001645

Gee, G. C., & Takeuchi, D. T. (2004). Traffic stress, vehicular burden and well-being: A multilevel analysis. *Social Science and Medicine, 59,* 405–414.

Geronimus, A. T., Bound, J., & Waidmann, T. A. (1999). Poverty, time, and place: Variation in excess mortality across selected US populations, 1980–1990. *Journal of Epidemiology and Community Health, 53,* 325–334.

Geronimus, A. T., Bound J., Waidmann, T. A, Colen, C. G., & Steffick, D. (2001). Inequality in life expectancy, functional status, and active life expectancy across selected black and white population in the United States. *Demography, 38*, 227–251.

Goldberg, J., Hayes, W., & Huntley, J. (2004, November). Health Policy Institute of Ohio. Understanding health disparities.

Grieco, E. M., & Cassidy, R. C. (2001). *Overview of race and Hispanic origin* (US Census Bureau, Census 2000 Special Report Series C2KBR/01-1). Washington, DC: US Government Printing Office.

Hobbs, F., & Stoops, N. (2002). *Demographic trends in the 20th century* (US Census Bureau, Census 2000 Special Report Series CENSR-4). Washington, DC: US Government Printing Office.

Iceland, J., Weinberg, D. H., & Steinmetz, E. (2002). *Racial and ethnic residential segregation in the United States: 1980–2000* (US Census Bureau, Series CENSR-3). Washington, DC: US Government Printing Office.

Institute of Medicine. (2001). *Health and behavior: The interplay of biological, behavioral, and societal influences.* Washington, DC: National Academies Press.

Jacobs, D. E., Clickner, R. P., Zhou, J. Y., Viet, S. M., Marker, D. A., Rogers, J. W., et al. (2002). The prevalence of lead-based paint hazards in US housing. *Environmental Health Perspectives, 110*, 599–606.

Juckett, G. (2005, December 1). Cross-cultural medicine. *American Family Physician.* Retrieved January 6, 2008, from http://www.aafp.org/afp/20051201/2267.html

Kessler, R. C., Mickelson, K. D., & Williams, D. R. (1999). The prevalence, distribution, and mental health correlates of perceived discrimination in the United States. *Journal of Health and Social Behavior, 40*(3), 208–30.

LaVeist, T. A. (1993). Segregation, poverty, and empowerment: Health consequences for African Americans. *The Milbank Quarterly, 71*, 41–64.

Lee, C. (2002). Environmental justice: Building a unified vision of health and the environment. *Environmental Health Perspectives, 110*(Suppl. 2), 141–144.

Lee, S. K., Sobal, J., & Frongillo, E. A. (2000, July). Acculturation and health in Korean Americans. *Social Science and Medicine, 51*(2), 159–173.

Logan, J. R. (2003). Ethnic diversity grows, neighborhood integration lags. In: B. Katz & R. E. Lang (Eds.), *Redefining urban and suburban America* (pp. 235–256). Washington, DC: Brookings Institution.

Massey, D. (2001). Residential segregation and neighborhood conditions in US metropolitan areas. In: N. J. Smelser, W. J. Wilson, & F. Mitchell (Eds.), *America becoming: Racial trends and their consequences* (pp. 391–434). Washington, DC: National Academies Press.

Massey, D., & Denton, N. A. (1993). *American apartheid: Segregation and the making of the underclass.* Cambridge, MA: Harvard University Press.

Mazumdar, S., Mazumdar, S., Docuyanan, F., & McLaughlin, C. M. (2000). Creating a sense of place: The Vietnamese-Americans and Little Saigon. *Journal of Environmental Psychology, 20*, 319–333.

McGinnis, J. M., Williams-Russo, J. M., & Knickman, J. R. (2002). The case for more active policy attention to health promotion. *Health Affairs, 21*(2), 78–93.

McKenzie, J. F., Pinger, R. R., & Kotecki, J. E. (2005). *An introduction to community health.* Sudbury, MA: Jones and Bartlett.

Mohai, P., & Bryant, B. (1992). Environmental racism: Reviewing the evidence. In: B. Bryant & P. Mohai (Eds), *Race and the incidence of environmental hazards: A time for discourse* (pp. 163–176). Boulder, CO: Westview.

Morello-Frosch, R., Pastor, M., Porras, C., & Sadd, J. (2002). Environmental justice and regional inequality in southern California: Implications for future research. *Environmental Health Perspectives, 110*(Suppl. 2), 149–154.

Morland, K., Wing, S., Diez-Roux, A. V., & Poole, C. (2002). Neighborhood characteristics associated with the location of food stores and food service places. *American Journal of Preventive Medicine, 22,* 23–29.

Morrison, R. S., Wallenstein, S., Natale, D. K., Senzel, R. S., & Huang, L. L. (2000). "We don't carry that"—failure of pharmacies in predominantly nonwhite neighborhoods to stock opioid analgesics. *New England Journal of Medicine, 3426,* 1023–1026.

National Association of Chronic Disease Directors. (2006). Retrieved September 1, 2007, from www.chronicdisease.org

National Center for Health Statistics. (2006). *NCHS data on health insurance and access to care.* Retrieved December 26, 2007, from http://origin.cdc.gov/nchs/data/factsheets/healthinsurance.pdf

National Diabetes Education Program. (2005). *The diabetes epidemic among American Indians and Alaska Natives.* Retrieved October 21, 2007, from http://ndep.nih.gov/diabetes/pubs/FS_AmIndian.pdf

Northridge, M. E., Stover, G. N., Rosenthal, J. E., & Sherard, D. (2003). Environmental equity and health: Understanding complexity and moving forward. *American Journal of Public Health, 93,* 209–214.

Office of Minority Health. (n.d.). *Minority populations.* Retrieved January 11, 2008, from http://www.omhrc.gov/templates/browse.aspx?lvl=1&lvlID=5

Office of Minority Health. (2001). *National standards for culturally and linguistically appropriate services in health care.* Washington, DC: US Department of Health and Human Services.

Ouis, D. (2001). Annoyance from road traffic noise: A review. *Journal of Environmental Psychology, 21,* 101–120.

Perera, F. P., Illman, S. M., Kinney, P. L., Whyatt, R. M., Kelvin, E. A., Shepard, P., et al. (2002). The challenge of preventing environmentally related disease in young children: Community-based research in New York City. *Environmental Health Perspectives, 110,* 197–204.

Rios, R., Poje, G. V., & Detels, R. (1993). Susceptibility to environmental pollutants among minorities. *Toxicology and Industrial Health, 9,* 797–820.

Senior, P. A., & Bhopa, R. (1994). Ethnicity as a variable in epidemiological research. *British Medical Journal, 309,* 327–300.

Sexton, K., Olden, K., & Johnson, B. L. (1993). "Environmental justice": The central role of research in establishing a credible scientific foundation for informed decision making. *Toxicology and Industrial Health, 9,* 685–727.

Stephenson, M. (2000). Development and validation of the Stephenson Multigroup Acculturation Scale (SMAS). *Psychological Assessment, 12,* 77–88.

Tran, T. V., Fitzpatrick, T., Berg, W. R., & Wright, R., Jr. (1996). Acculturation, health, stress, and psychological distress among elderly Hispanics. *Journal of Cross Cultural Gerontology, 11,* 149–165.

Tylor, E. B. (1924). *Primitive culture: Researches into the development of mythology, philosophy, religion, language, art, and custom* (7th ed). New York: Brentano. (Original work published 1871)

US Census Bureau. (n.d.). *American fact finder*. Retrieved November 11, 2007, from http://factfinder. census.gov/servlet/QTTable?_bm=y&-geo_id=01000US&-qr_name=DEC_2000_SF1_U_ DP1&-ds_name=DEC_2000_SF1_U

US Census Bureau. (2000). *The population profile of the United States: 2000 (Internet release)*. Retrieved October 21, 2004, from http://www.census.gov/population/www/pop-profile/profile2000.html

US Census Bureau. (2003). *Housing patterns*. Retrieved October 12, 2008, from http://www.census. gov/hhes/www/housing/resseg/tab7-1.html

US Department of Commerce. (1999). *Emerging minority marketplace*. Retrieved November 11, 2007, from http://faculty.washington.edu/mbarreto/courses/minoritypopulation2050.pdf

US Department of Health and Human Services. (2000). *Healthy People 2010: National health promotion and disease prevention objectives* (Conference ed. in 2 vols.) Washington, DC: Author.

Williams, D. R., Lavizzo-Mourey, R., & Warren, R. C. (1994). *The concept of race and health status in America*. Retrieved November 11, 2007, from http://www.pubmedcentral.nih.gov/picrender. fcgi?artid=1402239&blobtype=pdf

Williams, D. T. (2007). *Harvard public health review. Exposing the roots of health disparities*. Retrieved November 14, 2007, from www.hsph.harvard.edu/review/winter07/williams1.html

Winslow, C. E. A. (1920). The untilled field of public health. *Modern Medicine, 2,* 183–191.

Yen, I. H., & Syme, S. L. (1999). The social environment and health: A discussion of the epidemiologic literature. *Annual Review of Public Health, 20,* 287–308.

Zambrana, R. E., Scrimshaw, S. C. M., Collins, N., & Dunkel-Schetter, C. (1997). Prenatal health behavior and psychosocial risk factors in pregnant women of Mexican origin: The role of acculturation. *The American Journal of Public Health, 87,* 1022–1026.

PHOTO CREDITS

Chapter Opener ,
© Moth/Dreamstime.com

Unless otherwise indicated, all photographs and illustrations are under copyright of Jones and Bartlett Publishers, LLC, or have been provided by the author(s).

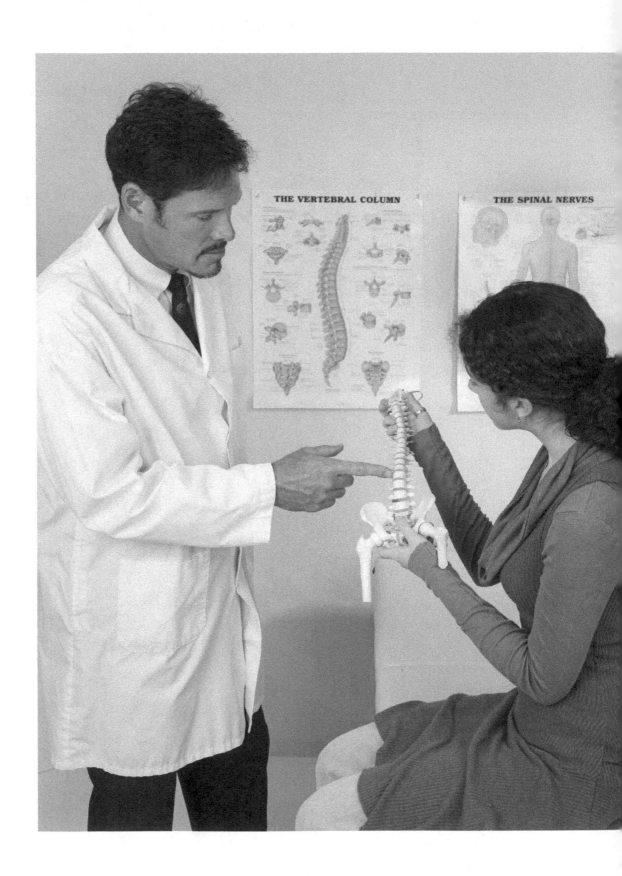

Complementary and Alternative Medicine

Everyone has a doctor in him or her; we just have to help it in its work.
The natural healing force within each one of us is the greatest force in getting well.
Our food should be our medicine.
Our medicine should be our food.

—Hippocrates

KEY CONCEPTS

- Complementary medicine
- Integrative medicine
- Doshas
- Prakriti
- Yoga
- Homeopathy
- Law of Similars (Principle of Similars)
- Principle of Infinitesimal Dose
- Principle of Specificity of the Individual
- Qi
- Five elements
- Yin and yang
- Meridians
- Acupuncture
- *Qigong*
- t'ai chi ch'uan
- Chiropractic
- Naturopathy
- Hydrotherapy
- Spirituality
- Meditation
- Mindfulness meditation
- Transcendental meditation
- Veritable energy
- Putative energy
- Magnet therapy
- Healing

CHAPTER OBJECTIVES

1. Identify the difference between complementary and alternative medicine practices.
2. Understand the various types of CAM practices.
3. Discuss the potential benefits and risks of CAM practices.
4. Appreciate the cultural influences on CAM practices.

HISTORY OF COMPLEMENTARY AND ALTERNATIVE MEDICINE

It is not entirely clear when humans began to develop modalities to deal with pain, injury, and disease. However, we know that these practices have been in existence for ages. The various practices to treat disease and injury have been passed down through the centuries from person to person and family member to family member. The practices have been influenced by observation and experimentation, as well as religious, social, and cultural practices. Over time the various forms of these practices have taken on the unique characteristics of the people and cultures that utilize them.

Previously these practices have been termed "folk medicine" by the mainstream science-based medical professions. It was believed that with the advent of the scientific approach to medicine the various traditional folk medicine practices would die out. However, that has not been the case. As new cultures immigrated to the United States, so did their traditional healing practices. Increased interest in these traditional practices has spurred research into their efficacy and recharacterized them as complementary and alternative medical practices.

Complementary medicine is considered to be treatments that are utilized in conjunction with conventional Western medical therapies that are prescribed by a physician. Alternative medicine has been defined as practices used instead of conventional medical intervention. However, studies have found that people have been using both alternative medicine and mainstream medicine concurrently. Consequently, the concept of **integrative medicine**, where complementary and alternative medicine practices are incorporated into conventional care, came into being. Complementary and alternative medicine (CAM) is a broad range of modalities outside the traditional Western medicine approach to care. Folk medicine, or the use of traditional remedies, is considered to be a form of complementary and alternative medicine. Folk remedies thus include not only the remedies passed down in families but also long-existing practices, such as Chinese medicine, acupuncture, and naturopathy, to name a few.

The history of CAM in the United States is convoluted. Prior to the latter part of the nineteenth century, medical care was provided by lay healers, naturopaths, homeopaths, midwives, and botanical healers. The nineteenth century advances in science that included germ theory, antisepsis, and anesthesia spurred the trend to scientific medical education. After Abraham Flexner's 1910 report on the need for standardization in medical education, the demise of practices that were not in compliance with the accepted medical model began. As a result, nonconventional treatments were marginalized in the first half of the twentieth century. Then interest in whole foods and dietary supplements in the 1950s began a resurgence of interest in alternative medical practices. The traditional health practices of immigrant cultures exposed Americans to alternatives, and the counterculture movements of the 1960s began the interest in natural healing practices. In the 1970s, the holistic health approach began incorporating Eastern medical traditions with conventional medical practices (White House Commission, 2002).

This resurgent public interest in modalities, characterized as folk medicine, has encouraged medical practitioners to investigate their efficacy and impact on conventional medical practices. It has been noted that many folk medicine traditions have common features. Hufford (1988, 1997) noted that folk traditions tend to view the cause of disease as an imbalance or lack of harmony; they are based on personal responsibility and connections between health and the person's environment; they tend to be complex practices that involve a holistic approach to disease; and they often include an energy that provides harmony and balance.

Being aware of cultural differences in beliefs regarding disease and treatment is imperative to a medical practitioner because those who engage in CAM practices may also seek intervention from Western medicine. It has long been thought that those who are more likely to seek folk medicine remedies tend to be less acculturated to the American culture and have a number of shared characteristics (Pachter, 1994), including the following:

- Living in ethnic areas
- Preference for native language
- Educated in their country of origin
- Migration to and from country of origin
- Close contact with older persons with a high level of ethnic identity

Although that remains the majority view, recent studies have provided very different and interesting information about the utilization of CAM practices in the United States. In 1990 a study was conducted to determine the prevalence, cost, and pattern of use of CAM therapies in the United States. The study was limited to people with telephones who could speak English, so many ethnic groups were not well represented. Notwithstanding, the results were enlightening. One in three respondents reported using at least one CAM modality in the last year. The highest numbers were among nonblack people aged 25 to 49 years. Most were utilized for chronic conditions, and 83% also sought treatment for the same problem from their physician, although 72% did not inform their physician of the nontraditional treatment (Eisenberg, et al., 1993). The researchers concluded that the incidence of utilization of nontraditional therapies was much higher than anticipated, and further research on the issue was indicated.

A follow-up study was conducted in 1997 to determine any changes in the previous data. That study found an increase in the use of CAM from 36.3% to 46.3% of respondents. It also found that more visits were made to alternative practitioners in the previous year than to Primary care physicians ("Trends in Alternative Medicine Use in the United States, 1990–1997").

These studies provide insight into the prevalence of CAM usage in the United States. Although they were unable to evaluate utilization by many ethnic groups because of language barriers, the studies question the previous medical conceptions about utilization of CAM. Complementary and alternative medicine practices are being used not just by ethnic minorities but by those enculturated in the United States as well. The information about the broad use of CAM provides a backdrop for recent governmental action.

More recently, the National Institutes of Health National Center for Complementary and Alternative Medicine (NCCAM, 2002) conducted a study to determine the extent of CAM use in the United States. This study was conducted in 2002 and specifically investigated who was using CAM, what CAM practices were most prevalent, and why CAM was being used. The results were significantly different from the previous beliefs, which were previously discussed (see Table 1).

TABLE 1 Most Common CAM Practices	
Prayer/self	43%
Prayer/others	24.4%
Natural products	18.9%
Deep breathing	11.6%
Prayer group	9.6%
Meditation	7.6%
Chiropractic	7.5%
Yoga	5.1%
Massage	5.0%
Diets	3.5%

Source: NCCAM, 2002.

TABLE 2 Domains of CAM

Biologically-based practices. Uses substances found in nature, like herbs or vitamins in doses that are not used in mainstream medicine

Energy medicine. Uses energy fields that are believed to surround and penetrate the body

Manipulative and body-based practices. Uses manipulation and movement of body parts

Mind–body medicine. Uses techniques to enhance the mind's ability to impact the body

Source: NCCAM, 2002.

Initially, the study noted that 36% of Americans had used a CAM practice in the last year. The NCCAM study showed greater use in different populations than previously thought. People with higher education, and more women than men, were more likely to use CAM. Also, people who were hospitalized in the last year and who were former smokers were also more likely to seek CAM treatments (NCCAM, 2002). The mind–body domain (see Table 2) was the most common domain utilized when prayer was included in the CAM treatments. When prayer was not included, biologically-based practices were the most prevalent.

The reasons reported for using CAM treatments included improved health, although conventional medical treatment was the most prevalent response. Many respondents thought it would be interesting to try or that conventional medicine would not help their problem. Finally, some participants responded that they were advised to try a CAM modality by a conventional medical practitioner or that conventional treatment was too expensive (see Table 3).

TABLE 3 CAM Use by Race/Ethnicity

	CAM with Megavitamins/Prayer	CAM without Megavitamins/Prayer
Asian	61.7%	43.1%
Black	71.3%	26.2%
Hispanic	61.4%	28.3%
White	60.4%	35.9%

Source: NCCAM, 2002.

Prayer was the most commonly utilized CAM treatment for health problems, and race or ethnicity did not change that outcome (see Tables 1 and 3). Most respondents used CAM for their own health needs, and only 12% used it for the needs of others.

The NCCAM study did not examine the efficacy or safety of CAM treatments and acknowledged that few studies exist on those issues. Further, the current information is inconclusive. The NCCAM study recommended further research into the safety of the varied CAM practices and whether or not they work.

The White House Commission on Complementary and Alternative Medicine Policy was convened to evaluate CAM utilization in the United States and to make recommendations regarding future governmental action. It noted that the use of CAM is very prevalent in the United States patient population, which indicates a patient interest in exploring therapeutic options for chronic conditions that are not offered by conventional medicine. The Commission produced 25 recommendations for further action by the government and private enterprises, which deal with coordination of research, education and training of health practitioners, CAM information and development and dissemination, access and delivery, coverage and reimbursement, and coordinating federal efforts (see Table 4). The Commission and its recommendations are clear indicators of the interest and concern regarding CAM practices in the United States today.

With the White House Commission's recommendations, the National Institutes of Health's National Center for Complementary and Alternative Medicine has created a strategic plan to specifically address racial and ethnic health disparities in the utilization of CAM practices. The report notes that little is known about the use of CAM in minority populations, and research is needed to determine the extent of use by specific groups of CAM, conventional medicine, or a combination of the two. To accomplish these objectives, NCCAM will conduct research in areas that include the following:

- Review epidemiologic studies of CAM use in racial and ethnic populations.
- Develop research methods to study CAM in minority populations.
- Study the use of traditional, indigenous medicine systems.
- Conduct outcome research on CAM in minority populations.

Understanding that many CAM therapies arise from cultures from which American minorities come, it is necessary to better understand those practices and how they are utilized by minority populations. With that in mind, we will now turn our attention to specific CAM therapies in practice in the United States today.

Coordination of Research

Recommendation 1: Federal agencies should receive increased funding for clinical, basic, and health services research on CAM.

Recommendation 2: Congress and the Administration should consider enacting legislative and administrative incentives to stimulate private sector investment in CAM research on products that may not be patentable.

Recommendation 3: Federal, private, and nonprofit sectors should support research on CAM modalities and approaches that are designed to improve self-care and behaviors that promote health.

Recommendation 4: Federal, private, and nonprofit sectors should support new and innovative CAM research on core questions posed by frontier areas of scientific study associated with CAM that might expand our understanding of health and disease.

Recommendation 5: Investigators engaged in research of CAM should ensure that human subjects participating in clinical studies receive the same protections as are required in conventional medical research and to which they are entitled.

Recommendation 6: The Commission recommends that state professional regulatory bodies include language in their guidelines stating that licensed, certified, or otherwise authorized practitioners who are engaged in research on CAM will not be sanctioned solely because they are engaged in such research if they:

1. Are engaged in well-designed research that is approved by appropriately constituted Institutional Review Boards.

2. Are following the requirements for the protection of human subjects.

3. Are meeting their professional and ethical responsibilities. All CAM and conventional practitioners, whether or not they are engaged in research, must meet whatever State practice requirements or standards govern their authorization to practice.

Recommendation 7: Increased efforts should be made to strengthen the emerging dialogue among CAM and conventional medical practitioners, researchers, and accredited research institutions; federal and state research, health care, and regulatory agencies; the private and nonprofit sectors; and the general public.

Recommendation 8: Public and private resources should be increased to strengthen the infrastructure for CAM research and research training at conventional medical and CAM institutions and to expand the cadre of basic, clinical, and health services researchers who are knowledgeable about CAM and have received rigorous research training.

TABLE 4 *(Continued)*

Recommendation 9: Public and private resources should be used to support, conduct, and update systematic reviews of the peer-reviewed research literature on the safety, efficacy, and cost–benefit of CAM practices and products.

Education and Training of Health Care Practitioners

Recommendation 10: The education and training of CAM and conventional practitioners should be designed to ensure public safety, improve health, and increase availability of qualified and knowledgeable CAM and conventional practitioners and enhance the collaboration among them.

Recommendation 11: The federal government should make available accurate, useful, and easily accessible information on CAM practices and products, including information on safety and effectiveness.

Recommendation 12: The quality and accuracy of CAM information on the Internet should be improved by establishing a voluntary standards board, a public education campaign, and actions to protect consumers' privacy.

Recommendation 13: Information on the training and education of providers of CAM services should be made easily available to the public.

Recommendation 14: CAM products that are available to U.S. consumers should be safe and meet appropriate standards of quality and consistency.

Recommendation 15: Provision of the Federal Food, Drug and Cosmetic Act, as modified by the Dietary Supplement Health and Education Act of 1994, should be fully implemented, funded, enforced, and evaluated.

Recommendation 16: Activities to ensure that advertising of dietary supplements and other CAM practices and products is truthful and not misleading should be increased.

Recommendation 17: The collection and dissemination of information about adverse events stemming from the use of dietary supplements should be improved.

Access and Delivery

Recommendation 18: The Department of Health and Human Services should evaluate current barriers to consumer access to safe and effective CAM practices and to qualified practitioners and should develop strategies for removing those barriers to increase access and to ensure accountability.

Recommendation 19: The federal government should offer assistance to states and professional organizations in (1) developing and evaluating guidelines for practitioner accountability and competence in CAM delivery, including regulation of practice, and (2) periodically reviewing and assessing the effects of regulations on consumer protection.

(Continues)

TABLE 4	White House Commission on Complementary and Alternative Medicine Policy Recommendations and Actions (*Continued*)

Recommendation 20: States should evaluate and review their regulation of CAM practitioners and ensure their accountability to the public. States should, as appropriate, implement provisions for licensure, registration, and exemption that are consistent with the practitioners' education, training, and scope of practice.

Recommendation 21: Nationally recognized accrediting bodies should evaluate how health care organizations under their oversight are using CAM practices and should develop strategies for the safe and appropriate use of qualified CAM practitioners and safe and effective products in these organizations.

Recommendation 22: The federal government should facilitate and support the evaluation and implementation of safe and effective CAM practices to help meet the health care needs of special and vulnerable populations.

Recommendation 23: Evidence should be developed and disseminated regarding safety, benefits, and cost-effectiveness of CAM interventions, as well as the optimum models for complementary and integrated care.

Recommendation 24: Insurers and managed care organizations should offer purchasers the option of health benefit plans that incorporate coverage of safe and effective CAM interventions provided by qualified practitioners.

Recommendation 25: Purchasers, including federal agencies and employers, should evaluate the possibility of covering benefits or adding health benefit plans that incorporate sage and effective CAM interventions.

Source: White House Commission on Complementary and Alternative Medicine Policy, 2002.

COMPLEMENTARY AND ALTERNATIVE HEALTH CARE MODALITIES

The White House Commission on Complementary and Alternative Medicine Policy noted that the major CAM systems have common characteristics that include focusing on individual treatment, a holistic approach to care, promotion of self-care and self-healing, and addressing spiritual influences on health. The Commission then created a classification model for CAM systems, which listed the various practices by their major domains (see Table 5). We will discuss the major modalities of complementary and alternative medicine and those that address specific cultural practices.

TABLE 5 CAM Systems of Health Care

I. Alternative health care systems
Ayurvedic medicine
Chiropractic
Homeopathic medicine
American Indian medicine (e.g., sweat lodge, medicine wheel)
Naturopathic medicine
Traditional Chinese medicine (e.g., acupuncture, Chinese herbal medicine)

II. Mind–body interventions
Meditation
Hypnosis
Guided imagery
Dance therapy
Music therapy
Art therapy
Prayer and mental healing

III. Biological-based therapies
Herbal therapies
Special diets (e.g., macrobiotics, extremely low fat or high carbohydrate diets)
Orthomolecular medicine (e.g., megavitamin therapy)
Individual biological therapies (e.g., shark cartilage, bee pollen)

IV. Therapeutic massage, body work, and somatic movement therapies
Massage
Feldenkrais
Alexander method

V. Energy therapies
Qigong
Reiki
Therapeutic touch

VI. Bioelectromagnetics
Magnet therapy

Source: White House Commission on Complementary and Alternative Medicine Policy, 2002.

Ayurvedic Medicine

Ayurveda, a Sanskrit word meaning science of life, was originally described in the ancient Hindu texts called Vedas. It was the major health care practice of India for thousands of years until the British raj emphasized its replacement with Western medical practices.

TABLE 6	The Doshas
Vata. Composed of air and ether
Pita. Composed of fire and water
Kapha. Composed of water and earth

It has experienced a resurgence of interest since Indian independence from Great Britain in the 1940s and, more recently, through the popular writer Dr. Deepak Chopra.

This ancient practice is based on the theory that the five great elements, ether, air, fire, water, and earth, are the basis for all living systems. The five elements are in constant interaction and are constantly changing. The elements combine in pairs to form **doshas**, the three vital energies that regulate everything in nature (see Table 6).

The doshas are combined at the time of conception in combinations unique to each individual. This combination is known as **prakriti**. A person's physiology, personality, intellect, and weaknesses are governed by two dominant doshas. If the doshas become imbalanced, the flow of prana, life energy, and agni, digestion, becomes upset. It is these imbalances that result in illness.

Ayurvedic practitioners seek to balance the doshas through herbal remedies, yoga, meditation, and massage. For example, Panchakarma is a remedy that consists of a purification process to remove impurities and restore balance to the doshas. Medicinal remedies are derived from minerals, herbs, and vegetables (Peters & Woodham, 2000).

Yoga

Yoga is an ancient system of exercises and breathing techniques designed to encourage physical and spiritual well-being. It incorporates a number of guidelines for well-being, including good nutrition and hygiene. The physical practice of yoga consists of going through asanas, or physical postures to improve the physical body and calm the nerves. Pranayamas are breathing techniques and meditations designed to improve spiritual well-being.

Some yoga practitioners teach that centers of energy, known as chakras, are connected to the nerves and spinal cord. It is believed that certain asanas and meditations can positively influence the chakras, improving physical and mental health. The exercise and relaxation techniques utilized in yoga are practiced by many people every day.

Homeopathy

Homeopathy is based on the **Law of Similars**, first postulated by the Greek healer Hippocrates. This concept that "like cures like" is premised on the belief in the body's ability to heal itself. This is accomplished by giving a person a substance that creates the symptoms of a disease in a healthy person. It is believed that this stimulates the body's natural healing properties to cure the disease.

Modern homeopathic practice was begun by German Samuel Hahnemann in the late eighteenth century from his experiments to cure malaria. His treatment concepts quickly spread throughout Europe and the United States. By 1900, 15% of U.S. physicians were homeopathic practitioners (Freeman, 2004). Not unlike other CAM practices, homeopathy suffered from the efforts of mainstream American medicine in the early twentieth century to squash its practice. However, homeopathy continued in other parts of the world and today is actively practiced in India, Germany, France, and Great Britain, and its practice has reemerged in the United States. Homeopathy is premised on three fundamental principles: the Principle of Similars, the Principle of Infinitesimal Dose, and the Principle of the Specificity of the Individual.

The **Principle of Similars** is based on the like cures like concept. If a substance is given to a healthy person and causes symptoms of a disease, then administering a smaller dose will cure the disease. This occurs through stimulation of the body's natural healing powers. Interestingly, this concept underlies Louis Pasteur's and Jonas Salk's work on immunity and vaccinations, the idea that exposure to a small amount of a disease will cause the body to create immunity to the disease. Also, allergies are often treated in mainstream Western medicine by exposing the patient to small amounts of an allergen to create resistance.

The **Principle of Infinitesimal Dose**, or the law of potentization, is the idea that the more a substance is diluted, the more potent it becomes for treatment. This reduces side effects from more potent doses, and practitioners believe that the more dilute a remedy, the longer its effect will last with fewer doses and the more effective the overall treatment will be. To achieve proper dilution, plant substances are dissolved in mixtures of alcohol and water and stored over a period of time so that the materials dissolve. The resultant solution is then repeatedly diluted in a process termed "potentization." This is a concept that raises questions regarding the effectiveness of homeopathy because through this process, little, if any, of the original substances are left in the ultimate remedy.

Finally, the **Principle of Specificity of the Individual** states that any condition must be matched to the distinctive symptoms of the person. This is termed "profiling" and involves evaluating the patient's physical, emotional, and mental characteristics to

TABLE 7 Hering's Laws of Cure
Constantine Hering was the father of American homeopathic practice. He developed the theory that healing progresses in a distinct pattern:
First, from the deepest part of the body to the extremities
Second, from the emotional and mental to the physical
Third, from the upper body to the lower body
Healing progresses in reverse order from the most recent problem to the oldest.

match his or her current condition to the correct remedy. Homeopathic practitioners have large resource materials to assist them in matching the person's symptoms to the proper remedy (see Table 7).

Homeopathic treatments have undergone study with varying results. Although there is disagreement on the mechanics of homeopathic treatment, studies have shown that homeopathic treatment can positively impact allergies, fibromyalgia, migraine, rheumatoid arthritis, and other conditions (Freeman, 2004).

Case Review and Analysis

Kistin and Newman (2007) reported a case wherein a healthy 28-year-old who had three previous pregnancies and one live birth began labor. She had no complications during her pregnancy, and she and her husband had created a birth plan with their doula, a birth coach. They desired a natural birth if at all possible.

The woman's labor proceeded well, and natural methods were used to stimulate labor. The well-being of the baby and mother were frequently monitored by the staff. A tablet of Caulophyllum 30C, a homeopathic remedy made from the herb blue cohosh, was given to help establish active labor. After nine hours of labor, the woman gave birth to a healthy baby boy. Kistin and Newman (2007) addressed the significance of this case as follows:

> The most recent Centers for Disease Control and Prevention (CDC) birth statistics from 2003 report that 20.6% of pregnant women undergo medical induction for labor, and an additional 17.0% are medically augmented. The methods for labor induction in hospital settings generally include intravenous oxytocin, oral or vaginal prostaglandins, and/or intracervical Foley bulb placement. Of these methods, intravenous oxytocin is the most widely-used agent.

Induction of labor for women with PROM at term reduces the risk of infectious morbidity without increasing the risk for cesarean or operative vaginal delivery. Induction of labor with oxytocin, however, is not without risk and may be associated with more complications in certain subpopulations, such as nulliparous women and women with an unripe cervix. Also, the use of oxytocin for induction of labor involves necessary additional interventions, including intravenous needle placement, continuous external or internal fetal monitoring, internal uterine pressure catheter, epidural anesthesia, and Foley catheter insertion, each of which carries added risks for the mother and fetus, as well as an additional monetary cost.

When induction of labor is indicated, women may be more accepting of a natural or nonpharmacologic method, and as with any intervention, it makes sense to use the least invasive, most effective method available. Homeopathic labor stimulants are potentially viable alternatives to oxytocin and prostaglandins for inducing and augmenting labor. Blue cohosh (*Caulophyllum thalictroides*) and black cohosh (*Actaea racemosa* [formerly *Cimicifuga racemosa*]) have been used as homeopathic labor stimulants around the world, especially in Europe and India. In the United States, there has been an upsurge in the use of homeopathic remedies, and a recent survey describing the use of complementary therapies among nurse–midwives in North Carolina reported that 30% recommend homeopathic substances for use during pregnancy. There is a rich history of positive experience with these remedies, but the evidence for the efficacy and safety is largely narrative and anecdotal. The purpose of this case study is to explore the role of homeopathic substances as potential alternatives to commonly used induction agents and to encourage further, rigorous clinical research into the safety and efficacy of use.

Reprinted from Kistin, S. J. & Newman, A. D. (2007). Introduction of labor with homeopathy: A case report. *Journal of Midwifery and Women's Health*, *52*(3), 5, with permission from Elsevier.

Traditional Chinese Medicine

"Traditional Chinese medicine" is the term used for a group of ancient healing practices that date back some 2,000 years to 200 BC. The concepts utilized have been adapted by the Koreans, Japanese, and Vietnamese into their own versions of treatment. The system includes, among other treatments, herbalism, acupuncture, *qigong*, and t'ai chi ch'uan.

Traditional Chinese medicine, or TCM, is based on diagnosis from the pattern of symptoms rather than on endeavoring to identify a specific illness. It is believed that the cause of disease must be cured, not just its symptoms. TCM considers a person's body, mind, spirit, and emotions as part of one complete whole rather than individual parts that are to be treated separately.

The Theories of Traditional Chinese Medicine

TCM is based on a number of interrelated theories: the theory of Qi, the theory of the Five Elements, the theory of Yin and Yang, and the Meridian theory. These theories inform the treatment modalities that include acupuncture, herbal medicine, t'ai chi ch'uan, and *qigong*.

The Theory of Qi **Qi**, pronounced "chee," is the vital life force that animates all things. Qi flows through the 12 meridians that run through the body. Physical, emotional, and mental harmony rely on the flow of qi. Qi has two parts, energy or power, and conscious intelligence. These parts are found in organ systems and allow them to perform their physical and energetic functions. Qi can also be described by how it functions. Qi creates all movement, protects the body, provides for harmonious transformation, such as water being turned into urine, keeps the organs and body parts in proper position, and warms the body. This theory holds that qi:

- Is spiritual in origin
- Makes up and moves through all living things
- Is available in infinite quantities, is positive in nature, and is important to all aspects of health
- Is present both inside the body and on its surface
- Flows throughout the body in specific channels
- Has its flow disturbed by negative thoughts or feelings

Qi deficiency can result in problems, such as what Western medicine calls chronic fatigue syndrome or a fever. Qi stagnation, where the energy cannot flow correctly, can result in what Western medicine calls pain.

The Five Elements Theory The **five elements** are based on the perception of the relationships between all things. These patterns are grouped and named for the five elements: wood, fire, earth, metal, and water. This theory states that the five organ systems are each tied to a particular element and to a broader group of phenomena that are associated with their elements, including the seasons, colors, emotions, and foods (see Table 8). This theory illustrates the interrelatedness between all things.

Each of the elements gives energy to one element and controls another element. When control and energy are properly balanced, a state of wellness exists. If the relationships become unbalanced, health problems will emerge.

TABLE 8 The Characteristics of the Five Elements

	Fire	Earth	Metal	Water	Wood
Season	Summer	Indian summer	Autumn	Winter	Spring
Taste	Bitter	Sweet	Pungent	Salty	Sour
Emotion	Joy	Worry	Grief	Fear	Anger
Body	Heart	Spleen	Lungs	Kidneys	Liver
	Small intestine	Stomach	Large intestine	Bladder	Gallbladder
	Tongue	Mouth	Nose	Hair	Tendons
	Blood vessels	Muscles	Skin	Bones	Eye
Energy/control	Melts metal	Dries water	Cuts wood	Douses fire	Breaks earth
	Water douses it	Wood breaks it	Fire melts it	Earth dries it	Metal cuts it

The Yin and Yang Theory The **yin and yang** theory holds that everything is made up of two polar energies. Neither can exist without the other, and they never separate. It is the principle of interconnectedness and interdependence. Yin and yang describe how things function in relation to one another and the important principle of harmony where things blend together into a whole.

Yin is female and associated with the moon and night, late afternoon, cold, rest, responsiveness, passivity, darkness, interiority, downwardness, inwardness, and decrease. Yang is male and associated with the sun and daytime, early morning, heat, stimulation, movement, activity, excitement, vigor, light, exteriority, upwardness, outwardness, and increase (see Figure 1).

The Meridian Theory **Meridians** are channels through which qi, blood, and information flow to all parts of the body. There are 12 meridians in the body; 6 are yin and 6 are yang. Although each meridian is attributed to, and named for, an organ or body function, the network of meridians connects the meridians to one another and all parts of the body, and they connect the body to the universe. When qi flows easily, the body is balanced and healthy. The meridians work to regulate the energy functions of the body and keep it balanced and in harmony.

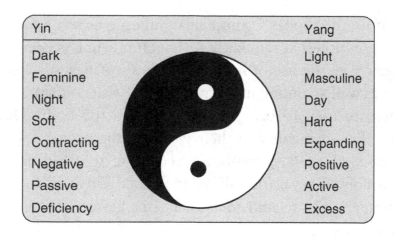

Yin	Yang
Dark	Light
Feminine	Masculine
Night	Day
Soft	Hard
Contracting	Expanding
Negative	Positive
Passive	Active
Deficiency	Excess

FIGURE 1 The symbol of yin and yang is a circle with two equal and opposite halves.

The Treatment Modalities of Traditional Chinese Medicine

Traditional Chinese Medicine encompasses many different treatment modalities. Here we will explore some of the treatment options utilized.

Acupuncture **Acupuncture** is *one* of the most researched and accepted complementary practices in the United States today. It is experiencing greater acceptance by traditional medical practitioners, and research of its efficacy in treating various conditions has been undertaken, although it has proven to be a difficult subject to study. Even though the research was challenging, the National Institutes of Health Consensus Conference on Acupuncture (1998) concluded that acupuncture is effective for various conditions, such as postoperative and chemotherapy-induced nausea and vomiting, and noted that it could be useful for treating a number of conditions, such as head or back pain and alcohol dependence.

Acupuncture involves stimulating specific points along the meridians to achieve a therapeutic purpose. The usual practice involves inserting a needle into one of the acupoints along a meridian associated with that organ or function. Besides puncturing the skin, practitioners also use other methods, including pressure, heat, friction, or electrical stimulation of the needle.

The TCM theory is that acupuncture works by bringing healing energy, qi, to the affected part of the body through the meridians. The stimulation of the appropriate meridian can assist in bringing the affected organ into balance.

Chinese Herbal Therapies Another significant aspect of traditional Chinese medicine is the use of herbal remedies. Although it is not as prevalent in the United States as acupuncture, the use of herbal remedies is widespread in China and other Asian countries as well as among immigrants from Asian countries. Like acupuncture, herbal remedies are used to bring balance back to the body. Herbs are classified according to the five elements and their yin and yang properties to determine how they will be used. Herbs are combined according to their properties to treat a particular disharmony. They are usually administered as teas, pills, powders, or creams. Safety and efficacy issues related to herbal remedies are discussed in the "Herbal Remedies" section.

Qigong The term *qigong* translates to "energy work." It is a part of traditional Chinese medicine that involves movement, breathing, and meditation, and it is intended to improve the flow of qi throughout the body. *Qigong* is an ancient technique that is practiced by millions of people every day. It involves a number of basic postures that are involved in daily practice, and a master can tailor the techniques to address specific problems.

The ancient noncombative martial art, **t'ai chi ch'uan**, is a form of *qigong*. The purpose of t'ai chi ch'uan is to improve the flow of qi through the body to encourage balance and harmony.

Case Review and Analysis

The following cases were reported on Acupuncture.com by two practitioners of acupuncture and traditional Chinese medicine in a discussion of the treatment of Alzheimer disease, stroke, and Parkinson disease (Chen & Zhang, 1997).

- *Case #1.* An 83-year-old female had a stroke two years ago. When she was first seen, she hobbled into the clinic, did not answer questions, and fell asleep. Clinical observation showed an extremely deficient and deep pulse. Her tongue was pink and slightly dusky with a greasy, yellow-green coat, which was much thicker on the left side. The patient was started on a regimen of Neuro Plus (Nao Wei Kang Wan) daily and received acupuncture treatment twice weekly. With treatment she improved rapidly. She can now lift her feet, smile, respond somewhat, and stay awake throughout the entire treatment. After four months of treatments she is able to speak, and her friends are happy because she can now talk with them on the phone.

- *Case #2.* The patient is a 64-year-old retired male who had complaints of poor attention span, hand tremor, stiff tongue, inability to hold a rice bowl or chopsticks, poor balance, difficulty walking, and partial urinary and fecal incontinence with frequent urination. A CT scan showed cerebral atrophy. The patient's condition dramatically improved after taking Neuro Plus (Nao Wei Kang Wan). His hand tremors stopped within a few days, and he felt more energetic. His walking improved and frequency of urination decreased. The patient stated that the treatment was like a "magic bullet."

Musculoskeletal Manipulation and Chiropractic

The modern practice of **chiropractic** has its origins in ancient practices. Many cultures have incorporated musculoskeletal manipulation in their healing practices, including the Chinese, Japanese, Indians, Egyptians, Mayans, Arabs, and American Indian tribes. The Greek healer and father of medicine, Hippocrates, included chapters on manipulation in his works on medicine. In Europe during the Middle Ages and Renaissance, bonesetters practiced musculoskeletal manipulation (Freeman, 2004).

The most prevalent contemporary practice of musculoskeletal manipulation is chiropractic, although musculoskeletal manipulation continues in other practices, such as osteopathic medicine. The term "chiropractic" is derived from Greek and translates to "done by hand." In its simplest terms, chiropractic diagnoses and treats disorders of the muscular, nervous, and skeletal systems with special emphasis on the spine. Spinal adjustment is the predominate treatment tool.

Begun in the late nineteenth century by Daniel David Palmer, an immigrant from Canada, chiropractic is founded on the belief that the spine is the key to health and that spinal misalignments affect the function of the entire body. Through manipulation, normal nerve function throughout the spine and nerves is restored and health is improved.

Chiropractic practice has three basic tenets (Chisolm, 2007):

1. The body has a powerful self-healing ability.
2. The body's structure (primarily that of the spine) and its function are closely related, and this relationship affects health.
3. Chiropractic therapy is concerned with the goals of normalizing this relationship between structure and function and assisting the body as it heals.

Early chiropractic theory held that misaligned vertebrae, called subluxation, disrupted nerve function, which could lead to disease and pain. Currently, the belief that the spine has a primary function in health remains, but theories have changed to accommodate advances in knowledge of physiology. Also, chiropractors emphasize that they do not treat disease but, rather, promote the body's ability to heal itself.

The hallmark treatment modality of chiropractic care is spinal manipulation, known as "adjustment." This term refers to any number of techniques utilized to correct misalignment of the spine and nerves, improving the patient's condition. Adjustment is utilized to correct subluxations and return the spine, and body, to better function. Additional therapies, such as heat and ice, massage, ultrasound or electrical stimulation, and traction, may be added depending on the person's need. It is not uncommon for chiropractic care to be combined with other CAM practices, such as homeopathy, naturopathy, or traditional Chinese medicine.

Chiropractic care is sought for any number of problems. The most common complaints are back pain, neck pain, and headache. Although chiropractic care is sought at greater and greater frequency for these chronic conditions, the scientific research has not definitively determined its efficacy.

Some chiropractic practitioners have utilized chiropractic techniques to treat a number of nonmusculoskeletal problems. The research on the efficacy of these interventions is scarce. It indicates that chiropractic may be helpful for menstrual pain, colic, and carpal tunnel syndrome, but it is contraindicated in the treatment of vascular problems, arteriosclerosis, tumors, arthritis, and metabolic disorders, among others.

Chiropractic is attractive to many people for the treatment of acute musculoskeletal injuries as well as chronic pain conditions. In the United States today, chiropractors are the second largest group of primary care providers, and chiropractic is the most widely utilized CAM modality in the country (Eisenberg, et al., 1993).

Naturopathy

Naturopathy, or natural medicine, has its origins in the late nineteenth century in Germany based on the ancient belief in the healing power of nature and that natural organisms have the ability to heal themselves and maintain health. Naturopaths believe that the body strives to maintain a state of equilibrium, known as homeostasis, and unhealthy environments, diets, physical or emotional stress, and lack of sleep or fresh air can disrupt that balance (see Table 9).

Naturopathic Treatments

Naturopaths believe that the body attempts to maintain optimum health. When homeostasis is upset, they utilize any number of treatments to return the body to balance.

TABLE 9	The Six Key Principles of Naturopathy
1. Promote the healing power of nature.	
2. Do no harm.	
3. Treat the whole person.	
4. Treat the cause.	
5. Prevention is the best cure.	
6. The physician is a teacher.	

Source: National Center for Complementary and Alternative Medicine. (2007a).

All treatments are designed to enhance the body's ability to heal itself. Modalities include diet, yoga, manipulation, massage, hydrotherapy, and natural herbs. Naturopathic practitioners take a holistic approach to treatment and focus on the cause of a disruption of homeostasis rather than treating only symptoms.

Herbal Remedies   Plants used for medicinal purposes are classified as medicinal herbs. Herbs have been used to treat diseases for centuries. Many conventional medications were originally developed from herbs. Naturopaths use herbs to restore homeostasis through treating the cause of diseases. Today the use of herbal remedies is the fastest growing CAM therapy.

Herbal preparations use either whole plants or parts of plants. Many herbalists believe in synergy, the idea that whole plants are more effective than their individual parts. Herbal remedies are prepared in pill or liquid form for ingestion or as tinctures, creams, or ointments for external use.

The World Health Organization estimates that 80% of the world's population uses some form of herbal remedies for their care (Freeman, 2004). The 10 most popular natural products in the United States are listed in Table   10. Consequently, the safety of herbal remedies is a concern because herbs can be dangerous in the wrong dose or when mixed with other herbs or medications.

In the United States, herbal products are sold as dietary supplements. They are regulated by the U.S. Food and Drug Administration (FDA) as foods. This means that they do not have to meet the same standards as drugs and over-the-counter medications for proof of safety, effectiveness, and what the FDA calls Good Manufacturing Practices (see Table   11).

TABLE 10   Ten Most Popular Natural Products

Echinacea, 40.3%. Used to stimulate the immune system for colds and chronic infections

Ginseng, 24.1%. Used to lower blood pressure and blood sugar and to increase energy

Gingko biloba, 21.1%. Used to aid memory and diminish dementia symptoms

Garlic supplements, 19.9%. Used to lower cholesterol and blood pressure

Glucosamine, 14.9%. Used for joint pain and degeneration

St. John's wort, 12.0%. Used for depression

Peppermint, 11.8%. Used for gastrointestinal complaints

Fish oils/omega fatty acids, 11.7%. Used to prevent cardiovascular disease

Ginger supplements, 10.5%. Used for nausea, especially in pregnancy and motion sickness

Soy supplements, 9.4%. Used for menopause, osteoporosis, and memory problems

The percentage reflects the number of Americans who use natural products.
Source: National Center for Complementary and Alternative Medicine. (2007b).

TABLE 11   About Dietary Supplements

Dietary supplements were defined in a law passed by Congress in 1994. A dietary supplement is a product that contains vitamins, minerals, herbs or other botanicals, amino acids, enzymes, and/or other ingredients intended to supplement the diet. The U.S. Food and Drug Administration has special labeling requirements for dietary supplements and treats them as foods, not drugs. Dietary supplements must meet all of the following conditions:

- It is a product (other than tobacco) intended to supplement the diet, which contains one or more of the following: vitamins, minerals, herbs or other botanicals, amino acids, or any combination of these ingredients.

- It is intended to be taken in tablet, capsule, powder, softgel, gelcap, or liquid form.

- It is not represented for use as a conventional food or as a sole item of a meal or diet.

- It is labeled as being a dietary supplement.

Source: National Center for Complementary and Alternative Medicine. (2009).

When considering using herbal remedies, it is important to consult a professional who is informed about the use of these remedies. Because a product is labeled "natural" does not mean it is safe or does not have harmful effects, or the product may not be recommended for a person's specific situation, such as pregnancy. It should be remembered that these remedies can act in the same way as many prescription or over-the-counter drugs and can cause side effects or interfere with the actions of other medications. As with any medication, herbal remedies are not without hazards, and their use must be properly monitored.

Case Review and Analysis

The patient was a 48-year-old woman who had rheumatic fever in the past that caused her to have an irregular heartbeat and damage to her mitral valve. She had a procedure done to repair the mitral valve and was placed on a blood thinning medication (known as an anticoagulant) to slow blood clotting after the procedure.

The patient was discharged home and began taking herbal preparations she had previously received from an herbalist. After a few weeks she became very ill with fevers, shortness of breath, and malaise. She was readmitted to the hospital, and it was determined that she was overanticoagulated and her blood was clotting much too slowly. She reported the herbs she had been taking, and it was suspected that she was suffering from an interaction between the herbs and the anticoagulant medication.

The physician researched the herbal preparations she had been taking and determined that one of the ingredients was danshen, which is an herbal remedy often used for heart-related complaints and is a component of many herbal preparations. It is known for its potency and its ability to potentiate the effect of the anticoagulant medication the patient was taking.

The herbal preparations were discontinued, and the patient was treated for the problems related to being overanticoagulated. She had a full recovery, although it took a number of weeks for her blood clotting to stabilize (Yee, Chan, & Sanderson, 1997).

Hydrotherapy **Hydrotherapy** is another treatment used by naturopathic practitioners based on the therapeutic effects of water. It was initially used in Germany and was thought to assist in ridding the body of waste and toxins. Hot and cold baths, compresses, wraps, and showers were used. Modern treatment uses the same modalities.

Water is known for its impact on the body. Cold water makes surface blood vessels restrict and inhibits inflammation, thus it reduces swelling and sends more blood to the internal organs. Hot water dilates blood vessels and is associated with relaxation and increased blood flow that relaxes muscles and stiffness. Some therapies use both hot and cold water either alternately or at the same time on different areas of the body.

Mind–Body Interventions

Mind–body interventions encompass an array of practices aimed at the relationship between the person's mind and physical function. These practices vary from emphasis on spiritual relations to psychological and emotional well-being.

Spirituality

In the NCCAM study (2007b) when prayer was included as a CAM therapy, it was the most often identified CAM practice used by respondents. Walker (2005) noted that the study provided further information regarding the importance of prayer to the respondents as follows:

- Respondents who used prayer for health reasons: 45%
- Respondents who prayed for their own health: 43%
- Respondents who had others pray for them: 25%
- Respondents who participated in a prayer group for health reasons: approximately 10%

Spiritual practices regarding health are not just limited to prayer. Beliefs in the ability of the supernatural to heal surfaced in shamanism thousands of years ago. Recorded history regarding spiritual healing includes Egyptian belief in the healing power of a particular holy site and Greek and Roman temples built to the healing gods. These types of practices are not unknown today. Shamanic traditions continue today in Africa, Central and South America, and among some American Indian tribes. Christians continue to make pilgrimages to holy sites that are believed to heal, like Lourdes. Scientific research has determined that spiritual practices positively impact health and increases longevity (Freeman, 2004). However, there is disagreement as to the mechanism of these benefits.

Spirituality is often described as a belief in a higher power, something beyond the human experience. Closely related but distinctive is religion, which is the acceptance of the specific beliefs and practices of an organized religion. A person may be spiritual without being religious, or they may be both. Research has shown that both spirituality and religious beliefs have positive effects on health (Freeman, 2004).

The scientific explanation for the positive influence of spirituality on health stems from a number of theories. One is the placebo effect, a beneficial response to a treatment that can't be explained on the basis of the treatment provided. Often the placebo effect is a response to suggestion of positive impact and the patient's belief in the treatment. Another scientific explanation for the positive impact of spirituality involves neurochemical or other physiologic changes.

Conversely, the religious explanation for the positive influence of prayer is due to connection to God and divine intervention in healing. Prayer, a petition to or contemplation of God, is the vehicle by which that divine connection is made. Prayer can be further subdivided into petitionary or intercessional prayer. Petitionary prayer is on one's personal behalf, and intercessional prayer is on behalf of another. Some form of prayer for connection with the Almighty is utilized in almost all cultures and religious tenets. Although there is disagreement between the scientific and religious worlds regarding the exact action of spirituality's and prayer's impacts on health, there is accord that they are beneficial.

Meditation **Meditation** refers to a group of mental techniques intended to provide relaxation and mental harmony, quiet one's mind, and increase awareness. It has been a practice in many cultures for thousands of years. Meditative practices are found in Christian, Jewish, Buddhist, Hindu, and Islamic religious traditions. Although meditation found its origins in religious practices, it is currently utilized for nonreligious purposes, such as improved emotional and physical health. Meditation is utilized to decrease stress and anxiety, decrease pain, improve mood, and positively impact heart disease and the symptoms of physical illness. Scientific research indicates that meditation decreases oxygen consumption, decreases heart and respiratory rates, and influences brain wave and hormone activity (Freeman, 2004).

Various techniques are used by different groups and religions. All techniques have some common factors, namely, use of a quiet location, assuming a comfortable position, focusing one's attention by concentrating on one's breath or a mantra (word or sound), and having an open attitude by not allowing distractions to disrupt focus. There are two common types of meditation practices: mindfulness meditation and transcendental meditation.

Mindfulness meditation originated in the Buddhist traditions. It is the concept of increasing awareness and acceptance of the present. During meditation one observes

TABLE 12	Relaxation Technique

1. Find a quiet place to sit.

2. Sit in a comfortable position with your feet on the floor, hands relaxed, and eyes closed.

3. Take three slow, deep breaths.

4. Begin to relax your muscles starting with your toes and progressing upward to your feet and ankles, then lower legs, then upper legs, etc., until you reach your face and head. Sometimes it is helpful to actually contract the muscles and then allow them to relax.

5. Breathe through your nose, concentrating on the breath going in and out. As you exhale, say a word in your mind like "calm" or "one."

6. Continue to concentrate on your breathing for 10 to 20 minutes. At the end of the time, sit quietly for a few minutes and gradually begin to arouse.

There is no failure in meditation. The benefit comes from maintaining a positive attitude and allowing relaxation to happen and ignoring distracting thoughts by gently pushing them from your mind when they appear.

thoughts and images in a nonjudgmental manner with the goal of learning to experience thoughts and feelings with greater balance and acceptance. This technique has been used to treat posttraumatic stress disorder, drug abuse, and chronic pain. It has also been found to increase cognitive function in the elderly.

Transcendental meditation found its origins in the Indian Vedic tradition. This practice is designed to allow the practitioner to experience ever finer levels of thought until the source of thought is experienced. A mantra is used to focus the mind, and the choice of mantra is vital to success. Transcendental meditation allows the mind to reach a quiet state and strives to create a state of relaxed alertness.

Transcendental meditation has been found to stimulate what is termed the "relaxation response," which is responsible for decreased blood pressure, muscular relaxation, decreased heart and respiratory rate, and a decrease in lactate levels, which are associated with anxiety. Research shows that a number of relaxation meditation techniques include four parts: a mental focus, passive attitude, decreased muscle tone, and a quiet environment (Freeman, 2004). One relaxation technique is described in Table 12.

Studies have shown that transcendental meditation has a positive affect on blood pressure, cardiovascular disease, and overall health. Mindfulness meditation is useful in the treatment of chronic pain and certain psychological disorders. The only situation where meditation is considered to be unsafe is in serious mental disorders like psychosis and schizophrenia. Otherwise, meditation has been determined to be a safe practice for almost everyone.

Hypnosis

Another mind–body intervention is hypnosis. As a technique, hypnosis has been present in many cultures for centuries. Its modern practice began with Franz Anton Mesmer in the eighteenth century, who studied and described "animal magnetism." It was from his efforts that the term "mesmerize" arose.

Hypnotism is a state of attentive, focused concentration associated with the suspension of some peripheral awareness. A person under hypnosis is induced to a state of deep relaxation and is susceptible to suggestions. Referencing a number of studies, Freeman (2004) described the major elements of a hypnotic state as:

- *Absorption*. The capacity to focus intently on a focal point or a theme
- *Relaxation*. Controlled alteration of the person's attention
- *Dissociation*. Capacity to compartmentalize different aspects of experience
- *Suggestibility*. Capacity for heightened responsiveness to instructions

Modern hypnosis is conducted by practitioners who are trained to induce a hypnotic state. It is believed that up to 90% of the population is capable of being hypnotized. Some people are more susceptible to hypnosis than others, as reflected in a classification system from low to high susceptibility. Although the great majority of the population is capable of being hypnotized, practitioners agree that people cannot be hypnotized against their will or without their consent. Although many theories exist regarding exactly how hypnosis works, no definitive determination has been made about its mechanism.

One of the earliest modern uses of hypnosis was for pain control during surgery prior to the advent of anesthesia. Hypnosis has been used very successfully for all types of pain control, and numerous studies have documented that effect. It is believed that hypnosis reduces anxiety, which contributes to the experience of pain, but, again, no definitive information exists on exactly how it works. Besides pain, hypnosis has been shown to be useful in the treatment of a number of conditions, especially those that are mediated or exacerbated by emotional overtones, such as irritable bowel syndrome, fibromyalgia, asthma, anticipatory or pregnancy-induced nausea, phobias, addictive behaviors, and anxiety.

Energy Therapies

Energy therapies focus on energy fields that are believed to have healing properties. We have discussed some of these already, such as qi in traditional Chinese medicine and the doshas in ayurvedic medicine. In these varied practices it is believed that vital energy exists and flows both outside and within the human body. Therapists in these modalities work with this energy, commonly called biofield, to either restore its flow or utilize it to restore health.

There are two classifications of energy therapy. The first, **veritable energy**, refers to the use of energy fields that can be physically experienced and/or measured. These include modalities such as magnet, sound, or light. **Putative energy** employs biofields for therapeutic effect and has not been measurable to current methods. These therapies include healing touch, therapeutic touch, and reiki. Kirlian photography, often called aura imaging, has been theorized to capture this energy; however, it is not apparent just what Kirlian photography actually represents. In the following sections, we will discuss a few of these modalities that have not been addressed elsewhere in this chapter.

Magnet Therapy

Magnet therapy involves the use of electromagnetic energy that is always present. The therapy often involves the application of static magnets over areas of pain. This is often accomplished by bracelets for arthritis or magnetic pads. Practitioners believe that this application impacts the body's natural magnetic field, thereby decreasing pain. No research on the efficacy of these treatments is available.

Pulsating electromagnetic therapy has been used by medical practitioners for many years. It is prescribed to treat nonunion fractures, and it is thought to improve arthritis and multiple sclerosis.

Healing (Laying on of Hands)

Healing, often called laying on of hands, has been characterized as both an energy and spiritual healing practice. In either event, it is an ancient practice that has modern application in many cultures and beliefs. In this therapy, a healer, known as a "worker," channels healing energy to the patient to stimulate natural healing. This can occur either in person or at a distance. Healing and laying on of hands is common to many cultures. Edgar Cayce was a well-known American practitioner of healing. He was reported to place himself into a trance and heal others who requested his

TABLE 13	Types of Healing Practices

Aura healing. A healer sees energy fields around a person, which indicate his or her state of health, then the healer touches the person and visualizes healing auras.

Spiritual healing. A healer connects with his or her internal energy, which connects the healer to a greater energy, and channels the energy to the patient.

Faith healing. A healer channels energy, and the patient must believe in the healer's ability or the power of the deity to heal.

Spiritualist healing. A healer establishes a connection to an entity in the spirit world that heals through the healer.

intercession either in person or at a distance. Today many people are proponents of what is termed "new age" philosophies, which have theories involving the existence of energy fields that have beneficial properties (see Table 13).

CHAPTER SUMMARY

This chapter has discussed complementary and alternative health care modalities that are associated with a number of cultures. Many are ancient practices that continue to exist despite the efforts of modern Western medicine to marginalize them. Although research on the efficacy of many of these practices is scarce, the prevalence of use indicates a need for further investigation of the risks and benefits of these practices.

REVIEW

1. Describe the advantages and disadvantages of three of the CAM modalities discussed in this chapter.
2. Discuss how meditation could be used in Western health care practice.
3. Describe the relationship between ethnic cultures and CAM in the United States.
4. Discuss how to inquire about CAM modalities used by patients during an initial interview.

GLOSSARY TERMS

complementary medicine

integrative medicine

doshas

prakriti

yoga

homeopathy

Law of Similars (Principle of Similars)

Principle of Infinitesimal Dose

Principle of Specificity of the Individual

qi

five elements

yin and yang

meridians

acupuncture

Qigong

t'ai chi ch'uan

chiropractic

naturopathy

hydrotherapy

spirituality

meditation

mindfulness meditation

transcendental meditation

veritable energy

putative energy

magnet therapy

healing

REFERENCES

American Medical Association. (1997). Report 13 of Council on Scientific Affairs. Retrieved March 26, 2008, from http://www.ama-assn.org/ama/pub/category/13644.html

Chen, J., & Zhang, H. (1997). *Treatment of neurodegenerative disorders. Alzheimers, stroke and Parkinson's disease.* Retrieved April 25, 2008, from http://acupuncture.com/conditions/alzandparkinson.htm

Chisolm, S. (2007). *The health professions: Trends and opportunities in US health care.* Sudbury, MA: Jones and Bartlett.

Eisenberg, D. M., Kessler, R.C., Foster, C., Norloci, F.E., Calkins, D.R and Delbanco, T.L. (1993, January 28). Unconventional medicine in the United States: Prevalence, costs and patterns of use. *The New England Journal of Medicine, 328,* 246–252.

Freeman, L. (2004). *Complementary and alternative medicine: A research-based approach* (2nd ed). St. Louis, MO: Mosby.

Hufford, D. J. (1988). Contemporary folk medicine. In N. Gevitz (Ed.), *Other healers: Unorthodox medicine in the United States.* Baltimore: Johns Hopkins University Press.

Hufford, D. J. (1997). Folk medicine and health culture in contemporary society. *Primary Care, 24,* 723–741.

Kistin, S., & Newman, A. (2007, May–June). Induction of labor with homeopathy: A case report. *Journal of Midwifery & Women's Health, 52*(3), 303–307. Retrieved April 25, 2008, from http://www.sciencedirect.com/science?_ob=ArticleListURL&_method=list&_ArticleListID =880293199&_sort=d&view=c&_acct=C000050221&_version=1&_urlVersion=0&_userid= 10&md5=357920d842ed02d9d59f2af944e52d36

National Center for Complementary and Alternative Medicine. (2002). *Office of Special Populations strategic plan to address racial and ethnic health disparities.* Retrieved April 28, 2008, from http://nccam.nih.gov/about/plans/healthdisparities

National Center for Complementary and Alternative Medicine. (2007a). *Backgrounder: An introduction to naturopathy.* Retrieved April 24, 2008, from http://www.nccam.nih.gov/health/naturopathy

National Center for Complementary and Alternative Medicine. (2007b). *The use of CAM in the United States.* Retrieved April 24, 2008, from http://www.nccam.nih.gov

National Center for Complementary and Alternative Medicine. (2009). *Using dietary supplements wisely.* Retrieved January 25, 2009, from http://nccam.nih.gov/health/supplements/wiseuse.htm

National Institutes of Health. (1998). National Institutes of Health consensus conference: Acupuncture. *Journal of the American Medical Association, 280,* 1518.

Pachter, L. M. (1994, March 2). Culture and clinical care. *Journal of the American Medical Association, 271*(9), 127–131.

Peters, D., & Woodham, A. (2000). *Encyclopedia of natural healing.* New York: Dorling Kindersley.

Trends in alternative medicine use in the United States, 1990–1997. Results of a follow-up national survey. (1998). *Journal of the American Medical Association, 280,* 1569–1575.

Walker, D. (2005). *Prayer and spirituality in health: Ancient practices, modern science.* Retrieved April 26, 2008, from http://nccam.nih.gov/news/newsletter/2005_winter/prayer.htm

What is traditional Chinese medicine? (2008). Retrieved April 12, 2008, from http://www.tcmworld.org/what_is_tcm/

White House Commission on Complementary and Alternative Medicine Policy. (2002). *Chapter 10: Recommendations and actions.* Retrieved March 27, 2008, from http://www.whccamp.hhs.gov/fr10.html

Yee, C., Chan, J., & Sanderson, J. (1997). Chinese herbs and warfarin potentiation by "Danshen." *Journal of Internal Medicine, 241,* 337–338.

PHOTO CREDITS

Chapter Opener , © Lisa F. Young/ShutterStock, Inc.

Unless otherwise indicated, all photographs and illustrations are under copyright of Jones and Bartlett Publishers, LLC, or have been provided by the author(s).

Religion, Rituals, and Health

Nothing is so conducive to good health as the regularity of life without haste and without worry which the rational practice of religion brings in its train.

—James J. Walsh

To prevent disease or to cure it, the power of truth, of divine Spirit, must break down the dream of the material senses.

—Mary Baker Eddy

KEY CONCEPTS

- Rituals
- Euthanasia
- Karma
- Ahimsa
- Living will

- Religion and health behaviors
- Religion and health outcomes
- Religion and medical decisions
- Shrines
- Animal sacrifice

CHAPTER OBJECTIVES

1. Describe the role that religion plays in the lives of Americans.
2. Explain how religion impacts health behaviors and the rationale behind these choices.
3. Describe ways that religion can have positive and negative effects on physical and mental health.
4. Explain how religion impacts medical decisions and the rationale behind these choices.
5. Describe religious differences in birthing and death rituals.

Have you ever prayed for a loved one or yourself when ill? If so, you fall within the majority of Americans. A national survey conducted by the federal government and published in 2004 found that 43% of Americans prayed for their own health, and 24% reported that other people were praying for their health (Dember, 2005). Seventy-nine percent of adults in the United States believe that spiritual faith can help people recover from illness, injury, or disease (McNicol, 1996).

Religion has a significant role in the United States and in the health of Americans. It has an impact on their social lives and health behaviors and, hence, their physical and mental well-being. Religion is a belief in and respect for a supernatural power or powers, which is regarded as creator and governor of the universe, and a personal or institutionalized system grounded in such belief and worship. Religion is divergent from spirituality, although there is overlap, because many people find spirituality in the form of religion. For many people spirituality means the life force within each one of us, and it refers to an individual's attempt to find meaning and purpose in life. Most of the research has focused on health and religion, as opposed to health and spirituality, primarily because religion is associated with behaviors that can be quantified (e.g., how often one prays or attends a place of worship), it can be categorized by type of religion, and there is more agreement about its meaning.

Religion and **rituals** overlap, but not all rituals are related to religion. Therefore, we discuss the two items separately in this chapter, but the reader should be aware that some rituals are related to religious practices, such as baptism, and other rituals are not tied to religion, such as the burning of ghost money when a person dies (a tradition in China). In the first part of the chapter we discuss religion and move into rituals, but the separation is not definitive. The opening topic is religion in America, and then we move into the subject of how religion impacts health. The second section of the chapter focuses on rituals related to health. Because these topics have such a vast scope, only the more common religious practices within the United States are covered.

RELIGION IN THE UNITED STATES

In 1999, about 95% of the population in the United States reported a belief in God or a higher power (Miller & Thoresen, 2003). In 2005, 57% of Americans said religion is very important in their lives, and another 28% said it is fairly important (Winseman, 2005). Church and synagogue attendance also reflects the importance of religion. Researchers have asked Americans how often they attend their place of worship, and since it was instituted in 1992, the question has produced consistent results (Saad, 2003). The survey results for 2003 are presented in Table 1. The most common self-identified religions in the United States can be found in Table 2.

Religion and ethnicity are linked, but it is important to not assume a person's religion based on his or her ethnicity. For example, in a 2002 study, 57% of people who identified themselves as Hispanic stated that they identified with the Catholic religion,

TABLE 1 Frequency of Church and Synagogue Attendance

How often do you attend church or synagogue: at least once a week, almost every week, about once a month, seldom, or never?

Once a Week	Almost Every Week	About Once a Month	Seldom	Never	No Opinion
31%	14%	14%	30%	10%	1%

Source: Saad, L. (2003).

which leaves 43% identifying with other religions or no religion (Kosmin, Mayer, & Keysar, 2001). It also is not safe to assume that a person strictly adheres to the practices of a religion. Adherence to religious practices exists on a continuum, with some strictly adhering to all of the guidelines and some having looser ties.

TABLE 2 Top 10 Religions in the United States, 2001

Religion	Percentage of United States Population in 2000	2001 Estimated Adult Population
1. Christianity	76.5%	159,030,000
2. Nonreligious/secular	13.2%	27,539,000
3. Judaism	1.3%	2,831,000
4. Islam	0.5%	1,104,000
5. Buddhism	0.5%	1,082,000
6. Agnostic	0.5%	991,000
7. Atheist	0.4%	902,000
8. Hinduism	0.4%	766,000
9. Unitarian Universalist	0.3%	629,000
10. Wiccan/pagan/druid	0.1%	307,000

Source: Adapted from Adherents.com.

RELIGION AND HEALTH BEHAVIORS

Lifestyle represents the single most prominent influence over our health today. It has been estimated that about 40% of the causes of early death are related to health behavioral patterns (Cottrell, Girvan, & McKenzie, 2006). As a result, the United States is seeing the need for more emphasis on prevention and behavior modification. People with religious ties have been shown to engage in healthier behavioral patterns, and these positive lifestyle choices lead to improved health and longer lives. The question is, Why do people with stronger religious ties have better health? The answer includes several possible factors, such as proscribed behaviors, social relationships, and improved coping mechanisms.

Health behaviors encouraged or proscribed by particular religions are one possible explanation for how religion can positively affect health. Some religions prohibit tobacco, alcohol, caffeine, and premarital sex, and some encourage vegetarianism, for example.

Social relationships are another potential explanatory factor for the connection between religion and improved health indicators. Social ties can provide both support and a sense of connectedness. Many churches and temples offer activities such as workshops, health fairs, and crafts fairs, which provide social interactions. Social relationships also are tied to coping mechanisms, because they provide support in multiple forms during times of stress. For example, they may provide financial support to people who have incurred a tragedy, such as a disability, loss of job, and house fire. Religious organizations also conduct fundraisers for families who have had a death or personal tragedy in the family. Churches and temples assist elders by providing transportation or taking communion or food to the homebound. Friendships and a sense of purpose also are methods of support.

Now that we have explained some possible reasons for religion impacting health, we are going to focus on specific behaviors.

Dietary Practices

Dietary practices have a long history of being incorporated into religions around the world. Some religions prohibit followers from consuming certain foods and drinks all of the time or on certain holy days; require or encourage specific dietary and food preparation practices and/or fasting (going without food and/or drink for a specified time); or prohibit eating certain foods at the same meal, such as dairy and meat products. Other religions require certain methods of food preparation and have special rules about the use of pans, plates, utensils, and how the food is to be cooked. Foods and drinks also may be a part of religious celebrations or rituals.

The restriction of certain foods and beverages may have a positive impact on the health of those engaged in such practices. For example, restricting consumption of animal products, such as beef and pork or all animal products, may reduce the risk of health problems. Many religions, such as Hinduism and Buddhism, practice or promote vegetarianism, and these diets have been shown to have several health effects, such as the reduction of heart disease, cancer, obesity, and stroke. Some religions help prevent obesity through beliefs that gluttony is a sin, only take what you need, and the need for self-discipline. Table 3 presents a list of religions, their related dietary practices and restrictions, and the rationale behind them.

Religions may incorporate some element of fasting into their practices. In many religions, the general purpose for fasting is to become closer to God, show respect for the body (temple) that is a gift from God, understand and appreciate the suffering that the poor experience, acquire the discipline required to resist temptation, atone for sinful acts, and/or cleanse evil from within the body (Advameg Inc., 2008). Fasting may be recommended for specific times of the day; for a specified number of hours; on designated days of the week, month, or year; or on holy days.

During times of fasting, most but not all religions permit the consumption of water. Water restriction can lead to a risk of dehydration. Some fasters may not take their medication during the fast, which may put their health at risk. Prolonged fasting and/or restrictions from water and/or medications may pose health risks for some followers. Because of these health risks, certain groups are often excused from fasting. These groups include people with chronic diseases, frail elderly, pregnant and lactating women, people who engage in strenuous labor, young children, and malnutritioned individuals.

Use of Stimulants and Depressants

In addition to foods, some religions prohibit or restrict the use of stimulants. A stimulant is a product (including medications), food, or drink that stimulates the nervous system and alters the recipient's physiology. Stimulants include substances that contain alcohol or caffeine, including tea, coffee, chocolate, and energy drinks. Caffeine is prohibited or restricted by many religions because of its addictive properties. Many religions also restrict spices and certain condiments, such as pepper, pickles, or foods with preservatives, because they are believed to be harmful by nature and flavor the natural taste and effect of foods (Advameg Inc., 2008).

Some religions prohibit the use of stimulants and depressants, but others use them during ceremonies. For example, Roman Catholics, Eastern Orthodox Christians, and certain Protestant denominations use wine as a sacramental product to represent

TABLE 3 Religions and Their Related Food and Substance Practices and Restrictions and Related Rationales

Type of Religion	Practice or Restriction	Rationale
Buddhism	• Vegetarian diet is desirable. • All foods in moderation.	• Natural foods of the earth are considered to be the most pure. • Encourage nonviolence (some Buddhists believe that the cause of human aggression is violence against animals).
Eastern Orthodox Christianity	• Restrictions on meat and fish. • Fasting selectively. • The ritual of the transubstantiation (changing) of bread and wine into the body and blood of Jesus Christ is believed to occur at communion.	• Observance of Holy Days includes fasting and restrictions to increase spiritual progress.
Hinduism	• Beef is forbidden. • Vegetarian diet is advocated. • Alcohol is avoided. • Numerous fasting days—may depend on the person's caste (or social standing) and the occasion.	• Cows are sacred and cannot be eaten, but the products of the "sacred" cow are pure and desirable. • Fasting promotes spiritual growth.
Islam	• Pork and certain birds are forbidden. • Alcohol is prohibited. • Coffee, tea, and stimulants are avoided. • Fasting from all food and drink during specific periods.	• Eating is for good health. • Failure to eat correctly minimizes spiritual awareness. • Fasting has a cleansing effect of evil elements.
Judaism	• Consumption of certain foods, including dairy products and fish, is subject to restrictions; for example, pork and shellfish are prohibited, and so is consuming meat and dairy at the same meal. • Leavened food is restricted. • Foods must be prepared in the right way to be kosher; for example, animals that provide meat must be slaughtered correctly. • Fasting is practiced.	• Land animals that do not have cloven hooves and that do not chew their cud are forbidden as unclean (e.g., hare, pig, camel). • The kosher process is based upon the Torah. • The Passover commemorates the birth of the Jewish nation, and the food eaten helps to tell the story of the exodus; for example, bitter herbs recall the suffering of the Israelites under Egyptian rule.

(Continues)

TABLE 3 Religions and Their Related Food and Substance Practices and Restrictions and Related Rationales (Continued)

Mormonism	• Caffeinated and alcoholic beverages are forbidden. • All foods should be consumed in moderation. • Fasting is practiced.	• Caffeine is addictive and leads to poor physical and emotional health. • Fasting is the discipline of self-control and honoring God.
Protestantism	• Few restrictions of food or fasting observations. • Moderation in eating, drinking, and exercise is promoted.	• God made all animal and natural products for humans' enjoyment. • Gluttony and drunkenness are sins to be controlled.
Rastafarianism	• Meat and fish are restricted. • Vegetarian diets only, with salts, preservatives, and condiments prohibited. • Herbal drinks are permitted; alcohol, coffee, and soft drinks are prohibited. • Marijuana used extensively for religious and medicinal purposes.	• Pigs and shellfish are unclean, they are viewed as scavengers. • Foods grown with chemicals are unnatural and prohibited. • Biblical texts support the use of herbs (marijuana and other herbs).
Roman Catholicism	• Meat is restricted on certain days. • Fasting is practiced. • The ritual of the transubstantiation (changing) of bread and wine into the body and blood of Jesus Christ is believed to occur at communion. • Fast for at least one hour prior to communion.	• Restrictions are consistent with specified days of the church year.
Seventh-day Adventist	• Expects adherence to kosher laws. • Pork is prohibited, and meat and fish is avoided. • Recommends vegetarian diet. • Alcohol and illegal drugs are discouraged. • Avoid caffeinated beverages.	• Diet is related to honoring and glorifying God.

Source: Adapted from Advameg Inc. (2008).

the blood of Christ in communion services (Advameg Inc., 2008). Rastafarians introduced marijuana into their religious rites because they consider it to be the "weed of wisdom", and they believe it contains healing ingredients (Advameg Inc., 2008). American Indians use tobacco and the hallucinogenic peyote as part of their spiritual ceremonies.

Other Health Behaviors

Research in adults and adolescents also has suggested a strong association between religious involvement and behaviors for which there is no specific religious teaching. For example, a national study of high school seniors in the United States found that religious students were more likely than their nonreligious peers to wear seatbelts, eat breakfast, eat fruit and green vegetables, get regular exercise, and sleep at least seven hours a night (Wallace & Forman, 1998 as cited in Williams & Sternthal, 2007). This research indicates that religious participation could have a general effect on lifestyle and not only a direct effect from the rules of the religion. Strawbridge and colleagues (2001) reviewed 28 years of data about people who lived in Alameda County, California, and they found that those who attended weekly services were more likely to quit poor health behaviors or adopt healthier behaviors (Hamilton, n.d.). In the same study, they found that weekly attendance also was associated with less depression and higher marital stability (Hamilton, n.d.).

RELIGION AND HEALTH OUTCOMES

As a result of religion's effects on health behaviors, it is not surprising that religion has been shown to have positive effects on both physical and mental health. Over the last several decades, a notable body of empirical evidence has emerged that examines the relationship between religion or religious practices and a host of outcomes. Most of the outcomes have been positive, but it is important to note that religion does not always have favorable effects on health. Next we briefly describe the potential negative effects and then move into a detailed description of the positive effects.

Religion can negatively impact health, because it has sometimes been used to justify hatred, aggression, and prejudice (Lee & Newberg, 2005). Religion can be judgmental, alienating, and exclusive. It also may cause the development of stressful social relations, and failure to conform to community norms may evoke open criticism by other congregation members or clergy. Feelings of religious guilt and the failure to meet religious expectations or cope with religious fears can contribute to illness

(Trenholm, Trent, & Compton, 1998). Parents' reliance on faith healing instead of appropriate medical care has led to negative outcomes and death for many children (Asser & Swan, 1998). Also, people may not participate in healthy behaviors because they believe that their health is in God's hands, so their behaviors will not change God's plan. This is referred to as a fatalistic attitude.

In terms of positive effects, there is an abundant amount of research that supports religion's constructive effect on health outcomes. A meta-analysis of 49 studies regarding religious coping found that positive forms of religious coping were related to lower levels of depression, anxiety, and distress, and negative forms of religious coping were associated with poorer psychological adjustment (Ano & Vasconcelles, 2005 as cited in Williams & Sternthal, 2007). Studies of adolescent behavior have found that higher levels of religious involvement are inversely related to alcohol and drug use, smoking, sexual activity, depressive symptoms, and suicide risk (Williams & Sternthal, 2007). These studies also found that spirituality and religion are positively related to immune system function. A review of 35 studies of the relationship between religion and health-related physiological processes found that both Judeo–Christian and Eastern religious practices were associated with reduced blood pressure and improved immune function; moreover, Zen, yoga, and meditation practices correlated with lower levels of stress hormones and cholesterol and better overall health outcomes in clinical patient populations (Seeman, Dubin, & Seeman, 2003 as cited in Williams & Sternthal, 2007).

Literature Review

In an important publication, Duke University researchers Harold Koenig and colleagues Michael McCullough and David Larson (2000) have systematically reviewed much of the research on religion and health. This lengthy and detailed review of hundreds of studies focuses on scholarship from refereed journals. In sum, the review demonstrates that the majority of published research is consistent with the notion that religious practices or religious involvement are associated with beneficial outcomes in mental and physical health (Johnson, Tompkins, & Webb, 2008). These outcome categories include hypertension, mortality, depression, alcohol use or abuse, drug use or abuse, and suicide. Reviews of additional social science research also confirm that religious commitment and involvement in religious practices are significantly linked to reductions not only in delinquency among youth and adolescent populations but also in criminality among adult populations. The following is a summary of the findings from an extensive literature review conducted by Johnson, Tompkins, and Webb (2008). This information is reprinted with permission from the Baylor Institute for Studies of Religion.

Hypertension

Hypertension, which afflicts 50 million Americans, is defined as a sustained or chronic elevation in blood pressure. It is the most common of cardiovascular disorders and affects about 20% of the adult population. Though there is strong evidence that pharmacologic treatment can lower blood pressure, there remains concern about the adverse side effects of such treatments. For this reason, social epidemiologists are interested in the effects of socioenvironmental determinants of blood pressure. Among the factors shown to correlate with hypertension is religion. In recent years, epidemiological studies have found that individuals who report higher levels of religious activities tend to have lower blood pressure. Johnson, Tompkins, and Webb's (2008) review of the research indicates that 76% of the studies found that religious activities or involvement tend to be linked with reduced levels of hypertension (see Table 4).

Mortality

A substantial body of research reveals an association between intensity of participation in religious activities and greater longevity. Studies reviewed for the report done by Johnson, Tompkins, and Webb (2008) examined the association between degree of religious involvement and survival (see Table 4). Involvement in a religious community is consistently related to lower mortality and longer life spans. Johnson, Tompkins, and Webb's (2008) review of this literature revealed that 75% of these published studies conclude that higher levels of religious involvement have a sizable

TABLE 4	Results of Religion and Health Outcomes Studies						
	Hypertension	Mortality	Depression	Suicide	Sexual Behavior	Alcohol Use	Drug Use	Delinquency
Beneficial outcomes	76%	76%	67%	87%	97%	88%	91%	76%
NA/mixed outcomes	20%	21%	27%	14%	3%	10%	8%	17%
Harmful outcomes	4%	3%	7%	0%	0%	3%	2%	2%

The data represents the percentage of published studies that were reviewed.
Source: Johnson, B. R., Tompkins, R. B., and Webb, D. (2008). Reprinted with permission from The Baylor Institutes for Studies of Religion.

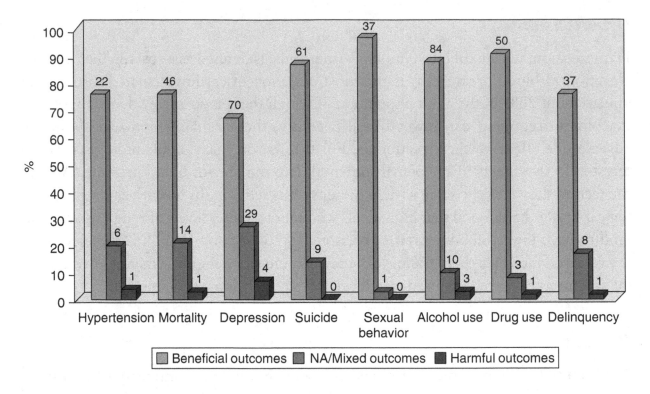

FIGURE 1 Research examining the relationship between religion and health outcomes (total of 498 studies reviewed).
Source: Johnson, B. R., Tompkins, R. B., and Webb, D. (2008). Reprinted with permission from The Baylor Institutes for Studies of Religion.

and consistent relationship with greater longevity (see Figure 1). This association was found to be independent of the effect of variables such as age, sex, race, education, and health. In a separate analysis, McCullough and colleagues conducted a meta-analytic review that incorporated data from more than 125,000 persons and similarly concluded that religious involvement had a significant and substantial association with increased length of life (McCullough, Hoyt, Larson, Koenig, & Thoresen, 2000 as cited in Johnson, Tompkins, and Webb, 2008). In fact, longitudinal research in a variety of different cohorts also has documented that frequent religious attendance is associated with a significant reduction in the risk of dying during study follow-up periods ranging from 5 to 28 years.

Depression

Depression is the most common of all mental disorders, and approximately 330 million people around the world suffer from it. People with depression also are at increased risk for use of hospital and medical services and for early death from physical causes. Over 100 studies that examined the religion–depression relationship were reviewed by Johnson, Tompkins, and Webb (2008), and they found that religious involvement tends to be associated with less depression in 68% of these articles (see Figure 1). People who are frequently involved in religious activities and who highly value their religious faith are at reduced risk for depression. Religious involvement seems to play an important role in helping people cope with the effects of stressful life circumstances. Prospective cohort studies and quasi-experimental and experimental research all suggest that religious or spiritual activities may lead to a reduction in depressive symptoms. These findings have been replicated across a number of large, well-designed studies and are consistent with much of the cross-sectional and prospective cohort research that has found less depression among more religious people (see Table 4).

Suicide

Suicide now ranks as the ninth leading cause of death in the United States. This is particularly alarming when one considers that suicides tend to be underestimated due to the fact that many of these deaths are coded as accidental. A substantial body of literature documents that religious involvement (e.g., measured by frequency of religious attendance, frequency of prayer, and degree of religious salience) is associated with less suicide, suicidal behavior, and suicidal ideation, as well as less tolerant attitudes toward suicide across a variety of samples from many nations. This consistent inverse association is found in studies using both group and individual-level data. In total, 87% of the studies reviewed on suicide found these beneficial outcomes (see Figure 1).

Promiscuous Sexual Behaviors

Out-of-wedlock pregnancy, often a result of sexual activity among adolescents, is largely responsible for the nearly 25% of children aged 6 years or younger who are below the federal poverty line. According to the Centers for Disease Control, unmarried motherhood is also associated with significantly higher infant mortality rates. Further, sexual promiscuity significantly increases the risk of contracting sexually transmitted diseases. Studies in the Johnson, Tompkins, and Webb (2008) review generally show that those who are religious are less likely to engage in premarital sex or extramarital affairs or to have multiple sexual partners (see Table 4). In fact, approximately 97% of the studies that were reviewed reported significant correlations between increased religious involvement and lower likelihood of promiscuous sexual behaviors (see Figure 1). None of the studies found that increased religious participation or commitment was linked to increases in promiscuous behavior.

Drug and Alcohol Use

The abuse of alcohol and illicit drugs ranks among the leading health and social concerns in the United States today. According to the National Institute on Drug Abuse, approximately 111 million persons in the United States are current alcohol users. About 32 million of these people engage in binge drinking, and 11 million Americans are heavy drinkers. Additionally, some 14 million Americans are current users of illicit drugs. Both chronic alcohol consumption and abuse of drugs are associated with increased risks of morbidity and mortality. Johnson, Tompkins, and Webb (2008) reviewed over 150 studies that examined the relationship between religiosity and drug use (n = 54) or alcohol use (n = 97) and abuse. The vast majority of these studies demonstrate that participation in religious activities is associated with less of a tendency to use or abuse drugs (87%) or alcohol (94%). These findings are consistent regardless of the population under study (i.e., children, adolescents, and adult populations) or whether the research was conducted prospectively or retrospectively (see Table 4). The greater a person's religious involvement, the less likely he or she will be to initiate alcohol or drug use or have problems with these substances if they are used (see Table 4). Only four of the studies that were reviewed reported a positive correlation between religious involvement and increased alcohol or drug use. Interestingly, these four tended to be some of the weaker studies with regard to methodological design and statistical analyses.

Delinquency

There is growing evidence that religious commitment and involvement helps protect youth from delinquent behavior and deviant activities. Recent evidence suggests that such effects persist even if there is not a strong prevailing social control against delinquent behavior in the surrounding community. There is mounting evidence that religious involvement may lower the risks of a broad range of delinquent behaviors, including both minor and serious forms of criminal behavior. There is also evidence that religious involvement has a cumulative effect throughout adolescence and thus may significantly lessen the risk of later adult criminality. Additionally, there is growing evidence that religion can be used as a tool to help prevent high-risk urban youths from engaging in delinquent behavior. Religious involvement may help adolescents learn prosocial behavior that emphasizes concern for other people's welfare. Such prosocial skills may give adolescents a greater sense of empathy toward others, which makes them less likely to commit acts that harm others. Similarly, when individuals become involved in deviant behavior, it is possible that participation in specific kinds of religious activities can help steer them back to a course of less deviant behavior and, more important, away from potential career criminal paths.

Research on adult samples is less common but tends to represent the same general pattern—that religion reduces criminal activity by adults. An important study by T. David Evans and colleagues found that religion, indicated by religious activities, reduced the likelihood of adult criminality as measured by a broad range of criminal acts (Johnson, Tompkins, and Webb, 2008). The relationship persisted even after secular controls were added to the model. Further, the finding did not depend on social or religious contexts. A small but growing body of literature focuses on the links between religion and family violence. Several recent studies found that regular religious attendance is inversely related to abuse among both men and women. As can be seen in Figure 1, 78% of these studies report reductions in delinquency and criminal acts to be associated with higher levels of religious activity and involvements.

Summary

In sum, Johnson, Tompkins, and Webb's (2008) review of the research on religious practices and health outcomes indicates that, in general, higher levels of religious involvement are associated with reduced hypertension, longer survival, less depression, lower level of drug and alcohol use and abuse, less promiscuous sexual behaviors, reduced likelihood of suicide, lower rates of delinquency among youth, and reduced criminal activity among adults. As can be seen in Figure 1, this substantial body of empirical evidence demonstrates a very clear picture: People who are most involved in religious activities tend to fare better with respect to important and yet diverse outcome factors. Thus, aided by appropriate documentation, religiosity is now beginning to be acknowledged as a key protective factor, reducing the deleterious effects of a number of harmful outcomes.

Well-Being

Well-being has been referred to as the positive side of mental health. Symptoms for well-being include happiness, joy, satisfaction, fulfillment, pleasure, contentment, and other indicators of a life that is full and complete (Koenig, H. G., McCullough, M. & Larson, D. B., 2001, as cited in Johnson, Tompkins, and Webb, 2008). Many studies have examined the relationship between religion and the promotion of beneficial outcomes (see Table 5). Many of these studies tend to be cross-sectional in design, but a significant number are important prospective cohort studies. As reported in Figure 2, Johnson, Tompkins, and Webb (2008) found that the vast majority of these

TABLE 5 Results of Religion and Well-Being Outcomes Studies				
	Well-Being	**Hope**	**Self Esteem**	**Educational Attainment**
Beneficial outcomes	81%	81%	68%	87%
NA/mixed outcomes	16%	16%	30%	10%
Harmful outcomes	4%	0%	5%	5%

The data represents the percentage of published studies that were reviewed.

Source: Johnson, B. R., Tompkins, R. B., and Webb, D. (2008). Reprinted with permission from The Baylor Institutes for Studies of Religion.

studies, some 81% of the 99 studies reviewed, reported some positive association between religious involvement and greater happiness, life satisfaction, morale, positive affect, or some other measure of well-being. The vast number of studies on religion and well-being have included younger and older populations as well as African Americans and Caucasians from various denominational affiliations. Only one study

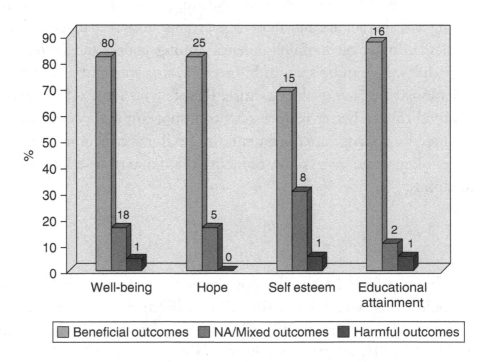

FIGURE 2 Research examining the relationship between religion and well-being outcomes (total of 171 studies reviewed). *Source:* Johnson, B. R., Tompkins, R. B., and Webb, D. (2008). Reprinted with permission from The Baylor Institutes for Studies of Religion.

found a negative correlation between religiosity and well-being, and this study was conducted in a small, nonrandom sample of college students.

Hope, Purpose, and Meaning in Life

Many religious traditions and beliefs have long promoted positive thinking and an optimistic outlook on life. Not surprisingly, researchers have examined the role religion may or may not play in instilling hope and meaning or a sense of purpose in life for adherents. Researchers have found, on the whole, a positive relationship between measures of religiosity and hope in varied clinical and nonclinical settings. In total, 25 of the 30 studies reviewed (83%) document that increases in religious involvement or commitment are associated with having hope or a sense of purpose or meaning in life (see Figure 2). Similarly, studies show that increasing religiousness also is associated with optimism as well as larger support networks, more social contacts, and greater satisfaction with support. In fact, 19 out of the 23 studies reviewed by Johnson, Tompkins, and Webb (2008) conclude that increases in religious involvement and commitment are associated with increased social support (see Table 5).

Self-Esteem

Most people would agree that contemporary American culture places too much significance on physical appearance and the idea that one's esteem is bolstered by their looks. Conversely, a common theme of various religious teachings is that physical appearance, for example, should not be the basis of self-esteem. Religion provides a basis for self-esteem that is not dependent upon individual accomplishments, relationships with others (e.g., who you know), or talent. In other words, a person's self-esteem is rooted in the individual's religious faith as well as the faith community as a whole. Of the studies Johnson, Tompkins, and Webb (2008) reviewed, 65% conclude that religious commitment and activities are related to increases in self-esteem (see Figure 2).

Educational Attainment

The literature on the role of religious practices or religiosity on educational attainment represents a relatively recent development in the research literature. In the last decade or so, a number of researchers have sought to determine if religion hampers or enhances educational attainment. Even though the development of a body of evidence is just beginning to emerge, some 84% of the studies reviewed concluded that religiosity or religious activities are positively correlated with improved educational attainment (see Figure 2).

Summary

To summarize, a review of the research on religious practices and various measures of well-being reveals that, in general, higher levels of religious involvement are associated with increased levels of well-being, hope, purpose, meaning in life, and educational attainment. As can be seen in Figure 2, this substantial body of evidence shows quite clearly that those who are most involved in religious activities tend to be better off on critical indicators of well-being. Just as the studies reviewed earlier (see Table 4 and Figure 1) document that religious commitment is a protective factor that buffers individuals from various harmful outcomes (e.g., hypertension, depression, suicide, delinquency, etc.), there is mounting empirical evidence to suggest that religious commitment is also a source for promoting or enhancing beneficial outcomes (e.g., well-being, purpose or meaning in life). This review of a large number of diverse studies leaves one with the observation that, in general, the effect of religion on physical and mental health outcomes is remarkably positive. These findings have led some religious health care practitioners to conclude that further collaboration between religious organizations and health services may be desirable. In an extensive literature review conducted by Johnson, Tompkins, and Webb (2008), Peterson (1983) noted that "we are convinced that a church with a vigorous life of worship, education, and personal support together with the promotion of wellness has more of an impact on the health of a community than an addition to the hospital or another doctor in town. Right now this is a hunch; in five years, we'll have the data to prove it" (p. 15). This enthusiasm notwithstanding, more research utilizing longitudinal and experimental designs is needed to further address important causal linkages between organic religion and myriad social and behavioral outcomes.

RELIGION AND MEDICAL DECISIONS

Medical decisions such as abortion, the use of birth control, allowance of blood transfusion, utilization of chemotherapy, advance directives, and euthanasia are difficult and life altering. Many people turn to religion to guide them with this process. Koenig (2004) stated that in a study of patients who visited the pulmonary disease clinic at the University of Pennsylvania, 66% of patients indicated that religious beliefs would influence their medical decisions should they become seriously ill, and 80% indicated that they would be receptive to inquiries about their religious beliefs. Religions provide guiding principles or direct rules about medical decisions. In this section we focus on two areas of medical decisions, beginning- and end-of-life decisions, but it is important to note that religion also affects many decisions between these two polar opposite life stages.

Beginning-of-Life Decisions

The beginning-of-life decisions, specifically abortion and birth control usage, have been a source of contradiction not only in religion, but in the United States legal system as well. Debates about whether abortion should be legal or not, when abortion can be performed, adolescents' access to birth control, and sex education in the schools are just a few of the legal and moral debates that continue today. Although laws regulate decisions about abortion and contraception use to some degree, so does religion.

Abortion

A central issue surrounding the morality of abortion is related to the core question about when life begins. Does it begin when the egg is fertilized, when the soul enters the fetus, when consciousness occurs, when the embryo becomes embedded in the uterine wall, when the fetus moves, or when the birth occurs? The answer to this question depends on whom you ask, and the answer one gives will shape his or her views on the morality of abortion. Some religions prohibit abortion on the basis of it being viewed as murder, bringing about bad karma, and it being an act of violence regardless of when or why the abortion takes place.

Many religions will approve of abortion under certain circumstances. These circumstances may include:

- The health of the mother being at risk if the pregnancy is continued
- The child may be born with a disability that will cause suffering
- In the case of rape or incest

Birth Control

With the exception of the emergency contraceptive, decisions surrounding the use of birth control center around the debate about the purpose of sexual intercourse. Is it for procreation or other reasons? The usage of birth control is prohibited for reasons such as men are not permitted to waste "their seed" and/or that it is a violation of the design built into the human race by God. Some religions permit the use of hormonal birth control methods such as pills, patches, injections, and implants, but they do not allow the use of birth control methods that block or destroy sperm, such as condoms and vasectomies. Condom use may be permitted to protect one from sexually transmitted infections, and birth control may be allowed when a woman needs a rest between pregnancies, when pregnancy poses a risk to the mother or baby, or when the man cannot financially support another child.

End-of-Life Decisions

In "The Parable of the Mustard Seed," the Buddha teaches a lesson that is valid for all cultures; human beings receive no exemption from mortality. Deep in the throes of grief after the death of her son, a woman seeks wisdom from the Buddha, who says that he does indeed have an answer to her queries. Before giving it, however, he insists that she must first collect a mustard seed from every house that has not been touched by death. She canvasses her entire community but fails to collect a single seed. Returning to the Buddha, she understands that, like all other living beings, we are destined to die.

Death is inevitable, but modern technology has changed the process through life-extending technologies. Organ transplantation, respirators, antibiotics, surgical procedures, and feeding tubes enable life to be prolonged. Other technologies, such as lethal injections, may hasten death. The decision to use these technologies is an individual choice. In some situations, the utilization of technology to prolong life may be contradictory to another fundamental human value, such as going against God's will. Human beings struggle with not overstepping these boundaries or playing God with life and death.

Decisions surrounding continuing treatment, discontinuing treatment, or hastening death are difficult and agonizing. As individuals and their families face these controversial questions and as many states consider revising their laws about end-of-life choices, religious traditions and values can offer guidance and insight, if not solutions, for some.

In the remainder of this section we cover the more controversial and general decisions, but there are many other end-of-life decisions to consider, such as burial versus cremation, timing of the burial, length of the mourning process, appropriate dress and behavior before and during the service and after the burial, and permission to conduct an autopsy.

Organ Donation

Organ donation is the removal of tissues of the human body from a person who has recently died or from a living donor for the purpose of transplanting or grafting them into other persons. Religion and organ donation is changing. Some religions that previously prohibited organ donation are now altering their views and seeing it as an act of compassion, but some continue to prohibit organ donation. Many of these latter religions prohibit organ donation because of their beliefs of life after death and resurrection. Some religions will consent to an organ donation if they are certain that it is for the health and welfare of the transplant recipient, but if the outcome is questionable, then the donation is not encouraged.

Euthanasia

Euthanasia is a Greek term that means "good death." Also called mercy killing, it is the act or practice of ending the life of an individual who is suffering from a terminal illness or an incurable condition by lethal injection or the suspension of extraordinary medical treatment. The person who is suffering from the painful and incurable disease or incapacitating physical disorder is painlessly put to death. Because there is no specific provision for it in most legal systems, it is usually regarded as either suicide (if performed by the patient) or murder (if performed by another person, which includes physician-assisted suicide).

Murder and suicide are against the belief systems of most religions, so in those systems it would be considered morally wrong (in some religions, such as Hinduism, suicide is acceptable if it is done by fasting because it is nonviolent). Other reasons for religious opposition is the concern for patients who may be in vulnerable positions because of their illness or their lack of social and economic resources. There is fear that patients who cannot afford expensive treatment, for example, will be pressured to accept euthanasia. There also is great concern about the moral nature of the doctor's professional self.

Karma and rebirth are other considerations for not supporting euthanasia. Karma is the total effect of a person's actions and conduct during the successive phases of the person's existence, regarded as determining the person's destiny. Karma extends through one's present life and all past and future lives as well. In Hinduism and Buddhism, human beings are believed to be captured in endless cycles of rebirth and reincarnation. In both traditions, all living creatures (humans, animals, plants, etc.) represent manifestations of the laws of karmic rebirth. To honor these laws, one must show great respect for the preservation of life and noninjury of conscious beings. Acts that are destructive of life are morally condemned by the principle of **ahimsa**, which is the conceptual equivalent of the Western principle of the sanctity of life. Religions may permit physicians to hasten death through legal injection but not by withholding care.

On the other side of the issue, most religions also consider acts of compassion and concern about the dignity of the dying person to be part of humanity. Concern for the welfare of others as one is dying is a consideration, because it can be seen as a sign of spiritual enlightenment. A person can decide to forego treatment to avoid imposing a heavy burden of caregiving on family or friends. He or she may also stop treatment to relieve loved ones of the emotional or economic distress of prolonged dying.

These two different perspectives lead to the dilemma of whether euthanasia is an act of compassion or murder. Religions answer the question differently, and debate exists within religions. This personal and difficult decision obviously needs to be made on an individual basis, but health care professionals should be aware of the conflicting perspectives and the rationale behind them.

Advance Directives and End-of-Life Care

Advance directives are legal documents that enable a person to convey his or her decisions about end-of-life care ahead of time. Advance directives include the **living will** and durable power of attorney, and they provide a way for patients to communicate their wishes to their family, friends, and health care professionals and to avoid confusion later in the event that the person becomes unable to do so.

A living will is a set of instructions that documents a person's wishes about medical care intended to sustain life. People can accept or refuse medical care. There are many types of life-sustaining care that should be taken into consideration when drafting a living will, such as:

- The use of life-sustaining equipment, such as dialysis and breathing machines
- Resuscitation if breathing or heartbeat stops
- Artificial hydration and nutrition (tube feeding)
- Withholding food and fluids
- Organ or tissue donation
- Comfort care

A durable power of attorney for health care is a document that names your health care proxy. The proxy is someone you trust to make health care decisions if you are unable to do so. Survey data suggest that about 20% of the United States population has advance directives, with significantly lower rates among Asian Americans, Hispanics, and blacks (Searight & Gafford, 2005). For example, about 40% of elderly white patients indicated that they have an advance directive, compared with only 16% of elderly blacks (Searight & Gafford, 2005). The low rates of advance directive completion among nonwhites may be because of distrust of the health care system, health care disparities, cultural perspectives on death and suffering, and family dynamics, such as parent–child relationships (Searight & Gafford, 2005). For example, whites may be concerned about dying patients undergoing needless suffering, and black physicians and patients are more likely to think of suffering as spiritually meaningful and being a display of religious faith (Searight & Gafford, 2005). Collectivist groups, such as Hispanics, may be reluctant to formally appoint a specific family member to be in charge because of concerns about isolating these persons or offending other relatives. Instead, a consensually-oriented decision-making approach appears to be more acceptable in this population. Among Asian Americans, aggressive treatment for elderly family members is likely to be frowned upon because family members should have love and respect for their parents and ancestors and because of their high respect for the elderly.

RITUALS

A ritual is a set of actions that usually are very structured and have a symbolic value or meaning. The performance of rituals are usually tied to religion or traditions, and their forms, purposes, and functions vary. These include compliance with religious obligations or ideals, satisfaction of spiritual or emotional needs of the practitioners, to ward off evil, to ensure the favor of a divine being, to maintain or restore health, demonstration of respect or submission, stating one's affiliation, obtaining social acceptance, or for the pleasure of the ritual itself. A ritual may be performed on certain occasions, at regular intervals, or at the discretion of individuals or communities. It may be performed by an individual, a small group, or the community, and it may occur in arbitrary places or specified locations. The rituals may be performed in private or public, or in front of specific people. The participants may be restricted to certain community members, with limitations related to age, gender, or type of activity (hunting and birthing rituals).

Rituals are related to numerous activities and events, such as birth, death, puberty, marriages, sporting events, club meetings, holidays, graduations, and presidential inaugurations, but rituals are not only related to major events. Handshaking, saying hello and good-bye, and taking your shoes off before entering a home are rituals. These actions and their symbolism are neither arbitrarily chosen by the performers nor dictated by logic or necessity, but they either are prescribed and imposed upon the performers by some external source or are inherited unconsciously from social traditions.

The biomedical system contains numerous rituals, including its own language filled with scientific terminology, jargon, and abbreviations (i.e., MRI, CAT scan). There are formal rules of behavior and communication, such as how physicians should be addressed and where the patient should sit. There are rituals such as hand washing, how to perform a physical examination, how to make a hospital bed, and how to document information in patient charts. The values and expectations include being on time for your appointment and adhering to the treatment regimen. People who are unaccustomed to this culture and these rituals can experience difficulty with them, and this includes maneuvering through the complex health insurance system, which is laden with unfamiliar rituals and rules. This can be particularly challenging if English is the patient's second language and if the patient did not come from a place with a similar system, such as socialized medicine.

In addition to rituals within health care systems, there are numerous rituals that are related to health. These rituals are discussed here to help prompt people who are working in health care to ask about, be sensitive to, and not be surprised about these key differences.

Objects as Rituals

There are numerous items that people wear to maintain their health. These may include amulets that may be worn on a necklace or strung around the neck, wrist, or waist. For example, people from Puerto Rico may place a bracelet on the wrist of a baby to ward off evil eye. In addition to being worn, amulets may be placed in the home. For example, items such as written documents, statues, crosses, or horseshoes may be hung on the home to protect the family's health as well as other factors. It is important to ask about removing these objects first because removal may cause great stress and concern for the person.

Shrines

For centuries people have described certain places as being holy or magic, as having a concentrated power, or having the presence of spirit. Ancient legends, historic records, and contemporary reports tell of extraordinary, even miraculous, happenings at these places. Different sacred sites have the power to heal the body, enlighten the mind, increase creativity, develop psychic abilities, and awaken the soul to a knowing of its true purpose in life. **Shrines** are located at some of these sacred sites. A shrine was originally a container, usually made of precious materials, but it has come to mean a holy or sacred place. Shrines may be enclosures within temples, home altars, and sacred burial places. Secular meanings have developed by association, and some of the associations are related to health and healing. People visit numerous shrines that represent health to maintain or restore health. Some examples of these shrines are Our Lady of La Leche, Our Lady of San Juan, and St. Peregrine. These shrines can be associated with healing for a specific disease or condition or with healing in general.

Animal Sacrifice

Animal sacrifice is not only practiced for food consumption but is believed to be needed for one to build and maintain a personal relationship with the spirit. It is also believed that it brings worshippers closer to their Creator or spirit and makes them aware of the spirit in them. Sacrifices are performed for events such as birth, marriage, and death. They are also used for healing. Animals are killed similarly to that of a kosher slaughter. Animals are cooked and eaten following all rituals, except in some healing and death rituals the animal is not eaten because it is believed that the sickness is passed into the dead animal.

Birthing Rituals

The birth of an infant is a life-altering event that is surrounded by many traditional and ancient rituals. These rituals are often related to protecting the health of the child, which includes protecting him or her from evil spirits. The rituals are related to events prior to, during, and after the birth. Because the rituals are so numerous, we have listed the general variations, but the list is not exhaustive.

Prior to birth:
- Food restrictions
- Wearing of amulets
- The fulfilling of food cravings
- Exposure to cold air
- Avoidance of loud noises or viewing certain types of people (i.e., deformed people)

During labor:
- How the placenta is discarded
- Silent birth (some cultures require that no words or sounds are spoken by the woman and/or family members)
- People present during labor
- Utilization of a midwife
- Place of delivery
- Medications used

After birth:
- Breastfeeding
- Amulets (placed on the baby, crib, or in the newborn's room)
- Female and male circumcision

- Baptism
- Animal sacrifice
- Cutting of child's lock of hair
- Bathing of baby
- Food restrictions
- When the naming of the baby occurs
- Rubbing the baby with oils or herbs
- Acceptance of postpartum depression
- Woman's and child's confinement period

Death Rituals

Responses to death vary widely across different cultures. Although some cultures may perform the same or similar rituals, they may have different meaning among the cultures. The rituals, in part, are related to beliefs about the meaning of life and life after death. Is death the end of existence or a transition to another life? Rituals play a role in behaviors, such as how people discuss death, respond to death, handle the deceased's body, the behaviors that occur at the funeral, and the mourning process.

Some general variations include:

- The method of disposing of the body
- Open versus closed casket
- The length of the mourning process and appropriate behavior
- Dress, including colors, at the funeral ceremony and afterwards
- Food restrictions or traditions
- Appropriate emotional responses
- The role of the family
- Use of prayer
- What is buried with the body
- Rituals engaged in before, during, and after the ceremony (i.e., burning of ghost money or candles, use of flowers)
- Animal sacrifice

CHAPTER SUMMARY

Religion plays a major role in the lives of Americans. It shapes our health behaviors and has been shown to have an overall positive effect on health behaviors. Religion also guides people when making difficult and sometimes life-altering decisions.

With technological advances, medical decisions can be complicated. Some people find the answers within their religion, but many people within religious sectors have differences in opinions. It is important for health care professionals not to assume someone's religion based upon their ethnicity and not to assume that everyone strictly adheres to the religious practices.

In this chapter we discussed how important religion is in the lives of Americans as well as the reasons why religion can impact health behaviors and decisions. We have discussed some reasons why people who are religious may have positive health habits and outcomes as well as the potential negative effects of religion. We ended the chapter with a discussion about rituals that are related to health. Many of those rituals are tied to religious beliefs, and health care professionals should make an effort to make provisions to adhere to these rituals.

REVIEW

1. Provide examples of how religion shapes health behaviors and the rationale behind them.
2. Explain some of the positive and negatives effects religion can have on health outcomes.
3. Provide examples of medical decisions that are made based on religion and the rationale behind them.
4. Explain issues that health care professionals should take into consideration related to beginning- and end-of-life transitions.

CASE STUDY

This case focuses on a Hasidic Judaism patient with cystic fibrosis and her family. Hasidic Judaism, sometimes referred to as Hasidic, refers to members of a Jewish religious movement founded in the eighteenth century in eastern Europe, which maintains that God's presence is in all of one's surroundings and that one should serve God in one's every deed and word. As you read through this story, pay particular attention to the multiple cultural and religious factors that influence this child's medical management.

Judy Cohen is 6 years old. Much of her life in the Hasidic Jewish community revolves around the neighborhood synagogue, her extended family, and their Hasidic Jewish community. She lives with her parents and four siblings in a house packed closely against her grandparents' house next door. The Cohen house is awash in the smells of Mrs. Cohen's cooking, the sounds of Yiddish prayer and conversation, and the laughter of children. The Cohens speak English fluently, but they prefer to speak their native language. They speak English only when necessary.

Judy's mother stays home to care for Judy and her four siblings, ages 3, 7, 9, and 10 years. Judy's father, Mr. Cohen, works for a family business. His job does not provide medical coverage, so the family is covered by Medicaid insurance. When the father is not working, he is usually praying, socializing, and consulting with the rabbi at the synagogue.

When she was 12 months old, Judy was diagnosed with cystic fibrosis (CF), which is an inherited chronic disease that affects the lungs and digestive system. At the time, the medical team that specialized in CF recommended that her siblings have sweat tests, which is the test used for diagnosing cystic fibrosis. Judy's parents declined because they believed that their children's health was in God's hands. Judy's condition was stable then, and she and her mother attended regularly scheduled appointments with the CF team. Judy's father, although he was concerned, did not usually come to Judy's appointments.

When Judy was 18 months old, she went to the clinic with an increased cough and weight loss. The team recommended that she be hospitalized. Judy's parents initially declined but agreed a week later after her cough had worsened.

At age 4 years, Judy again went into the hospital for pneumonia. Mr. and Mrs. Cohen reluctantly agreed to the hospital admission. When Judy appeared to be responding to the intravenous antibiotics, her parents convinced the medical team to allow Judy to complete her regimen of antibiotics at home. When she was home, the family did have their daughter complete the course of antibiotics that was recommended, but they refused visiting nurse services because they did not want the neighbors to know about Judy's illness.

When Mrs. Cohen became pregnant with her fifth child, the medical team strongly suggested that she go for genetic counseling and possibly testing. After discussing the issue with their rabbi, Mr. and Mrs. Cohen decided not to have genetic testing. Again, they believed that "whatever will be, will be" and that the unborn child's health was in God's hands.

Today, Judy went to the clinic for a routine follow-up appointment. This is her first visit since beginning school. Her respiratory status is good, but she's having more frequent stools. After being questioned, Mr. and Mrs. Cohen admit that they don't want the school to give Judy the required enzymes, which are recommended so that she can digest her food. They haven't told anyone at school that Judy has CF.

There are several issues to consider about this case:

- What are the various ways in which religious beliefs can affect the understanding of illness?
- How did the Cohen's Hasidic belief system impact Judy's treatment?
- What are some of the main tenets of Hasidic Judaism?
- Do you believe that the Cohens should have been required to have genetic testing done?
- Do you think the Cohens mishandled Judy's illness?

Source: Cross Cultural Health Care. (2003).

GLOSSARY TERMS

rituals	living will
euthanasia	shrines
karma	animal sacrifice
ahimsa	

REFERENCES

Adherents.com. (2005). *Largest religious groups in the United States of America.* Retrieved February 22, 2008, from www.adherents.com/rel_USA.html#religions

Advameg Inc. (2008). *Religion and Dietary Practices.* Retrieved on March 15, 2009 from http://www.faqs.org/nutrition/Pre-Sma/Religion-and-Dietary-Practices.html

Ano, G. G., & Vasconcelles, E. B. (2005). Religious coping and psychological adjustment to stress: A meta-analysis. *Journal of Clinical Psychology, 61,* 461–480.

Asser, S. M., & Swan, R. (1998). Child fatalities from religion-motivated medical neglect. *Pediatrics, 101,* 625–629.

Cottrell, R. R., Girvan, J. T., & McKenzie, J. F. (2006). *Principles and foundations of health promotion and education.* San Francisco: Pearson Benjamin Cummins.

Cross Cultural Health Care. (2003). *The case of Rivka Cohen.* Retrieved June 16, 2008, from http://support.mchtraining.net/national_cccE/case4/case.html

Dember, A. (2005, July 25). A prayer for health. *Boston Globe.* Retrieved February 3, 2008, from http://www.boston.com/news/globe/health_science/articles/2005/07/25/a_prayer_for_health/

Hamilton, S. R. (n.d.). American Society on Aging. *Studies show religious attendance brings added longevity.* Retrieved February 21, 2008, from www.asaging.org/at/at-226/religious.html

Johnson, B. R., Tompkins, R. B., & Webb, D. (2008). *Assessing the effectiveness of faith-based organizations: A review of the literature.* Waco, TX: Baylor University.

Koenig, H. G. (2004, December). Religion, spirituality, and medicine: Research findings and implications for clinical practice. *Southern Medical Journal, 97*(12), 1194–1200.

Koenig, H. G., McCullough, M. E., & Larson, D. B. (2000). *Handbook of religion and health*. New York: Oxford University Press.

Kosmin, B. A., Mayer, E., & Keysar, A. (2001). *American religious identification survey 2001*. Retrieved December 10, 2007, from www.gc.cuny.edu/faculty/research_studies/aris.pdf

Lee, B. Y., & Newberg, A. B. (2005). Religion and health: A review and critical analysis. *Zygon, 40,* 443–468.

McCullough, M. E., Hoyt, W. T., Larson, D. B., Koenig, H. G., & Thoresen, C. E. (2000). Religious involvement and mortality: A meta analytic review. *Health Psychology, 19,* 211–222.

McNicol, T. (1996, April 7). Where religion and medicine meet: The new faith in medicine. *USA Weekend.*

Miller, W. R., & Thoresen, C. E. (2003). Spirituality, religion, and health: An emerging research field. *American Psychologist, 58,* 24–35.

Peterson, B. (1983). Renewing the church's health ministries: Reflections on ten years' experience. *Journal of Religion and the Applied Behavioral Sciences, 17.*

Saad, L. (2003). *Religion is very important to majority of Americans*. Retrieved December 20, 2007, from http://www.gallup.com/poll/9853/Religion-Very-Important-Majority-Americans.aspx

Searight, H. R., & Gafford, J. (2005, February). Cultural diversity at the end of life: Issues and guidelines for family physicians. *American Family Physician*. Retrieved December 30, 2007, from http://www.aafp.org/afp/20050201/515.html

Seeman, T. E., Dubin L. F., & Seeman, M. (2003). Religiosity/spirituality and health. A critical review of the evidence for biological pathways. *American Psychologist, 58,* 53–63.

Strawbridge, W. J., Shema, S. J., Cohen, R. D. (2001). Religious attendance increases survival by improving and maintaining good health behaviors, mental health, and social relationships. *Annals of Behavioral Medicine, 23,* 68–74.

Trenholm, P., Trent, J., & Compton, W. C. (1998). Negative religious conflict as a predictor of panic disorder. *Journal of Clinical Psychology, 54,* 59–65.

Wallace, J. M., Jr., & Forman, T. A. (1998). Religion's role in promoting health and reducing risk among American youth. *Health Education and Behavior, 25,* 721–741.

Williams, D. R., & Sternthal, M. J. (2007). Spirituality, religion and health: Evidence and research directions. *The Medical Journal of Australia*. Retrieved February 22, 2008, from http://www.mja.com.au/public/issues/186_10_210507/wil11060_fm.html

Winseman, A. L. (2005). *Religion "very important" to most Americans*. Retrieved December 20, 2007, from http://www.gallup.com/poll/20539/Religion-Very-Important-Most-Americans.aspx

PHOTO CREDITS

Chapter Opener   ,   © Janetto/Dreamstime.com

Unless otherwise indicated, all photographs and illustrations are under copyright of Jones and Bartlett Publishers, LLC, or have been provided by the author(s).

Hispanic and Latino American Populations

Her days are slow, days of grinding dried snake into powder, of crushing wild bees to mix with white wine. And the townspeople come, hoping to be touched by her ointments, her hands, her prayers, her eyes. She listens to their stories, and she listens to the desert, always to the desert.

—Pat Mora

Preservation of one's own culture does not require contempt or disrespect for other cultures.

—Cesar Chavez

KEY CONCEPTS

- Empacho
- Santeria
- Espiritismo
- Orishas

CHAPTER OBJECTIVES

1. Provide an overview of the social and economic circumstances of Hispanics in the United States.
2. Provide an overview of Hispanic beliefs about the causes of illness.
3. Describe at least three unique diseases among Hispanics.
4. Describe Hispanics' health risk behaviors and common illnesses.
5. List at least six tips for working with Hispanic populations.

An unresolved debate is the use of the terms "Hispanic" and "Latino." Which is the politically correct term? Is there a difference? It depends on whom you ask. Some say it is a personal preference, and others argue that there are differences related to places of origin.

The argument against using the term "Hispanic" is that this term is based upon the Spanish word "hispano," which literally means "from Spain." Some people believe that the term "Hispanic" is incorrect because Hispanic American heritage goes further than just Spain. The Hispanic market is composed of people who come from as many as 20 different countries. The reason Hispanics speak Spanish is because of Spain's influence in history. Spaniards brought not only their language but also religion to different regions of the world. Most Hispanics are Catholic or Christian, and similar religions tend to translate into similar values. Therefore, the argument against this term is that Hispanics speak Spanish, but they are not all from Spain. What they do share is language and values.

The term "Latino" includes everyone from Latin America and therefore includes people from Brazil (who speak Portuguese). A commonality of Hispanics and Latinos is that they speak Spanish, yet the people in the largest country in South America do not speak Spanish. Brazil was colonized by Portugal and not by Spain, thus its inhabitants are of Portuguese descent. Brazilians speak Portuguese, which makes them Latin but not Hispanic. "Latino" also is not a genuine Spanish word, unlike "Hispanic." Some people believe that the term "Latino" is more derogatory than the word "Hispanic", because Latino refers to the Latin language of the Romans who conquered Spain.

In the United States, the term "Hispanic" gained acceptance after it was picked up by the government and used in forms and census to identify people with Spanish heritage. Hispanic is not a race but an ethnic distinction because Hispanics come from a variety of geographic regions and are not genetically related. The ethnic label "Hispanic" was the result of the desire to quantify the Spanish-speaking population for the U.S. Census Bureau. For years, the U.S. Census Bureau considered Hispanic to be a race. They changed that definition before the 1970 census, and in 1977 the U.S. racial classifications became American Indian, Alaskan Native, Asian or Pacific Islander, Black, and White. The government added ethnic classifications of "Hispanic Origin" and "Not of Hispanic Origin."

The term "Chicano" is a more exclusive term used solely in reference to people of Mexican descent and is used to describe only an American with Mexican heritage (Mexican American). Originally, "Chicano," which is an abbreviation of the word "Mexicano," was used by non-Hispanics as a racial slur. Around the 1950s, however, Mexican Americans adopted the word "Chicano." The word changed from a derogative to a source of confidence for Mexican Americans. Although the term "Chicano" is an old word, many elderly Hispanics of Mexican descent do not like it because the term had been used, long ago, as derogatory reference to Mexican people.

If you are trying to figure out how to refer to a group of people, the one concept on which most Hispanics and Latinos agree is that they prefer to be called by their immediate ethnic group. If you are referring to Mexican Americans, use that phrase instead of Hispanic or Latino. Because most Hispanics or Latinos in the United States are from Mexico and not Latin America, and "Hispanic" is the term more commonly used by the U.S. government, we will use the term "Hispanic" throughout this chapter unless the data source identifies the ethnic group differently.

HISTORY OF HISPANICS IN THE UNITED STATES

People often hold the misconception that Hispanics are a recent group to migrate to the United States. This erroneous perception is mostly due to the media attention given to Hispanic groups in the 1980s, when the census revealed that Hispanics were the fastest growing group in the United States. The reality is that Hispanics have a long history in the United States.

Mexican Americans were once concentrated in the states that formerly belonged to Mexico, primarily California, Arizona, New Mexico, Texas, and Colorado. Racial discrimination led to lynchings of Mexicans and Mexican Americans in the Southwest, which has long been overlooked in American history. Between 1848 and 1928, mobs lynched at least 597 Mexicans (Carigan, 2003). Mexicans were lynched at a rate of 27.4 per 100,000 of population between 1880 and 1930. This statistic is second only to that of the African American community during that period, which suffered an average of 37.1 per 100,000 population (Carigan, 2003). The Texas Rangers were an organized group known to brutally repress the Mexican American population in Texas. Historians estimate that hundreds, perhaps even thousands, of Mexicans and Mexican Americans were killed by the Texas Rangers (Carigan, 2003). Anti-Mexican mob violence and intimidation resulted in Mexicans being displaced from their lands, denied access to natural resources, and becoming politically disenfranchised. Mexican American identity has changed drastically over time. They have campaigned for voting rights, stood against educational and employment discrimination, and stood for economic and social advancement.

On the other side of the continent, many Cubans have desired to come to the United States because living in a socialist country under the dictatorship of Fidel and Raúl Castro has brought about inequality. These individuals seek more political freedom, a democratic form of government, and/or to live in a land of capitalism where there are fewer restrictions and more opportunities. To get to the United States, many Cubans turn to smugglers who charge high fees, or they may resort to making homemade boats and even rafts for the 90-mile journey from Cuba to Florida. Others fly to countries such as Mexico to enter the United States via that country. Not all are successful, and children and adults sometimes end up losing their lives in their efforts to reach American soil. In 1994 there was a wave of over 30,000 Cubans who tried to enter the United States. This caused the United States and Cuban governments to work out an immigration agreement. Cuba agreed to do a better job of patrolling their seas to prevent Cubans from leaving their country. If they were not successful in reaching Florida soil and were intercepted by the U.S. Coast Guard, which is responsible for overseeing America's seas and shores, the Cuban government also agreed that there would be no reprisal against the Cubans who were returned. However, in reality Cubans who are returned usually face some kind of punishment by the Cuban government, like imprisonment. The general rule is that when an individual reaches American soil, not American waters, they are allowed to remain in the United States. In 1994 the United States set a quota of 20,000 immigrant visas annually for Cubans, of which 5,000 come from a lottery system. One of the biggest incentives is that in a period of five years or less, Cuban immigrants may gain eligibility to apply for United States citizenship. However, there are some requirements as to who can apply for the lottery. The screening process is conducted to ensure that the prospective immigrants will not become a burden to the United States government. Lottery winners are entitled to bring their spouse and children younger than 21 years of age.

Puerto Rico is a territory of the United States. At the end of the Spanish-American War in 1898, the United States acquired Puerto Rico and has retained sovereignty ever since, and a large influx of Puerto Rican workers to the United States began. The Jones-Shafroth Act in 1917 made the move easier, because the U.S. Congress declared that all Puerto Ricans are U.S. citizens, enabling a migration free from all immigration barriers.

HISPANICS IN THE UNITED STATES

Hispanics are the fastest-growing major population group in the United States (New Century Foundation, 2006). According to the U.S. Census Bureau, they will account for one in four of the American population by 2050 (New Century Foundation, 2006). According to the 2006 U.S. Census Bureau population estimate, there are roughly 44.3 million Hispanics living in the United States (see Figure 1). This group represents almost 15% of the United States total population, and they experienced a 61% increase from 1990 to 2000 (U.S. Census Bureau, 2004). In 2004, among Hispanic

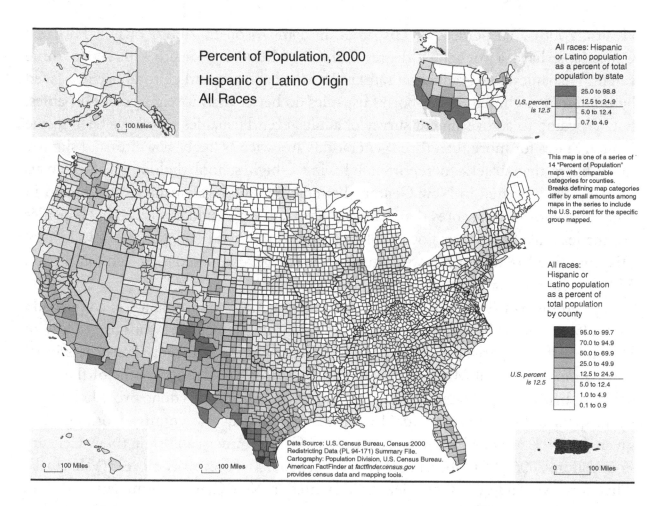

FIGURE 1 Percentage of population: Hispanic or Latino Origin, 2000.
Source: U.S. Census Bureau, Population Division (2008), http://www.census.gov/main/www/citation.html.

subgroups, Mexicans rank as the largest at 66%. The other 34% includes Central and South Americans (13%), Puerto Ricans (9.4%), and Cubans (3.9%); the remaining 7.5% are people of other Hispanic origins (U.S. Census Bureau, 2004).

States with the largest Hispanic populations are California (13 million) and Texas (8 million) (Office of Minority Health, 2008). The Hispanic population is younger than any other group. In 2000 the median age for Hispanics was 26.0 years, compared to 35.4 years for the total population (U.S. Census Bureau, 2004). Among Hispanics, Mexicans have the largest proportion of people under age 18 years (36%) (Office of Minority Health, 2008).

According to a 2006 U.S. Census Bureau report, 55% of Hispanics, in comparison to 85% of non-Hispanic Caucasians, have a high school diploma (Office of Minority

Health, 2008). Ten percent of Hispanics, in comparison to 24.6% of non-Hispanic Caucasians, have a bachelor's degree (Office of Minority Health, 2008). To some extent, Hispanics' low graduation rates reflect the language and cultural barriers faced by immigrants. United States–born Hispanics do better than foreign-born Hispanics, but according to a government survey of adults, even Hispanics who have been in the United States for more than three generations are twice as likely as whites and slightly more likely than blacks to report not having a high school diploma (U.S. Census Bureau, 2006 as cited in New Century Foundation, 2006). Hispanics who remain in school have lower test scores than whites (New Century Foundation, 2006). Hispanics are the least likely of the major population groups to attend college. In 2003, 28% of Hispanics aged 18 to 24 years were enrolled in college, compared to 38% of blacks and 52% of whites (New Century Foundation, 2006).

According to a 2004 U.S. Census Bureau report, 24.6% of Hispanics, in comparison to 13.4% of non-Hispanic Caucasians, work within service occupations; 16.8% of Hispanics, in comparison to 39.1% of Caucasians, work in managerial or professional occupations (Office of Minority Health, 2008). Casual day labor is some of the most difficult, badly compensated work in the United States, and it is done overwhelmingly by Hispanics. Of the estimated 118,000 day laborers in the country working on a given day, 59% are of Mexican and 28% are of Central American origin (New Century Foundation, 2006). Day laborers can earn about $15,000 if they work all year (Valenzuela, Theodore, Meléndez, & Gonzalez, 2006 as cited in New Century Foundation, 2006).

According to a 2004 study, 22.5% of Hispanics, in comparison to 8.2% of non-Hispanic Caucasians, were living at the poverty level (Office of Minority Health, 2008). Hispanics represented 14% of the total U.S. population but constituted 21.8% of the population living in poverty (Office of Minority Health, 2008). Fifty percent of Hispanic households use some form of welfare, which is the highest rate of any major population group (New Century Foundation, 2006).

It is significant to note that Hispanics have the highest health uninsured rates of any racial or ethnic group within the United States. In 2004 the Centers for Disease Control and Prevention reported that private insurance coverage among Hispanic subgroups varied as follows: 39.1% of Mexicans, 47.3% of Puerto Ricans, 57.9% of Cubans, and 45.1% of other Hispanic and Latino groups. Those without health insurance coverage varied among Hispanic subgroups: 37.6% of Mexicans, 20.4% of Puerto Ricans, 22.8% of Cubans, and 32.3% of other Hispanic or Latino groups (Office of Minority Health, 2008).

With regard to crime, Hispanics are 3.3 times more likely to be in prison than whites; they are 4.2 times more likely to be in prison for murder and 5.8 times more likely to be in prison for felony drug crimes (New Century Foundation, 2006). Young Hispanics are 19 times more likely than young whites (and slightly more likely than young blacks) to be in youth gangs (New Century Foundation, 2006). Hispanic incarceration rates are especially high for violent crimes, motor vehicle theft, and drug offenses (New Century Foundation, 2006). High drug offense rates reflect Mexico's role as an important source of drugs; 92% of the cocaine sold in the United States comes through Mexico, and it is our largest supplier of marijuana and second largest supplier of heroin (Placido, 2005 as cited in New Century Foundation, 2006). Hispanics are 2.9 times more likely to die from homicide than whites and are 3.4 times more likely than whites to die from gunshot wounds (New Century Foundation, 2006).

After they come to the United States, Mexicans retain longer and stronger attachments to their country of origin than do immigrants who have come greater distances. Thirty-three percent of citizens of Hispanic origin consider themselves to be Americans first (New Century Foundation, 2006). The rest consider themselves to be Hispanic/ Latino or their former nationality first (New Century Foundation, 2006). Only 34% of Mexicans who are eligible for U.S. citizenship actually become Americans, the lowest figure for any national group (González, 2006 as cited in New Century Foundation, 2006). When they become citizens, Hispanics remain emotionally attached to their countries of origin.

With regard to their social structure, Hispanics tend to view the family as a primary source of support. Families are very close, broadly defined, and emotionally and financially supportive. Family often includes non-blood-related persons. Some non-Hispanics interpret these family characteristics as overinvolvement or dependence. The eldest male is typically the authority figure, and gender roles are traditional. Important decisions are made by the whole family, not the individual, because they tend to have a collectivist type of social structure. Elders should be shown respect, and they are viewed as authority figures within the community. Elders often provide child care for the grandchildren (Rhode Island Department of Health, n.d.).

Hispanics place higher value on individuals as opposed to institutions. They tend to trust and cooperate with individuals they know personally, and many dislike impersonal and formal structures. Hispanic customers may identify a health care worker by name rather than by job title or institution. In a professional situation, many Hispanics expect to be addressed formally (e.g., Mrs. Martinez), but also personally (e.g., How are your children?) (Rhode Island Department of Health, n.d.). The length of the social interaction is often viewed to be less important than the quality (Rhode Island Department of Health, n.d.).

With regard to communication, Hispanics tend to avoid conflict and criticism, because they prefer smooth social relations based on politeness and respect (Rhode Island Department of Health, n.d.). Overt disagreement is not considered to be appropriate behavior. Many Hispanics are characterized by warm, friendly, and affectionate relationships. Personal space is close and frequently shared with family members or close friends. Many Hispanics, particularly if they were not raised in the United States, may avoid direct eye contact with authority figures or in awkward situations. Many will nod affirmatively but not necessarily mean agreement. Silence may mean failure to understand and embarrassment about asking or disagreeing.

Modesty and privacy are important; therefore, health issues that are stigmatized should be discussed through an interpreter and not family members. Legally, family members should not be used as interpreters, but when one is used as interpreter, if the issue is personal, try to use a family member of the same gender. Sexuality issues are hard to discuss. Often the word for sex (*sexo*) is not even used; *tener relaciones* (to have relations) is used instead (Rhode Island Department of Health, n.d.).

BELIEFS ABOUT CAUSES OF HEALTH AND ILLNESS

Health is generally viewed by Hispanics as being and looking clean, being able to rest and sleep well, feeling good and happy, and having the ability to perform in one's expected role as mother, father, worker, etc. (Rhode Island Department of Health, n.d.). In Puerto Rico, the phrase *llenitos y limpios* (clean and not too thin) is used (Rhode Island Department of Health, n.d.). A person's well-being depends upon a balance in emotional, physical, and social factors, and when they are not in balance, illness occurs. Some attribute physical illness to *los nervios*, believing that illness results from having experienced a strong emotional state. Thus, they try to prevent illness by avoiding intense rage, sadness, and other emotions (Rhode Island Department of Health, n.d.). Depression is not talked about openly.

There are many unique illnesses that Hispanics diagnose that are not part of the Western medical system. Some common illnesses and their causes are listed in Table 1.

Hispanic cultures view illnesses, treatments, and foods as having hot or cold properties, although how these are ascribed may vary by country. Some cultures consider health to be the product of balance among four body humours (blood and yellow bile are hot, phlegm and black bile are cold). One would balance a hot illness with cold medications and foods, etc. This might result in not following a doctor's advice to drink lots of fluids for a common cold, if one believes such drinks add more coldness to the body. Instead, hot liquids (tea, soup, broth) could be recommended

TABLE 1 Common Illnesses in the Hispanic Culture and Their Characteristics and Causes

Illness	Characteristics	Cause(s)
Ataque de nervios (nervous attack)	Intense and brief expression of shock, anxiety, or sadness	Believed to be caused by family conflict or anger (e.g., screaming, kicking)
Bilis (bile rage)	Vomiting, diarrhea, headaches, dizziness, migraine, nightmares, loss of appetite, inability to urinate; brought on by livid rage and revenge fantasies	Believed to stem from bile pouring into bloodstream in response to strong emotion
Caida de la mollera (fallen fontanel)	Childhood condition characterized by irritability and diarrhea	Believed to be caused by abrupt withdrawal from the mother's breast
Empacho	Lack of appetite, stomachache, diarrhea, vomiting, constipation, cramps, or vomiting	Caused by poorly digested or uncooked food or overeating
Fatiga (shortness of breath or fatigue)	Asthma symptoms (especially in Puerto Rican usage) and fatigue	
Frio de la matriz (frozen womb)	Pelvic congestion and decreased libido believed to be caused by insufficient rest after childbirth	
Mal aire (bad air)	Cold air that is believed to cause respiratory infections and earaches	
Mal de ojo (evil eye)	Vomiting, fever, crying, restlessness	A hex cast on children, sometimes unconsciously, that is believed to be caused by the admiring gaze of someone more powerful
Mal puesto (sorcery)	Unnatural illness that is not easily explained	
Pasmo (cold or frozen face; lockjaw)	Temporary paralysis of the face or limbs or spasm of voluntary muscle	Exposure to cold air when body is overheated; caused by a sudden hot–cold imbalance
Susto (fright)	Anorexia, insomnia, hallucinations, depression, weakness, painful sensations	Traumatic experiences or shock

Sources: Adapted from Rhode Island Department of Health. (n.d.) and Juckett. (2005).

TABLE 2 Hot versus Cold Latino Diagnoses

Cold Conditions
- Cancer
- Colic
- Empacho (indigestion)
- Frio de la matriz (frozen womb)
- Headache
- Menstrual cramps
- Pneumonia
- Upper respiratory infections

Hot Conditions
- Bilis (bile, rage)
- Diabetes mellitus
- Gastroesophageal reflux or peptic ulcer
- Hypertension
- Mal de ojo (evil eye)
- Pregnancy
- Sore throat or infection
- Susto (soul loss)

Source: Juckett. (2005).

(Rhode Island Department of Health, n.d.). In Table 2 a list of hot and cold illnesses are provided.

Susto is illness that occurs from a frightful experience, and it is similar to anxiety in Western medicine. Symptoms include withdrawal from social interactions, listlessness, not sleeping well, and loss of appetite. Most people who believe in susto deem that anyone can get it; both adults and children can be affected. The soul leaves the body due to a frightening experience, and the body becomes susceptible to illness and disharmony. It can be caused by events such as the sudden, unexpected barking of a dog, tripping over an unnoticed object, having a nighttime encounter with a ghost who keeps your spirit from finding its way back into your body before you wake, or being in a social situation that causes you to have fear or anger, for example.

Mal de ojo, sometimes called "evil eye," is the illness that is a result of an envious glance from another individual. It mostly affects children. It has been defined as a hex caused by a gaze from a more powerful or stronger person looking at a weaker person (usually an infant or child but sometimes a woman). It may be someone from outside the family looking at the child with envy, or a stare from a powerful person who is admiring the child. It is usually caused inadvertently. Those affected may suffer symptoms including headaches, high fever, diarrhea, not sleeping well, increased fussiness, and weeping. It is not fully known what diseases in Western medicine correlate with mal de ojo; however, in severe cases the symptoms are similar to those of sepsis (the presence of pathogenic organisms or their toxins in the blood or tissues) and should warrant a medical evaluation. Cases of mal de ojo with frequent crying and no other symptoms are thought to be similar to colic.

Empacho describes stomach pains and cramps that are believed to be caused by a ball of food clinging to the stomach due to altered eating habits, eating spoiled food, overeating, and swallowing chewing gum. The disease state of empacho has often been defined as a perceived stomach or intestinal blockage. In most cases, it is not an actual obstruction but rather indigestion or gastroenteritis. Abdominal pain and bloating are symptoms of empacho. Some Hispanic populations also add nausea, vomiting, diarrhea, and lethargy as symptoms that may occur in some cases. It tends to occur more in young children, but people of all ages are susceptible. Empacho is considered to be a cold illness. Folk medicines used to treat empacho include greta (lead monoxide) and azarcón (lead tetroxide), which are dangerous and can cause lead poisoning. There have been case reports of deaths from these substances.

The ideology about illness and health is rooted in the fabric of the culture, and it is the fundamental element of traditional values. Even though the Mexican American culture utilizes Western medicine, they rely primarily on folk practitioners to treat traditional illnesses.

HEALING TRADITIONS

Some treatments for illness are provided by family members, but illness also may be treated by nonfamily members. Hispanic healing traditions include curanderismo in Mexico and much of Latin America, **Santeria** in Brazil and Cuba, and **Espiritismo** in Puerto Rico. Most of these traditions distinguish natural illnesses from supernatural illnesses. The healing traditions include a variety of methods as shown in Table 3.

Curanderos

A curandero (or curandera for a female) is a traditional folk healer or shaman who is dedicated to curing physical and/or spiritual illnesses. The curandero is often a

TABLE 3 Traditional Latino Diagnoses and Their Related Treatment Methods

Diagnosis	Traditional Treatment
Ataque de nervios (nervous attack)	No immediate treatment other than calming the patient
Bilis (bile, rage)	Herbs, including wormwood
Caida de la mollera (fallen fontanel)	Holding the child upside down or pushing up on the hard palate
Empacho (indigestion or blockage)	Treated by massaging the stomach and drinking purgative tea, or by azarcón or greta, medicines that have been implicated in some cases of lead poisoning
Fatiga (shortness of breath or fatigue)	Herbal treatments, including eucalyptus and mullein (gordolobo), steam inhalation
Frio de la matriz (frozen womb)	Damiana tea, rest
Mal aire (bad air)	Steam baths, hot compresses, stimulating herbal teas
Mal de ojo (evil eye)	The hex can be broken if the person responsible for the hex touches the child or if a healer passes an egg over the child's body
Mal puesto (sorcery)	Magic
Pasmo (cold or frozen face; lockjaw)	Massage
Susto (fright-induced soul loss)	Treatment may include a barrida (spiritualistic cleansing by sweeping the body with eggs, lemons, and bay leaves), herb tea, prayer; repeated until the patient improves

Source: Adapted from Juckett. (2005).

respected member of the community and is highly religious and spiritual. In Spanish the word curandero means healer. These healers often use herbs and other natural remedies to cure illnesses, but their primary method of healing is the supernatural because they believe that the cause of many illnesses are lost malevolent spirits, a lesson from God, or a curse. There are different types of curanderos/curanderas. Curanderos (traditional healers) use verbal charms or spells to produce a magic effect and herbs, sobadores practice manipulation, parteras are midwives, and abuelas (literally "grandmothers," although they are not necessarily related to the patient) provide initial care. Yerberos are primarily herbalists, and hueseros and sabaderos are bone/muscle therapists who emphasize physical ailments.

Curanderos treat ailments such as espanto (Spanish for shock), empacho (Spanish for surfeit, which means to feed in excess), susto (fright illness), mal aire (literally bad air), and mal de ojo (evil eye) with religious rituals, ceremonial cleansing, and prayers. Often curanderos contact certain spirits to aid them in their healing work. The remedies of the curanderos are often helpful but sometimes have negative effects on the health of their patients. For example, a common method of healing mollera caída, a condition in which an infant's fontanelle has sunken, is to hold the infant's feet with its head down and perform a ceremonial ritual. Some other traditional treatments, such as azarcón and greta (lead salts) and azogue (mercury), are also harmful because of their lead and mercury content. Other remedies are harmless. For example, a common method of treating mal de ojo (evil eye) is to rub an egg over the body of the sick to draw out the evil spirit that is causing the disease.

These methods of treating health problems often lead to conflict with modern medicine because doctors reject the curandero's healing as superstitious and worthless. As a result, curanderos have often experienced discrimination and been likened to witches by the medical profession and non-Hispanic communities. However, these remedies are important to the Hispanic culture, and disbelief may lead to insult, conflict, or the rejection of modern medicine. Other medical doctors, recognizing the benefits of the spiritual and emotional healing offered by curanderos, have begun to work in conjunction with them, supporting their use of rituals and ceremonies in the healing of the sick while insisting that patients receive modern medical attention as well.

Santeria

Santeria, also known as the "Way of the Saints," is an Afro-Caribbean religion based on beliefs of the Yoruba people in Nigeria, Africa. The traditions have been influenced by Roman Catholic beliefs. Santeria incorporates elements of several faiths and is therefore called a syncretic religion. It has grown beyond its Yoruba and Catholic origins to become a religion in its own right and a powerful symbol of the religious creativity of Afro-Cuban culture. For a long time, Santeria was a secretive underground religion, but it is becoming increasingly visible in the Americas. It was once considered to be a ghetto religion practiced only by the Caribbean poor and uneducated, but now Santeria has a growing following among middle-class professionals and other ethnic groups, such as whites, blacks, and Asian Americans.

Because of the history of secrecy, it is not known how many people follow Santeria. There is no central organization for this religion, and it is practiced in private, which makes it more difficult to determine the number of followers. There are no scriptures for this religion, and it is taught through word of mouth. The Santeria tradition is composed of a hierarchical structure according to priesthood level and authority.

Santeria practices include animal offerings, dance, and appeals for assistance sung to the **orishas**, which resemble the Catholic saints and are spirits that reflect one of the manifestations of Olodumare (God). Animal sacrifice also is a part of Santeria and is very controversial. Followers of Santeria point out that ritual slaughter is conducted in a safe and humane manner by the priests who are charged with the task. Furthermore, the animal is cooked and eaten afterwards by the community. In fact, chickens, a staple food of many African-descended and Creole cultures, are the most common sacrifice; the chicken's blood is offered to the orisha, and the meat is consumed by all.

Followers believe that orishas will help them in life, if they carry out the appropriate rituals, and enable them to achieve the destiny that God planned for them before they were born. This is very much a mutual relationship, because the orishas need to be worshipped by human beings if they are to continue to exist. In a Supreme Court case in 1993, Justice Kennedy said in his decision that:

> The Santeria faith teaches that every individual has a destiny from God, a destiny fulfilled with the aid and energy of the orishas. The basis of the Santeria religion is the nurture of a personal relation with the orishas, and one of the principal forms of devotion is an animal sacrifice. According to Santeria teaching, the orishas are powerful but not immortal. They depend for survival on the sacrifice. (*Church of Likumi Babalu Aye v. City of Hialeah*, 508 U.S. 520 (1993))

Drum music and dancing are a form of prayer and will sometimes induce a trance state in an initiated priest, who becomes possessed and will channel the orisha.

Espiritismo

Espiritismo is the Spanish word for "Spiritism." It is the belief in Latin America and the Caribbean that good and evil spirits can affect human life, such as one's health and luck. An opinion, doctrine, or principle (tenet) of Espiritismo is the belief in a supreme God who is the omnipotent creator of the universe. There also is a belief in a spirit world inhabited by discarnate spiritual beings who gradually evolve intellectually and morally.

Espiritismo has never had a single leader or epicenter of practice, so practice varies greatly between individuals and groups. Espiritismo has absorbed various practices from other religious and spiritual practices endemic to Latin America and the Caribbean, such as Roman Catholicism, curanderismo, Santeria, and voodoo.

A ritual associated with Espiritismo de Corzon, which is a form of Espiritismo that is practiced primarily in Cuba, is physically, mentally, and emotionally difficult. Those participating in the ritual stand in a circle holding hands while walking in a counterclockwise fashion (Olmos & Paravisini-Gebert, 2003). At the same time, they chant and beat the floor with their feet and swing their arms forcefully until they fall into a trance (Olmos & Paravisini-Gebert, 2003). The heavy breathing and stamping, which is heavily associated with chanting in African cults, serve one specific purpose (Olmos & Paravisini-Gebert, 2003). The noises create a hypnotic sound that leads the medium into a trance. Upon reaching this particular state of mind, the medium can contact the spirits for solutions to problems or aliments (Olmos & Paravisini-Gebert, 2003).

Puerto Rican Espiritismo shares many similarities in its origins to Cuban Espiritismo. Educated Puerto Ricans used Espiritismo as a way of justification in their mission to free the country from the grasp of Spanish colonialism (Olmos & Paravisini-Gebert, 2003). However, the religious movement encountered many setbacks in its early years in Puerto Rico. Those who were caught practicing it were punished by the government and ostracized by the Catholic Church (Olmos & Paravisini-Gebert, 2003). The movement, despite all the roadblocks, continued to spread in the country. The attempt to achieve spiritual communication through a medium was widely practiced all over the island.

BEHAVIORAL RISK FACTORS AND COMMON HEALTH PROBLEMS _____

The behaviors described here are linked to the common health problems that Hispanics face, but it is important to note that some of their illnesses are not related to behaviors. Their health problems are related to other social factors as well, such as poverty or lack of access to care.

Hispanics' typical diet is high in fiber with beans and grains (rice) as staple foods, and they rely on beans as a source of protein rather than meat. Leafy green vegetables and dairy are not a usual part of their diet (Rhode Island Department of Health, n.d.). Generally, Hispanics eat a lot of tropical fruits, fruit juices, and starchy root vegetables (e.g., potatoes, cassava, and plantains). The food pyramid for the traditional Latino diet can be found in Figure 2.

According to the 2003 to 2004 National Health and Examination Survey (American Health Association, n.d.), 73.1% of Mexican American males and 71.7% of Mexican

The Traditional Healthy Latin American Diet Pyramid

Daily Beverage Recommendations:
6 Glasses of Water

Alcohol in moderation

MEAT SWEETS & EGGS — WEEKLY

PLANT OILS

FISH & SHELLFISH — DAIRY — POULTRY — DAILY

WHOLE GRAINS, TUBERS, PASTA, BEANS & NUTS — AT EVERY MEAL

FRUITS — VEGETABLES

Daily Physical Activity

FIGURE 2 Food pyramid for traditional Latino diet.
Source: © 2000 Oldways Preservation & Exchange Trust. www.oldwayspt.org. Reproduced with permission.

American females are overweight or obese, and of these, 27.3% of males and 38.4% of females are obese.

Hispanics have lower rates of smoking than most racial and ethnic groups. In 2005, 16.2% of Hispanics smoked (American Lung Association, 2007). There are significant variations in smoking rates among Hispanic subgroups. In 2005, 16.7% of Cuban Americans smoked, compared to 23.6% of Puerto Ricans, 21.2% of Mexican Americans, 14.3% percent of Dominicans, and 12.2% of Central and South Americans (American Lung Association, 2007).

Hispanic males have high rates of alcohol consumption. In 2000, 8.7% of Hispanics indicated excessive alcohol consumption. Excessive alcohol drinkers were defined as those who had more than 12 drinks of any type of alcoholic beverage in their lifetime and consumed more than 5 drinks on one occasion at least 12 times during the past 12 months, compared to 9.4% of non-Hispanic whites and 6.9% of non-Hispanic blacks (Centers for Disease Control and Prevention, n.d.). One possible explanation for the high drinking rate among males is the cultural ideology of machismo. Men strive to appear strong and masculine by drinking large amounts of alcohol.

There are substantial differences in drinking patterns among Hispanics. For example, Cuban Americans have lower rates of drinking than Mexican Americans and Puerto Ricans (Caetano, Clark, & Tam, 1998). Among Hispanics, those born in the United States were approximately three times more likely to engage in drinking and driving than those who were born elsewhere (Caetano & Clark, 1998). Hispanic men also had higher rates of having been arrested for driving under the influence of alcohol (19%), compared to white men (13%) and black men (11%) (Caetano & Clark, 1998).

QUICK FACTS

Cancer

- In 2004, Hispanic men were 13% less likely to have prostate cancer than non-Hispanic white men.
- In 2004, Hispanic women were 33% less likely to have breast cancer than non-Hispanic white women.
- Hispanic men and women have higher incidence and mortality rates for stomach and liver cancer.
- In 2003, Hispanic women were 2.2 times as likely as non-Hispanic white women to be diagnosed with cervical cancer.

Diabetes

- Mexican American adults were two times more likely than non-Hispanic white adults to have been diagnosed with diabetes by a physician.
- In 2002, Hispanics were 1.5 times as likely to start treatment for end-stage renal disease related to diabetes, compared to non-Hispanic white men.
- In 2004, Hispanics were 1.5 times as likely as non-Hispanic whites to die from diabetes.

Heart Disease

- In 2005, Hispanics were 10% less likely to have heart disease, compared to non-Hispanic whites.
- In 2004, Mexican American men were 30% less likely to die from heart disease, compared to non-Hispanic white men.
- Mexican American women were 1.3 times more likely than non-Hispanic white women to be obese.

HIV–AIDS

- Hispanics accounted for 18% of HIV–AIDS cases in 2005.
- Hispanic males had more than three times the AIDS rate than non-Hispanic white males.
- Hispanic females had more than five times the AIDS rate than non-Hispanic white females.
- Hispanic men were 2.6 times as likely to die from HIV–AIDS than non-Hispanic white men.
- Hispanic women were four times as likely to die from HIV–AIDS than non-Hispanic white women in 2004.

Immunization

- In 2005, Hispanic adults aged 65 years and older were 10% less likely to have received the influenza (flu) shot in the past 12 months, compared to non-Hispanic whites of the same age group.
- In 2005, Hispanic adults aged 65 years and older were 50% less likely to have ever received the pneumonia shot, compared to non-Hispanic white adults of the same age group.
- Although Hispanic children aged 19 to 35 months had comparable rates of immunization for hepatitis, influenza, MMR, and polio, they were slightly less likely to be fully immunized, compared to non-Hispanic white children.

Infant Mortality

- In 2004, infant mortality rates for Hispanic subpopulations ranged from 4.6 per 1,000 live births to 7.8 per 1,000 live births, compared to the non-Hispanic white infant mortality rate of 5.7 per 1,000 live births.
- In 2004, Puerto Ricans had 1.4 times the infant mortality rate of non-Hispanic whites.
- Puerto Rican infants were twice as likely to die from causes related to low birth weight, compared to non-Hispanic white infants.
- Mexican American mothers were 2.5 times as likely as non-Hispanic white mothers to begin prenatal care in the third trimester or not receive prenatal care at all.

Stroke

- In 2004, Hispanic men were 14% less likely to die from a stroke than non-Hispanic white men.
- In 2004, Hispanic women were 30% less likely to die from a stroke than non-Hispanic white women.

Source: Office of Minority Health. (2008).

CONSIDERATIONS FOR HEALTH PROMOTION AND PROGRAM PLANNING

The following are some concepts to consider when planning and implementing a health promotion program for this target audience.

- Preventive medicine is not a norm for most Hispanics. This behavior may be related to the Hispanic here-and-now orientation, as opposed to a future-planning orientation. It also is related to their fatalistic belief system.
- Some commonly known Hispanic sayings suggest that events in one's life result from luck, fate, or other powers beyond an individual's control. For example:
  - *Que será, será.* (What will be will be.)
  - *Que sea lo que Dios quiera.* (It's in God's hands.)
  - *Esta enfermedad es una prueba de Dios.* (This illness is a test of God.)
  - *De algo se tiene que morir uno.* (You have to die of something.)
- Persons with acute or chronic illness may regard themselves as innocent victims of malevolent forces. Severe illness may be attributed to God's design, bad behavior, or punishment. Genetic defects in a child may be attributed to the parents' actions.
- Consider sitting closer to Hispanic patients and clients than you would with people from other cultures.
- Be particularly aware of your nonverbal communication messages.
- Be aware that Hispanics often have higher exposure rates to environmental hazards due to living in urban environments, and males have high exposure due to their jobs.
- Family and friends may indulge patients, allowing them to be passive, which is an approach that may conflict with the Western view that active participation is required to prevent or heal much disease.
- Some Hispanic sayings support health promotion and illustrate the considerable status given to health and prevention:
  - *La salud es todo o casi todo.* (Health is everything, or almost everything.)
  - *Es mejor prevenir que curar.* (An ounce of prevention is worth a pound of cure.)
  - *Ayúdate que Dios te ayudará.* (Help yourself and God will help you.)
- "Helping yourself" may lead to placing responsibility for cure with the entire family. The challenge for health care professionals is to assess the amount of control patients believe they have over their health and to design interventions that build on traditional support systems.
- Vaccination is very important and adhered to for children.

- Western medicine is expected and preferred in case of severe illness, but some Hispanics also may use native healers, and the educator and provider should inquire about the utilization of other healers.
- Use appropriate titles to show respect, such as *señor* and *señorita*.
- A botanica is a resource store for herbs and other traditional remedies. Some Hispanics may go there before going to a physician or clinic. In many Latin American countries, pharmacists prescribe medications, and a wider range of medications is available over the counter. People may share medicines or write home for relatives to send them medications. Individuals may discontinue medication if it does not immediately alleviate symptoms or after their symptoms abate. Many Hispanics believe that taking too much medicine is harmful.
- When providing nutritional advice or education, use positive examples from Hispanic cultural foods.
- Consider suggesting family-based methods for increasing physical activity, such as dancing or walking with family members.
- If you have the patient's permission, involve the family members in the consultation because it may assist with increasing the listener's adherence to the recommendation(s).
- Consider using peer educators (promotoras) as community outreach workers for community-based efforts, because they have been shown to be successful with this community.
- Check for understanding and agreement, because Hispanics tend to avoid conflict and are hesitant to ask questions.
- Inquire about complementary and alternative treatments being used, because they are frequently utilized by Hispanics.
- Because of historic events, some Hispanics may distrust the health care system (many Puerto Rican women experienced involuntary sterilization and were adversely affected by birth control pill trials), view the health care system as an extension of a repressive government (Central Americans), or fear deportation, especially if they are not in the country legally.
- Some Hispanics confuse public health programs with welfare and avoid them due to stigma.

CHAPTER SUMMARY

Many people are not aware of the violent history of Hispanics in this country. Hispanics are the largest minority group in the United States, a group that is rapidly growing. They have strong ties to their country of origin, and many Hispanics, even after living here for a long period of time, do not view themselves as American. They have strong family ties and have held on to their cultural belief systems and practices. Hispanics have many unique features to their health belief systems and healing practices, and have types of healers that are not seen in other cultures, therefore, there are major differences that need to be considered when providing health care services to this population.

In this chapter, we have provided an overview of the history of Hispanics, including the fact that part of the United States previously belonged to Mexico. Many of the unique illnesses have been discussed, such as empacho and susto, along with treatment modalities, which include the treatment of hot and cold illnesses. Various types of healing systems have been discussed, such as curanderismo and Espiritismo. Common health behaviors and illnesses among this group have been explained, along with issues for consideration when developing health promotion and education efforts for this target population.

REVIEW

1. Explain the terms "Hispanic" and "Latino" and the reasons why they are not considered to be a race.
2. Provide an overview of the history of Hispanics in the United States.
3. Explain the socioeconomic conditions of Hispanics in the United States.
4. What are susto, empacho, and mal de ojo?
5. What are curanderismo, Santeria, and Espiritismo?
6. What are some of the common health risk behaviors and diseases among Hispanics in the United States?

CASE STUDY

This case focuses on a low-income, non-English speaking Latino patient and family. As you read through this story, pay special attention to issues involved in medical decision making, such as gender roles and values and interest in treatments outside of traditional Western medicine based on culturally constructed folk illness beliefs.

When Alejandro Flores was born, his parents were ecstatic and very proud. Alejandro was their first child born in the continental United States, in a world far away from their tradition and family in Puerto Rico. The Flores family had worked very hard to move to the northeast a year before Alejandro's birth, and they felt that his arrival helped connect them with their new home.

It is four years after Alejandro's birth, and the Flores family has grown even larger. There are now five children (three older than Alejandro and one 20-month-old baby) and Alejandro's grandmother living in the same apartment. Alejandro's mother, Señora Flores, takes care of her family as best she can, and she feels lucky to have her mother there to give her advice and a helping hand. Señor Flores works very hard as a custodian at a local school to provide his family with enough income. He has picked up a little English at work, but only Spanish is spoken at home.

Serious asthma problems run in the Flores family, and Alejandro is no exception. Although he looks healthy, Alejandro has had severe asthma for several years. When he was 2 years old, a series of awful wheezing episodes sent him to the hospital multiple times. His parents do their best to care for him, but they are both spread pretty thin and have limited time available. To help with all of Alejandro's asthma problems, the Flores family recently relocated to a new apartment that has air conditioning, and Sr. Flores has limited his smoking to outside on the patio. The family has two dogs, which could be a problem, but they just couldn't see getting rid of two loved members of their family.

Alejandro also takes a lot of medications for his asthma symptoms. His parents have been taught about asthma and have been given an asthma action plan—all in Spanish. They were told to call the clinic if at any time Alejandro's symptoms worsened. Despite these actions, Alejandro still continues to have heavy wheezing and a tight cough, especially at night.

With Alejandro continuing to have asthma problems, Sra. Flores became skeptical that the medications were not working. Under the guidance of her mother, she took Alejandro to an espiritista (in curanderismo, the Mexican American healing system, an espiritista is a healer who serves as a medium for exorcisms and is adept at facilitating the help of benevolent spirits and removing malevolent spirits that surround the client). At the espiritista's advice, Sra. Flores stopped giving Alejandro all of the prescribed medications and began giving him an herbal tea that she believed, along with prayer, would take Alejandro's asthma symptoms completely away.

Alejandro and his parents attended their regularly scheduled visit to the clinic to see if the new medications were helping to control Alejandro's symptoms. This is the second visit since Alejandro's last hospitalization six months ago. Sra. Flores has not contacted anyone at the clinic about Alejandro's asthma getting worse, so the clinic staff assumes the best.

There are several issues to consider about this case:

- Why might Sra. Flores have chosen to consult an espiritista rather than call the clinic when Alejandro was not getting better?
- Do you think that traditional Latino gender roles might have some affect on this child and family's experience with the health care system?

- How might it be possible to incorporate alternative folk remedies with mainstream Western medicine in developing a treatment plan for Alejandro?

Source: Cross Cultural Health Care Case Studies. (n.d.).

MODEL PROGRAM

Sembrando Salud

Sembrando Salud is a culturally sensitive, community-based tobacco and alcohol-use prevention program in San Diego County, California, that is specifically adapted for migrant Hispanic adolescents and their families. The program is designed to improve parent–child communication skills as a way of developing and maintaining healthy decision making. Designed for youths 11 to 16 years old, the intervention consists of eight weekly two-hour sessions where adolescents meet in small groups. Sessions usually take place during the evenings at school or at other community-based organizations. Sessions are run by trained group leaders, all of whom are bilingual Mexican Americans. Group leaders are trained over 10 weekly sessions and are monitored throughout the intervention to ensure consistency and quality of program implementation.

The program interventions are a mix of interactive teaching methods, including videos, demonstrations, skill practice, group discussions led by a leader, and role-playing. All interventions include three central components: (1) information about the health effects of tobacco/alcohol use, (2) social influences on tobacco/alcohol use, and (3) training in refusal skills. Further, adolescents are exposed to how problems can be identified and analyzed, solutions can be generated, and decisions can be made, implemented, and evaluated. There is an additional emphasis on developing parental support for the healthy discussions and behaviors of adolescents through enhanced parent–child communications. Parental communication skills—such as listening, confirmation, and reassurance—also are developed. The program reinforces new behavioral skills, such as communicating with peers and adults and refusing alcohol and tobacco offers.

Evaluation

A randomized pretest–posttest control group study was implemented to determine whether the intervention held true to its design and affected parent–child communication. Schools within geographic regions were prerandomized to a treatment condition (tobacco and alcohol use prevention) or an attention-control condition (first aid/home safety). Each condition was designed to be equivalent in all respects (except for the content) and included eight weekly, two-hour sessions, with parents attending three of the eight sessions jointly with their adolescent. Each week was formatted into small-group evening sessions held on school grounds or at a neighborhood community agency.

Outcome

This culturally sensitive, family-based intervention for migrant Hispanic youth was found to be effective in increasing perceived parent–child communication in families with few children. Specifically, parents and children enrolled in the treatment condition reported greater improvements in communication than those in the attention-control condition. The intervention appeared to be more effective in smaller families, presumably because of the increased opportunity for parents to monitor and communicate with participating youths.

The study had notable limitations, so the results may not be generalized. First, the study targeted a hard-to-reach population, with 60% of those eligible not participating. This factor makes it difficult to generalize the findings to those who were not reached. Additional limitations include the short-term nature of the follow-up, which does not allow any determination of long-term effects, and reliance on self-report measures, which raises the concern that the promising results of the intervention are due to the desire of parents and their children to be presented in a positive light. That being said, it certainly is a noteworthy, promising practice.

Source: Office of Juvenile Justice and Delinquency Prevention. (n.d.).

GLOSSARY TERMS

empacho   orishas
Santeria   Espiritismo

REFERENCES

American Heart Association. (n.d.). *Statistical fact sheet—risk factors.* Retrieved March 31, 2008, from http://www.americanheart.org/downloadable/heart/1136820021462Overweight06.pdf

American Lung Association. (2007). *Smoking and Hispanics fact sheet.* Retrieved March 31, 2008, from http://www.lungusa.org/site/pp.asp?c=dvLUK9O0E&b=36002

Caetano, R., & Clark, C. L. (1998). Trends in alcohol-related problems among whites, blacks, and Hispanics: 1984–1995. *Alcoholism: Clinical and Experimental Research, 22,* 534–538.

Caetano, R., Clark, C. L., & Tam, T. (1998). *Alcohol consumption among racial/ethnic minorities.* Retrieved March 31, 2008, from http://www.hawaii.edu/hivandaids/Alcohol%20Consumption%20Among%20RacialEthnic%20Minorities%20%20%20%20%20Theory%20and%20Research.pdf

Carigan, W. D. (2003). The lynching of persons of Mexican origin or descent in the United States, 1848 to 1928. *Journal of Social History.* Retrieved March 28, 2008, from http://findarticles.com/p/articles/mi_m2005/is_2_37/ai_111897839/pg_1

Centers for Disease Control and Prevention. (n.d.). National Health interview surrey, 2000. Retrieved April 19, 2009, from http://www.cdc.gov/nchs/data/nhis/measure09.pdf.

Church of Likumi Babalu Aye v. City of Hialeah, 508 US 520 (1993).

Cross Cultural Health Care Case Studies. (n.d.). *The Case of Alejandro Flores.* Retrieved June 16, 2008, from http://support.mchtraining.net/national_ccce/case3/case.html

Juckett, G. (2005). Cross-cultural medicine. *American Family Physician.* Retrieved March 30, 2008, from http://www.aafp.org/afp/20051201/2267.html

New Century Foundation. (2006). *Hispanics: A statistical portrait.* Retrieved March 8, 2008, from http://www.amren.com/Reports/Hispanics/HispanicsReport.htm

Office of Juvenile Justice and Delinquency Prevention. (n.d.). *Programs guide. Sembrando Salud.* Retrieved January 16, 2008, from http://www.dsgonline.com/mpg2.5//TitleV_MPG_Table_Ind_Rec.asp?id=626

Office of Minority Health. (2008). *Hispanic/Latino profile.* Retrieved March 8, 2008, from http://www.omhrc.gov/templates/browse.aspx?lvl=2&lvlid=54

Oldways Preservation & Exchange Trust. Latino Nutrition Coalition. (n.d.). *Latin American diet food.* Retrieved March 17, 2008, from http://www.oldwayspt.org/

Olmos, M. F., & Paravisini-Gebert, L. (2003). *Creole religions of the Caribbean: An introduction from vodou and Santeria to obeah and Espiritismo.* New York: New York University Press.

Rhode Island Department of Health. (n.d.). *Latino/Hispanic culture & health.* Retrieved March 17, 2008, from http://www.health.ri.gov/chic/minority/lat_cul.php

US Census Bureau. (2004). *We the people: Hispanics in the United States.* Retrieved March 8, 2008, from http://www.census.gov/prod/2004pubs/censr-18.pdf

PHOTO CREDITS

Chapter Opener , © Richard Gunion/Dreamstime.com

Unless otherwise indicated, all photographs and illustrations are under copyright of Jones and Bartlett Publishers, LLC, or have been provided by the author(s).

American Indian and Alaska Native Populations

What we see as science, Indians see as magic. What we see as magic, they see as science. I don't find a hopeless contradiction. If we can appreciate each others views, we can see the whole picture more clearly.

—Hammerschlag (1988, p. 14)

Everything on the earth has a purpose, every disease an herb to cure it, and every person a mission. This is the Indian theory of existence.

—Mourning Dove Salish

KEY CONCEPTS

- Sweat lodges
- Talking circles
- Peyote
- Sand painting
- Medicine wheel
- Medicine bundle

CHAPTER OBJECTIVES

1. Provide an overview of the social and economic circumstances of American Indians and Alaska Natives in the United States.
2. Provide an overview of American Indian and Alaska Native beliefs about the causes of illness.
3. Describe at least three American Indian and Alaska Native healing practices.
4. Describe American Indian and Alaska Native health risk behaviors and common illnesses.
5. List at least six tips for working with American Indian and Alaska Native populations.

The terms "American Indian" and "Alaska Native" refer to people descended from any of the original peoples of North and South America (including Central America) and who maintain tribal affiliation or community attachment (US Census Bureau, 2002). There is a wide range of terms used to describe these groups, such as Native Indians, American Indians, Native American Indians, Indians, Indigenous, Aboriginal, Native Alaskans, and Original Americans. It is important to note that not all Native Americans come from the contiguous United States. Native Hawaiians, for example, also can be considered Native American, but it is not common to use such a designation. In this book we have chosen to use the same terminology as the 2000 United States census, which are American Indians and Alaska Natives, unless the data source uses other terms. Much of the data on these two groups have been gathered collectively, and when available, the data will be reported separately in this chapter.

The American Indian and Alaska Native populations are diverse, geographically dispersed, and economically disadvantaged (Management Sciences for Health, n.d.). Disease patterns among American Indians and Alaska Natives are associated with negative consequences of poverty, limited access to health services, and cultural dislocation (Management Sciences for Health, n.d.). Inadequate education, high rates of unemployment, discrimination, and cultural differences all contribute to unhealthy lifestyles and disparities in access to health care for many American Indian and Alaska Native people (Management Sciences for Health, n.d.).

American Indians and Alaska Natives also are very self-determined and proud people. In a special message on Indian affairs delivered on July 8, 1970, to Congress, President Richard Nixon declared:

> But the story of the Indian in America is something more than the record of the white man's frequent aggression, broken agreements, intermittent remorse and prolonged failure. It is a record of enormous contributions to this country—to its art and culture, to its strength and spirit, to its sense of history and its sense of purpose (President Nixon, July 8, 1970).

In this chapter we provide a brief history of American Indian and Alaska Native populations, information about their current status in the United States, their beliefs about the causes of illness and healing practices, behavioral risk factors, and the common health problems that they face. The first part of the chapter is focused on American Indians and the second section is about Alaska Natives, and then we combine the groups when we discuss key points to consider when working with these populations.

HISTORY OF AMERICAN INDIANS IN THE UNITED STATES

The American Indians are descendents of the first humans who migrated from Asia and Europe to North America about 30,000 years ago. Christopher Columbus "discovered" North America in 1492 during his voyage in search for the East Indies. He used the name "Indians" to describe the native people of the land.

The European invasion that began in the fifteenth century changed the lives of American Indians. In addition to the aggressive violence and wars against the American

Indians, new diseases, such as smallpox and measles, were introduced, and the indigenous Americans had no immunities to them. In addition, the Europeans' racism, genocide, and ethnocentrism prevented them from accepting the Indians as equals. The American Indians were viewed as a problem with the solution being to eradicate them through wars and to push any survivors westward.

In the nineteenth century, the westward expansion of the United States caused large numbers of American Indians to resettle farther west, often by force, almost always reluctantly. The United States Congress, under President Andrew Jackson, passed the Indian Removal Act of 1830, which authorized the president to conduct treaties to exchange American Indian land east of the Mississippi River for lands west of the river. As many as 100,000 Native Americans eventually relocated in the West as a result of this Indian Removal Act. In theory, relocation was supposed to be voluntary, but in practice great pressure was put on American Indian leaders to sign removal treaties. President Jackson told people to kill as many bison as possible to cut out the Plains Indian's main source of food (Kelman, 1999). At one point, there were fewer than 500 bison left in the Great Plains (Kelman, 1999).

Many steps were taken to "civilize" American Indians, such as not permitting them to speak their native language and creating Indian boarding schools. The Indian Citizenship Act of 1924 gave U.S. citizenship to American Indians, in part because of an interest by many to see them merged with the American mainstream and also because of the service of many Native American veterans in World War I.

AMERICAN INDIANS IN THE UNITED STATES

American Indians in the United States comprise a large number of distinct tribes. There are 561 federally recognized tribal governments in the United States. In addition, there are a number of tribes that are recognized by individual states but not by the federal government. The rights and benefits associated with state recognition vary from state to state. Being federally recognized is important to the tribes, because it describes the right of federally recognized tribes to govern themselves (called tribal sovereignty) and creates the existence of a government-to-government relationship with the United States. Thus, a tribe is not a ward of the government but an independent nation with the right to form its own government, enforce criminal and civil laws, levy taxes within its borders, establish its membership, and license and regulate activities. Nonrecognized tribes do not have these powers. Limitations on tribal powers of self-government include the same limitations applicable to states; for example, neither tribes nor states have the power to make war, engage in foreign relations, or

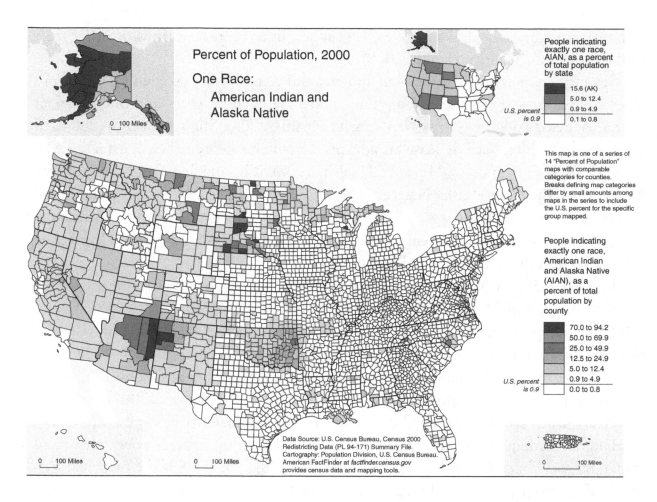

FIGURE 1 Percentage of population: American Indian and Alaska Native, 2000.

Source: U.S. Census Bureau, Population Division (2008), http://www.census.gov/main/www/citation.html.

coin money (this includes paper currency). The federal government has a trust responsibility to protect tribal lands, assets, resources, and treaty rights. Others reasons why federal recognition is important is that the tribe has the right to label arts and crafts as Native American and apply for grants that are specifically reserved for American Indians.

According to the U.S. Census Bureau (2002), in 2000, 1.5% of the population reported being American Indian or Alaska Native. Forty-three percent live in the West, 31% in the South, 17% in the Midwest, and 9% in the Northeast (see Figure 1). California has the largest American Indian and Alaska Native population, followed by Oklahoma, Arizona, Texas, New Mexico, and New York (US Census Bureau, 2002). California and Oklahoma combined include about 25% of the total American Indian and Alaska Native population (US Census Bureau, 2002). As of 2000, the largest tribes in the United States by population were Cherokee, Navajo, Latin American, and Choctaw, respectively (US Census Bureau, 2002). As of 2006, of the 4.5 million

American Indians and Alaska Natives, 1.8 million lived on reservations or other trust lands (Office of Minority Health, 2008).

Seventy-six percent of American Indians and Alaska Natives aged 25 years and older have at least a high school diploma, and 14% aged 25 years and older have at least a bachelor's degree (Office of Minority Health, 2008). Slightly over 50,000 aged 25 years and older have at least an advanced graduate degree (i.e., master's, PhD, medical, or law) (Office of Minority Health, 2008). The median family income for American Indians and Alaska Natives is $33,627, with 26% of American Indians and Alaska Natives aged 16 years and older working in management and professional occupations. Twenty-five percent of American Indians and Alaska Natives live at the poverty level (Office of Minority Health, 2008).

In 2003, 45% of American Indians and Alaska Natives had private health insurance coverage, and 21.3% relied on Medicaid coverage (Office of Minority Health, 2008). Thirty percent had no health insurance coverage in 2005 (Office of Minority Health, 2008). The Indian Health Service (IHS), an agency within the U.S. Department of Health and Human Services, is responsible for providing federal health services to American Indians and Alaska Natives (Indian Health Service, 2007). The provision of health services to members of federally-recognized tribes grew out of the special government-to-government relationship between the federal government and Indian tribes. This relationship was established in 1787. The IHS is the principal federal health care provider and health advocate for Indian people, and its goal is to raise their health status to the highest possible level. The IHS currently provides health services to approximately 1.5 million American Indians and Alaska Natives. Approximately 57% of American Indians and Alaska Natives living in the United States rely on the Indian Health Service to provide access to health care services in 46 hospitals and over 600 other facilities (Indian Health Service, 2007).

Many of the American Indian and Alaska Native languages have become extinct since the invasion of the Europeans. Only eight indigenous languages of the continental United States currently have a population of speakers in the United States and Canada large enough to populate a medium-sized town (Rehling, n.d.). Navajo is the largest American Indian language still spoken, with about 149,000 speakers, followed by Cree, Ojibwa, Cherokee, Dakota, Apache, Blackfoot, and Choctaw (Rehling, n.d.).

American Indians believe in a Supreme Creator; most tribes also have lesser deities like Mary or Jesus figures and mediators between the spirit world and the earth (similar to saints in Christianity). They believe that people should try to maintain constant, daily harmony and contact with the Creator, follow all sacred teachings, and treat all life (people, animals, plants, rocks, rivers, rainbows, etc.) with respect.

American Indians are family-based people. American Indians are taught to respect their elders and obey their orders. The elders are seen as people with much knowledge and are considered to be the head of the household. After the elders, men are considered to be the leaders of the house. In addition to being the chiefs of the house, men also are viewed as the leaders of the tribe, protectors, and fighters. Traditionally, the men would go out and hunt to bring food for the whole community; as a result, they are still seen as the providers for the family.

Women are still viewed as the people who do all of the housework, gather materials, and take care of the home, and they teach the children the ways of the American Indians. The children have to learn the traditions of the tribe and community and have to respect the elders. The older family members keep an eye on the new generation to make sure that they are following traditions.

Besides believing in close family relations, American Indians also believe in living in a community. Many different tribes live together in one community. To be a member of the community, a person does not need to be from the same tribe or even have blood relations with anyone from the community. As many as 80 different tribes can live together in one community (West Virginia Division of Culture and History, 2008). The elders are in charge of teaching and guiding the community in the ways of the tribes and have the responsibility to pass on their history orally. They also teach the community the traditional ways of the tribe. They show the new generation how to make traditional arts and crafts and show them the traditional rituals.

One of the rituals is storytelling or experiencing stories through songs or other performances. Songs play an important part of the American Indians' lives. The songs the American Indians execute are usually ancestral songs that tell the story of the ancestors and of hardships they had to face. Many of the songs are related to nature and hunting. The songs are considered to be the property of the person who dreamt it or of the community after that person passes away. If someone wants to reenact the song, they must obtain special permission from the community.

Music and dance are often linked together in performances. Everyone who attends the performance has to take part in it one way or another. The American Indians believe that even witnessing a performance is considered having participated in the performance. The dances are a way the American Indians express themselves and what surrounds them. The dances are done to celebrate an occasion and to promote unity and togetherness. During the dance, the dancers make lots of noise and wear certain kinds of clothes, depending on the event. For example, they might dress up as animals or like spirits to honor them.

With regard to their dietary practices, American Indians believe that certain foods are sacred. For example, some American Indians believe the Great Spirit

Hashtali gave the American Indians corn as a present, so it is considered to be sacred. Corn is used quite frequently for meals because it can be easily grown and does not require a lot of work. The American Indians use corn to make flour and bread, and it can be eaten as is or dried. Another sacred food is blood soup, which is made from a mixture of blood and corn flour cooked in broth. Blood soup may be used as a sacred meal during the nighttime Holy Smoke ceremony of the Sioux, which is a celebration of Mother Earth that involves the use of the peace pipe (Advameg, 2007). Wolves and coyotes are the only animals that are not hunted for food, because they are regarded as teachers or pathfinders and held as sacred by all tribes (Advameg, 2007). At marriage ceremonies, the bride and groom exchange food instead of rings (Advameg, 2007). The groom brings venison or some other meat to indicate his intention to provide for the household, and the bride provides corn or bean bread to symbolize her willingness to care for and provide nourishment for the household (Advameg, 2007).

American Indian diets and food practices have changed possibly more than any other ethnic group in the United States. Although the current diet of American Indians may vary by tribe and by personal traits such as age, it closely resembles that of the U.S. white population. There is no statistically significant difference in the overall diet quality of American Indians and the rest of the U.S. population, but the majority of American Indians do consume too much fat (62% of their diet is fat) (Advameg, 2007). On any given day, only 21% of American Indians eat the recommended amount of fruit, 34% eat the amount of vegetables that are recommended, 24% eat the recommended amount of grains, and 27% consume the recommended amount of dairy products (Advameg, 2007). American Indians also are four times more likely to report not having enough to eat than other U.S. households (Advameg, 2007).

The U.S. Department of Agriculture (USDA) food guide for American Indians can be found in Figure 2. The bald eagle is shown on the pyramid because almost all American Indians attach special significance to the eagle and its feathers. Images of eagles and their feathers are used on many tribal logos as symbols of the American Indians. To be given an eagle feather is the highest honor that can be awarded within indigenous cultures. Bald and golden eagles (and their feathers) are highly revered and considered to be sacred within American Indian traditions, culture, and religion. They represent honesty, truth, strength, courage, wisdom, power, and freedom. Because these birds roam the sky, they are believed to have a special connection to God. According to traditional American Indian beliefs, the Creator made all the birds of the sky when the world was new. Of all the birds, the Creator chose the eagle to be the leader . . . the Master of the Sky. The eagle is considered to be a messenger to God (American Eagle Foundation, n.d.).

FIGURE 2 Native American food guide.

Source: CANFIT, Berkeley, CA. For more information, call 510-644-1533 or info@canfit.org. Used with permission.

BELIEFS ABOUT CAUSES OF HEALTH AND ILLNESS AMONG AMERICAN INDIANS

To American Indians, health is a continual process of staying strong spiritually, mentally, and physically. This strength keeps away or overcomes the forces that cause illness. People must stay in harmony with themselves, other people, their natural environment, and their Creator. Adhering to traditional and tribal beliefs and obeying tribal religious codes is another part of staying healthy because violating tribal tenets or laws has consequences like physical or mental illness, disability, ongoing bad luck, or trauma. The violation must be set right before harmony and health can be restored. American Indians believe illness is the price to be paid either for something that happened in the past or for something that will happen in the future; therefore, each person is responsible for his or her health. Illness is not looked upon as abnormal.

This group does not believe in biomedicine or germ theory, because they believe illness is caused by personal responsibility, qualities, and spirits (Spector, 2004). There are three distinct causes of illness to trigger patient suffering: (1) by a hostile spirit thrusting a foreign object, such as a sharp stone, insect, or a tangled thread, into the person; (2) by the patient's soul leaving the body on its own accord; (3) and by the patient's soul being stolen away by enemy spirits (Haas, 2007).

HEALING TRADITIONS AMONG AMERICAN INDIANS

Most American Indian tribes have healing traditions that are not based on Western science and are related to their beliefs about the causation of illness and disease. Therefore, many healing traditions and rituals focus on harmony, and the overall purpose is to bring participants into harmony with themselves, their tribe, and all of life. Healing occurs when someone is restored to harmony and connected to universal powers. Traditional healing is holistic. It focuses on the person, not the illness, so the process does not focus on symptoms or diseases, because it addresses the total individual.

Traditional healing practices are still used frequently. Marbella, Harris, Diehr, Ignace, and Ignace (1998) conducted semistructured interviews in an urban setting to gain an understanding of the prevalence, utilization patterns, and practice implications of the use of Native American healers together with the use of physicians. Thirty tribal affiliations were represented. These researchers found that 38% of the patients see a healer, and of those who do not, 86% would consider seeing one in the future. Most patients reported seeing a healer for spiritual reasons. Among those seeing healers, the most frequently mentioned were spiritual healers (50.9%), herbalists (42.1%), and medicine men (28.1%). These percentages add up to more than 100% because some patients reported seeing more than one type of healer (Marbella et al., 1998). More than a third of the patients seeing healers received different advice from their physicians and healers. The patients rate their healer's advice higher than their physician's advice 61.4% of the time. Only 14.8% of the patients seeing healers tell their physician about their use of healers (Marbella et al., 1998).

In the following section we discuss **sweat lodges**, **talking circles**, plants and herbs, healing ceremonies, and types and practices of healers. The information has been divided into these categories to help organize the information for the reader, but the categories are arbitrary to some extent. For example, healers use plants and herbs, but we have put them into separate categories for educational purposes.

Sweat Lodges

Sweat lodges are used for healing and balancing. American Indians consider sweat lodges to be a good way to clean one's body and sweat out illness or disease (Bonvillain, 1997). Hot stones covered in water are placed in a small, confined, dark enclosure, creating a steam bath. The stones, considered by American Indians to be their oldest living relatives, are usually lava rocks that do not break when heated. Sweating removes toxins from the body, stimulates the endocrine glands, and makes the heart pump more blood. American Indians believe that sweat lodges also bring balance and health to spirit, mind, and body. They use sweat lodges in many ways, such as before spiritual undertakings, to bring clarity to a problem, to call upon helpful spirits, and to reconnect with the Great Spirit.

Even the building of a sweat lodge is sacred and symbolic. As shown in Figure 3, willow saplings are bent and tied together to form a square with four sides, which

FIGURE 3 Sweat lodge.
Source: Courtesy of Kirk Shoemaker.

represents the sacred four directions. There usually is a single entryway that faces either west or east. The connected poles create a frame that looks like an overturned basket, which symbolically represents items such as the womb or arch of the sky. In some tribes there are 28 poles, which represent either the ribs of a woman, a female bear or turtle, or the lunar cycle. The framework is covered in the skins of buffalo or other animals that represent the animal world. The interior of sweat lodges can be created out of many different materials depending on what is available to the community. The interior can be made out of furs, grasses, or various types of bark from trees. A small pit, or alter, is dug in the center of the lodge for the stones. A branch that represents the tree of life is placed in the middle of the alter and is surrounded by small stones. Antlers to move the hot stones and a medicine pipe are placed near the alter.

Before the sweat lodge is used, "The One Who Pours the Water" purifies the surrounding area by smearing it with sacred herbs to ensure that positive spirits will be present. A stone tender stays outside the lodge, heating stones and passing them inside when summoned by The One Who Pours the Water. One heated stone is not used; it is left for the spirits to sweat with and honors the spirits who have come to the ceremony.

Talking Circles

Talking circles are highly regarded among American Indian people, because they reflect the circle of life. To American Indians, the circle represents that all life is cyclical in nature, such as the changing of the seasons, the phases of the moon, the shape of the world, and the shape of the universe. All parts in the circle are equal.

Traditionally, the group gathers in a circle, and the facilitators provide a list of general but important questions for discussion. These questions may be used as a guide for discussion, but they also are useful to facilitate opportunities for casual, informal conversation and storytelling. The group passes around what is called a "talking feather." Whoever has the feather states what is on his or her mind but has not been said. When that person is finished talking, the feather is handed to the next person in a clockwise direction, and the next person says what has been left unsaid. The person who holds the feather cannot be interrupted. Traditionally, an eagle feather, which is a sacred symbol, was passed around the circle. Sometimes other objects are used. Today the practice is so ingrained in the behavior of Indian people that it is not always necessary to use an object in the circle.

Plants and Herbs

American Indians use herbs to purify the spirit and bring balance to people who are unhealthy in spirit, mind, or body. They learned about the healing powers of herbs by watching sick animals. They use a wide variety of plants and herbs for healing. In fact, there are so many that books have been written on them. A few of the herbs will be covered here, but describing all of them is beyond the focus of this book.

One plant they use is sage, which is believed to protect against bad spirits and to draw them out of the body or the soul. American Indians use sage for many purposes, such as to heal problems of the stomach, colon, nasal passages, kidneys, liver, lungs, pores of the skin, bones, and sex organs; to heal burns and scrapes; as an antiseptic for allergies, colds, and fever; as a gargle for sore throat; and as a tea to calm the nerves. Cedar, a tall evergreen tree, is a milder medicine than sage. It is combined with sage and sweetgrass, a plant that grows in damp environments like marshes or near water, to make a powerful mixture used in sacred ceremonies. Cedar fruit and leaves are boiled and then drank to heal coughs. For head colds, cedar is burned and inhaled. Some of the other herbs that are used include acacia, prickly pear, saw palmetto, sunflower, yerba mansa, cliffrose, and cayenne.

Tobacco, often smoked in medicine pipes, is one of the most sacred plants to American Indians, and it is used in some way in nearly every cure. It is smoked pure and is not mixed with chemicals. When American Indians smoke sacred tobacco and other herbs, their breath, which they consider to be the source of life, becomes visible. When smoke is released, it rises up to the Great Spirit carrying prayers. People who share a pipe are acknowledging that they share the same breath. There are many different types of medicine pipes; some are for war, sun, and marriage, and there are tribal, personal, ceremonial, and social pipes. The pipe itself, made of wood with a soft pithy center, is symbolic, and some are shaped like animals. The bowl represents the female aspect of the Great Spirit–Mother Earth. The stem represents the male aspect of the Great Spirit–Father Sky. Together, the bowl and stem represent the union that brings forth life. The bowl in which tobacco is burned also symbolizes all that changes. The stem signifies all that is unchanging. Smoking the pipe is a central component in all ceremonies because it unites the two worlds of spirit and matter.

Another important plant that is used is peyote, which is a hallucinogenic drug. **Peyote** is a spineless, dome-shaped cactus (*Lophophora williamsii*) that is native to Mexico and the southwest United States. It has buttonlike tubercles that are chewed fresh or dry. Peyote has a history of ritual religious and medicinal use among certain indigenous American Indian tribes going back thousands of years. Peyote is legal only on Indian reservations because of its spiritual and healing properties (Bonvillain, 1997). It is viewed by American Indians as an agent that allows one to encounter spirits and receive visions or messages from spirits or Gods. American Indians also believe that peyote "can be used to make a person throw up and thus this would expel the illness from the body" (Bonvillain, 1997).

Healing Ceremonies

Ceremonies are used to help groups of people return to harmony, and they are not used for individual healing. The ceremonies used by the tribes vary, and there are differences in the way they practice medicine.

For example, the Navajo heal through their **sand painting**, see Figure 4. Sitting on the floor of a house, the medicine person begins painting at sunrise using ground colored rocks and minerals. The paintings depict the gods, elements of the heavens, and religious objects. After the painting which includes complex forms and designs in great detail, is completed, the patient is placed in the center of the painting. The healing

FIGURE 4 Sand painting.
Source: © Bestweb/ShutterStock, Inc.

ceremony, which includes rituals and chants, is performed. Before sunset, the medicine person destroys the painting. The sands are sent to the desert and scattered on the four winds.

The Iroquois practice medicine through their False Faces, a religious society. Each spring and fall, when most illnesses occur, society members wear strange and distorted masks to drive illness and disease away from the tribe. Wearing these masks and ragged clothes and carrying rattles made from tortoise shells, they perform a dance. After the dance, society members go from house to house to rid the community of evil.

Some tribes use medicine wheels, see Figure 5. The medicine wheel's large circle measures 213 feet around. The 28 spokes radiating from its center represent the number of days in the lunar cycle. A medicine wheel is a metaphor or symbol that represents the circle of life and the individual journey each person must take to find his or her own path. Within the medicine wheel are the four cardinal directions and the four sacred colors. The wheel is typically separated into four sections, which represent the north, south, east, and west. The Mother Earth is below the wheel and the Father Sky is above it. The south (white) represents fire and passion, and the animals that are

Content removed due to copyright restrictions

FIGURE **5** Medicine wheel.
Source: © Dana White/PhotoEdit, Inc.

associated with it, such as the eagle and lion, represent pride, strength, and courage. The north (blue) represents air and flight and is associated with winged animals that fly, such as the owl and hummingbird. The west (black) is associated with water and emotions and is associated with animals that work in teams and prepare for winter, such as the snake (because it sheds its skin) and the beaver. The east (red) is linked to the earth and wisdom and is related to animals that have layers of fat to sustain them during the winter, such as the buffalo. The wheel helps American Indians to see exactly where they are and in which areas they need to develop to realize and fulfill their potential. They see that people are all connected to one another, and by showing the intricacies of the interwoven threads of life, they can envision their role in life. It helps them understand that without their part in the tapestry, the bigger picture is not as it should be. It is a model to be used to view self, society, or anything that one could ever think of looking into.

Healers

Medicine men are prominent healers in the American Indian community. Medicine men can be male or female. They have knowledge about the interrelationships of human beings, the earth, the universe, plants, animals, the sun, the moon, and the stars (Spector, 2004). These healers are in tune with the way human beings interact with the world around them, and they are able to use their environment to help provide treatment. A healer is held in high regard because it has taken him or her many years of training and apprenticeship to be able to heal the community. Many American Indians first consult a medicine man before seeking other health professionals because of their belief that the treatment they receive from the traditional healer is better than treatment from health care establishments (Spector, 2004).

Medicine men have power that other members of the tribe do not have. Their power comes from visions that lead them into studying medicine or by being born into a family with many generations of medicine people. In many tribes, both men and women can serve as medicine people, but in some, like the Yurok in California, only women can be medicine people. Some medicine people are also shamans (holy men and women). A shaman is a healer who goes on a "soul journey" or a "soul flight" to the spirit world, aided by the power of songs, drums, rattles, and other objects, to communicate with spirits then performs a healing ceremony (Haas, 2007). All medicine people are considered to be learned and are respected members of the tribe.

Medicine people have naturalistic skills. Some medicine people specialize in areas like herbal medicine, bone setting, midwifery, or counseling. Often the medicine man cures people simply because they believe in him or her (placebo effect). Medicine people bring hope, understanding, and confidence to patients, which are often as powerful as modern medicine could have been. They work in the unseen world of good and bad spirits to restore harmony and health.

American Indians believe that they are related to all forms of life. Medicine people make medicine tools out of materials from nature, including fur, skins, bone, crystals, shells, roots, and feathers. They use these tools to evoke the spirit of what the tool has been made of, which helps strengthen their inner powers. For example, a medicine drum is made of wood and animal skins. When medicine people play the drum, they can call up the assistance of the spirits of the tree and the animal from which the drum was made.

Medicine people keep their medicine tools in a **medicine bundle**, see Figure 6. This is a large piece of cloth or hide that they tie securely with a thong, piece of yarn, or string. The contents of the medicine bundle are sacred. Each medicine person may own or share different medicine bundles: one's own, the tribe's, and bundles for special purposes, like seeking visions, hunting, or protection in battle. Some are passed down from one generation to the next. Personal medicine bundles are private, and asking about another person's medical tools is forbidden. Some medicine bundles are small enough to be worn around the neck. Medicine bundles that belong to tribes are often called the "grandmothers", because they have the power to nourish and nurture the tribe and promote continued well-being. Tribal medicine bundles grow stronger with each passing year.

Tribes carefully guard the knowledge of their medicine people. Members of the tribe who want to become medicine people must first serve a long apprenticeship with an experienced medicine person. In many tribes, medicine men cannot charge for their services. Gifts, however, are expected. Some tribes do require payment and have set lists of standard gifts. Nearly all tribes recognize tobacco as a gift of respect.

One way medicine men help heal the community is by using various forms of plants and herbal remedies. Medicine men spend many years during their apprenticeship in mastering the uses of plants and herbal remedies to be able to cure disease (Bonvillain, 1997). They know which various plants or teas cure different illnesses. For example, one type of plant medicine men used during the 1500s to cure scurvy, caused by a deficiency of vitamin C, was white pine or hemlock (Bonvillain, 1997). Hemlock is an excellent source of vitamin C, according to Frankis (2006). The most widely used plant in healing the American Indian community is tobacco. Tobacco has many useful purposes, such as treating burns, earaches, stomach cramps, and inflammation (Bonvillain, 1997).

FIGURE 6 Medicine bundle.
Source: © Khumina/ShutterStock, Inc.

Certain people in each tribe are recognized as healers. They receive special teachings. Healing traditions are passed from one generation to the next through visions, stories, and dreams. Healing does not follow written guidelines. Healers work differently with each person they help. They use their herbs, ceremony, and power in the best way for each individual. Healing might involve sweat lodges, talking circles, ceremonial smoking of tobacco, herbalism, animal spirits, or vision quests. Each tribe uses its own techniques. The techniques by themselves are not considered to be "traditional healing." They are only steps toward becoming whole, balanced, and connected.

BEHAVIORAL RISK FACTORS AND COMMON HEALTH PROBLEMS AMONG AMERICAN INDIANS

The major behavioral health risk factors for American Indians are seat belt nonuse, cigarette smoking, heavy drinking, sedentary lifestyles, being overweight or obese, and lack of preventive behaviors, such as health screenings. These risk factors have led to American Indians' disproportionately high mortality from alcoholism, tuberculosis, diabetes, injuries, suicide, heart disease, stroke, cancer, lung disease, and homicide. The leading causes of death among American Indians and Alaska Natives in 2003 were as follows (National Center for Health Statistics, 2006):

- Diseases of the heart
- Malignant neoplasms
- Unintentional injuries
- Diabetes mellitus
- Chronic liver disease and cirrhosis
- Cerebrovascular diseases
- Chronic lower respiratory disease
- Influenza and pneumonia
- Suicide
- Nephritis, nephrotic syndrome, and nephrosis

It is important to note that these behavioral risk factors and common health problems in American Indians vary greatly among the tribes and regions. For example, Denny, Holtzman, and Cobb (2003) found that the prevalence of current cigarette smoking ranged from 21.2% in the Southwest to 44.1% in the Northern Plains, and the awareness of diabetes was lower in Alaska than in other regions. Therefore, it is important for health care professionals to gather data about the specific tribe and geographic region prior to developing any individual or community-based interventions.

American Indians have a high risk of motor vehicle deaths and injuries, which is caused by several factors. One factor is that they have the lowest rate of using seat belts in the nation. The other reason is their high rate of drinking and driving.

Denny et al. (2003) defined cigarette smoking as the respondent having ever smoked more than or equal to 100 cigarettes in his or her life and currently smoking.

These researchers found that cigarette smoking was highest in the Northern Plains (44.1%) and Alaska (39.0%) and lowest in the Southwest (21.2%). American Indian and Alaska Native respondents were more likely to report cigarette smoking (32.2%) than respondents of other racial and ethnic groups (22.3%) (Denny et al., 2003). The lands of American Indians do not impose taxes, and they do not have laws that prevent the sale of alcohol and tobacco products to minors. Because of this, the young population easily uses alcohol and tobacco products. American Indians believe that tobacco is sacred, and it is therefore more often used in ceremonies.

Diabetes also has become a problem within the American Indian community. American Indians and Alaska Natives are 2.2 times as likely to have diabetes as non-Hispanic whites (American Diabetes Association, n.d.). As illustrated in Figure 7, among other ethnicities, American Indians have the highest rate of diabetes.

The American Indian population has suffered from many suicide deaths. American Indian and Alaska Native males in the 15- to 24-year-old age group have the highest suicide rate, 27.99 per 100,000, compared to white (17.54 per 100,000), black

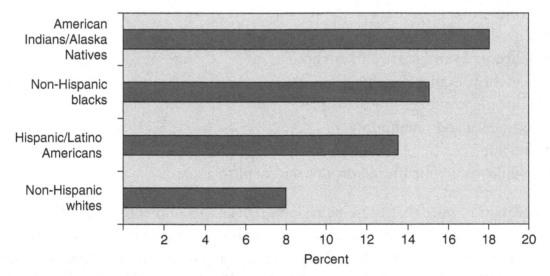

Footnote: *For American Indians/Alaska Natives, the estimate of total prevalence was calculated using the estimate of diagnosed diabetes from the 2003 outpatient database of the Indian Health Service and the estimate of undiagnosed diabetes from the 1999-2002 National Health and Nutrition Examination Survey. For the other groups, 1999-2002 NHANES estimates of total prevalence (both diagnosed and undiagnosed) were projected to year 2006.*

FIGURE 7 Estimated age-adjusted total prevalence of diabetes in people aged 20 years or older, by race/ethnicity: United States, 2005.

Source: Centers for Disease Control and Prevention. (2006).

(12.8 per 100,000), and Asian and Pacific Islander (8.96 per 100,000) males of the same age (Suicide Prevention Resource Center, n.d.). Suicide was the leading cause of death for American Indians and Alaska Natives between the ages of 10 and 34 years (Suicide Prevention Resource Center, n.d.).

QUICK FACTS

Cancer
- In 2002, American Indian/Alaska Native men were 30% less likely to have prostate cancer as non-Hispanic white men.
- In 2002, American Indian/Alaska Native women were 30% less likely to have breast cancer as non-Hispanic white women.
- American Indian/Alaska Native men were twice as likely to be diagnosed with stomach and liver cancers as white men.
- American Indian women were 20% more likely to die from cervical cancer, compared to white women.

Diabetes
- American Indian/Alaska Native adults were 2.3 times as likely as white adults to be diagnosed with diabetes.
- American Indians/Alaska Natives were twice as likely as non-Hispanic whites to die from diabetes in 2003.
- American Indian/Alaska Native adults were 1.6 times as likely as white adults to be obese.
- American Indian/Alaska Native adults were 1.3 times as likely as white adults to have high blood pressure.

Heart Disease
- American Indian/Alaska Native adults are 1.2 times as likely as white adults to have heart disease.
- American Indian/Alaska Native adults are 1.4 times as likely as white adults to be current cigarette smokers.
- American Indian/Alaska Native adults are 1.6 times as likely as white adults to be obese.
- American Indian/Alaska Native adults are 1.3 times as likely as white adults to have high blood pressure.

HIV–AIDS
- American Indian/Alaska Natives have a 40% higher AIDS rate than their non-Hispanic white counterparts.
- American Indian/Alaska Native men have a 10% higher AIDS rate, compared to non-Hispanic white men.
- American Indian/Alaska Native women have three times the AIDS rate of non-Hispanic white women.

(Continues)

263

Immunization

- In 2005, American Indian/Alaska Native children aged 19 to 35 months received the recommended doses of vaccines for measles, mumps, rubella, Hib-Imune, polio, and chicken pox at the same rate as non-Hispanic white children.
- In 2005, American Indian/Alaska Native adults aged 18 to 64 years were slightly more likely than their non-Hispanic white counterparts to have received the influenza (flu) shot in the past 12 months.

Infant Mortality

- American Indians/Alaska Natives have 1.5 times the infant mortality rate as non-Hispanic whites.
- American Indian/Alaska Native babies are 2.2 times as likely as non-Hispanic white babies to die from sudden infant death syndrome (SIDS), and they are 1.4 times as likely to die from complications related to low birth weight or congenital malformations, compared to non-Hispanic whites babies.
- American Indian/Alaska Native infants are 3.6 times as likely as non-Hispanic white infants to have mothers who began prenatal care in the third trimester or did not receive prenatal care at all.

Stroke

- In general, American Indian/Alaska Native adults are 60% more likely to have a stroke than their white adult counterparts.
- American Indian/Alaska Native women have twice the rate of stroke as white women.
- American Indian/Alaska Native adults are more likely to be obese than white adults, and they are more likely to have high blood pressure, compared to white adults.

Source: Office of Minority Health. (2008).

HISTORY OF ALASKA NATIVES IN THE UNITED STATES

The natives of Alaska are one of the oldest civilizations, and they have experienced numerous conflicts in relation to land possession and redistribution. Alaska Natives were living on their land when Russians arrived to make their claims on the land. After years of Russian rule, Alaska was purchased by the United States in 1867. In 1906 the Homestead Act established land to the following individuals: "Indian or Eskimo of full or mixed blood who resides in and is a native of said district, and who is the head of a family, or is 21 years of age; and the land so allotted shall be deemed the homestead of the allotted and his heirs in perpetuity, and shall be inalienable and non-taxable until otherwise provided by Congress" (Alaska Native Heritage Center, 2000). This act was the first to establish land for Alaska Natives, but it left out many tribes.

Discrimination and segregation was prevalent in Alaska, especially between Alaska Natives and whites (Russians and Americans). In 1945, Alaska passed a law that ended legal segregation, and this marked the start of a new beginning. According to the Alaska Native Claims Settlement Act of 1971, 40 million acres of land and nearly a billion dollars was awarded to Alaska Natives.

ALASKA NATIVES IN THE UNITED STATES

Alaska Natives include people from villages or tribes such as Aleut, Inupiat, Yupik, Eskimo, and Athabaskan peoples. Today Alaska Natives face difficulty in conforming to the American culture. Many natives have been forced to live outside their accustomed villages due to a lack of resources. As a result, some native families have been affected by these demographic changes. Alaska Natives who choose to move to the city no longer hunt or fish and are adopting unhealthy American food standards. These types of changes may contribute to some of the health disparities that Alaska Natives face. Even though Alaska Natives have faced a turbulent past, traditional Alaska Native culture can still be seen within their social environment.

There are many different languages that Alaska Natives use to communicate. The Alaska Native Language Center currently reports 20 known native languages. However, this organization also reports that many languages will go extinct by the next generation (Palca, 2002). Unfortunately, because there is a variety of languages, it is difficult to accommodate all of them in the public education system. Cultural and linguistic differences are one of the root causes of why Alaska's education system is failing its native students.

Villages consist of mostly related families; however, if residents are not related, they are still treated as one big family. Alaska Natives typically develop close-knit relationships with one another. Village members watch out for one another, and food is always shared when an animal is caught. Alaska Natives believe that if a person shares his or her food, the person will catch more animals in the future. When a young male experiences his first kill, it is tradition for him to give the entire kill to the elders, who are highly respected and are needed to pass on traditions from generation to generation. The tradition of sharing and giving is a major part of Native Alaskan culture.

Hunting, fishing, and gathering are the way of life in rural Alaska (Alexandria, 1994). Native Alaskans' diet mainly consists of fish, deer, moose, whale, seal, caribou, duck, walrus, and sea lion. Alaska Natives consume about 40% protein in their daily diet. They typically suffer some deficiencies in their diet, such as calcium, vitamin D, and vitamin C (Nobmann, Byers, Lanier, Hankin, & Jackson, 1992). However, there are some plants that can be eaten to make up for the deficiency if they grow in the surrounding environment. Usually, the men do the strenuous hunting, and the women gather berries and plants that will aid in nutrition. Women also prepare and store the food after it is gathered. The common methods for food preparation have caused the highest rates of *Clostridium botulinum* outbreaks in the world (Shaffer, Wainwright, Middaugh, & Tauxe, 1990). Currently, prevention efforts are in place to stop the growth of the toxic bacteria, which is also found naturally in the soil.

Religion was never a big part of life in a native village. Currently, the main religions of Alaska include Russian Orthodox and Christianity. However, years ago Native Alaskans were focused on survival instead of organized religion.

BELIEFS ABOUT CAUSES OF HEALTH AND ILLNESS AMONG ALASKA NATIVES

Despite the fact that some Alaska Natives are nonreligious, traditional natives believe that the cause of illness is derived from spirits (Alexandria, 1994). To get rid of an illness, a shaman is needed to remove the ill spirit and restore health. Healing ceremonies can take place in public, and the shaman encourages village members to participate to get rid of the bad spirit that is causing the illness. In addition, some shamans have medical skills, such as treating burns with fat, cleaning wounds with urine, amputating frozen gangrenous limbs, and setting broken bones. Traditional natives believe that shamans have the ability to fly and reach the heavens.

Currently, beliefs about the causes of illness are beginning to shift. Alaska Natives noticed that they were less likely to get sick when they traveled in small nomadic bands. However, when Alaska Natives began to settle, they noticed that people were more likely to become ill and die. As a result, they have begun to lean toward the germ theory. Shamans are still used today, because it is often difficult to reach health care clinics. In some instances, both a shaman and Western medicine are used in combination to treat illness.

HEALING TRADITIONS AMONG ALASKA NATIVES

There are many ancient traditions for healing that are used by Alaska Natives.

> Alaska Native traditional healing practices are rooted in a 10,000 year history and are re-emerging today as an holistic healing approach for individuals and communities. These methods are often used in combination with western-based medical therapies for the purpose of health promotion, disease prevention, pain reduction and enhancement of psychological wellness. (Corral, 2007)

Alaska Native traditional healing may indeed be pairing up with Western medicine in some regions of Alaska where that is plausible, and there are some specific examples of this phenomenon. For example, Alaska Natives refer to traditional healers as "traditional healers" and "tribal doctors." Though they may sound as if they are one of the same, there is one very important distinction: Traditional healers are members of the communities who learn the traditional healing methods by observing other traditional healers over a number of years. Formal standardized training or apprenticeship does not exist. Tribal doctors are similar to traditional healers in the sense that they are very knowledgeable about native traditional healing modalities. The difference is that tribal doctors go through some sort of formal standardized training, and they most often work under the supervison of or in alliance with physicians. This alliance that tribal doctors have formed with physicians clearly demonstrates the connection between Native Alaskan traditional healing modalities and Western medicine (Corral, 2007).

Despite the emergence of a complementary relationship between Alaskan traditional healing and Western medicine, traditional healing practices are quite distinguishable when compared to the Western medicine mode of treatment.

> While allopathic medicine focuses on identifying and treating a specific diagnosis, traditional healing strives to restore the patient's sense of natural balance and harmony with self, community and culture. Traditional healing attempts to nurture the mind–body–spirit connection, and to actively involve the patient in finding renewed commitment to lifelong health and wellness. (Corral, 2007)

Medicinal plants, such as roots, berries, leaves, and flowers, have historically been used as healing agents throughout Alaska's many regions. These medicinal plants are used in numerous ways to heal everything from the common cold, flesh wounds, and mouth sores, to promoting healthy pregnancy, to many other applications (Corral, 2007). A common medicinal plant that is widely used in Alaska and British Columbia for treating a variety of ailments, including arthritis, fever, and diabetes, is known as Devil's Club (*Oplopanax horridus* [OH]). According to Tai and colleagues (2006), ethanolic extract of OH has antiproliferative (meaning that it prevents the spread and growth of cells) effects on several types of cancer cells, and it has strong antioxidant activity. The medicinal plants are aimed more at healing the bodily ailments, but other traditional healing modalities are also focused on the spirit and the mind.

Drumming, dancing, and singing are known to be very powerful sources of healing among Alaska Natives. The ceremonies incorporate music, movement, and drum rhythms to penetrate the people involved and aid them in fully expressing emotion, increasing physical energy, making a strong connection with life and one another, and promoting happiness. This also helps to promote overall well-being and a sense of love among the community. These ceremonies can be used to prevent drug and alcohol abuse, domestic violence, and suicide, which are some of the most prevalent problems among Alaska Natives (Corral, 2007).

BEHAVIORAL RISK FACTORS AND COMMON HEALTH PROBLEMS AMONG ALASKA NATIVES

Unfortunately, many of the issues that Alaska Natives struggle with are due to unhealthy and risky behaviors. The top behavioral risk factors are alcohol consumption, smoking and chewing tobacco, drug use, inadequate exercise, obese body weight, unhealthy diet, violence, and suicide.

Alcohol has caused health problems and behavioral issues in many societies, but Alaska Natives have been struck much harder than most. There are many theories as to why alcohol is such a major issue in Alaska, but one study conducted by the National Center for American Indian and Alaska Native Mental Health Research goes back to the beginning. According to this study, alcohol was not a part of Alaska's culture until it was introduced by the Russians, who used it to abuse the natives and take advantage of them. Alcohol quickly became a problem in small villages, spreading like wildfire. The immediate effect was an increase in spouse abuse and neglect of daily chores. This behavior led to shame and guilt, which was often dealt with by more drinking. This behavior is learned by the children in the home, and the cycle continues. The average starting age for drinking is now at around 9 years old (Seale, Shellenberger, & Spence, 2006). Seale et al. (2006) sum up the cultural effects in this statement: "The stress, confusion, and depression caused by the dramatic cultural changes of the twentieth century were described as a major influence on alcohol consumption" (p. 11). The traditional culture for many Alaska Natives is gone, and they are left to live with limited resources for success. Without adequate health education and easy access to medical or mental health care, it has become a difficult task to fight a problem of alcohol abuse.

Alcohol abuse has been linked to many health problems, both directly and indirectly. One deadly health outcome associated with alcohol is suicide, which is the fourth leading cause of death among Alaska Natives (Alaska Native Epidemiology Center, 2007). "Suicide is a particularly critical problem among male Alaska Natives, who are 14 to 40 times more likely to commit suicide than any other United States male in the same age group" (Seale, et al., 2006, p. 2).

Another behavioral risk factor that is extremely prevalent among Alaska Natives is the use of tobacco. Smoking and/or chewing tobacco is practiced by half of all

Alaska Natives older than the age of 12 years. "Of those patients who were screened for tobacco use during 2006, 46% were smokers. Fifty-nine percent used some form of tobacco" (Alaska Native Epidemiology Center, 2007, p. 30).

Obesity is a problem among Alaska Natives. Twenty-three percent of U.S. whites are obese, compared to 31% of Alaska Natives (Alaska Native Epidemiology Center, 2007). In addition, Alaska Native adults get less than half the amount of some sort of physical activity as that of U.S. whites: 25% and 51%, respectively (Alaska Native Epidemiology Center, 2007).

Like all cultural groups in the United States, Alaska Natives suffer from many health problems that greatly affect their way of life. These health problems result in an overall lower life expectancy. The 10 leading causes of death for Alaska Natives between 1989 and 1998 in order of frequency were cancer, unintentional injuries, heart disease, suicide, cerebrovascular disease, chronic obstructive pulmonary disease, pneumonia and influenza, homicide and legal intervention, chronic liver disease, and diabetes (Lanier, Ehrsam, & Sandidge, 2002).

Unintentional injuries and suicides are ranked second and fourth among Alaska Natives, and both of these health disparities are preventable. "Unintentional injuries are the leading cause of death in children and young adults and are responsible for the greatest number of years of life lost in Alaska" (Alaska Department of Health & Social Services, 2002, p. 4). The high rate of alcohol abuse among Alaska Natives contributes to the toll of injuries (Alaska Department of Health & Social Services, 2002). Some of the other contributing factors to the high rate of unintentional injuries are the prevalence of guns in homes, no laws that require helmets, and inadequate seat belt laws. "Firearm death rates for Alaska Natives are more than four times the national rate" (Alaska Department of Health & Social Services, 2002, p. 4). "Guns are readily available in many homes in Alaska due to recreational and subsistence hunting" (Alaska Department of Health & Social Services, 2002, p. 4). In Alaska there are no laws that require people to wear helmets while they are riding a motorcycle, snowmobile, all-terrain vehicle (ATV), or bicycle (Alaska Department of Health & Social Services, 2002). The absence of these laws is very unfortunate because the use of a helmet could reduce the death rate. "The state of Alaska does have a seat belt law, but police officers are not allowed to issue a citation unless they have another reason to pull over the vehicle" (Alaska Department of Health & Social Services, 2002, p. 6). Unfortunately, these laws are not very proactive in combating the problems that Alaska Natives face.

Mental health problems contribute to the accident and suicide rates as well. "Estimates project about 10 percent of Alaska's children and youths (age 5 to 18) have severe emotional disturbances, and 6.2 percent of Alaska's adult population under age 55 suffer from severe mental illness" (Alaska Department of Health & Social Services,

2002, p. 4). "Together, accidents and suicides accounted for about 72 percent of all deaths in the 15–34 age group" (Alaska Department of Health & Social Services, 2002, p. 6). It is awful that there is such a high prevalence of mental health problems among Alaska Natives, and yet 175 villages in Alaska have no local mental health services other than the occasional itinerant provider (Alaska Department of Health & Social Services, 2002). "Around 90 percent of all people who kill themselves have a mental or substance abuse disorder or a combination of disorders" (Alaska Department of Health & Social Services, 2002, p. 5).

CONSIDERATIONS FOR HEALTH PROMOTION AND PROGRAM PLANNING

The following are some concepts to consider when planning and implementing a health promotion program for this target audience.

- Native peoples use their tribal names when referring to themselves, so it is advised that health care professionals ask individuals or groups how they prefer to be addressed.
- Recognize that there are varying degrees of acculturation levels, so health care professionals need to assess where the patient or client is on the continuum of acculturation.
- Recognize that there is great diversity among the tribes, so do not make assumptions.
- Holistic thinking is common and should be used to identify appropriate and acceptable prevention and treatment plans.
- Try to accommodate complementary and alternative forms of healing.
- Do not be surprised or offended by a hand shake that is softer or gentler than you are accustomed to.
- Be patient with silence, and give the listener time to reflect on what you said prior to responding.
- Prolonged eye contact should be avoided, because it is viewed as being disrespectful.
- Work with the families and remember that elders are respected.
- Do not encourage or try to reward competitive behavior, because cooperation is valued by these cultures.
- Do not appear to be in a hurry, because it may give a negative impression of you.
- Do not interrupt the person who is speaking, because it is considered to be extremely rude.

- Keep nonverbal communication to a minimum.
- With the exception of a hand shake, touch is not usually acceptable.
- Remember that listening is more valued than speaking.
- Be aware that suspicion and mistrust may exist.
- When developing community programs, involve the community members.
- Be aware of superstitions such as unlucky and lucky numbers and colors.
- Consider the incorporation of talking circles into your program.

CHAPTER SUMMARY

American Indians and Alaska Natives have a history of being conquered by other nations, having foreign cultures impose upon their way of life, and being the victims of discrimination. Fortunately, they have been able to hold on to their traditional culture in many ways. They continue to express their traditional values within their villages by maintaining close-knit families and using traditional healing modalities to prevent and heal illness. Unfortunately, both groups experience major health disparities, such as high incidence of suicide, alcoholism, cancer, unintentional injuries, diabetes, and mental illness. Through quality and culturally-sensitive health promotion programs, perhaps one day American Indians and Alaska Natives will experience better health and gain access to quality health care.

In this chapter we discussed the challenges that these populations encountered historically. We learned that these populations do not believe in the germ theory as the cause of disease, although some Alaska Natives are adopting this belief system. We learned about their various approaches to healing, such as sweat baths and ceremonies, and their common behaviors, risk factors, and illnesses. General tips for working with these populations were provided, but we caution that there is a vast amount of diversity within these groups, so it is important not to generalize.

REVIEW

1. Describe the histories of American Indians and Alaska Natives in the United States.
2. According to American Indian and Alaska Native beliefs, how is illness caused?
3. What are sweat lodges, talking circles, and medicine wheels?
4. Describe some plants and herbs that are used for healing.
5. Describe what medicine men are and their approach to healing.

CASE STUDY

Don is a 45-year-old, full-blood Indian who is married and has five children. The family lives in a small, rural community on a large reservation in New Mexico. Don was sent to boarding school for high school, and then he served in the war. He recently was treated through Veterans Affairs (VA), which is where he participated in a posttraumatic stress disorder (PTSD) support group. Don suffers from alcoholism. It began soon after his initial patrols in the war, which involved heavy combat and, ultimately, physical injury. He exhibits the hallmark symptoms of PTSD, including flashbacks, nightmares, intrusive thoughts on an almost daily basis, marked hypervigilance, irritability, and avoidant behavior.

Don is fluent in English and his native language, which is spoken in his home. He is the descendant of a family of traditional healers. Consequently, the community expected him to assume a leadership role in its cultural and spiritual life. However, boarding school interrupted his early participation in important aspects of local ceremonial life. His participation was further delayed by military service and then forestalled by his alcoholism. During boarding school, Don was frequently harassed by non-Indian staff members for speaking his native language, for wearing his hair long, and for running away. Afraid of similar ridicule while in the service, he seldom shared his personal background with fellow infantrymen. Don was the target of racism and was called "Chief" and "blanket ass."

Some 10 years after his return from the war, Don began cycling through several periods of treatment for his alcoholism in tribal residential programs. It was not until one month after he began treatment for his alcoholism at a local VA facility that a provisional diagnosis of PTSD was made. Upon completing that treatment, he transferred to an inpatient unit that specialized in combat-related trauma. Don left the unit against medical advice, sober but still experiencing significant symptoms.

Don's tribal members frequently refer to PTSD as the "wounded spirit." His community has long recognized the consequences of being a warrior, and indeed, a ceremony has evolved over many generations to prevent as well as treat the underlying causes of these symptoms. Within this tribal worldview, combat-related trauma upsets the balance that underpins someone's personal, physical, mental, emotional, and spiritual health. Don did not participate in these and other tribal ceremonies until after he was diagnosed at the VA with PTSD. His sobriety has been aided by involvement in the Native American Church, with its reinforcement of his decision to remain sober and its support for positive life changes.

Though Don has a great deal of work ahead of him, he feels that he is now ready to participate in the tribe's major ceremonial intended to bless and purify its warriors. His family, once alienated but now reunited, is excited about that process.

There are several issues to consider about this case:

- What cultural issues exist in this scenario?
- How did Don's culture help and hinder his situation?
- Are there steps that could have been taken to help prevent Don's alcohol problem?

Source: Adapted from National Alliance on Mental Illness. (2003).

MODEL PROGRAM

American Indian Life Skills Development

The American Indian Life Skills Development curriculum is a school-based, culturally-tailored, suicide-prevention curriculum for American Indian adolescents. Tailored to American Indian norms, values, beliefs, and attitudes, the curriculum is designed to build self-esteem, identify emotions and stress, increase communication and problem-solving skills, and recognize and eliminate self-destructive behavior, including substance abuse. The curriculum provides American Indian adolescents with information on suicide and suicide-intervention training and helps them set personal and community goals.

Each lesson in the curriculum contains standard skills training techniques for providing information about the helpful or harmful effects of certain behaviors, modeling of target skills, experimental activities, behavior rehearsal for skill acquisition, and feedback for skills refinement. The curriculum can be delivered three times a week over 30 weeks during the school year or as an after-school program.

Evaluation

The research design was nonrandom, quasi-experimental with two conditions: an intervention and a no-intervention condition. A multimethod approach was used to assess the effectiveness of the curriculum. It included a pretest and posttest self-report survey of risk factors associated with suicide, behavioral observations of suicide intervention skills targeted in the curriculum judged by two American Indian graduate students, and peer ratings of classmates' skills and abilities relevant to suicide intervention. Freshman students enrolled in a required language arts class were eligible for the study, and juniors were included to increase the sample size. Sophomores were expressly excluded because of their participation in a program pilot test the previous year. Sixty-nine students were assigned to the intervention condition, and 59 students were assigned to the no-intervention condition. The sample was 64% female and 36% male. A pretest indicated that 81% of the sample was in the moderate to severe range on the Suicide Probability Scale. Forty percent of students reported that a relative or friend had committed suicide, and 18% reported having personally attempted suicide. Moreover, 79% of those students who attempted suicide in the past had attempted two times or more, 70% had tried within six months of the pretest, 17% had required medical attention, and 22% had informed no one about the attempt. Posttests were conducted eight months after the pretest.

Outcome

Overall, the evaluation produced evidence to suggest the curriculum succeeded in creating a healthier psychological profile. Students exposed to the curriculum scored better (lower) than the no-intervention group at posttest on suicide probability and hopelessness, and the intervention group showed greater ability to perform problem-solving and suicide intervention skills in a behavioral assessment. However, the evaluators noted potential threats to validity because of the coexistence of the two groups throughout the intervention.

Source: Helping America's Youth. (n.d.).

GLOSSARY TERMS

sweat lodges

shaman

talking circles

medicine bundle

peyote

REFERENCES

Advameg. (2007). *Diet of Native Americans*. Retrieved March 9, 2008, from http://www.faqs.org/nutrition/Met-Obe/Native-Americans-Diet-of.html

Alaska Department of Health & Social Services. (2002). *Healthy Alaskans 2010, volume 1: Targets for improved health*. Retrieved February 7, 2008, from http://www.hss.state.ak.us/dph/targets/ha2010/volume_1.htm

Alaska Native Epidemiology Center. (2007). Regional health profile for Yukon-Kuskokwim Health Corp. Retrieved February 12, 2008, from http://www.anthc.org/cs/chs/epi/upload/Regional_Health_Profile_YKHC_0707.pdf

Alaska Native Heritage Center. (2000). *Information about Alaska Native cultures*. Retrieved February 16, 2008, from http://www.akhistorycourse.org/articles/article.php?artID=195

Alexandria, V. (1994). *People of the ice and snow*. Richmond, VA: Time Life.

American Diabetes Association. (n.d.). *Total prevalence of diabetes and pre-diabetes*. Retrieved February 7, 2008, from http://www.diabetes.org/diabetes-statistics/prevalence.jsp

American Eagle Foundation. (n.d.). *American eagle & Native American Indian*. Retrieved March 10, 2008, from http://www.eagles.org/native_american.htm

Bonvillain, N. (1997). *Native American medicine*. Philadelphia: Chelsea House.

Centers for Disease Control and Prevention. (2006). *National diabetes fact sheet*. Retrieved December 1, 2006, from http://www.cdc.gov/diabetes/pubs/estimates05.htm#prev4

Corral, K. (2007). *Alaska Native traditional healing*. Retrieved February 2, 2008, from http://altmed.creighton.edu/AKNative

Denny, C. H., Holtzman, D., & Cobb, N. (2003). Surveillance for health behaviors of American Indians and Alaska Natives: Findings from the behavioral risk factor surveillance system, 1997–2000. *Morbidity and Mortality Weekly Report, 52*(SS07), 1–13. Retrieved March 16, 2008, from http://www.cdc.gov/mmwr/preview/mmwrhtml/ss5207a1.htm

Frankis, M. P. (2006). *Picea sitchensis (Bongard)*. Retrieved February 14, 2008, from http://www.conifers.org/pi/pic/sitchensis.htm

Haas, M. J. (2007). *Shaman song*. Retrieved February 2, 2008, from http://www.shamansong.com/gpage.html3.html

Hammerschlag, C. A. (1988). *The dancing healers: A doctor's journey of healing with Native Americans*. San Francisco: Harper.

Helping America's Youth. (n.d.). *American Indian life skills development*. Retrieved October 31, 2008, from http://guide.helpingamericasyouth.gov/programdetail.cfm?id=635

Indian Health Service. (2007). *Indian health service introduction*. Retrieved March 13, 2008, from http://www.ihs.gov/PublicInfo/PublicAffairs/Welcome_Info/IHSintro.asp

Kelman, S. (1999). *American government*. New York: Holt-Rinehart & Winston.

Lanier, A. P., Ehrsam, G., & Sandidge, J. (2002). Alaska Native mortality. Retrieved March 25, 2008, from http://surveillance.cancer.gov/documents/disparities/native/ANMortality.pdf

Management Sciences for Health. (n.d.). *American Indians & Alaska Natives: Health disparities overview*. Retrieved March 3, 2008, from http://erc.msh.org/mainpage.cfm?file=7.3.0.htm&module=provider&language=English#readmoe

Marbella, A. M, Harris, M. C., Diehr, S., Ignace, G., & Ignace, G. (1998). Use of Native American healers among Native American patients in an urban Native American health center. *Archives of Family Medicine, 7*, 182–185.

National Alliance on Mental Illness. (2003). American Indian and Alaska Native. Retrieved on March 18, 2009, from http://www.nami.org/Content/ContentGroups/Multicultural_Support1/CDResourceManual.pdf

National Center for Health Statistics. (2006). *Health, United States, 2005*. Retrieved March 17, 2008, from http://www.ncbi.nlm.nih.gov/books/bv.fcgi?rid=healthus05.table.379

Nixon, President Richard. (1970). *Special Message on Indian Affairs*. Retrieved from http://www.undeclaredutes.net/pdf/nixonmessage.pdf

Nobmann, E. D., Byers, T., Lanier, A. P., Hankin, J. H., & Jackson, M. Y. (1992). The diet of Alaska Native adults: 1987–1988. *American Journal of Clinical Nutrition, 55*, 1024–1032.

Office of Minority Health. (2008). *American Indian/Alaska Native profile*. Retrieved March 8, 2008, from http://www.omhrc.gov/templates/browse.aspx?lvl=2&lvlid=52

Palca, J. (2002). *Saving Alaska's native languages*. Retrieved February 9, 2008, from http://www.npr.org/programs/morning/features/2002/mar/alaska/

Rehling, J. (n.d.). *Native American languages.* Retrieved March 8, 2008, from http://www.cogsci.indiana.edu/farg/rehling/nativeAm/ling.html

Seale, J., Shellenberger, S., & Spence, J. (2006). Alcohol problems in Alaska Natives: Lessons from the Inuit. *American Indian and Alaska Native Mental Health Research: The Journal of the National Center, 13*(1), 1–31. Retrieved February 18, 2008, from Academic Search Premier database.

Shaffer, N., Wainwright, R. B., Middaugh, J. P., & Tauxe, R. V. (1990). Botulism among Alaska Natives: The role of changing food preparation and consumption practices. *The Western Journal of Medicine, 153,* 390–393.

Spector, R. E. (2004). *Cultural diversity in health and illness.* Upper Saddle River, NJ: Pearson Education.

Suicide Prevention Resource Center. (n.d.). *Suicide among American Indians/Alaska Natives.* Retrieved February 7, 2008, from http://www.sprc.org/library/ai.an.facts.pdf

Tai, J., Cheung, S., Cheah, S., Chan, E., & Hasman, D. (2006, November 24). In vitro anti-proliferative and anti-oxidant studies on Devil's Club *Oplopanax horridus. Journal of Ethnopharmacology, 108*(2), 228–235.

US Census Bureau. (2002). *The American Indian and Alaska Native population: 2000.* Retrieved March 4, 2008, from http://www.census.gov/prod/2002pubs/c2kbr01-15.pdf

US Census Bureau. (2008). *Population density of the United States, and selected maps of race and Hispanic origin: 2000.* Retrieved November 9, 2008, from http://www.census.gov/population/www/censusdata/2000maps.html

US Department of Agriculture. (2007). *Ethnic/cultural food guide pyramid.* Retrieved March 7, 2008, from http://fnic.nal.usda.gov/nal_display/index.php?info_center=4&tax_level=3&tax_subject=256&topic_id=1348&level3_id=5732

West Virginia Division of Culture and History. (2008). *Native American communities in West Virginia.* Retrieved February 5, 2008, from http://www.wvculture.org/arts/ethnic/native.html

PHOTO CREDITS

Chapter

Opener , © Jose Gil/Dreamstime.com

Unless otherwise indicated, all photographs and illustrations are under copyright of Jones and Bartlett Publishers, LLC, or have been provided by the author(s).

African American Populations

I have a dream that my four little children will one day live in a nation where they will not be judged by the color of their skin, but by the content of their character.

—Martin Luther King, Jr.

If I'd known I was going to live this long, I'd have taken better care of myself.

—Eubie Blake

KEY CONCEPTS

- Tuskegee study
- Voodoo
- Candomblé

CHAPTER OBJECTIVES

1. Provide an overview of the social and economic circumstances of African Americans in the United States.
2. Provide an overview of African American beliefs about the causes of illness.
3. Describe at least three African American healing practices.
4. Describe African American health risk behaviors and common illnesses.
5. List at least six tips for working with African American populations.

The term "black people" usually refers to humans with dark skin color, so the term has been used to categorize a number of diverse populations into one common group. Some definitions of the term include only people of relatively recent sub-Saharan African descent. Others extend the term to any of the populations characterized by dark skin color, a definition that also includes certain populations in geographic regions such as South Asia and Southeast Asia. African Americans are defined as people who have origins in any of the black racial groups in Africa. Historically identified by a number of terms (Negro, colored, black) over the decades, the current politically correct term to refer to anyone who has roots in any of the African countries is African American. This term also is preferable to the younger members (aged 30 years and younger) of this group. However, older members (aged 60 years and older) may still prefer to be called Negro or colored, and middle-aged members (aged 30 to 60 years) may prefer to be called black. It is acceptable to ask African Americans what ethnic term they personally prefer (Nobles & Goddard, 1990). In the literature the terms "African American" and "black" are used. The term "black" incorporates a broader population. For example, black Caribbean Islanders fall within the category of black but not African American. In this chapter, we focus on African Americans, but when we refer to research, the term used in the original source is used.

In this chapter we discuss the unique history of African Americans, which includes forced migration. This history plays a role in the following parts of the chapter, which includes a discussion about their current position within the United States, beliefs about the causes of illness and how to treat it, health behaviors, and common health problems. Then we move into a discussion about how to create a successful community health program taking these factors into consideration.

HISTORY OF AFRICAN AMERICANS IN THE UNITED STATES

The slave trade, which was called the "transatlantic slave trade," was the forced migration of Africans to the New World, which occurred in or around the Atlantic Ocean (The New York Public Library, 2007). It lasted from the sixteenth century to the nineteenth century, and an estimated 12 million men, women, and children were forced to migrate to the United States from their homeland of Africa. The majority of the ancestors of African Americans came from a part of Africa bounded by the Senegal River in the north and by Angola in the south. This area also was called the area of catchment, which is the known area from which the slaves were taken (Perry, 1998). Africans were taken by force, made to be slaves, and shipped to other countries against their will (Perry, 1998). Under these circumstances it is very unlikely that families stayed intact. With the influx of Africans to America came a new culture and a new way of life for the future generations of African Americans.

African indentured and enslaved laborers assisted with the European colonial expansion in North America as they cleared the land, erected shelters, and constructed forts. They raised subsistence crops, gathered lumber, raised cattle and hogs, and harvested exports that supported the colonial economies. People of African descent, free and bound, helped defend the colonies against Indians and against other European colonial powers' attempts at territorial expansion. After the British colonies established territorial dominance along the Atlantic coast, people of African descent—many second and third generation Americans, some free or near-free indentured servants, and some bound in slavery—involved themselves in the politics of revolution.

They fought in the wars of rebellion and participated in the birth and growth of the United States.

Even though African Americans made these great contributions to North America, they faced horrific acts and mistreatment, sexual assault, lynching, and other forms of violent acts and discrimination. During the time of slavery, slave overseers were authorized to whip and brutalize noncompliant slaves. Each state had laws (known as slave codes) that defined the status of slaves and the rights of masters; the codes gave slave owners near-absolute power over the rights of their human property. These codes indemnified or even required the use of violence and were condemned by people who opposed slavery as being evil. In addition to physical abuse and murder, slaves were at constant risk of losing members of their families if their owners decided to trade them for profit, punishment, or to pay debts. A few slaves retaliated by murdering owners and overseers, burning barns, killing horses, or staging work slowdowns. After slavery and the Civil War ended, black codes were used to regulate the freedoms of former slaves. The black codes outraged people in the North because it seemed that the South was creating a form of quasi-slavery to evade the results of the war. After winning the 1866 elections, the Republicans put the South under military rule. The new governments repealed all the black codes, and they were never reenacted. Even with the changes in laws, African Americans still faced unequal treatment and discrimination, which continues into the present day.

AFRICAN AMERICANS IN THE UNITED STATES

African Americans constitute almost 13% of the American population (Centers for Disease Control and Prevention [CDC], 2008), and they live throughout America but are mostly concentrated in southern states (see Figure 1). In 2006, the 10 states with the largest black populations were New York, Florida, Texas, Georgia, California, Illinois, North Carolina, Maryland, Virginia, and Michigan (Office of Minority Health, 2008). African Americans are the second largest minority population, following the Hispanic/Latino population. At the time of the 2000 census, 58% of African Americans lived in urban areas (CDC, 2008).

With many African Americans living in urban cities, overcrowding in some urban areas has added to the stress for many residents. These areas tend to be surrounded by the symptoms of poverty, high crime, and inadequate housing (Walker, 1996). In fact, murder is the leading cause of death among young African American males (Campinha-Bacote, 1998). These impoverished neighborhoods often lack adequate health care institutions, such as hospitals, clinics, and pharmacies.

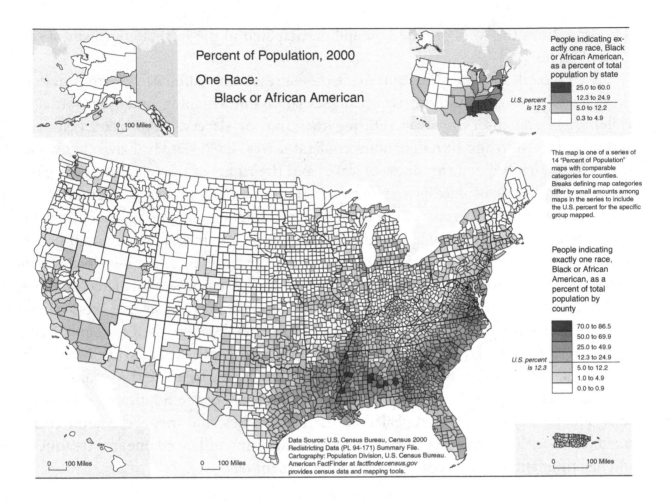

FIGURE 1 Percentage of population: Black or African American, 2000.
Source: U.S. Census Bureau, Population Division (2008), http://www.census.gov/main/www/citation.html.

African Americans have to contend with higher poverty levels. In 2006, the U.S. Census Bureau reported that 20% of African Americans, in comparison to 8% of non-Hispanic Caucasians, were living at or below the poverty level (Office of Minority Health, 2008). This represents a large number of single African American women with children. The effect of poverty on one's health is extensive. In this country the poor are more likely to be sick, compared to those with higher incomes who live longer and healthier lives (Office of Minority Health, 2008). Poverty itself is a hardship because it is related to marital stress and dissolution, health problems, low educational attainment, deficits in psychological functioning, and crime. According to a U.S. Census Bureau report (2006), the average African American family's median income was $31,969, in comparison to $52,423 for non-Hispanic Caucasian families

(Office of Minority Health, 2008). In 2006, the unemployment rate for blacks was twice that for non-Hispanic whites (8% and 4%, respectively) (Office of Minority Health, 2008). Poverty confronts African Americans with daily problems and forces them to be concerned with the present necessities of life rather than the future. Sometimes obtaining medical care has to wait while money is allocated to food, shelter, and other basic needs (Leininger, 1995).

A lower percentage of African Americans have health insurance coverage than whites. In 2006, 17.3% of African Americans, in comparison to 12% of non-Hispanic Caucasians, were uninsured (Office of Minority Health, 2008). In 2004, 55% of African Americans, in comparison to 78% of non-Hispanic Caucasians, used employer-sponsored health insurance (Office of Minority Health, 2008). Also in 2004, 24.6% of African Americans, in comparison to 7.9% of non-Hispanic Caucasians, relied on public health insurance (Office of Minority Health, 2008).

In 2004, 74% of blacks received a high school diploma, compared to 81% of non-Hispanic whites (Office of Minority Health, 2008). The percentage of all white adults over the age of 25 years in 2003 who held a graduate degree was 9.8%, compared to the percentage of all African American adults, which was 5.3% (US Census Bureau, 2006). Even when African Americans progress educationally, it has been found that only 47% who are college graduates earn as much as Anglo-Americans who are high school graduates only (US Department of Health and Human Services, 2000).

Most African American children live in a single-parent household. Sixty-eight percent of African American births are to unmarried parents, compared to whites (29%) and Hispanics (44%) (Christopher, 2006). Sixty-two percent of all African American households are headed by a single parent, compared to 27% of white and 35% of Hispanic households, and 61% of black children live in low-income families (Christopher, 2006).

Because of the high percentage of female-headed households in the African American community, when women are unable to handle various situations they usually rely on grandmothers, mothers, aunts, and godmothers to provide assistance (Campinha-Bacote, 1998). Large, extended family networks are the norm for most African Americans. It is not uncommon to have children grow up in the same household as their grandparents and around the comer from several aunts, uncles, and cousins (Ladner & Gourdine, 1992). This is in keeping with the tradition of the matriarchal lineage in many African villages and the fact that in slavery times many fathers were taken away from the family and sold (Ladner & Gourdine, 1992).

African American people have a deep reliance on faith. Spirituality plays a major role in African American culture and is often expressed through religious practices and activities. The black church has been a cornerstone in the African American community, serving as an organizing place and stabilizing entity. It has been noted that health screening programs may best be initiated through community and church activities where the entire family is usually present (Jennings, 1996 as cited in Fields, 2001).

In general, there is a mistrust of the health care system by most African Americans. This mistrust has been fueled by incidences, such as the **Tuskegee study**, in which the U.S. Public Health Service conducted a study from 1932 to 1972 on hundreds of black men with syphilis. The men were not treated with antibiotics that would have cured the disease, and indeed, most of them died (Clarke-Tasker, 1993). The scientific and medical communities reacted with shock after the study was exposed; however, most African Americans universally saw the study as a blatant act of genocide perpetrated against blacks by whites. As a result, many people in the African American community believe that health care professionals simply do not value their lives.

The number of African American health care professionals is low, which further compounds the issues of mistrust in the African American community. In 1999 only 3.6% of all physicians and 4.9% of registered nurses were African American (U.S. Department of Health and Human Services, n.d.). These numbers are not in proportion to the overall African American population.

The distrust in the medical system is not a paranoid reaction. Research shows that blacks commonly receive disrespect in health care settings (Welch, 2003). Many blacks experience adverse encounters due to negative assumptions and images (Welch, 2003). The most common assumption is related to women's sexual promiscuity (Welch, 2003). Consider the experience of Betty, a 40-year-old black woman who works in health care. Here she describes her experience with a health care provider during a visit for a Pap smear:

> I went to this doctor. I had an infection. . . . She said, "How many sex partners do you have?" I said "Gulp" and just looked at her. . . . She said, "Oh, you don't know how many". . . . I felt like I was a little piece of garbage. I was just . . . stereotyped: "There was a little black woman who's out havin' all of these men who comes in here with an infection. . . ." (Welch, 2003)

Subtle insults and comments make blacks feel inferior in health care settings. This mistrust is what leads African Americans to rely on traditional healing methods or to not seek care until it can no longer be avoided.

African Americans experience discrimination in other areas outside of the health care system as well. People who are constantly treated unfairly tend to have more stress, which can lead to emotional, physical, and behavioral problems. When people face discrimination during adolescence, they tend to have behavioral problems that lead to antisocial behavior. Teens can feel out of place among their peers, and because they choose not to talk about it, they act out their frustration that they keep inside. They may engage in aggressive and/or illegal acts, such as fighting and shoplifting. As a young teen, one may feel that there is nowhere to turn, which pushes one to consider suicide. Often when adults go through depression because of racial discrimination, they develop abnormal behaviors, such as being irritable and hostile toward others for no reason, having insomnia, and discriminating against others around them. Growing up around discrimination usually causes adolescents to have a hard time concentrating in school and achieving their goals. As adults it can lead to low self-esteem because they become less satisfied with their lives, thinking that every other race is better than theirs. Sometimes when people have had some kind of interaction with racial discrimination, they tend to think the world is out to get them. Everywhere they go, they think there's racial discrimination, even when there isn't any sign of discrimination. Physically, there are many effects of racial discrimi- nation. It causes stress, which can lead to problems such as high blood pressure and a weakened immune system. Another physical effect of racial discrimination is obesity and diabetes. Due to racial discrimination, many unhealthy behaviors arise, such as smoking, drinking, drug use, and binge eating. Another unhealthy behavior is that someone experiencing racial discrimination can verbally abuse someone or be very discriminating toward other people outside of their race. People who experience racial discrimination are usually from lower socioeconomic status (SES). This is partially a result of discrimination that occurs when seeking employment and in the work place.

BELIEFS ABOUT CAUSES OF HEALTH AND ILLNESS

Many low-income blacks traditionally separate illnesses into two categories: natural and unnatural illnesses (Welch, 2003). *Natural illness* occurs as a result of God's will or when a person comes into unhealthy contact with the forces of nature, such as expo- sure to cold or impurities in the air, food, or water. Natural illness also can occur as a punishment for sins (Welch, 2003). Cures for natural illness include an antidote or other logical protective actions. *Unnatural illness*, on the other hand, is considered to be the result of evil influences that alter God's intended plan (Welch, 2003). These illnesses are often founded on a belief in witchcraft, in which individuals exist who possess power to mobilize the forces of good and evil. The use of voodoo healers among Haitians and other West Indian blacks is an example. Treatment or cures for unnatural illness can be found in religion, magic, amulets, and herbs. Many of these beliefs are African in origin, and aspects of them may be seen among African Americans of all backgrounds (Welch, 2003).

Many African Americans believe that health is a gift from God; illness is a result of something that was not pleasing to God (Sadler & Huff, 2007). African Americans have historically believed that illness may be due to their failure to live according to God's will. Some African Americans even believe that illness comes directly from Satan (Roberson, 1985 as cited in Fields, 2001). Although most African American communities rely on religion and their relationship with God as a main reason for illness, some community members do not. As with any community, it is difficult to truly determine how the African American community perceives the cause of disease, illness, or injury because no two African Americans are alike.

Like all cultures, there are many different beliefs from the past that continue to the present. Many of the beliefs are not supported by medical research. For example, some African American beliefs and traditions surrounding pregnancy and birth include the following (Moore, 2007):

- A pregnant woman is not supposed to hold her hands up over her head. It is believed she will strangle the baby.
- A pregnant woman should not cross her legs when sitting. This will cause hemorrhoids.
- A pregnant woman should indulge her food cravings or the baby will have unpleasant physical or personality traits that match the characteristics of the food.
- Babies are not named until it is known if they will survive. It is believed that spirits of the dead cannot see and therefore cannot harm a child who does not have a name.
- The placenta has a spirit of its own and must be secretly buried where it will never be disturbed and negatively affect the child.
- A small portion of the umbilical cord is wrapped in paper and put away to ensure the newborn will not get colic.
- Talismans are used for protection and to connect the child to ancestral powers and the spirits of nature.

- New mothers are to rest and be cared for in the initial four to eight weeks after birth, assisted by their family and the community.
- Henna body art is used during the postpartum period. The henna beautification lifts the new mother's spirits, wards off depression, and signifies the mother's new and higher social status.

HEALING TRADITIONS

African American healing traditions encompass a variety of beliefs and practices. Some of them were brought through slavery and ancestral roots. The ancestral roots from West Africa brought many herbal and spiritual healing techniques. Types of healers that African Americans use include faith or spiritual healers. African American healers may choose to use rituals, charms, and/or herbs. Today, African Americans can choose if they want to be seen by a biomedical doctor or a traditional healer. Although they have the freedom to choose their practitioner, certain factors can affect their choice, such as trust, access to care, insurance, as well as other socioeconomic factors.

Prayer is the most common treatment for illness among people who believe that illness is caused by God's will. Roberson (1985 as cited in Fields, 2001) stated that spiritual beliefs form a foundation for the health belief systems of African Americans. Instead of going to the doctor when they are ill, some African Americans will pray for their actions that caused them to get sick, giving God a chance to make them healthy before having to seek the help of Western medicine (University of Washington Medical Center, 2007).

Herbs and remedies are another important aspect of the healing traditions of African Americans. Most home remedies are learned from caregivers, such as mothers or grandmothers (Warner, 2005). Some herbs and remedies that are used include the following (Ansorge, 1999; Spector, 2004; Warner, 2005):

- St. John's wort is used for scrapes, strains, and burns. Today it is known for being a mild treatment for depression.
- Petals from an African plant called okra are used to cure boils.
- Wild yam is used to cure indigestion.
- Rectified turpentine with sugar is used to treat a cough.
- Nine drops of turpentine nine days after intercourse may act as a contraceptive.
- Sugar and turpentine are used to get rid of worms.
- Dried snake ground up and brewed as tea is used to treat blemishes.

- Cool baths, isopropyl alcohol (topically), warming the feet, and cool drinks or Popsicles are used to treat fever.
- Catnip, senna extract, chamomile, cigarette smoke, and walking are used to treat colic.
- Whiskey, pennies, eggs, and ice cubes or popsicles alleviate teething.

In addition, another type of remedy that African Americans commonly use is wearing bad-smelling objects, such as bags containing gum resin or asafetida (rotten flesh), around the neck. Although this traditional method does not have any healing properties, it is said to ward off infectious disease (Ansorge, 1999).

The goal of treatment for unnatural illness is to remove evil spirits from the body. Traditional healers, who are usually women, are consulted. These women possess knowledge regarding the use of herbs and roots as well as mystical voodoolike powers. Some African Americans who believe that they have been hexed will often seek out a voodoo-type healer in addition to or instead of a licensed medical provider (Leininger, 1995 as cited in Fields, 2001).

Voodoo (from *vodoun*, meaning spirit) originated in Africa nearly 10,000 years ago (Dakwar, 2004). Although its origins remain mysterious and elusive, scholars are fairly certain that its birthplace was somewhere in West Africa. It is recognized as one of the world's oldest religions (Dakwar, 2004). Voodoo was brought to this country in 1724 with the arrival of slaves from the West African coast (Spector, 2004). Historian Sharla Fett identified four themes that link the medical practices of Southern slaves to those of the West and Central African cultures. The four themes include beliefs that medicine posses a spiritual force, preparing medicine brings the healer closer to spiritual power, healing maintains relationships between the living and the world of ancestors, and power can be used for healing and harming (Savitt, 2002). Voodoo is divided into two types: white magic and black magic. White magic is known to be harmless and includes the use of powders and oils that are pleasantly scented. On the other hand, black magic is quite rare but dangerous and includes the use of oils and powders with a foul and vile odor (Spector, 2004). The practice involves candle-lit rituals and spiritual ceremonies, most commonly held by women. Chest pain, luck, success, attracting money, and evil intentions are just a few examples of reasons why people practice voodoo (Spector, 2004). Today, it is most commonly practiced in areas of the South and in Northern cities with large populations of African Americans (Ansorge, 1999).

During the nineteenth and twentieth centuries, voodoo suffered persecution in both America and the Caribbean (Dakwar, 2004). The practice of voodoo was made illegal, and the spiritual tools of voodoo—fetishes, rods, and sculptures—were confiscated and destroyed (Dakwar, 2004). Simultaneously, a campaign to discredit and disparage voodoo in the public eye began; this led to the popular understanding of voodoo as malicious, dark, foolish, primitive, dangerous, and violent, which continues to this day. Today, voodoo is practiced by millions of people in Africa, America, and the Caribbean (Dakwar, 2004).

Santeria, which was described in Chapter 7, also is practiced by African Americans. In fact, the religion is based on the West African religions that were brought to the New World by slaves, who were imported to the Caribbean to work the sugar plantations. These slaves carried with them their own religious traditions, including a tradition of possession trance for communicating with the ancestors and deities, the use of animal sacrifice, and the practice of sacred drumming and dance. Those slaves who landed in the Caribbean and Central and South America were nominally converted to Catholicism. However, they were able to preserve some of their traditions by fusing together various Yoruban beliefs and rituals with elements from the surrounding Catholic culture. In Cuba this religious tradition has evolved into what we know today as Santeria, the Way of the Saints. Today, hundreds of thousands of Americans participate in this ancient religion. Many are of Hispanic and Caribbean descent, but as the religion moves out of the inner cities and into the suburbs, a growing number of followers are of African American and European American heritage.

Another religion tied to the days of slavery is **Candomblé**, which was developed in Brazil by enslaved Africans who attempted to recreate their culture on the other side of the ocean. The rituals involve animal sacrifices, healing, dancing, drumming, and the possession of participants by orishas, which are religious deities that are said to represent human characteristics such as bravery, love, and honor. Today, Candomblé is widely practiced in Brazil, but because of its secrecy it is unknown how widespread it is in the United States.

Attempts at spiritual healing may be concealed from Western health care providers to avoid the stigma attached to such practices, which may be labeled as devil worshipping or mumbo jumbo by mainstream European American culture (Welch, 2003). When such medical or health-related information is revealed, providers should place it in its proper cultural context.

BEHAVIORAL RISK FACTORS AND COMMON HEALTH PROBLEMS _____

Some of the adverse behaviors that particularly affect the African American community are drug use, smoking, nutritional habits, and limited physical activity. The consumption and trafficking of drugs such as alcohol and cocaine in the African American community is market driven and stimulated by unemployment, poverty, despair, alienation, depression, hopelessness, and dependency (addiction). Alcoholism is the most significant social and health problem within the African American population. Studies have shown that 60% of homicides in the African American community are alcohol related (Hill, 2007). Despite years of protest from African Americans, their communities are still plastered with billboards that have messages about alcohol. African American youth continue to be shown more alcohol advertisements than any other youth group in the United States (Hill, 2007).

With regard to smoking, African Americans smoke approximately 35% fewer cigarettes per day than do whites (Ellis, 2005). They are not considered to be heavy smokers. In fact, the average African American adult smokes significantly fewer cigarettes than the average white adult. However, despite the fact that African Americans start smoking later in life and smoke fewer cigarettes, they have a greater likelihood of becoming sick and getting lung cancer. This is in part because African Americans have a preference for mentholated brands, which are high in tar and nicotine (Ellis, 2005). Eighty percent of African American smokers smoke mentholated cigarettes, but only 25% of white smokers smoke mentholated cigarettes. The use of menthol is associated with increased health risks and has resulted in significantly poorer health status for African Americans (Ellis, 2005).

A family tradition of soul food may be problematic for some African Americans. Soul foods traditionally have a high fat, sugar, and sodium content (Andrews, 2007). Many American-born African Americans enjoy consuming pork products with high salt content, fried foods, and heavy gravy. "Because African Americans on average have high-fat, lower-fiber diets than whites, they should be encouraged to adopt alternative diets that maintain cultural traditions where possible" (Welch, 2003).

Studies have shown that African American diets stress the consumption of meat and eggs, which results in a high-cholesterol and saturated-fat diet. African American foods also tend to be lower in complex carbohydrates and dietary fiber. This may contribute to their high incidence of being overweight. Sixty percent of African American men and 78% of African American women are considered to be overweight, and 28.8% of African American men and 50.8% of African American women are considered to be obese (Andrews, 2007). A food guide pyramid has been developed to reflect the cultural foods that African Americans eat and to help them improve their nutrition status (see Figure 2).

The African American pyramid of foods has a foundation of biscuits, corn (corn breads, grits, and hominy), pasta, and rice. In urban communities, store-bought

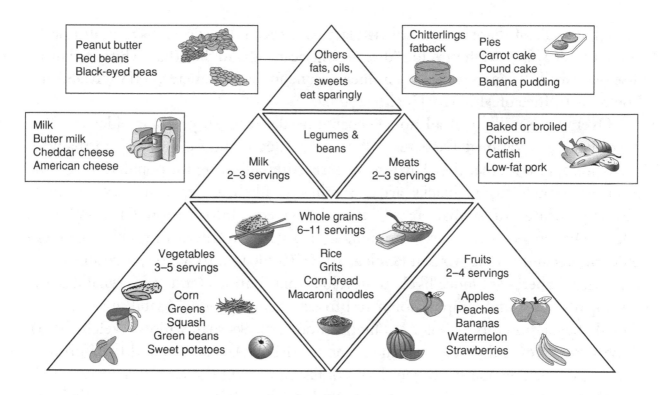

FIGURE 2 African American food pyramid.

Source: Adapted from sedma.org and Oldways Preservation and Exchange Trust.

breads have replaced biscuits. Vegetables (green leafy vegetables—chard, collard, kale, mustard greens—corn, okra, sweet potatoes, and yams) and fruits (apples, bananas, berries, peaches, and watermelon) make up the middle of the pyramid. Fruit consumption by today's African Americans is considered to be low when compared to other groups. Pork (chitterlings, intestines, ham hocks, and sausages) remains the primary protein source, and frying is still the most popular way of preparing foods. Fruit drinks and tea are the drinks of choice over milk (which is consumed in puddings and ice cream) (Welch, 2003).

There are many reasons that African Americans choose to eat a diet high in fat and sodium. African Americans in general accept larger body sizes, feel less guilt about overeating, and are less likely to practice unhealthy dieting behaviors, such as overexercising or purging (Andrews, 2007). Although African Americans have a healthy acceptance of a wider range of body sizes, their tolerance may lead to more obesity and serious obesity-related health problems. One problem with consuming a diet high in fat and sodium is the risk of high blood pressure. African Americans have higher rates of hypertension than any other race (Andrews, 2007).

As a result of these behavioral risk factors, African Americans have health problems. In 2003, the death rate for African Americans was higher than whites for heart diseases, stroke, cancer, asthma, influenza, pneumonia, diabetes, HIV–AIDS, and homicide (Office of Minority Health, 2008).

Over three million of all non-Hispanic blacks aged 20 years or older (13.3%) have diabetes (National Diabetes Information Clearinghouse, 2005), and many of them are not aware that they have the disease. After adjusting for population age differences, non-Hispanic blacks are 1.8 times as likely to have diabetes as non-Hispanic whites of similar age (National Diabetes Information Clearinghouse, 2005). Diabetes is particularly common among African American middle-aged and older adults and among women (Welch, 2003). Compared to whites, African Americans with diabetes are more likely to develop complications (end-stage renal disease, retinopathy, and limb amputations) and to experience greater disability as a result. The diabetes mortality rate is 27% higher among blacks than whites (Welch, 2003). Type II diabetes is the most common among African Americans, and their primary risk factors include obesity, higher levels of fasting insulin (hyperinsulinemia), gestational diabetes, and lack of physical activity (Welch, 2003). Among these risks, obesity is the most significant, and there is a disproportionate number of African Americans with both diabetes and obesity (Welch, 2003). Obesity is also believed to contribute to Type I diabetes (non-insulin-dependent diabetes) in 50% to 90% of cases (Welch, 2003).

In 2004, African Americans had 2.4 times the infant mortality rate as non-Hispanic whites. African American infants were almost four times as likely to die from causes related to low birth weight, compared to non-Hispanic white infants. They also had 2.1 times the sudden infant death syndrome mortality rate as non-Hispanic whites. African American mothers were 2.6 times more likely than non-Hispanic white mothers to begin prenatal care in the third trimester or not receive prenatal care at all (Office of Minority Health, 2008).

Heart disease is the leading cause of death for black women in the United States (CDC, 2008). As a whole, African American men and women are more likely than people of other races to have heart failure and to suffer from more severe forms of it. Also, they are more likely to have symptoms at a younger age for heart disease, have those symptoms get worse faster, have more hospital visits due to heart failure, and die from heart failure (National Heart Lung and Blood Institute, 2008).

The HIV epidemic is most prominent among African Americans. In 2005, blacks accounted for 18,121 of the estimated 37,331 new HIV/AIDS diagnoses (49%) in the United States (CDC, 2008). For African American men, the primary transmission category was sexual contact with other men, followed by injection drug use and high-risk heterosexual contact, whereas for African American women, the primary transmission category was high-risk heterosexual contact followed by injection drug use (CDC, 2008).

In addition to being at risk from sharing needles, casual and chronic substance users are more likely to engage in high-risk behaviors, such as unprotected sex (CDC, 2008). The Centers for Disease Control ranks African Americans with the highest rates of sexually transmitted diseases; furthermore, African Americans are about 18 times more likely than whites to have gonorrhea and about five times as likely to have syphilis (CDC, 2008). Linked to unprotected sex is the number of teenage pregnancies. Although the number of teenage pregnancies has declined over the years, teen pregnancy rates vary widely by race and ethnicity. In 2002, the pregnancy rate for non-Hispanic white teens was 49 per 1,000 women aged 15 to 19 years; the rate for Hispanic teens was 135.2; and for African American teens it was 138.9 (Ventura, Abma, Mosher, & Henshaw, 2006).

In 2001, the Centers for Disease Control (CDC) reported that homicide is the leading cause of death for African Americans aged 15 to 24 years and that the rate of homicide among African Americans is one of the primary reasons for the differences in life expectancy between blacks and whites (Roberts, n.d.). In an analysis of mortality data from 1998, the CDC concluded that although it is only the thirteenth leading cause of death in the United States, homicide was the third-ranking cause of death in contributing to the difference in life expectancy between blacks and whites (Roberts, n.d.). Despite making up only about 12% of the nation's population, blacks constituted 38% of all arrests for violent crime in 2002 (Roberts, n.d.). Blacks made up a disproportionate amount of arrests for aggravated assault (34.2%) and forcible rape (34%) and half of all arrests for murder and nonnegligent manslaughter (Roberts, n.d.). For individuals younger than age 18 years, blacks made up an even greater percentage of arrests for violent crimes (42%). Although arrest rates do not completely represent rates of violent acts because many acts go unreported and arrests do not always mean guilt, the tremendous disparity in the rates of arrests for violent crimes among blacks does likely indicate a higher rate of violence (Roberts, n.d.). In addition, overall, African Americans were victimized by intimate partners at significantly higher rates than persons of any other race between 1993 and 1998 (Rennison & Welchans, 2000). Black females experienced intimate partner violence at a rate 35% higher than that of white females and about 22 times the rate of women of other races (Rennison & Welchans, 2000). Black males experienced intimate partner violence at a rate about 62% higher than that of white males and about 22 times the rate of men of other races (Rennison & Welchans, 2000).

QUICK FACTS

Cancer

- In 2003, African American men were 1.4 times as likely to have new cases of lung and prostate cancer, compared to non-Hispanic white men.
- African American men were twice as likely to have new cases of stomach cancer as non-Hispanic white men.
- African American men had lower five-year cancer survival rates for lung and pancreatic cancer, compared to non-Hispanic white men.
- In 2004, African American men were 2.4 times as likely to die from prostate cancer as non-Hispanic white men.
- In 2003, African American women were 10% less likely to have been diagnosed with breast cancer than non-Hispanic white women; however, they were 36% more likely to die from breast cancer, compared to non-Hispanic white women.
- In 2003, African American women were 2.3 times as likely to have been diagnosed with stomach cancer, and they were 2.2 times as likely to die from stomach cancer, compared to non-Hispanic white women.

Diabetes

- African American adults were 1.8 times more likely than non-Hispanic white adults to have been diagnosed with diabetes by a physician.
- In 2002, African American men were 2.1 times as likely to start treatment for end-stage renal disease related to diabetes, compared to non-Hispanic white men.
- In 2003, diabetic African Americans were 1.8 times as likely as diabetic whites to be hospitalized.
- In 2004, African Americans were 2.2 times as likely as non-Hispanic whites to die from diabetes.

Heart Disease

- In 2004, African American men were 30% more likely to die from heart disease, compared to non-Hispanic white men.
- African Americans were 1.5 times as likely as non-Hispanic whites to have high blood pressure.
- African American women were 1.7 times as likely as non-Hispanic white women to be obese.

HIV–AIDS

- African Americans accounted for 47% of HIV–AIDS cases in 2005.
- African American males had more than eight times the AIDS rate of non-Hispanic white males.
- African American females had more than 23 times the AIDS rate of non-Hispanic white females.
- African American men were more than nine times as likely to die from HIV–AIDS as non-Hispanic white men.
- African American women were more than 21 times as likely to die from HIV–AIDS as non-Hispanic white women.

(Continues)

Immunization

- In 2005, African Americans aged 65 years and older were 40% less likely to have received a influenza (flu) shot in the past 12 months, compared to non-Hispanic whites of the same age group.
- In 2005, African American adults aged 65 years and older were 30% less likely to have ever received a pneumonia shot, compared to non-Hispanic white adults of the same age group.
- Although African American children aged 19 to 35 months had comparable rates of immunization for hepatitis, influenza, MMR, and polio, they were slightly less likely to be fully immunized, compared to non-Hispanic white children.

Infant Mortality

- In 2004, African Americans had 2.4 times the infant mortality rate of non-Hispanic whites.
- African American infants were almost four times as likely to die from causes related to low birth weight, compared to non-Hispanic white infants.
- African Americans had 2.1 times the sudden infant death syndrome mortality rate as non-Hispanic whites.
- African American mothers were 2.6 times as likely as non-Hispanic white mothers to begin prenatal care in the third trimester or not receive prenatal care at all.

Stroke

- African American adults were 50% more likely than their white adult counterparts to have a stroke.
- African American males were 60% more likely to die from a stroke than their white adult counterparts.
- Analysis from a CDC health interview survey reveals that African American stroke survivors were more likely to become disabled and have difficulty with activities of daily living than their non-Hispanic white counterparts.

Source: Office of Minority Health. (2008).

CONSIDERATIONS FOR HEALTH PROMOTION AND PROGRAM PLANNING

The following are some concepts to consider when planning and implementing a health promotion program for this target audience.

- Be aware and sensitive to the distrust of the medical community and the government that may exist among African American community members.
- Consider utilizing churches to disseminate information or as a place to conduct health screenings and educational interventions.
- Be aware that peer educators have not been shown to be effective in developing health programs to African American audiences.

- Develop interventions that focus on positive health changes instead of attempting to instill change through fear or negative messages.
- Until invited otherwise, greet African Americans with formal titles.
- Take special care to have congruent verbal and nonverbal communication patterns.
- Be aware of different terminology because there are various regional terms used to describe medical conditions. Among immigrants from Haiti, Jamaica, and the Bahamas, and among many Southern blacks, for example, blood may be characterized as *low* or *high*, referring to anemia as opposed to hypertension. *Spells*, also called *falling outs*, are perceived to be a result of *low blood*; elderly blacks especially may refer to *having had a spell*. *Shock* is a common term for a stroke. Other common terms include *having sugar*, *sweet blood*, or *thin blood*, referring to diabetes (Welch, 2003).
- Understand that occasional outbursts of laugher may appear to be inappropriate for the situation because African Americans find solace in laughter and playfulness.

CHAPTER SUMMARY

African Americans initially came to the United States primarily through the slave trade. Some of their beliefs about causes of illness and treatment approaches are related to their religious practices and ancestral roots, which is why some African Americans choose to use faith or spiritual healers rather than a biomedical doctor. The main behavioral risks associated with African Americans are smoking, alcohol consumption, weight management, and lack of physical activity. African Americans also experience high levels of poverty, discrimination, and violence.

In this chapter we discussed the unique aspects of the history of African Americans and how their history has had a negative impact on their trust in the medical system. We learned that religion plays a central role in this community and how that is integrated into their health belief system and practices. General tips for working with these populations were provided, but as usual we caution that there is a vast amount of diversity within this community, so it is important not to generalize.

REVIEW

1. Explain the history of African Americans in the United States.
2. Provide an overview of African Americans' socioeconomic situation.
3. Why is there is general mistrust by African Americans in the medical system?
4. What are some of the behavior risk factors and common diseases that African Americans experience?

CASE STUDY

The number of infants who die before their first birthday is much higher in the United States than in other countries, and for African Americans the rate is nearly twice as high as for white Americans. Even well-educated black women have birth outcomes worse than white women who haven't finished high school. Why?

We meet Andrea Jackson, a successful lawyer, executive, and mother. When Andrea was pregnant with her first child, she, like so many others, did her best to ensure a healthy baby; she ate right, exercised, abstained from alcohol and smoking, and received good prenatal care. Yet two and a half months before her due date, she went into labor unexpectedly. Her newborn weighed less than three pounds. Andrea and her husband were devastated. How could this have happened?

We know that, in general, health follows wealth; on average, the higher on the socioeconomic ladder you are, the lower your risk of cancer, heart disease, diabetes, infant death, and preterm deliveries. For highly-educated African American women like Andrea, the advantages of income and status do make a difference for her health, but there's still something else at play: racism.

There are several issues to consider about this case:

- How may have Andrea's race and culture played a role in her having a low-birth-weight baby?
- Are there any culture-specific protective factors that may have helped Andrea cope with the racism she has faced?

MODEL PROGRAM

SISTERS

The goal of the SISTERS program is to provide much-needed peer-oriented outreach, support, and case management to ensure the coordination of drug treatment, prenatal care, postpartum care, pediatric services, and family support services for pregnant and postpartum women. The program particularly targets African American or Hispanic women who are on public assistance, are mandated to treatment, report having experienced more than four violent traumas (e.g., sexual assault, death of a loved one), and have smoked crack cocaine during their last pregnancy. Program strategies include coordinated services, such as relapse prevention counseling, acupuncture detoxification, prenatal care, housing, transportation, child care, nutrition, assistance with child welfare, Medicaid, and sponsorship for attendance at Narcotics Anonymous meetings.

Program counselors, or "SISTERS," are women in recovery who have experienced many years of addiction, abusive relationships, life on the streets, birth of infants with positive toxicology, and removal of their child by protective services. These women have turned their lives around by getting help through available social service agencies. The SISTERS cultivate a trusting relationship with clients while serving as peer counselors. Those SISTERS who have received licensure as New York State Certified Acupuncturists administer acupuncture detoxification treatments to their clients. Additional tasks for the SISTERS include providing assistance to their clients concerning infant health services, housing, food, transportation, helping read and understand medical forms, promoting positive attitudes about the use of health and social services, and abstaining from alcohol and substance abuse.

SISTERS must qualify appropriately in five criteria: (1) professional experience or education, (2) race, ethnicity, and culture, (3) experience, age, and maturity, (4) gender, and (5) interpersonal and helping skills. Additional requirements include (1) a desire for the position, (2) having given birth to a baby with positive drug toxicology, (3) successful completion of treatment, (4) maintenance of sobriety for at least one year, and (5) the unqualified endorsement of supervisory staff in the clinic.

Evaluation

The evaluation was designed to demonstrate the effectiveness of peer counseling through (1) availability and use of services, (2) substance abuse abstinence and psychosocial functioning, and (3) birth outcomes and parenting attitudes. A repeated-measures (intake, two months, six months) evaluation design with a comparison group of non-SISTERS clients from the clinic was used. Data collection involved focus groups, individual client satisfaction surveys, and in-person interviews conducted by a social worker for which clients received stipends. Urine toxicology data from the clinic's information system was used to assess sobriety outcomes.

Outcome

Major program outcomes include the following:

- Urine samples of SISTERS clients became significantly cleaner over a one-year period, compared to the control group.
- Change scores for SISTERS clients significantly improved for measures of depression and self-efficacy in contrast to the non-SISTERS group.
- SISTERS clients, when compared to non-SISTERS clients, experienced a significant decrease in parental stress and rigidity of parenting style.

- SISTERS clients used more services than non-SISTERS clients.
- SISTERS clients were more likely to use warm expressions of empathy to describe their counselors.
- Seventy-eight percent of SISTERS clients gave birth to babies weighing at least 2,500 grams. More active clients had significantly heavier babies than less active clients.
- Eighty percent of infants born to SISTERS clients were toxicologically clean at birth.
- SISTERS clients continually regained custody of their children; at intake 60% had no children living at home, but at the end of the project this decreased to 18%. All SISTERS clients who obtained custody of their babies kept them for the duration of the program.

Source: Helping America's Youth. (n.d.).

GLOSSARY TERMS

Tuskegee study
voodoo

Candomblé

REFERENCES

Andrews, L. C. (2007). NetWellness. *African Americans and diet.* Retrieved February 10, 2008, from http://www.netwellness.org/healthtopics/aahealth/healthybody.cfm

Ansorge, R. (1999). Herbs and roots are in African-American folk medicine. *Colorado Springs Gazette.* Retrieved February 8, 2008, from http://www.texnews.com/1998/1999/ads/ads/health2/roots.html

Campinha-Bacote, J. (1998). African-Americans. In L. D. Purnell & B. J. Paulanka (Eds.), *Transcultural health care: A culturally competent approach* (pp. 53–73). Philadelphia: F. A. Davis.

Centers for Disease Control and Prevention. (2008). *Fact sheet on African Americans.* Retrieved February 11, 2008, from http://www.cdc.gov/hiv/topics/aa/resources/factsheets/aa.htm

Christopher, G. C. (2006). Strengthening black families. *Chicago Defender,* p. 13 (Document ID: 1106558821). Retrieved February 9, 2008, from Ethnic NewsWatch.

Clarke-Tasker, V. (1993). Cancer prevention and detection in African-Americans. In M. Frank-Stromburg & S. J. Olsen (Eds.), *Cancer prevention in minority populations: Cultural implications for health care professionals.* St. Louis, MO: Mosby.

Dakwar, E. (2004). Creighton University Medical Center. Complementary and Alternative Medicine. *Voodoo therapy.* Retrieved March 24, 2008, from http://altmed.creighton.edu/voodoo/

Ellis, G. (2005). Cigarette companies target African-Americans. *Philadelphia Tribune,* p. 5B (Document ID: 791096531). Retrieved February 9, 2008, from http://www.highbeam.com/doc/1P1-105266359.html

Fields, S. D. (2001). Health belief system of African-Americans: Essential information for today's practicing nurses. *The Journal of Multicultural Nursing & Health*. Retrieved from http://findarticles .com/p/articles/mi_qa3919/is_200101/ai_n8931688?tag=content;col1

Helping America's Youth. (n.d.). *SISTERS*. Retrieved October 31, 2008, from http://guide. helpingamericasyouth.gov/programdetail.cfm?id=423

Hill, P. J. (2007). Legacy of addiction, incarceration feeds itself. *Call & Post*, pp. 9–11 (Document ID: 1369714311). Retrieved February 9, 2008, from Ethnic NewsWatch.

Jennings, K. (1996). Getting black women to screen for cancer: Incorporating health beliefs into practice. *Journal of the American Academy of Nurse Practitioners, 8*(2), 53–59.

Ladner, J., & Gourdine, R. (1992). Adolescent pregnancy in the African-American community. In R. Braithwaite & S. Taylor (Eds.), *Health issues in the black community* (pp. 206–221). San Francisco: Jossey-Bass.

Leininger, M. (1995). *Transcultural nursing: Concepts, theories, research and practice* (2nd ed.). New York: McGraw-Hill.

Moore, J. (2007). Hawaii Community College. *Traditional health beliefs*. Retrieved June 18, 2008, from http://www.hawcc.hawaii.edu/nursing/transcultural.html

National Diabetes Information Clearinghouse. (2005). *National diabetes statistics*. Retrieved June 18, 2008, from http://diabetes.niddk.nih.gov/dm/pubs/statistics/index.htm

National Heart Lung and Blood Institute. (2008). *African American health*. Retrieved February 10, 2008, from http://www.nhlbi.nih.gov/health/index.htm

Nobles, W. W., & Goddard, L. L. (1990). The Institute for the Advanced Study of Black Family Life and Culture. *An African-centered model of prevention for African-American youth at high risk*. Retrieved March 1, 2009, from http://www.iasbflc.org/Articles/AfricanModel/africanmodel01.htm

Office of Minority Health. (2008). *African-American profile*. Retrieved February 13, 2004, from http://www.omhrc.gov/

Perry, J. A. (1998). African roots of African-American culture. *Black Collegian Online*. Retrieved June 18, 2008, from http://www.black-collegian.com/issues/1998-12/africanroots12.shtml

Rennison, C. M., & Welchans, S. (2000). US Department of Justice. *Intimate partner violence* (NCJ 178247). Retrieved November 8, 2008, from http://www.ojp.usdoj.gov/bjs/pub/ascii/ipv.txt

Roberson, M. (1985). The influence of religious beliefs on health choices of Afro-Americans. *Topics in Clinical Nursing, 7*(3), 57–63.

Roberts, S. (n.d.). Black Youth Project. *Black youth, health, and society*. Retrieved November 8, 2008, from http://blackyouthproject.uchicago.edu/primers/reviews/health.pdf

Sadler, C., & Huff, M. (2007). *African-American women: Health beliefs, lifestyle, and osteoporosis*. Retrieved February 10, 2008, from http://www.nursingcenter.com/prodev/ce_article.asp?tid=710316

Savitt, T. L. (2002). *Medicine and slavery: The diseases and healthcare of blacks*. Champaign, IL: University of Illinois Press.

Spector, R. E. (2004). *Cultural diversity in health and illness* (6th ed.). Upper Saddle River, NJ: Pearson Education.

The New York Public Library. (2007). *In Motion: The African-American migration experience*. Retrieved February 11, 2008, from http://www.inmotionaame.org/home.cfm

University of Washington Medical Center. (2007). *African American culture clues: Communicating with your African American patient*. Retrieved February 9, 2008, from http://www.depts.washington .edu/pfes/pdf/AfricanAmericanCultureClue4_07.pdf

US Census Bureau. (2006). *Facts for features: African-American history month*. Retrieved February 11, 2008, from http://www.census.gov/Press-Release/www/2000/ff00-01.html

US Census Bureau. (2008). *Population density of the United States, and selected maps of race and Hispanic origin: 2000*. Retrieved November 9, 2008, from http://www.census.gov/population/www/censusdata/2000maps.html

US Department of Health and Human Services. (n.d.). *Changing demographics and the implications for physicians, nurses, and other health workers*. Washington, DC: Author. Retrieved April 19, 2009, from http://bhpr.hrsa.gov/healthworkforce/reports/changedemo/composition.htm

US Department of Health and Human Services. (2000). *Healthy People 2010: National health promotion and disease prevention objectives*. Washington, DC: Author.

Ventura, S. J., Abma, J. C., Mosher, W. D., & Henshaw, S. K. (2006, December 13). *Recent trends in teenage pregnancy in the United States, 1990–2002. Health E-stats*. Hyattsville, MD: National Center for Health Statistics.

Walker, A. (1996). Health and illness in African (black) American communities. In R. E. Spector (Ed.), *Cultural diversity in health and illness* (4th ed., pp. 191–214). New York: Appleton-Century-Crofts.

Warner, J. (2005). Folk remedies part of African American tradition. *Fox News*. Retrieved February 9, 2008, from http://www.foxnews.com/story/0,2933,149791,00.html

Welch, M. (2003). *Care of blacks and African Americans*. Retrieved June 17, 2008, from http://www.acponline.org/fcgi/search?q=welch+care+of+blacks&site=ACP_Online&num=10

PHOTO CREDITS

Chapter Opener , ©
Oscar C. Williams/ShutterStock, Inc.

Unless otherwise indicated, all photographs and illustrations are under copyright of Jones and Bartlett Publishers, LLC, or have been provided by the author(s).

Asian American and Pacific Islander Populations

Keeping your body healthy is an expression of gratitude to the whole cosmos—the trees, the clouds, everything.

—Thich Nhat Hanh

Always aim at complete harmony of thought and word and deed. Always aim at purifying your thoughts and everything will be well.

—Mahatma Gandhi

Sickness is a thing of the spirit.

—Japanese proverb

KEY CONCEPTS

- Hmong
- aAma and aDuonga
- Kior chi force
- Timbang
- Kava
- Betel nut
- Mana
- Lokahi
- Kahunas

CHAPTER OBJECTIVES

1. Discuss the social and economic circumstances of the various Asian Americans and Pacific Islanders in the United States.
2. Describe the beliefs about the cause of illness for Asian American and Pacific Islander cultures.
3. Discuss risk factors and illnesses that Asian Americans and Pacific Islanders are prone to.
4. Describe beliefs about healing practices for Asian Americans and Pacific Islanders.

HISTORY OF ASIAN AMERICANS AND PACIFIC ISLANDERS IN THE UNITED STATES

The experience of Asian Americans and Pacific Islanders differs depending on their country of origin, culture, and when they arrived in this country. The historical background for many of these groups is discussed below.

Chinese Americans

The background of Chinese Americans is difficult to track because no immigration records exist prior to 1820. However, stories claim that Chinese persons were brought to America as slaves by the Spanish conquistadors in the seventeenth century. There are documents that show Chinese names on the East Coast in the late eighteenth century.

Although agreement on when the first Chinese people arrived in North America cannot be reached, there is little disagreement about when their immigration exploded. When gold was discovered in California in 1849, word spread to China and immigrants flooded the West Coast. When the gold rush diminished, Chinese immigrants began working on the transcontinental railroad. They settled in great numbers in California and worked as farm laborers, in various businesses, and in factories.

Due to anti-Chinese discrimination, Chinese Americans tended to live in racially segregated areas and established enduring social structures that continue to the present. Immigration decreased for a long period as a result of the Chinese Exclusion Act of 1882, which suspended immigration and naturalization for Chinese people. This discriminatory practice was continued until the McCarran-Walter Act of 1952 made naturalization available to all races. After the reforms of the Immigration and Naturalization Act of 1965, immigration of Chinese people increased dramatically and created the basis for the strong Chinese American presence today.

Vietnamese Americans

The Vietnamese presence in the United States occurred in waves related to the American involvement in the Vietnam war. It was the continuing conflicts in Southeast Asia that led to the immigration of Laotians and Cambodians to the United States as well.

Vietnamese people who worked with the United States during that conflict fled to the United States when the Thieu government lost power in 1975. It is thought that 130,000 Vietnamese people came to the United States in 1975 alone. Most of those immigrants were young, well-educated, English-speaking city dwellers.

The second wave of immigrants was spawned by the invasion of Laos and Cambodia by Vietnamese troops. Between 1979 and 1983, 455,000 Vietnamese, Laotian, and Cambodian refugees came to the United States. These refugees tended to be made up of different ethnic groups and were more rural, less educated, and not as familiar with Western ideas as the first wave of immigrants (LaBorde, 1996).

The third group of refugees from Southeast Asia arrived from 1985 to 1991. This group tended to include both Vietnamese and Chinese people who were admitted to the country in family reunification programs (LaBorde, 1996).

Korean Americans and Asian Indians

Korean immigration to the United States began in the early twentieth century when Koreans immigrated to Hawaii to work on the plantations. Thereafter, a significant wave of immigration was related to the Korean War in the 1950s. That immigration brought many more Koreans to the U.S. mainland where most settled in the western states (Beller, Pinker, Snapka, & Van Dusan, n.d.).

Asian Indians do not have the same immigration patterns as many other Asian immigrants. Their immigration was not necessarily related to a war. Instead, they have been immigrating to the United States in greater numbers during the latter part of the twentieth century as the population in India has increased. Most came to the United States looking for greater educational and employment opportunities, and to escape the poverty of their native country.

Japanese Americans

Many Japanese people began immigrating to the United States in the nineteenth century. At first they moved to Hawaii and the Western United States to work on plantations, farms, and in the fishing and canning industry. During World War II, in one of the more shameful events in American history, Japanese Americans were interned in concentration camps because of their race and concerns that they would collaborate with the Imperial Japanese government. Even in the face of this discrimination, many Japanese Americans enlisted to assist the country in the war effort. In fact, the U.S. Army's 442nd Regimental Combat Team was composed of Japanese Americans who fought in Europe and was the most decorated unit in U.S. military history. Since the end of World War II, Japanese Americans have grown in their influence on American culture, and currently the U.S. government is engaged in a program of reparation for the suffering endured by Japanese Americans in the camps during World War II.

Native Hawaiians and Pacific Islanders

These varied islands sit in the vastness of the Pacific Ocean and were some of the last areas on Earth to be inhabited by humans. For the majority of the time during which the islands were inhabited, the people were content to remain there. It was not until recently that migration from these islands to the United States has occurred. The largest immigrations occurred after World War II and in the 1980s, with economic opportunity being the prime motivation.

The relationship of Native Hawaiians and the United States is much more controversial, because Native Hawaiians had a very distinct and proud history prior to becoming part of the union. The Hawaiian Islands were ruled by hereditary monarchs, the most famous being Kamehameha the Great, who unified the islands prior to the arrival of Captain James Cook in 1778.

After the islands were discovered by Cook, American and European traders and planters began arriving, and the traditional way of life in the islands changed. For most of the nineteenth century, the islands were ruled by a series of monarchs descended from Kamehameha. In the latter part of the nineteenth century, the last of these monarchs, Queen Liliuokalani, was overthrown by a group of mostly Americans backed by U.S. troops. In 1898, Hawaii was annexed to the United States, and the territory of Hawaii was established. Thereafter, Hawaii became infamous for the attack on Pearl Harbor in 1942 that ushered the United States into World War II and its strategic role during that conflict.

Hawaii became the fiftieth state of the union in 1959. However, the events that led to annexation and statehood remain controversial among Native Hawaiians. A Hawaiian sovereignty movement continues to be strong and active in the islands today and pride in the Hawaiian language and traditions, such as hula, is resurging.

ASIAN AMERICANS AND PACIFIC ISLANDERS IN THE UNITED STATES

Asian Americans and Pacific Islanders (AAPI) comprise the most diverse ethnic group in the United States. According to U.S. Census Bureau data, Asians are people with origins in a number of areas of the world: the Far East, Southeast Asia, and South Asia, also known as the Indian Subcontinent. Native Hawaiians and Pacific Islanders trace their origins to Hawaii and various Pacific Islands (see Table 1). According to the 2004 U.S. Census Bureau data, Hawaiian and Pacific Islanders collectively comprise 5% of the population of the United States, and Asians comprise 4.2% of that number. This represents an increase of 63% from the 1990 census. These groups speak more than 100 different languages. They are the fastest growing racial/ethnic group in the United States, and it is estimated that they will comprise 1 in 10 Americans by 2050 (Office of Minority Health, 2008a).

TABLE 1 Asian American and Pacific Islander Origins

Far East. China, Japan, Korea, Mongolia, Okinawa, Taiwan

Southeast Asia. Borneo, Brunei, Burma, Cambodia, Celebes, Philippines, Java, Indonesia, Laos, Malaysia, Singapore, Thailand, Vietnam

South Asia (Indian Subcontinent). Afghanistan, Bangladesh, Bhutan, India, Maldives, Nepal, Pakistan, Sri Lanka, Tibet

Pacific Islands. The Flag Territories: American Samoa, Territory of Guam, Commonwealth of the Northern Mariana Islands; The Freely Associated States: Federated States of Micronesia, the Republic of Palau, the Republic of the Marshall Islands

Source: U.S. Census Bureau. (n.d.).

Notwithstanding their growing presence in the U.S. population, these groups have historically been overlooked when health research has been undertaken. Often this was due to the "myth of the model minority," a belief that Asians were quiet and did not complain and, therefore, did not have health care needs. Although these people are grouped together, they have varied cultures, traditions, religions, ancestry, languages, and health beliefs and needs. We will discuss some of what these varied peoples have in common and the specifics for many of the individual ethnic groups by exploring their history, traditional beliefs related to health and illness, risk factors, and health care needs.

QUICK FACTS

Asian Americans

Overview (demographics). Asian Americans are defined as people who have origins in any of the original peoples of the Far East, Southeast Asia, or the Indian Subcontinent. According to the 2007 U.S. Census Bureau population estimate, there are 15.2 million Asian Americans living in the United States. Asian Americans account for 5% of the nation's population. This number represents an increase of 63% from the 1990 census, thus making Asian Americans the fastest growing of all major racial/ethnic groups. In 2007, the following states had the largest Asian American populations: California, New York, Hawaii, Texas, New Jersey, and Illinois.

Language fluency. The percentage of persons aged 5 years or older who do not speak English at home varies among Asian American groups: 62% of Vietnamese, 50% of Chinese, 24% of Filipinos, and 23% of Asian Indians are not fluent in English.

Educational attainment. According to 2006 U.S. Census Bureau data, roughly 83% of all Asian Americans and all people in the United States aged 25 years and older had at least a high school diploma. However, 42% of Asian Americans, compared to 27% of the total U.S. population, had earned at least a bachelor's degree. Among Asian American subgroups, Asian Indians had the highest percentage of bachelor's degree attainment at 64%. In regards to employment, about 45% of Asian Americans were employed in management, professional, and related occupations, compared to 34% of the total population. In addition, the proportions of Asian Americans employed in highly-skilled and managerial sectors varied from 13% for Laotians to 60% for Asian Indians.

Economics. According to 2007 U.S. Census Bureau data, the median family income of Asian American families is $15,600 higher than the national median income for all households. Ten percent of Asian Americans, compared to 8.2% of non-Hispanic whites, live at the poverty level, and 2.2% of Asian Americans, compared to 1.3% of Caucasians, live on public assistance.

Source: Office of Minority Health. (2008a).

QUICK FACTS

Native Hawaiians and Pacific Islanders

Overview (demographics). Native Hawaiians and Pacific Islanders (NHPI) refers to people who have origins in any of the original peoples of Hawaii, Guam, Samoa, or other Pacific Islands. According to a 2007 U.S. Census Bureau estimate, there are roughly 1,118,000 NHPIs who reside within the United States. This group represents about 0.1% of the U.S. population. Of that number, 269,306 NHPIs reside in Hawaii. Some other states that have significant NHPI populations are California, Washington, Texas, New York, Florida, and Utah. It is also significant to note that 30% of this group is younger than 18 years of age.

Language fluency. Forty-two percent of NHPIs speak a language other than English at home.

Educational attainment. Eighty-four percent of NHPIs have high school diplomas; 10% of NHPIs have a bachelor's degree, compared to 27% of Caucasians; and 4% of NHPIs have obtained graduate degrees, compared to 11% of Caucasian Americans.

Economics. The average size of an NHPI family is four people. The median household income for this group is $50,992.

Source: Office of Minority Health. (2008b).

Geographic Distribution

As a group, Asian Americans and Pacific Islanders tend to live in the Western United States, although data indicates an increase in their populations in the East and South.

Asian Americans

Although 75% of Asian Americans resided in the 10 states shown in Table 2, approximately half (51%) resided in California, New York, and Hawaii. By region, 49% of Asian Americans lived in the West, 20% in the Northeast, 19% in the South, and 12% in the Midwest, as shown in Figure 1 (Office of Minority Health, 2008a).

Interestingly, the highest growth states for Asian Americans are not the highest population states, pointing to the emergence of new settlement and migratory patterns. The states that have exhibited some of the highest Asian American growth rates since 1990 are Nevada (219%), North Carolina (173%), Georgia (171%), Arizona (130%), and Nebraska (124%) (Office of Minority Health, 2008a).

Most Asian Americans are second and third generation in the United States. The groups with the highest percentage of foreign-born nationals living in the United States are Japanese, Pakistani, and Asian Indian (Bennett & Reeves, 2004). The largest Asian American subgroups are Filipino, Chinese, and Asian Indian (see Figure 2).

Native Hawaiians and Pacific Islanders

By region, approximately 73% of NHPIs lived in the West, 14% in the South, 7% in the Northeast, and 6% in the Midwest. A majority of NHPIs (58%) lived in Hawaii

TABLE 2 Top 10 States with Highest Number of Asian Americans

State	Population (Inclusive)
California	4,155,685
New York	1,169,200
Hawaii	703,232
Texas	644,193
New Jersey	524,356
Illinois	473,649
Washington	395,741
Florida	333,013
Virginia	304,559
Massachusetts	264,814

Source: Office of Minority Health. (2008a).

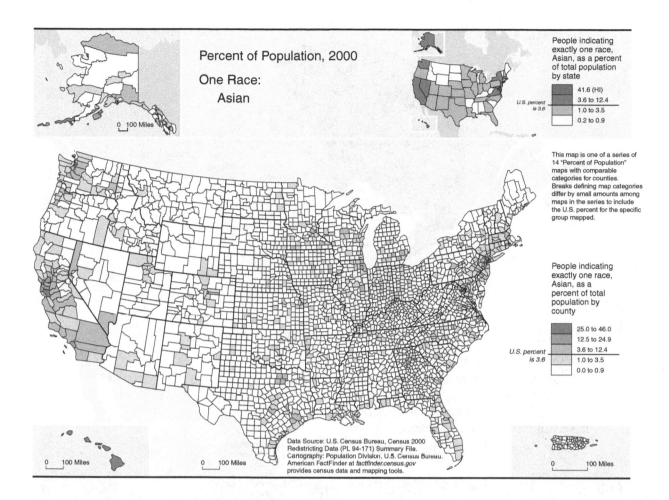

FIGURE 1 Percentage of population: Asian, 2000.

Source: U.S. Census Bureau, Population Division (2008). http://www.census.gov/main/www/citation.html

and California. Hawaii was home to 282,667 NHPIs (23% of the state's population), and California was home to 221,458 NHPIs (0.7% of the state's population) (see Table 3 and Figure 3).

The states with the highest growth rates for NHPIs includes both the traditionally high population states as well as some newer emerging areas. California, with the second largest NHPI population in the nation, showed one of the lowest rates of growth for NHPIs, but Nevada showed astounding growth. The NHPI population in Nevada increased 461%, and the state's total population grew 66% (U.S. Census Bureau, 2008).

Language Data

According to the 2000 census, there were over four million Asian Americans and Pacific Islanders in the United States who have limited English proficiency (LEP), which is defined as individuals who do not speak English very well.

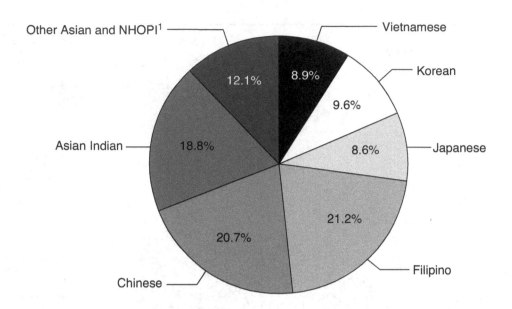

FIGURE   2   Percentage distribution of Asian subgroups for non-Hispanic Asian adults aged 18 years and older: United States, 2004–2006.

[1]NHOPI is Native Hawaiian or Other Pacific Islander. Estimates are age adjusted using the projected 2000 U.S. population as the standard population. Estimates are based on household interviews of a sample of the civilian noninstitutionalized population.

Source: Centers for Disease Control and Prevention. (2008).

TABLE 3 Top 10 States with Highest Number of NHPIs	
State	**Population (Inclusive)**
Hawaii	282,667
California	221,458
Washington	42,761
Texas	29,094
New York	28,612
Florida	23,998
Utah	21,367
Nevada	16,234
Oregon	16,019
Arizona	13,415

Source: Office of Minority Health. (2008b).

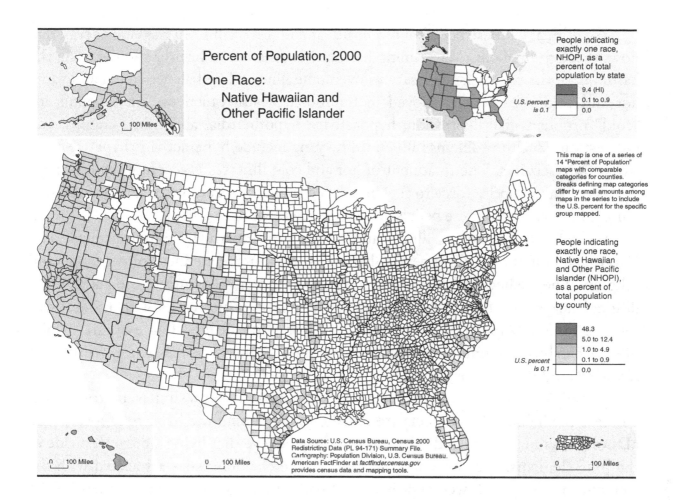

FIGURE 3 Percentage of population: Native Hawaiian and other Pacific Islander, 2000.
Source: U.S. Census Bureau. (2008). http://www.census.gov/main/www/citation.html

The 2000 census also revealed that 73% of Asian Americans speak a language other than English in their homes. This represents a rate that is four times higher than the national average (18%) and more than 12 times the rate for whites (6%). When Asian Americans were disaggregated by subgroup, the results showed that many subgroups have significantly higher rates; in seven subgroups, over 90% speak a non-English language at home (Carrasco & Weiss, 2005).

BELIEFS ABOUT CAUSES OF HEALTH AND ILLNESS

Asian beliefs regarding health and illness vary from country to country and often among districts within a country. However, a common thread through many Asian health practices is the belief that the body must remain balanced to remain healthy. Many Asian cultures are incorporating Western medical systems with traditional practices.

Traditional Chinese beliefs about health and illness stem from the vital energy that flows through the body. Maintaining harmony is essential to health, and restoring the harmony of the energy is necessary to overcome illness. The balance of yin and yang, hot and cold, are often employed in traditional health practices. Yin accounts for "cold" problems like depression, hypoactivity, hypothermia, abdominal cramps, and indigestion. Health problems influenced by yang include hyperactivity, hyperthermia, stroke, and seizures. The treatment of hot and cold illnesses is accomplished through the use of the opposite force to regain balance (Beller, Pinker, Snapka, & Van Dusan, n.d.). The specifics of these beliefs are discussed at length in Chapter 3.

Vietnamese theories of illness and health vary greatly by ethnic groups. The **Hmong** mountain-dwelling people believe in the interrelatedness of medicine and religion. They believe sickness is due to being cursed or the wrath of the gods. A traditional healer is a priest who exorcises bad spirits or intercedes with the gods to remove disease. Amulets are also employed for good health. For example, babies often wear bua, an amulet of cloth containing a Buddhist verse that is worn on a string around the wrist or neck.

Urban Vietnamese people utilize a health system very similar to traditional Chinese medicine. These beliefs are based on maintaining the balance of **aAma and aDuonga**, similar to yin and yang theory. They believe that living things are made of the four elements: fire, air, water, and earth. The characteristics associated with the elements are hot, cold, wet, and dry. Treating an illness requires employment of the opposite characteristic to the one that is causing the sickness. Like Chinese medicine herbal remedies, massage, thermal treatments, and acupuncture are utilized to treat illness (LaBorde, 1996).

For traditional Koreans, illness is often seen as one's fate, and hospitalization may be seen as a sign of impending death. Illness is often attributed to yin and yang, just as in Chinese medicine. Also, the **Kior chi force**, the life force similar to chi in traditional Chinese medicine, is important in maintaining health, and efforts are made to balance this force and to not engage in activities that could diminish it. Herbal remedies are utilized for illness.

Filipino health practices incorporate a number of ideas, such as **timbang**, which is described as follows by McBride (n.d.):

> This is a key indigenous health concept that includes a complex set of fundamental principles. A range of "hot" and "cold" beliefs regarding humoral balances in the body, food, and dietary balances includes the following:
>
> - Rapid shifts from "hot" to "cold" lead to illness.
> - "Warm" environment is essential to maintain optimal health.

- Cold drinks or cooling foods should be avoided in the morning.
- An overheated body (as in childbirth or fever) is vulnerable; and heated body or muscles can get "shocked" when cooled suddenly.
- A layer of fat ("being stout") is preferred to maintain "warmth" and protect vital energy.
- Heat and cooling relate to quality and balance of air (hangin, "winds") in the body.
- Sudden changes in weather patterns, cool breezes or exposure in evening hours to low temperature, presence of hot sun immediately after a lengthy rain, or vapors rising from the soil, all may upset the body balance by simply blowing on the body surface (McBride, (n.d.), p. 3).

In the article, "Health and Illness in Filipino Immigrants", in a special issue of the *Western Journal of Medicine,* James Anderson (1983) explains that physical and mental illnesses are considered to be caused by different factors:

1. **Mystical** causes are often associated with experiences or behaviors such as retribution from ancestors for unfulfilled obligations. Some believe in soul loss and that sleep related to the wandering of the soul out of body, known as bangungot or nightmares after a heavy meal may result in death.
2. **Personalistic** causes may be attributed to social punishment or retribution by supernatural beings such as an evil spirit, witch, or mankukulam (sorcerer). A stronger spirit such as a healer or priest may counteract this force. For protection, using holy oils, wearing religious objects or an anting anting (amulet or talisman) may be recommended.
3. **Naturalistic** causes include a range of factors from nature events (thunder, lightning, drafts, etc.), excessive stress, incompatible food and drugs, infection, or familial susceptibility.

For Filipinos it is important to prevent illness by avoiding inappropriate behaviors and restoring health through the balance of the life force and the causes of illness.

Asian Indians often practice ayurvedic medicine. This ancient practice is based on the theory that the five great elements, ether, air, fire, water, and earth, are the basis for all living systems. The five elements are in constant interaction and are constantly changing. Ayurvedic medicine is discussed in detail in Chapter 3. Asian Indians also employ Western medicine.

HEALING TRADITIONS

Healing traditions among Pacific Islanders revolve around the use of naturally occurring substances, such as plant extracts and herbs. Many Pacific Islanders use **kava** root and **betel nut** for various cultural, medicinal, and ceremonial purposes. These substances are thought to overcome social barriers, ease social interactions, and cure afflictions, and they accompany ceremonial rituals. Kava is usually brewed into a tea and has been used for healing since ancient times. Betel nut is chewed and has a narcotic-like effect.

Although many Native Hawaiians utilize Western medicine for their health care needs, traditional practices continue to influence many. Like other aspects of their culture, Hawaiian health beliefs are closely related to nature. They consider the mind, body, and spirit to be one, and the body cannot maintain health without a healthy spirit. Native Hawaiians have a great regard for nature and believe the environment impacts their health through **mana**, the healing energy of the island. Thus, the concept of **lokahi**—harmony between people, nature, and the gods—is critical to maintaining health and preventing illness.

Native Hawaiian healing is practiced by **kahunas**, "keepers of the secret." Various treatments are employed, including massage and herbalism. Different types of kahunas treat different problems, not unlike specialization within Western medicine.

Many Asian Americans and Pacific Islanders use techniques discussed in Chapter 3, such as traditional Chinese medicine and ayurvedic medicine. Cambodians use coining, cupping, and pinching to treat many problems associated with "wind illness," forms of respiratory illness. Coining is rubbing or scratching the skin of the back, neck, upper chest, and arms with a coin. Cupping and pinching function in the same manner, to bring blood to an area of the body. Before or during rubbing, they apply Tiger Balm, herbal liquid medicine, skin lotion, or water on the skin. The technique helps to smooth the skin and is believed to improve the coining outcome.

BEHAVIORAL RISK FACTORS AND COMMON HEALTH PROBLEMS _____

Data regarding significant risks and health disparities for Asian Americans, Native Hawaiian, and Pacific Islanders include the following (Centers for Disease Control and Prevention [CDC], Office of Minority Health and Disparities, 2006):

- In 2006, the five-year relative survival rate for all cancers for Native Hawaiians was 47%, compared to 57% for whites and 55% for all races.
- In 2003, Asian American women older than age 18 years were less likely to have a Pap smear than other ethnic groups.
- In 2002, Native Hawaiians and Japanese and Filipino residents of Hawaii older than age 20 years were two times more likely to be diagnosed with diabetes as white residents of Hawaii.
- In 2002, the infant mortality rate for Native Hawaiians was 9.6 per 1,000 live births, higher than that of all other populations.
- In 2003, new AIDS cases reported among Asian Americans and Pacific Islanders was up 34.7% over the 1999 level.

- In 2001, Asian Americans and Pacific Islanders older than age 40 years were 2.5 times more likely to have hepatitis B than non-Hispanic whites.
- In 2004, Asian Americans were 5.6 times more likely to have tuberculosis than the general American population, and Native Hawaiians and Pacific Islanders were 3.3 times more likely to have the disease.

Asian Americans

Barnes, Adams, and Powell-Griner (2008) researched the utilization of health resources among Asian Americans. They found that Korean Americans were the most likely among the Asian populations to be without a regular source of health care. Vietnamese Americans were more likely than other groups to consider a clinic as their primary place for health care. Asian American adults were more likely to have never seen a dentist, compared to white or black adults, and a large percentage of Korean Americans had not been to a dentist in the last year.

Interestingly, the rate of Asian Americans who did not seek health care because of cost was relatively low. However, of this population, Korean Americas had the highest rate of not seeking care because of financial concerns (Barnes, Adams, Powell-Griner, 2008).

Data from the census and recent research has provided a much better picture of the health behaviors of Asian Americans and the common health problems they encounter. The data indicates that Asian American populations have differing personal practices and susceptibilities to disease.

Most Asian American adults have never smoked; however, for those who do, the highest rate of smoking was among Korean American and Japanese American adults. Japanese American adults also were more likely to be current moderate or heavy drinkers. Vietnamese American adults had the highest incidence of alcohol abstinence over a lifetime, and Asian Indian Americans were a close second. Most Asian American adults were in an appropriate weight range, but Filipino American adults were more likely to be obese, compared to other Asian American adults. Finally, few Asian Americans reported doing regular physical activity, and Vietnamese Americans were most likely to be inactive during their leisure time (Barnes, Adams, Powell-Griner, 2008).

Sixty percent of Asian Americans reported being in excellent or very good health (Barnes, Adams, Powell-Griner). No difference between males or females was reported for most Asian American groups. Vietnamese Americans had the highest rate of poor health, and Vietnamese American women were twice as likely to be in poor health than Vietnamese American men (see Figure   4).

Asian American adults are less likely to report being diagnosed with hypertension and high blood pressure than black, white, or Hispanic adults. Among Asian American

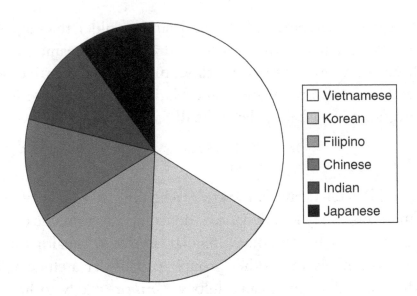

FIGURE **4** Asian American adults reporting fair to poor health for 2004–2006.
Source: Barnes, Adams, and Powell-Griner. (2008).

populations, Filipino Americans and Japanese Americans are more likely to be diagnosed with hypertension than Chinese Americans, Korean Americans, or Asian Indian Americans. Asian Americans were also less likely to have diabetes than black or Hispanic Americans. However, within the Asian American population, Asian Indian Americans had a significantly greater incidence of diabetes than Chinese or Japanese Americans. Compared to white, black, and Hispanic Americans, Asian Americans are less likely to suffer from migraines. Among the Asian American population, Vietnamese Americans and Filipino Americans have the highest incidence of migraines.

Immunization rates for Asian American populations are lower than the other groups overall. Asian Americans were less likely to have received a pneumonia vaccine. They received the hepatitis B vaccine at the same rate as white and black adults, but they were less likely to obtain HIV testing. Asian Americans report psychological distress less frequently than white, black, or Hispanic adults (Barnes, Adams, Powell-Griner, 2008).

Asian Americans are most at risk for a number of health problems, including cancer, heart disease, stroke, diabetes, and unintentional injuries. They also have a high incidence of chronic obstructive pulmonary disease, hepatitis B, HIV–AIDS, smoking, tuberculosis, and liver disease (CDC, 2006).

Although heart disease occurs less frequently among Asian Americans than any other minority group, it is still a leading cause of death among Asian Americans (see Table   4). Asian Americans are at risk for silent heart attacks, a painless form of the disease that can lead to a fatal outcome as a result of the lack of warning of a problem.

TABLE	4	Ten Leading Causes of Death in Asian American and Pacific Islander Populations

1. Cancer	6. Influenza and pneumonia
2. Heart disease	7. Chronic lower respiratory disease
3. Stroke	8. Suicide
4. Unintentional injuries	9. Kidney disease
5. Diabetes	10. Alzheimer disease

Source: Centers for Disease Control and Prevention, Office of Minority Health and Disparities. (2007).

Stroke within the Asian American population is higher than within the white American population.

In addition to the various pathologies that Asian Americans are susceptible to, there are other factors that negatively impact their health. They tend to avoid visits to medical practitioners because of language and cultural barriers, fear of deportation, and lack of insurance (Office of Minority Health, 2008a). Figure 5 depicts

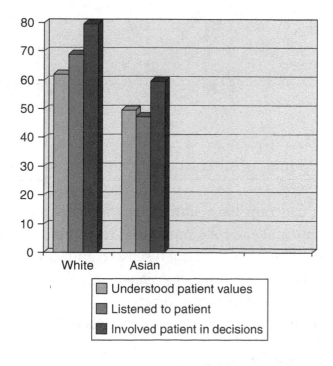

FIGURE 5 Asian Americans' and white Americans' perceptions of relationship with physicians.
Source: Ngo-Metzger, Legedza, and Phillips. (2004).

319

TABLE 5 Comparison of Eastern and Western Values

Values	Eastern/Traditional	Western/Modern
Societal orientation	Family	Individual
Family makeup	Extended	Nuclear
Primary relationship	Parent–child	Marital
Family values	Well defined	Flexible
Relationship emphasis	Interpersonal and harmony	Self-fulfillment and development
Gender roles	Male dominant	Opportunity for females
Control	Authoritative	Democratic
Emotional expression	Suppressive	Expressive
Beliefs	Fatalism/karma	Personal control
	Harmony with nature	Control of nature
	Cooperation	Competition
	Spiritualism	Materialism

Source: Carrasco and Weiss. (2005).

Asian Americans' perceptions of interactions with physicians, compared to white Americans' perceptions.

Asian Americans as a group have similar perspectives on mental health issues. Many traditional Asian cultural and religious beliefs view mental health problems to be shameful and disgraceful. They often are not discussed and, consequently, seeking help is often avoided. These views also instruct Asians' view of the world and the differences between Asian cultures and Western societies. Table 5 compares the differing approaches to society, family, and behavioral issues between Asian and Western societies.

Native Hawaiians and Pacific Islanders

Native Hawaiians and Pacific Islanders (NHPI) have poorer health than the American population as a whole. The most common health disorders for Pacific Islanders include cancer, diabetes, heart disease, and obesity. Some of the leading causes of death are cancer, heart disease, stroke, and unintentional injuries, and premature death is caused by obesity, cardiovascular disease, cancer, and diabetes (CDC, 2006) (see Table 4). Some other health conditions and risk factors that are prevalent among NHPIs are hepatitis B, HIV–AIDS, and tuberculosis.

It is significant to note that in comparison to other ethnic groups, NHPIs have higher rates of smoking, alcohol consumption, and obesity. This group also has little access to cancer prevention and control programs (Office of Minority Health, 2008b).

The infant mortality rate (deaths per 1,000 live births) for Native Hawaiians in 2002 was 9.6, higher than the rate for all Asian American and Pacific Islander groups combined (4.8 deaths per 1,000 live births) and for the general population (7.0 deaths per 1,000 live births). The tuberculosis rate (cases per 100,000 patients) for NHPIs in 2007 was 21 times higher than the white population; the NHPI rate was 23.0 cases per 100,000, compared to 1.1 cases per 100,000 for the white population (Office of Minority Health, 2008b).

QUICK FACTS

Cancer
- In 2004, NHPI men were 40% less likely to have prostate cancer than non-Hispanic white men.
- In 2004, NHPI women were 30% less likely to have breast cancer than non-Hispanic white women.
- NHPI men and women have higher incidence and mortality rates for stomach and liver cancer.

Diabetes
- In Hawaii, Native Hawaiians have more than twice the rate of diabetes as whites.
- NHPIs are 20% less likely than non-Hispanic whites to die from diabetes.
- In Hawaii, Native Hawaiians are more than 5.7 times as likely as whites to die from diabetes.
- In Hawaii, Filipino Americans have more than three times the death rate of whites.

Heart Disease
- Overall, NHPI adults are less likely than white adults to have heart disease, and they are less likely to die from heart disease.
- NHPIs are 40% more likely to be diagnosed with heart disease, compared to non-Hispanic whites.

(Continues)

Diet

As a group, Asian Americans are not as concerned with nutrition as people from Western cultures. The texture, flavor, color, and aroma of food is much more important in Chinese cooking. The balance of yin and yang, hot and cold, is much more important than food groups.

Because many Asian Americans are lactose intolerant, dairy products are not a large part of their diet. Soy milk and tofu are the staples that provide protein and calcium. The primary food groups for Asian Americans are grains, vegetables, fruit, and meat or fish, and rice and noodles are daily staples (see Figure   6).

The Asian Indian diet and cooking involves the use of aromatic spices. Asian Indian dietary practices have religious influences from the Hindu and Muslim traditions. Hindus are vegetarians and believe that food was created by a Supreme Being for the benefit of man. Muslims have several dietary restrictions (Bhungalia, Kelly, VanDeKeift, & Young, n.d.).

Pacific Islanders have been experiencing poor nutrition related to dietary changes that incorporate more Western practices like fast food and highly processed foods. Coupled with more sedentary lifestyles, these dietary changes have placed more Pacific Islanders at risk for obesity and diabetes.

The Traditional Healthy Asian Diet Pyramid

Daily Beverage Recommendations:

6 Glasses of Water or Tea

Sake, Wine, or Beer in moderation

MEAT — Monthly

SWEETS
EGGS & POULTRY — Weekly

FISH & SHELLFISH or DAIRY — Optional Daily

VEGETABLE OILS

FRUITS — LEGUMES, SEEDS & NUTS — VEGETABLES — Daily

RICE, NOODLES, BREADS, MILLET, CORN & OTHER WHOLE GRAINS

Daily Physical Activity

FIGURE 6 Asian food pyramid.
Source: © 2000 Oldways Preservation & Exchange Trust. www.oldwayspt.org. Reproduced with permission.

CONSIDERATIONS FOR HEALTH PROMOTION AND PROGRAM PLANNING

Health promotion for Asian Americans and Pacific Islanders creates a unique challenge given the varied cultures and traditions involved. Points to consider for Asian American and Pacific Islander programs should include:

- Ensure good communication by thorough explanation and language translation where necessary.

- Show respect for family relationships and their needs, and include family in discussions.
- Provide dietary-appropriate meals.
- Inquire about other treatments used for health problems and obtain specific information regarding herbs and other substances that are being used.

CHAPTER SUMMARY

The term "Asian American" is a generality for many people who trace their heritage to numerous countries, cultures, and traditions across Asia. They continue the traditions of their ancestors and experience health care issues unique to their heritage.

Pacific Islanders and Native Hawaiians also have many cultural backgrounds. Many people in the United States are unaware of the history of Hawaii and its controversial entry into the United States. This chapter has provided an introduction to the varied cultures and health practices that comprise Asian Americans, Pacific Islanders, and Native Hawaiians through a discussion of their heritage, history in America, traditional health practices, and common health risks.

REVIEW

1. Discuss Asian Americans' and Pacific Islanders' history in the United States and the influence it has had on their health.
2. What cultural influences impact the health of Asian Americans and Pacific Islanders?
3. Discuss the health behaviors of Asian Americans and how those behaviors impact their health.
4. Discuss the health behaviors of Pacific Islanders and how those behaviors impact their health.

CASE STUDIES

Case #1. An elderly Japanese American woman lived alone in her apartment. Recently it was noted that she was not keeping her apartment and garden up as she did in the past, she has locked herself out of her apartment four times this year, she has forgotten to pay the rent, and last week she left the stove on and burned a pot.

Her friends and family made an appointment for her with a geriatric consultant through her health care provider. She was evaluated by a social worker, and a Caucasian caregiver was hired to assist her with activities of daily living. Since the caregiver has been cooking, the woman has been experiencing diarrhea, cramping, and abdominal pain. She has been using over-the-counter medications for the problem and is being evaluated at the hospital for her symptoms.

Among the things to be considered by the doctors is the possibility that the woman is lactose intolerant, which is prevalent among Japanese people. Because a non-Japanese caregiver now cooks her meals, she may be eating food she is not used to that possibly contains lactose, and she may not be able to discuss this with the caregiver due to communication problems.

Consider the following:

- What can be done to assist this woman in a manner more appropriate to her traditions?

Case #2. A healthy Japanese American man was declared brain dead after a motor vehicle accident. His children consented to donate his organs. The decedent's siblings arrived from Japan and were very upset that his organs had been donated. They believed the decedent would not have wanted that, and they could not understand how he had died because his heart was still beating. They made overtures that the children had improperly let him die, and a terrible split occurred within the family.

Organ donation among traditional Japanese is not well received. Education and counseling is needed to assist the family during the loss of a loved one.

Consider the following:

- How could the health care providers have helped to reduce the likelihood of the family rift?
- How might health care providers deal with family members who don't understand the decisions that were made?

Source: Tanabe. (n.d.).

MODEL PROGRAMS

Families In Good Health

The Families in Good Health Program was designed in Long Beach, California to improve cardiac health by decreasing the sedentary lifestyle among Southeast Asians. The program focused on families and spent considerable effort in identifying the needs of the various communities. Since the main place for socialization was the temples and churches attended by the various groups, fitness activities were developed and offered at those sites.

Activities offered included health education, traditional dances, youth classes, walking groups, water aerobics for elders, and an exercise cassette with traditional music and nutritional information for those who could not read English. Community groups donated exercise equipment, and the YMCA worked with the program to lower costs for program participants.

Source: National Institutes of Health, Office of Prevention, Education, and Control. (2000).

Strengthening Hawaii Families

The Strengthening Hawaii Families program is a culturally relevant, family-focused program designed to prevent substance abuse and other problems through improving parenting skills, family relations, and reducing childhood behavioral problems.

Evaluation

The program consists of 14 weeks of training in parenting, child skills, and family skills. Topics covered include family values, culture and generational continuity, goal setting, communication problem solving, anger management, and wellness, among others.

Outcomes

At the end of the program, follow-up found that the program had the following positive outcomes:

- Significant reduction in family conflict
- Significant improvement in family cohesion and organization
- Significant improvement in family communication

Source: SAMHSA's National Registry of Evidence-based Programs and Practices. (2009).

GLOSSARY TERMS

Hmong	betel nut
aAma and aDuonga	mana
Kior chi force	lokahi
timbang	kahunas
kava	

REFERENCES

Anderson, J. (1983). Health and illness in Filipino immigrants. In Cross-Cultural Medicine [Special issue]. *Western Journal of Medicine, 139*(6), 811–819.

Barnes, P., Adams, P., & Powell-Griner, E. (2008). *Health characteristics of the Asian Adult population: United States, 2004–2006.* Advance data from vital and health statistics, no. 394. Hyattsville, MD: National Center for Health Statistics. Retrieved May 22, 2008, from http://www.meps.ahrq.gov/mepsweb/data_files/publications/st224/stat224.pdf

Beller, T., Pinker, M., Snapka, S., & Van Dusan, D. (n.d.). *Korean-American health care beliefs and practices.* Retrieved April 25, 2008 from http://bearspace.baylor.edu/Charles_Kemp/www/korean_health.htm

Bennett, C., & Reeves, T. (2004, December). *We the people: Asians in the United States. Census 2000 special reports.* Retrieved May 16, 2008 from http://www.census.gov/prod/2004pubs/censr-17.pdf

Bhungalia, S., Kelly, T., VanDeKeift, S., & Young, M. (n.d.). *Indian health care beliefs and practices.* Retrieved April 25, 2008, from http://bearspace.baylor.edu/Charles_Kemp/www/korean_health.htm

Carrasco, M., & Weiss, J. (2005). NAMI. *Asian American and Pacific Islander outreach resource manual.* Retrieved April 25, 2008, from http://www.NAMI.org/Content/ContentGroups/Multicultural_Support1/AAPIManual.pdf

Centers for Disease Control and Prevention. (2008). *CDC advance data from vital and health statistics, number 394. Health characteristics of the Asian adult population: United States, 2004–2006.* Retrieved May 22, 2008, from http://www.cdc.gov/nchs/data/ad/ad394.pdf

Centers for Disease Control and Prevention, Office of Minority Health and Disparities. (2006, May). *Highlights in minority health & health disparities May 2006; Asian American Pacific Islander heritage month 2006.* Retrieved April 25, 2008, from http://www.cdc.gov/omhd/Highlights/2006/HMay06AAPI.htm

Centers for Disease Control and Prevention, Office of Minority Health and Disparities. (2007). *Asian American populations.* Retrieved April 25, 2008, from http://www.cdc.gov/omhd/Populations/AsianAm/AsianAm.htm

Hilgenkamp, K., & Pescaia, C. (2003). Traditional Hawaiian healing and western influence [Special issue: Hawaii]. *California Journal of Health Promotion, 1,* 34–39. Retrieved May 30, 2008, from http://www.hawaii.edu/hivandaids/Traditional_Hawaiian_Healing_and_Western_Influence.pdf

LaBorde, P. (1996, July). *Vietnamese cultural profile.* Retrieved April 25, 2008, from http://www.ethnomed.org/ethnomed/cultures/vietnamese/vietnamese_cp.html

McBride, M. (n.d.). *Health and health care of Filipino American elders.* Retrieved May 23, 2008, from http://www.stanford.edu/group/ethnoger/filipino.html

National Institutes of Health, Office of Prevention, Education, and Control. (2000). *Addressing cardiovascular health in Asian Americans and Pacific Islanders* (NIH Publication No. 00-3647).

Ngo-Metzger, Q., Legedza, A., & Phillips, R. (2004). Asian Americans reports of their health care experiences. *The Commonwealth Fund.* Retrieved May 16, 2008, from http://www.commonwealthfund.org/Content/Publications/In-the-Literature/2004/Feb/Asian-Americans-Reports-of-Their-Health-Care-Experiences.aspx

Office of Minority Health. (2008a). *Asian American/Pacific Islander profile.* Retrieved April 25, 2008, from http://www.omhrc.gov/templates/browse.aspx?lvl=2&lvlid=53

Office of Minority Health. (2008b). *Native Hawaiians/other Pacific Islanders profile.* Retrieved November 21, 2008, from www.omhrc.gov/templates/browse.aspx?lvl=2&lvlID=71

Oldways Preservation & Exchange Trust. (2008). *Asian diet pyramid.* Retrieved July 23, 2008, from http://www.oldwayspt.org/asian_pyramid.html

SAMHSA's National Registry of Evidence-based Programs and Practices. (2009). *Strengthening Hawaii families.* Retrieved January 26, 2009, from http://nrepp.samhsa.gov/legacy_fulldetails. asp?LEGACY_ID=1038

Tanabe, M. (n.d.). *Health and health care of Japanese-American elders.* Retrieved May 23, 2008, from http://www.stanford.edu/group/ethnoger/japanese.html

US Census Bureau. (n.d.). *Race and Hispanic origin in 2005.* Retrieved May 27, 2008, from http://www.Census.gov/population/pop-profile/dynamic/RACEHO.pdf

US Census Bureau. (2008). *Population density of the United States, and selected maps of race and Hispanic origin: 2000.* Retrieved November 9, 2008, from http://www.census.gov/population/www/censusdata/2000maps.html

PHOTO CREDITS

Chapter Opener , © Serguei Bachlakov/Dreamstime.com

Unless otherwise indicated, all photographs and illustrations are under copyright of Jones and Bartlett Publishers, LLC, or have been provided by the author(s).

Caucasian American Populations

Sometimes God calms the storm, but sometimes God lets the storm rage and calms his child.

—Amish proverb

May God give you luck and health.

—Roma (Gypsy) blessing

It is well to give when asked, but it is better to give unasked, through understanding.

—Kahlil Gibran

KEY CONCEPTS

- Rumspringa
- Brauche
- Ellis-van Creveld syndrome
- Romany
- Gadje
- Wuzho
- Marime
- Drabarni

CHAPTER OBJECTIVES

1. Describe the cultural impact on health for the Amish, Roma, and Arab Americans.
2. Discuss the common health risks for these groups.
3. Describe the behavioral health challenges for these groups.

The U.S. Census Bureau's term "white" applies to a person having origins among any of the original peoples of Europe, the Middle East, or North Africa. That is a very broad area that encompasses numerous ethnic and cultural groups. Much has been written about the dominant European groups that inhabit the United States. Figure 1 illustrates the distribution of non-Hispanic whites in the United States. In this chapter we will discuss some of the cultural and health care issues that impact cultures and ethnic groups that are less well known.

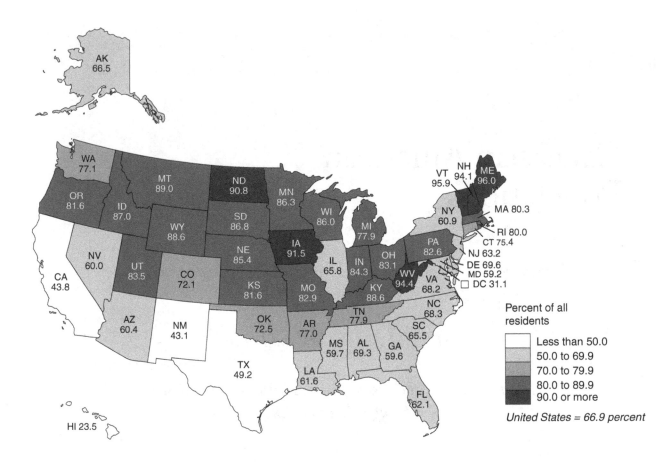

FIGURE 1 Percentage of non-Hispanic whites (single race) in the United States: 2005. *Source:* Reprinted from U.S. Census Bureau. (2005a).

HISTORY OF AMISH AMERICANS IN THE UNITED STATES

Jakob Amman, a Swiss Anabaptist leader, is the namesake of the Amish. Their religion can be traced back to sixteenth century Europe during Martin Luther's Protestant Reformation. Questions about whether the government or the Bible should be the supreme authority arose, and further divisions occurred, resulting in a new religious sect, the Anabaptists. The Anabaptists would experience further subdivision, resulting in groups we know today as the Amish, Mennonites, Church of the Brethren, Hutterites, and many more. The Amish have five religious orders: Old Order, New Order, Andy Weaver, Beachy, and Swartzentruber, with Old Order being the most traditional.

AMISH AMERICANS IN THE UNITED STATES

Religious persecution forced the Amish and Mennonites to find a safe haven in the New World. In the 1730s, a group of Amish immigrants joined Mennonite colonists who had already established a community in Lancaster, Pennsylvania. Lancaster houses the oldest Amish community in North America. "More than 90 percent of Lancaster's Amish are affiliated with the Old Order Amish" (Kraybill, 2001, p. 12).

Amish families live in common geographic areas. In the present day, they have established 1,300 congregations and have grown to a population of about 180,000 throughout 24 states, as well as Ontario, Canada. Although the oldest settlement is found in Pennsylvania, the most heavily populated area is Ohio, where over 150 congregations exist, and 70% of the Amish are found in Indiana, Ohio, and Pennsylvania. (Kraybill, 2001). They speak a specific Pennsylvania German dialect commonly called Pennsylvania Dutch.

The Amish strive for homogeneity. They have deep agricultural roots and believe that farming is the glue that holds their communities together. Traditionally, farming has also leveled the occupational profiles of the Amish. Although increases in land values and new business ventures have challenged the level of equality in Amish communities, the society is still a relatively egalitarian one; thus, great monetary wealth and relative poverty are nearly nonexistent. Consequently, the Amish frown upon the use of government assistance in times of need. Their society is structured such that any assistance required is provided by the community itself. This isolation from mainstream society makes it difficult to track Amish poverty levels in terms of federal poverty guidelines.

Unlike typical Western societies, social class and education are not revered in the Amish community; preserving religion and way of life is of primary importance. Traditionally, Amish children attended one-room public schools where the curriculum reflected Amish values. The Amish believe that education in evolution, science, and sex education is contradictory to their value system and consider higher education to be vain. For the most part, the Amish have successfully resisted governmental and societal movements to change their educational practices. Today, most Amish students in Lancaster, Pennsylvania still attend one-room private schools taught by Amish teachers. In 1972, the Supreme Court ruled in favor of allowing Amish families to remove their children from school at the conclusion of eight years of education.

The Amish social environment, including the family structure, child-rearing practices, religion, communication, and pregnancy beliefs, greatly influences the health of this population. The Amish live a simple lifestyle that abstains from material luxuries and resembles the lifestyle of sixteenth century European peasants. For example, they still utilize horses and buggies for transportation, and their lifestyle is agriculturally based. Their unique heritage is ingrained in a belief system that seeks to retain their traditional values while avoiding the influences of the dominant culture. The two most valued aspects of their lives include their family and their church district.

The Amish generally have large families, mostly because they do not routinely practice birth control. Children are believed to be economic blessings, because they help with maintaining the farm and household. It is not unusual for generations of family members to live in the same house and operate as one unit. Single people and single-parent homes are rare: "Only five percent of Amish households are single-person units, compared to twenty percent for the county" (Kraybill, 2001, p. 100). The average number of people in a household is 12, which may include extended family.

The gender roles within the family are traditional; the males are the dominant figures within the household, directing the farming operations and overseeing their children's work in the fields. Many husbands will assist in child care, lawn care, and gardening, but they usually do not assist in other household work. Wives are responsible for washing, cooking, canning, sewing, mending, and cleaning. Church leaders teach that wives must submit to the authority of their husbands according to religious doctrine. Women are not usually employed outside of the home. Their main duties revolve around raising the children, gardening, and assisting with barn chores. They find opportunities to host quilting parties and attend special events like weddings to maintain some form of socialization. The women who have their own businesses like their male counterparts, which include nearly 15% of the business owners in the Amish community, are believed to be acting in direct violation of God's created order (Kraybill, 2001). They are believed to be more susceptible to divorce, having unruly children, and disrupting the family order. The Amish are such strong believers in a patriarchal society that if divorce occurs because a woman does not subject herself to her defined gender role, she can be excommunicated from the community. Likewise, a man that chooses to divorce his wife must also be excommunicated. His wife can remain in the church, but she cannot remarry until her former husband dies.

The Amish religion is deeply integrated with their family structure. The Amish believe that the Bible is a guide for parents to teach their children the values of their religion while training them to conform to the Amish ways. Cultural beliefs are passed down through the generations in such a way that young Amish children are not exposed to cultural diversities that modern youth outside of the Amish community are exposed.

The church district is the other primary location of activity besides the home. The Amish practice a religion that has its roots in Christianity but has no specific identification. Some Amish would consider themselves to be conservative Protestant, but the majority would consider themselves to be Anabaptist. The ordained leaders of the church are always men and are usually elderly. Old age is respected among the Amish community as a symbol of wisdom and knowledge. Congregations meet to worship and attend baptisms, weddings, excommunications, and funerals. Sinful members must confess their major sins before other members of the congregation. One bishop, two or three ministers, and a deacon usually lead two congregations in two separate districts. The power that bishops have is the ability to recommend an excommunication and the ability to reinstate a penitent member upon approval of the congregation through a majority vote. Bishops are also responsible for making their own interpretations of religious doctrine for a district. Some bishops are more lenient than others. For example, some bishops will permit power lawn mowers, but others do not. The role of the ministers is to preach to the congregation and provide spiritual direction. These ministers do not need to have credentials or special training to become a minister; they are selected by the congregation to serve the people without monetary compensation. Ministers earn their livelihood by farming, carpentry, or other related occupations, including business (Kraybill, 2001).

Technology and electricity are believed to be products of modernity and are addressed and integrated into the Amish community under meticulous law. Amish people may use technology to communicate with one another or with non-Amish acquaintances, but the technology must be kept at a distance yet be easily accessible to all individuals within the Amish community. For example, a telephone may be located at the end of a lane and used by all families within that vicinity (Armer & Radina, 2006). Certain electric appliances are used more often by men who work in the barns than women who work in the kitchen or house. Electric mixers, blenders, dishwashers, microwave ovens, and clothes dryers are usually banned from the kitchen. Washing machines, sewing machines, mixers, beaters, and blenders are operated by air pressure.

A unique part of the Amish culture is **Rumspringa**, which means "running around." This practice is the focus of a documentary directed by Lucy Walker entitled *Devil's Playground*. Walker describes Rumspringa as a time when adolescents are free to explore the world outside of the Amish culture. Rumspringa is practiced by young males and females between the ages of 16 and 21 years. During this period, individuals may partake in activities of their choosing, which may include drinking alcohol, using illicit drugs, and experimenting with sexual activities. Rumspringa ends when the young person makes the decision to either live in the outside world or become baptized within the Amish community (Cantor & Walker, 2002).

BELIEFS ABOUT CAUSES OF HEALTH AND ILLNESS AMONG AMISH AMERICANS

The Amish believe that sin is the cause of illness; therefore, their approach to health care in the United States is unique compared to other white Americans (Palmer, 1992). The way in which the Amish make decisions about health is affected by their separation from the world and modern technology.

Health care practitioners should be sensitive to the unique perspective of their Amish patients. For example, considering that the Amish have little contact with medical professionals and technology, health care practitioners should convey descriptions of treatment procedures accordingly, avoiding complex medical language (Lee, 2005). Moreover, health care professionals should expect to talk to spouses and family members who are likely to gather in support of the patient. Finally, as much treatment as possible should take place in one visit due to transportation difficulties. These issues should be considered to provide Amish patients with the best possible health care outcomes (Lee, 2005).

HEALING TRADITIONS AMONG AMISH AMERICANS

The Amish tend to approach health care as organically as possible with the use of holistic, natural, herbal, and folk medicine, which are readily accessible in Amish communities (Palmer, 1992). Basic natural and herbal remedies may include iron pills, vitamins E and C, herbal tea, and sage tea. Other natural remedies include corn silk tea for an enlarged prostate, aloe vera gel for minor trauma, and poho oil (peppermint oil in a petrolatum base) for respiratory problems (Kriebel, 2000). Additionally, the Amish have been known to utilize reflexology, which is the practice of applying pressure to specific parts of the feet and hands to affect the nervous system (Julia, 1996). The Amish utilize chiropractic procedures and **brauche** practices in which the brauche healer lays his hands over a patient's head or stomach while quietly reciting verses to "pull out" the ailment (Wenger, 1995).

Amish women try to limit their use of technology, even during pregnancy and while giving birth. For example, amniocentesis and other invasive prenatal diagnostic tests are not acceptable. Amish women prefer to use nurse midwives and lay midwives, and to have home deliveries, because it limits the use of technology as well as reduces the number of visits to the doctor, which may be costly (Lemon, 2006).

Women practice certain folk traditions during pregnancy to prepare themselves for giving birth. These practices include not walking under a clothesline because that is believed to cause a stillbirth. Another practice includes not climbing through a window or under a table because both can cause the umbilical cord to wrap around the baby's neck (Lemon, 2006). Women use a medley of herbs, called 5-W, five weeks before their pregnancy ends. These herbs include a mixture of red raspberry leaves, black cohosh root, butcher's broom root, dong quai root, and squaw vine root. The formula is believed to ease the labor by quieting the nerves and relaxing the uterus (Lemon, 2006).

BEHAVIORAL RISK FACTORS AND COMMON HEALTH PROBLEMS AMONG AMISH AMERICANS

The Amish have few behavioral risk factors due to various health-promoting behaviors, which, among the adult population, include low rates of tobacco use and alcohol consumption, high levels of physical activity, and low levels of obesity. However, the Amish are cautious and conservative and may refuse health care services (Armer & Radina, 2006). Furthermore, Amish youth are prone to alcohol abuse, which inspired the Drug Abuse Resistance Education (D.A.R.E.) program to conduct outreach in Amish communities (Ohio Department of Alcohol and Drug Services, 2005).

Amish children and adolescents live in nontechnological farming communities, which results in a population that is physically active and that has a low rate of obesity (Basset, Schneider, & Huntington, 2004). Amish adults also showed very high levels of physical activity, which includes consistently walking at moderate to vigorous levels and farming daily. This type of lifestyle, one that promotes physical activity, results in the low prevalence of obesity and positive health outcomes in general for the Amish community (Basset, et al., 2007).

The Amish do not completely prohibit the use of modern medical technology, but they tend to be extremely cautious and may refuse intervention if it is not approved by community leaders. For example, Amish families vary in receptivity to the practice of immunizations for communicable diseases, leading to increased vulnerability to those illnesses. Although the Amish account for less than 0.5% of the national population, they were responsible for nearly all cases of rubella reported in the United States in 1991 (Armer & Radina, 2006). Moreover, the lack of immunizations puts the Amish at risk when they travel outside of their communities, because they may not be protected against diseases to which they become exposed.

According to the *Encyclopedia of Medical Anthropology*, certain Amish communities live by laws and precepts that have been passed down for generations. Such customs include marrying within their own community and allowing first cousins to marry. Consequently, a growing number of distinctive genetic recessive disorders among the

Amish have arisen (Ember & Ember, 2004). Individuals who have a genetic recessive disorder, such as **Ellis-van Creveld syndrome** (EVC), receive a defective recessive gene from each parent. EVC, a form of dwarfism, is an autosomal recessive disorder in which individuals exhibit postaxial polydactyly of the hands; this is indicated by an extra digit located next to the fifth digit. In addition, EVC is characterized by individuals having short forearms and legs as well as congenital heart failure (Leach, 2007).

Cartilage-hair hypoplasia, another form of dwarfism, is a genetic disorder that is rarely seen outside of Amish communities (ClinicalTrials.gov, 2007). This rare disorder was not recognized until the mid-1960s when Amish children began to present with features similar to, but more pronounced than, EVC. These signs include fine and underdeveloped hair (hypoplasia of the hair) and underdeveloped cartilage (hypoplasia of the cartilage), resulting in skeletal abnormalities and an inability to fully extend the upper limbs (McKusick, 2000). Researchers are currently attempting to verify the causes of such health problems to find solutions to these disorders. As the homogenous Amish population continues to grow, further research is necessary to understand their propensity toward genetic recessive disorders (ClinicalTrials.gov, 2007).

Another rising health concern, particularly among young Amish community members, is the use of drugs and alcohol. It has been noted that the use of drugs and alcohol was not initially taken seriously because of the Amish adolescent participation in the Rumspringa ritual (Donnermeyer & Lora, 2002).

For some individuals, the use of drugs and alcohol during the period of Rumspringa has been linked with depression (Donnermeyer & Lora, 2002). Drug- and alcohol-related depression may exist in part because of the pressure to either join the church or become shunned and leave the community (Cantor & Walker, 2002). This issue has become so severe in Holmes County, Ohio, that Amish church elders set up a private mental health center for their community. Because the center is not directed by the outside medical community, the elders are responsible for counseling members who suffer from depression or other mental illnesses (Donnermeyer & Lora, 2002). Although teen depression has risen within Amish communities, depression among adults has not been an issue. Studies have revealed that Amish adults tend to live relatively stress-free lives (Cantor & Walker, 2002).

Humility and simplicity are characteristics that form the underpinning of Amish society in the United States. The Amish practice a conservative form of Christian idealism, which was founded on early Anabaptist practices (Kraybill, 2001). The Amish interpret the Bible literally and strive to retain their traditional values while avoiding the influences of outside norms. The Amish limit their contact with the dominant culture and generally reject the use of modern technology (Armer & Radina, 2006).

The Amish tend to prefer natural home remedies; however, they may seek health care services from medical doctors and complementary health providers, such as reflexologists and chiropractors (Julia, 1996). Due to a relatively stress-free and active lifestyle, positive health outcomes among the population include low rates of obesity, smoking, and cancer (Ferketich, et al., 2008). As a result of the lack of vaccinations among the Amish, they are more susceptible to communicable diseases (Armer & Radina, 2006). Finally, common health problems found among the Amish are birth defects as a result of recessive genetic disorders due to intermarriage practices (Leach, 2007).

CONSIDERATIONS FOR HEALTH PROMOTION AND PROGRAM PLANNING FOR AMISH AMERICANS

When working with members of the Amish community, the following recommendations should be considered to improve cultural understanding:

- Be cognizant of the cultural differences this group has with society as a whole.
- Recognize the importance of privacy.
- Recognize that Amish people might not understand things you consider to be everyday occurrences.
- Be cognizant of the formality of family relationships.
- Explain all procedures and instructions to ensure understanding.

HISTORY OF ROMA AMERICANS IN THE UNITED STATES

A cultural group that is very misunderstood and often overlooked is the Roma. Commonly known as Gypsies, that term is considered a pejorative by these people, and the proper term for this group is the Roma or the Romani. They are an isolated group that maintains a strong social and cultural bond separate and apart from everyday American society.

The Roma are originally from northern India and migrated throughout middle and eastern Europe beginning around 1000 AD. They immigrated to the United States mainly in two stages: in the eighteenth century as a result of being deported from various European countries and at the end of the nineteenth century primarily from Eastern Europe.

They speak primarily **Romany**, a language derived from Sanskrit, and English as a second language. Interestingly, until recently Romany was a wholly spoken language.

Most older Roma are not literate, and some younger members have some education. Written forms of the Romany language have been occurring with the education of the younger generations.

ROMA AMERICANS IN THE UNITED STATES

It is difficult to determine the exact number of Roma in the United States, because they do not believe in recording births and deaths, and no census data exists. However, it is estimated that there are between 200,000 and 500,000 members of various Roma groups in the United States (Sutherland, 1992). Roma populations are concentrated in urban areas such as San Francisco, New York, Los Angeles, Chicago, Boston, Atlanta, Seattle, and Houston.

Roma Americans have a very complicated social structure to their culture. In general they have four loyalties to their nation, clan, family, and vista. They are first divided into nations; the most common nations are the Machwaya, Kalderasham, Churara, and Lowara. The nations are further divided into clans. A clan is a group of families united by ancestry, profession, and historic ties. Each clan has a leader, but there is no such thing as "Gypsy kings" as characterized in popular lore. Some clans are further divided into tribes, but most are composed of families. It is the family that is the most important social group for the Roma. A vista is extended family (Ryczak, Zebreski, May, Traver, & Kemp, n.d.).

Roma Americans purposely isolate themselves from the larger community and tend to be ethnocentric. They maintain separation from people and things that are **gadje**, non-Roma, who are considered to be unclean. The strict code that they live by limits acculturation.

BELIEFS ABOUT CAUSES OF HEALTH AND ILLNESS AMONG ROMA AMERICANS

Roma Americans' beliefs regarding health and illness stem from two concepts: impurity and fortune. The first concept is related to the ideas of **wuzho** (pure) and **marime** (impure). Roma Americans have very strict traditions about what is polluted and how things are to be kept clean. Secretions from the upper half of the body are not polluted, but secretions from the lower half of the body are. Therefore, separate soap and towels are used for the upper and lower halves of the body. Failing to keep the two secretions separate can result in serious illness. Also, because gadje (non-Romas) do not practice body separation, they are considered to be impure and diseased.

Fortune also plays a role in health. Good fortune and good health are thought to be related. Illness can be caused by actions that are considered to be contaminating and, therefore, create bad fortune.

Roma Americans distinguish between illnesses that are of a gadje cause and those that are part of their beliefs. Gadje illnesses can be cured by gadje doctors. Hospitals are avoided by Roma Americans because they are unclean and are separate from Roma society. Illness is a problem to be dealt with by the entire clan. Therefore, if a clan member is hospitalized, family and clan members are expected to stay with them and provide curing rituals and protect them. An exception to the aversion to hospitals is childbirth. Women are considered to be unclean during pregnancy and for a number of weeks after delivery. Childbirth should not happen in the family home because it can cause impurity in the home. Therefore, delivery in hospitals is accepted in the culture.

Finally, older members of a family are very important in health care decision making. They are considered to be the authority in the family and carry great weight in all decisions.

HEALING TRADITIONS AMONG ROMA AMERICANS

As previously discussed, illnesses can be characterized as those of the Roma or those that are gadje. Roma health treatment is the prerogative of the older women of the clan who are known as **drabarni**, women who have knowledge of medicines. Roma diseases are not connected to gadje diseases and can only be cured by Roma treatments. Some diseases are caused by spirits or the devil. One spirit, called Mamioro, spreads disease among dirty houses, so keeping a clean home is imperative. The devil has been known to cause nervous diseases. Herbs and rituals are utilized to address these problems.

BEHAVIORAL RISK FACTORS AND COMMON HEALTH PROBLEMS AMONG ROMA AMERICANS

There are reports that the life expectancy of Roma Americans is reduced from the general population. A European study found they have a life expectancy of less than 50 years (Ryczak, et al., n.d.). It has been reported that the life expectancy of a Roma person in the United States is between age 48 and 55 years (Sutherland, 1992). In Romani culture, the larger a person is, the luckier he or she is considered to be. A fat person is considered to be healthy and fortunate, and a thin person is considered to be ill and to have poor luck. This belief and other cultural beliefs are sources of health concerns for this group.

As a group, Roma Americans are resistant to immunization because it does not comport with their beliefs regarding purification. Thus, they are at risk for many communicable diseases.

The Roma American diet is high in fat and salt. A great percentage of Roma Americans smoke and are obese. These practices put them at risk for cardiovascular disease, hypertension, and diabetes. The closeness of living conditions leads to an increased risk of infectious diseases such as hepatitis. Romani children are more likely to be born prematurely or with low birth weight, and the increased incidence of consanguineous marriages has led to an increased risk of birth defects (Ryczak, Zebreski, May, Traver, Kemp, n.d.).

CONSIDERATIONS FOR HEALTH PROMOTION AND PROGRAM PLANNING FOR ROMA AMERICANS

In working with Roma Americans, the following issues should be considered:

- Understand that illness is an issue for the entire society, and the entire clan will be involved in visiting the sick person in the hospital.
- Recognize the primacy of the elders in the family and the clan in making decisions.
- Always remember the importance of what is considered to be clean and unclean and provide separate soap, washcloths, and towels for the upper and lower body parts.
- Understand that this population is mistrustful of non-Roma people and things.
- Understand that Roma Americans are an ethnocentric culture and believe that they must be provided with the best doctors and treatment even if such treatment is not indicated.

HISTORY OF ARAB AND MIDDLE EASTERN AMERICANS IN THE UNITED STATES

Being Arab is not based on race. Arabs are usually associated with the geographic area extending from the Atlantic coast of Northern Africa to the Arabian Gulf. The people who descend from this area are classified as Arabs based largely on a common language (Arabic) and a shared sense of geographic, historic, and cultural identity. Arabs include peoples with widely-varied physical features, countries, or origin and religions.

There are 10 Arab countries in Africa (Algeria, Djibouti, Egypt, Eritrea, Libya, Mauritania, Morocco, Somalia, Sudan, and Tunisia) and 11 countries in Asia (Bahrain, Iraq, Jordan, Kuwait, Lebanon, Oman, Qatar, Saudi Arabia, Syria, United Arab Emirates, and Yemen), including the Palestinian people who live either in Israeli territory or under semiautonomous conditions in the West Bank and Gaza (Ahmad, 2004).

Although it is believed that between 2–3 million Arabs live in the United States, the 2000 U.S. census found that only 850,000 people in the country voluntarily reported Arab ancestry, which is 0.3% of the total population, an increase from 0.2% in 1990 (see Figure   2). More than half of the respondents were American born, and 46% of foreign-born respondents arrived in the United States between 1990 and 2000 (see Figure   3).

Middle Easterners who trace their ancestry to Iran are not considered to be Arab. They are of Persian descent, and their primary language is Farsi. However, Arab and

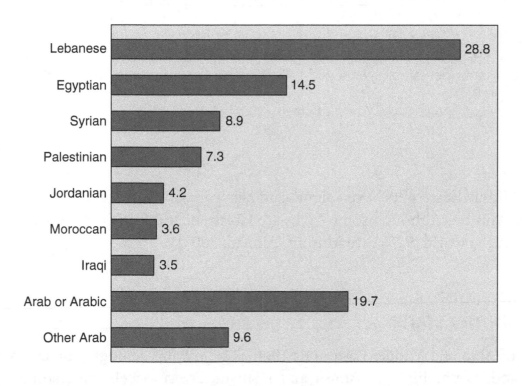

FIGURE   2 Arab population by ancestry: 2000.

Percent distribution. Data based on sample. For information on confidentiality protection, sampling error, nonsampling error, and definitions, see www.census.gov/prod/cen2000/doc/sf4.pdf.

Other Arab (9.6%) includes Yemeni, Kurdish, Algerian, Saudi, Tunisian, Kuwaiti, Libyan, Berber, Emirati (United Arab Emirates), Omani, Qatari, Bahraini, Alhuceman, Bedouin, Rio de Oro, and the general terms Middle Eastern and North African.

Source: Reprinted from U.S. Census Bureau. (2005b).

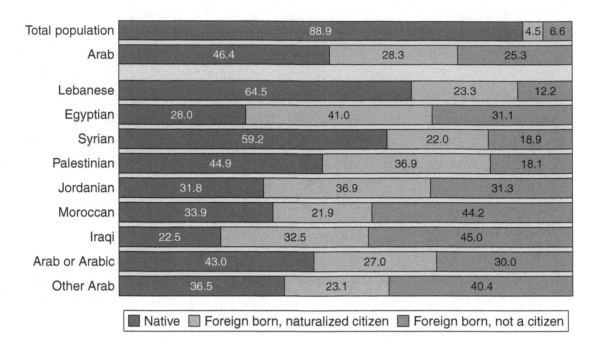

FIGURE 3 Nativity and citizenship status: 2000.

Percent distribution. Data based on sample. For information on confidentiality protection, sampling error, nonsampling error, and definitions, see www.census.gov/prod/cen2000/doc/sf4.pdf.

Source: Reprinted from U.S. Census Bureau. (2005b).

Persian Middle Easterners have a significant factor in common: The great majority of them are Muslim. Although some Arabs are Christian and Jewish, the great majority of Arabs in the world (92%) are Muslim (Ahmad, 2004).

ARAB AND MIDDLE EASTERN AMERICANS IN THE UNITED STATES

Persons of Arab and Middle Eastern descent are a growing demographic in American society and, not unlike the Amish and Romani, are not well understood by the larger society. This cultural group has also experienced increased discrimination and suspicion since 9/11 events.

Arabs immigrated to the United States in three waves. The first occurred between the late 1800s and World War I from the area of Palestine for economic reasons. Many of these immigrants were Christians, and their descendants have become firmly acculturated. The second wave began after 1948 and the establishment of the State of Israel. This group included many professionals and Muslims. This wave tended to settle in the Midwest and accounts for the large concentration of Arab descendants in the Detroit and Chicago areas. The third wave began with the 1967 Arab–Israeli War and continues today. This group fled political instability. Today the area with the largest Arab population is the Dearborn, Michigan area (Ahmad, 2004).

Because the vast majority of Arabs are Muslim, the tenets of the Islamic religion are very influential in Arab Americans' lives. Arab American culture is centered around family relationships. The simplest relationship is the nuclear family, but each Arab American belongs to a large, extended family and often to an even more extended clan that is related by blood kinship (Hammad, Kysia, Rabah, Hassoun, & Connelly, 1999).

The Arab American family is the center of Arab American culture. It is a paternalistic structure, but women are respected, especially mothers. Marriage is highly valued and is considered to be the basic structure of society. Divorce is highly discouraged. Having children is very important in the Arab American culture, and a marriage with many children is considered to be highly blessed. Sickness, birth, and death are events that involve participation by the community.

Cleanliness is a basic tenet of Islam. The Quran, the Islamic holy book, proscribes eating certain foods, including pork or pork products, meat of dead animals, blood, and all intoxicants. Fasting from dawn to dusk every day during the month of Ramadan is required by the religious tenets (Athar, n.d.).

BELIEFS ABOUT CAUSES OF HEALTH AND ILLNESS AMONG ARAB AND MIDDLE EASTERN AMERICANS

Middle Eastern health beliefs arise from the long-standing traditions of the great Islamic healers of the seventh and eighth centuries. Western theories from Hippocrates and Galen came to Arab medicine through trading routes and were incorporated into the Arabs' knowledge base. They advanced human knowledge of anatomy, physiology, and medical treatments. Thus, the tenets of allopathic medicine form the basis of most Arab beliefs about health and illness.

However, traditional religious-based beliefs still exist. There is a tradition that bad thoughts toward someone can cause illness and that the evil eye can cause adverse consequences. Amulets and verses from holy works are utilized to offset the effect. Such beliefs are not uncommon in the Middle East and may be found among those who live in the United States (Hammad, et al., 1999).

Muslims consider an illness to be atonement for their sins, and they receive illness and death with patience and prayers. Death is part of their journey to meet Allah (God) (Athar, n.d.).

HEALING TRADITIONS AMONG ARAB AND MIDDLE EASTERN AMERICANS

The great majority of Arab and Middle Eastern Americans utilize the Western allopathic medical care, much of which derived from the great Arab healers of the past, but there are a few traditional practices still in evidence. Traditional practitioners are in existence in the Arab world, although not frequently within the United States. The most utilized traditional practitioners are bonesetters, who are considered to be superior in skill to Western providers. Midwives are used for childbirth, although birth in hospitals is considered to be more prestigious (Hammad, et al., 1999).

Almost all Middle Eastern people believe in maintaining good health through hygiene and a healthy diet. Women and men are modest and may refuse treatment by practitioners of the opposite gender.

Iraqis have a significant history of traditional healing practices. Some common practices include the following (Iraqi Refugees, 2002):

- Cumin, in conjunction with various other ingredients, is used to treat fever, abdominal pain, and tooth pain.
- Respiratory complaints are treated with honey and lemon.
- Infertility can be treated by a placenta being placed over the doorway of the infertile couple's home.
- Henna is believed to have magic healing properties and will be painted on the body to protect against the evil eye and spirits.

Middle Eastern diets have the following characteristics (Nolan, 1995):

- *Dairy products.* The most common dairy products are yogurt and cheese; feta cheese is preferred. Milk is usually only used in desserts and puddings.
- *Protein.* Pork is eaten only by Christians and is forbidden by religion for Muslims and Jews. Lamb is the most frequently used meat. Many Middle Easterners will not combine dairy products or shellfish with the meal. Legumes, such as black beans, chickpeas (garbanzo beans), lentils, navy beans, and red beans, are commonly used in all dishes.
- *Breads and cereals.* Some form of wheat or rice accompanies each meal.
- *Fruits.* Fruits tend to be eaten as dessert or as snacks. Fresh, raw fruit is preferred. Lemons are used for flavoring. Green and black olives are present in many dishes, and olive oil is most frequently used in food preparation.
- *Vegetables.* Vegetables are preferred raw.

The Mediterranean diet pyramid is shown in Figure 4.

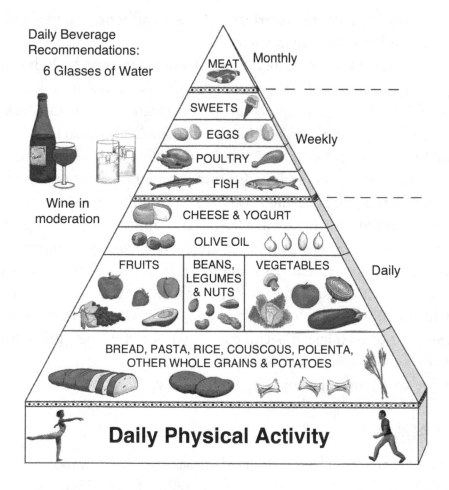

FIGURE 4 Mediterranean diet pyramid.
Source: © 2000 Oldways Preservation & Exchange Trust. www.oldwayspt.org. Reproduced with permission.

BEHAVIORAL RISK FACTORS AND COMMON HEALTH PROBLEMS AMONG ARAB AND MIDDLE EASTERN AMERICANS

As a group, Arab and Middle Eastern Americans face the same health concerns as the majority of Caucasian American citizens. Recent immigrants may be at greater risk for certain inborn genetic disorders as a result of interfamily marriages. Otherwise, their health risks mirror the majority of the population, with heart disease and cancer among the major morbidity factors.

CONSIDERATIONS FOR HEALTH PROMOTION AND PROGRAM PLANNING FOR ARAB AND MIDDLE EASTERN AMERICANS

A number of points that should be considered when dealing with Arab and Middle Eastern Americans in health care include the following:

- Arab and Middle Eastern Americans prefer treatment by a medical provider of the same gender, especially for women.
- Arab and Middle Eastern Americans consider nurses to be helpers, not health care professionals, and their suggestions and advice are not taken seriously.
- Arab and Middle Eastern Americans prefer treatment that involves prescribing pills or giving injections rather than simple medical counseling.
- For orthodox Muslims, follow a halal (Muslim diet), which prohibits some types of meat, like pork, and medications and foods that contain alcohol. Meat needs to be prepared according to Islamic requirements. Also, provide for religious requirements for prayer as often as five times a day, starting before sunrise and ending at night, and provide fasting during the holy month of Ramadan between sunrise and sunset. Although those who are ill are exempted from this practice, devout Muslims may desire to fast anyway.
- Allow for receipt of food into the right hand for Muslim patients. The left hand is considered to be unclean because it is used for cleaning during toileting.
- Respect modesty and privacy.
- Allow for visits and input by the imam, a prayer leader.

CHAPTER SUMMARY

People who are characterized as white or Caucasian are not composed of just those of northern European descent. They contain people of very divergent backgrounds, such as the Amish, Roma, and those of Arab and Middle Eastern descent. It is important to remember that culture and ethnicity have a significant impact on people's health activities and perspectives on health, and merely characterizing a person as white does not describe those beliefs.

REVIEW

1. Describe the health and illness beliefs of the Amish and Roma Americans.
2. Prepare three recommendations to provide culturally competent care for a clinic that deals with Amish or Roma American clients.
3. Describe how Arab American clients might view American health practices differently than other patients.

CASE STUDIES

Case #1. After his wife gave birth, an Arab man would not allow a male lab technician to enter his wife's room to draw blood. The nurses explained to the man the need for the blood test, and the man eventually agreed to allow the technician into the room. He made sure his wife was completely covered in the bed and exposed only her arm for the lab technician to draw the blood. This protected his wife's modesty and the family honor.

Male providers should be aware of these sensitivities when dealing with Arab American families. In this situation the family's concerns were addressed and respected.

Case #2. A nurse found an Iranian patient on the floor when she entered her room. The nurse was concerned that the patient had fallen, and the patient became upset when the nurse tried to help her out. Because the patient did not speak English, she could not explain to the nurse what she was doing. The nurse later learned that the patient was praying.

Muslims pray to Mecca five times per day. The patient was merely practicing her religious tenets. It is important to be aware of such practices when treating ethnic patients.

Source: Fernandez and Fernandez. (2005).

MODEL PROGRAM

Dental Services for Amish Families

In the late 1990s a team from Indiana University organized a program to provide dental services to families of the local Amish communities. They obtained a grant from the Robert Wood Johnson Foundation to undertake dental screening, care, education, and ongoing access. The primary goal of the program was to address serious deficiencies in oral health among the Amish community related to cultural isolation, economics, and transportation problems. The Amish bishop was enlisted to assist in spreading the word about the services and to encourage participation.

The program focused on four areas:

- A series of dental clinics that provided direct dental care
- Testing area water wells for fluoride levels
- Dental education
- Creating a fluoride rinse program in 25 schools

The plan further called for the Amish community to create a plan to provide for their dental needs after the end of the grant. That resulted in the Amish community building and equipping a dental clinic to provide ongoing services to the community.

Source: Robert Wood Johnson Foundation. (2005).

GLOSSARY TERMS

Rumspringa

brauche

Ellis-van Creveld syndrome

Romany

gadje

wuzho

marime

drabarni

REFERENCES

Ahmad, N. (2004). *Arab-American culture and health care*. Retrieved June 16, 2008, from http://www.case.edu/med/epidbio/mphp439/Arab-Americans.htm

Armer, J. M., & Radina, M. E. (2006). Definition of health and health promotion behaviors among Midwestern old order Amish families. *The Journal of Multicultural Nursing & Health, 12*(3), 44–53.

Athar, S. (n.d.). *Information for health care providers when dealing with a Muslim patient*. Retrieved June 12, 2008, from http://www.islam-usa.com

Basset, D., Jr., Schneider, P. L., & Huntington, G. E. (2004, January). Physical activity in an old order Amish community. *Medicine & Science in Sports & Exercise, 36*(1), 79–85.

Basset, D. R., Jr., Tremblay, M. S., Esliger, D. W., Copeland, J. L., Barnes, D., & Huntington, G. E. (2007, March). Physical activity and body mass index of children in an older Amish community. *Medicine & Science in Sports & Exercise, 39*(3), 410–415.

Cantor, S. (Producer), & Walker, L. (Director). (2002). *Devil's playground* [Documentary]. United States: Stick Figure Productions.

ClinicalTrials.gov. (2007, September). *Genetic studies in the Amish and Mennonites*. Retrieved May 23, 2008, from http://clinicaltrials.gov

Donnermeyer, J. F., & Lora, F. (2002). Amish society: An overview reconsidered. *Journal of Multicultural Nursing & Health*. Retrieved May 24, 2008, from http://findarticles.com/p/articles/mi_qa3919/is_200610/ai_n17194972

Ember, C. R., & Ember, M. (2004). *Encyclopedia of medical anthropology: Health and illness in the world's culture* (Vol. 2). New York: Kluwer/Plenum.

Ferketich, A. K., Katz, M. L., Paskett, E. D., Lemeshow, S., Westman, J. A., Clinton, S. K., et al. (2008, Winter). Tobacco use among the Amish in Holmes County, Ohio. *Journal of Rural Health, 24*(1), 84–90.

Fernandez, V. M., & Fernandez, K. M. (2005). *Transcultural nursing: The Middle Eastern community*. Retrieved June 16, 2008, from http://www.culturediversity.org/mide.htm

Hammad, A., Kysia, R., Rabah, R., Hassoun, R., & Connelly, M. (1999). Arab Community Center for Social and Economic Services. *Guide to Arab culture: Health care delivery to the Arab American community*. Retrieved June 16, 2008, from http://www.accesscommunity.org/site/DocServer/health_and_research_cente_21.pdf?docID=381

Iraqi Refugees. (2002). Retrieved June 19, 2008, from http://www3.baylor.edu:80~Charles_Kemp/Iraqi_refugees.htm

Julia, M. C. (1996). *Multicultural awareness in the health care professions*. Needham Heights, MA: Simon and Schuster.

Kraybill, D. B. (2001). *The riddle of Amish culture*. Baltimore: Johns Hopkins University Press.

Kriebel, D. W. (2000). *Belief, power, and identity in Pennsylvania Dutch brauche, or powwowing.* Ann Arbor, MI: UMI

Leach, B. (2007, February 1). Scienceline. *The road to genetic cures.* Retrieved May 23, 2008, from http://www.scienceline.org/2007/02/01/biology-hapmaps-leach/

Lee, D. (2005). *Our Amish neighbors: Providing culturally competent care* (Multicultural Health Series) [Videotape and handout]. UMHS, PMCH, Cultural Competency Division.

Lemon, B. C. (2006, Fall). Amish health and belief systems in obstetrical settings. *The Journal of Multicultural Nursing & Health,* 1–7.

McKusick, V. A. (2000). Ellis-van Creveld syndrome and the Amish. *Nature Genetics.* Retrieved May 24, 2008, from http://www.nature.com/ng/journal/v24/n3/full/ng0300_203.html

Nolan, J. (1995). *Cultural diversity: Eating in America. Middle Eastern.* Retrieved June 12, 2008, from http://ohioline.osu.edu/hyg-Fact/5000/5256.html

Ohio Department of Alcohol and Drug Services. (2005, Spring/Summer). Amish D.A.R.E. program shining example of SDFSC funds, innovation at work. *Perspectives, 3*(1), 5–6.

Oldways Preservation and Exchange Trust. (2000). Retrieved February 4, 2009, from www.oldwayspt.org.

Palmer, C. V. (1992). The health beliefs and practices of an old order Amish family. *Journal of the American Academy of Nurse Practitioners, 4,* 117–122.

Robert Wood Johnson Foundation. (2005). *Providing modern dentistry for folk who cling to old ways.* Retrieved January 23, 2009, from http://www.rwjf.org/reports/grr/035938.htm

Ryczak, K., Zebreski, L., May, M., Traver, S. & Kemp, C. (n.d.). *Gypsy (Roma) culture health refugees immigrants.* Retrieved June 16, 2008, from http://bearspace.baylor.edu/Charles_Kemp/www/gypsy_health.htm

Sutherland, A. (1992). Cross-cultural medicine: A decade later. Gypsies and healthcare. *The Western Journal of Medicine, 157,* 3. Retrieved June 16, 2008, from http://www.pubmedcentral.nih.gov/picrender.fcgi?artid=1011276&blobtype=pdf

US Census Bureau. (2005a). *Race and Hispanic origin in 2005.* Retrieved June 10, 2008, from http://www.census.gov/population/www/pop-profile/files/dynamic/RACEHO.pdf

US Census Bureau. (2005b). *We the people of Arab ancestry in the United States. Census 2000 special reports.* Retrieved June 16, 2008, from http://www.census.gov/prod/2005pubs/censr-21.pdf

Wenger, A. F. Z. (1995). Cultural context, health and health care decision making. *Journal of Transcultural Nursing, 7*(1), 3–14.

PHOTO CREDITS

Chapter Opener ,   © Ralph R. Echtinaw/
ShutterStock, Inc.

Unless otherwise indicated, all photographs and illustrations are under copyright of
Jones and Bartlett Publishers, LLC, or have been provided by the author(s).

Nonethnic Populations: Lesbian, Gay, Bisexual, and Transgender (LGBT) Individuals; Migrant Farmworkers

Gay and lesbian people fall in love. We settle down. We commit our lives to one another. We raise our children. We protect them. We try to be good citizens.

—Senator Sheila Kuehl

If God had wanted me otherwise, He would have created me otherwise.

—Johann Wolfgang von Goethe

We draw our strength from the very despair in which we have been forced to live. We shall endure.

—Cesar Chavez

KEY CONCEPTS

- Sexual identity
- Gender identity
- Homosexual
- Transgender
- Bisexual
- Gay
- Lesbian

CHAPTER OBJECTIVES

1. Describe the differences among lesbian, gay, bisexual, and transgender (LGBT) persons.
2. Discuss the health risks encountered by LGBT persons.
3. Describe the problems often encountered by LGBT persons in accessing health care services.
4. Discuss steps that can be taken to improve cultural competence within the medical community in caring for LGBT patients and their families.
5. Describe the challenges migrant farm workers encounter in obtaining health care.
6. Discuss ways to decrease migrant farm workers' health risks.

Although culture can be easily identified in ethnic and racial groups, it also exists in other human relationships. Culture is not restricted to race, ethnicity, or heritage; it includes customs, beliefs, values, and knowledge that influence our behavior and impact our health. Therefore, understanding the health influences on nonethnic cultural groups is necessary to complete a discussion of cultures and health.

This concept of culture becomes clear when we examine the lesbian, gay, bisexual, and transgender communities, as well as migrant farmworkers, and how these cultural relationships impact health.

INTRODUCTION TO LESBIAN, GAY, BISEXUAL, AND TRANSGENDER (LGBT) INDIVIDUALS

Lesbian, gay, bisexual, and transgender (LGBT) individuals exist in all cultures, communities, and subgroups of American society. Therefore, LGBT persons tend to be as different as the varied cultures from which they arise. LGBT culture has its own values, beliefs, traditions, and behaviors. Unlike other cultures, however, LGBT culture is often concealed within society as a result of homophobia, heterosexism, prejudice, and discrimination.

It is difficult to identify members of this culture without their self-identification or resorting to stereotypical prejudices. LGBT culture, to a great extent, remains hidden from the larger society and is not taught or transmitted through usual cultural vehicles, such as family and society. Historically, the secrecy of the culture has been an effort at self-preservation. Today, the LGBT culture is emerging and demanding a place in society.

Perhaps we should begin our discussion of this unique and varied cultural group by defining some terms. **Sexual identity** is usually defined as a person's physical, romantic, emotional, and/or spiritual attraction to another person. **Gender identity** references a person's internal, personal sense of being male or female, boy or girl, man or woman. Gender identity and sexual identity are not the same thing. **Homosexual** individuals' gender identity is consistent with their physical sexual characteristics, but their sexual identity is to persons of the same sex. For transgender people, their physical, birth-assigned gender does not match their internal sense of their gender. **Transgender** is usually defined as individuals who live full- or part-time in the gender role opposite to the one in which they were physically born. They may be heterosexual or homosexual. **Bisexual** refers to those whose sexual identity is to both men and women. Finally, the term **gay** refers to homosexuals in general, and it is usually used to refer to male homosexuals more specifically. **Lesbian** refers to homosexual women specifically.

HISTORY OF LGBT AMERICANS IN THE UNITED STATES

History has references to homosexuality throughout the ages. It was not until the twentieth century in the United States that homosexuals began to emerge as a culture and demand their rights. For the greatest part of American history, homosexual activity has been outlawed through state sodomy laws. The members of the LGBT community lived underground to avoid legal entanglements.

LGBT AMERICANS IN THE UNITED STATES

In the post–World War II, anticommunist era of the 1950s, small groups of gay men and lesbian women began to form to end discrimination. Most notably were the Daughters of Bilitis, which is credited as the first lesbian rights group, and the Mattachine Society, the first group to advocate on behalf of gay men.

Societal changes in the 1960s heralded a new wave of gay activism. As civil rights were being obtained by black Americans, gay Americans were beginning to object to the restraints placed by the law on their lives. Years of resentment came to a head in the Stonewall riots in 1969. Prior to this event, it was common for police to raid gay and lesbian bars and arrest the patrons. In a New York bar named the Stonewall Inn, the patrons protested and a riot broke out. Over the next few days, gays and lesbians continued to riot, demanding their right to assembly. This event sparked gay and lesbian activism across the country, resulting in the birth of the gay rights movement, which overturned many laws and other restrictions on personal activity.

LGBT persons have made significant strides in obtaining equal status in the United States; however, discriminatory practices still exist. In 1973 the American Psychiatric Association declassified homosexuality as a mental disorder. The diagnosis of "ego-dystonic homosexuality" was removed from the *Diagnostic and Statistical Manual of Mental Disorders (DSM)*, and for the first time homosexual Americans were no longer considered to be mentally ill. Legal advances, though slow, have been made as well. Many states have overturned their sodomy laws and now offer domestic partner benefits to same-sex couples. As this book is being written, the California Supreme court has followed the lead of the Massachusetts Supreme Court in ruling that depriving same-sex couples the right to marry is a denial of equal protection under the state constitution. In response, a proposition was placed on the California ballot for the November 2008 election to limit marriage to a man and a woman. That initiative passed and its constitutionality is being reviewed by the California Supreme Court as this book is being printed. Despite these legislative changes, homosexuality is still criminalized by sodomy laws in 16 states. Thus, the struggle for equality within the LGBT community continues, and discrimination based on homophobia and heterosexism continues in basic civil rights, employment, and housing.

HEALING TRADITIONS AMONG LGBT AMERICANS

A major hurdle to understanding the interaction of the LGBT community and health care is that little research is available to guide the discussion. In fact, there is not even good data on the number of LGBT persons in the United States. The classic assumption about the size of the LGBT population comes from the 1949 Kinsey Report. There it was postulated that 10% of the male population and 5% to 6% of the female population of the United States was homosexual. The 1990 U.S. census allowed respondents to classify themselves as unmarried partners. Of those over the age of 15 years, 1.63% reported themselves as the unmarried partner of the householder (Gay & Lesbian Medical Association, 2001). There is no data on the number of transgender individuals in the United States, but 25,000 have undergone sexual reassignment surgery, and another 60,000 consider themselves to be candidates for the surgery (Gay & Lesbian Medical Association, 2001).

Due to their minority status and history of discrimination, clinical and public health studies regarding the needs of LGBT persons are infrequent. Therefore, researchers have to depend on small studies that are often uninformative in describing the needs of this community.

It is widely reported that LGBT persons experience discrimination in health care. It has been reported that they encounter substandard care and often do not report important health issues because of fear of stigmatization. One study reported that 40% of responding physicians were uncomfortable providing care to LGBT patients. In a survey of LGBT physicians, 67% of the respondents reported their belief that they had seen gay and/or lesbian patients receive substandard care or be mishandled as a result of their sexual orientation (Dean, et al., 2000).

Access to care is often a major problem for this group. Although as a group LGBT persons have higher education levels than average, they experience a lower socioeconomic status than heterosexuals. Those in committed relationships experience difficulty with insurance companies recognizing them, and they are often denied the privileges that are extended to married partners (O'Hanlan, Cabaj, Schatz, Lock, & Nemrow, 1997). Discrimination in insurance and public entitlement programs creates roadblocks to public programs, and they often do not cover needed services. Even if an LGBT couple can obtain insurance coverage through employment, they are often reluctant to utilize it for fear that it would expose their sexual orientation and submit them to job discrimination.

		Disclosure of Sexual Orientation	Prejudice/ Discrimination	Concealed Sexual Identity
Sexuality	**Cultural**			
HIV–AIDS	Socialization Parenting	Family conflicts	Health care provider bias	Reluctance to seek care
Hepatitis	Nulliparity in women	Psychological problems	Harassment	Delayed treatment
Human papillomavirus		Depression Anxiety Suicide	Limited access	Suppression of medical information
Sexually transmitted disease			Violence Pathologizing of behavior	
Anal cancer				

Source: Dean, et al. (2000).

Stigmatization, lack of sensitivity, and reluctance to address sexual issues has been reported as interfering with mental health care. LGBT persons report discriminatory care in nursing homes and senior centers (Dean, et al., 2000). Table 1 describes many social and behavioral factors that are of significant concern to this community.

LGBT couples encounter difficulty obtaining the rights granted to married couples in health care settings, such as hospitals. Unless they have a signed durable power of attorney for health care or an advance directive, authorization for medical treatment will be made by the closest relative, not the homosexual partner. Further, those same family members could override the decision of the partner, even in circumstances where the partner is in a much better position to know what the sick individual would want.

LGBT persons report difficulty in communication with health care providers. LGBT persons find it difficult to discuss their sexual history and related health needs with their health care providers. A 1990 survey of Michigan lesbians found that 61% of the respondents felt they could not disclose their sexual identity to their provider (Dean, et al., 2000). Medical education has not informed providers about the health needs of this population. Removing the barriers to communication and educating practitioners about the unique health needs of the LGBT community is imperative.

More specifically, misconceptions and assumptions about lesbians' health and their health care needs have been identified. Lesbians' care can be compromised as a result of their sexual orientation. Lesbians are less likely to receive Pap smears for cervical cancer due to a false assumption that because they are not currently sexually active with men, they are not at risk for developing the disease. They remain at risk for sexually transmitted diseases, specifically human papillomavirus, which has been associated with cervical cancer. Therefore, they should be treated for all risks (U.S. Department of Health and Human Services, Office on Women's Health [HHS OWH], 2000).

The Office on Women's Health of the U.S. Department of Health and Human Services has identified the need for research to improve the health care of lesbians and to identify health conditions for which they are at risk. It was noted that improved cultural competency, with physicians being better informed about lesbian health issues and more understanding of lesbians' reluctance to seek care due to homophobia, was needed (HHS OWH, 2000).

To investigate U.S. hospitals' policies and procedures related to LGBT concerns, the Human Rights Campaign Foundation and the Gay and Lesbian Medical Association devised the Healthcare Equality Index to evaluate how the health care community responds to the needs of the LGBT community. The focus of the inquiry was on five criteria: patient nondiscrimination, hospital visitation, decision making, cultural competency training, and employment policies.

The project began in 2007, and all participants were given anonymity for their responses. Requests for participation were sent to 1,000 hospitals. Responses from 78 hospitals in 20 states were obtained. The results showed that 50 hospitals had policies providing the same access to same-sex partners as is provided to married spouses, 56 allowed the designation of a domestic partner or someone else as medical surrogate, only 45 had a policy allowing same-sex parents the same access to medical decision making for their minor children as married spouses, and 57 provided staff training on specific issues impacting the LGBT patients and their families (HRC, GLMA, 2007).

The 2008 results were provided by 88 hospitals in 21 states. Forty-five of the responding hospitals responded affirmatively to the 10 survey questions. The question with the most positive results involved having a patient bill of rights with a nondiscrimination policy, including sexual orientation. The question with the least affirmative responses involved having equal employment opportunity policies that include gender identity and/or expression (HRC, GLMA, 2007).

BEHAVIORAL RISK FACTORS AND COMMON HEALTH PROBLEMS AMONG LGBT AMERICANS

The LGBT community is at risk for unique health problems. These risks can be exacerbated by misunderstanding and stigmatization.

HIV–AIDS

The onset of acquired immunodeficiency syndrome (AIDS) in the 1980s brought devastation to the lives of gay men. Since the early 1980s, it is estimated that 702,000 Americans have been diagnosed with the disease, and 54% of that number are men who have had sexual interactions with other men. African and Latino men have constituted the majority of cases reported since 1998 (Dean, et al., 2000). Although discrimination and a belief that these men deserved their fate was the initial response to the epidemic, with time, a better understanding of the disease and its risk factors have enlightened the discussion. The importance of distinguishing between sexual identity and sexual behavior has been emphasized in dealing with this disease.

Recent research has found that men who have sex with men are most at risk. Those men characterize themselves as gay, bisexual, and heterosexual. Therefore, focus must be placed on behaviors and not labels. Studies have shown that bisexual behavior in men was associated with a reduced use of condoms and a weaker perception of safe sexual practices. Also, bisexual men were often unlikely to disclose their bisexuality to their female partners (Dean, et al., 2000).

Impacting behavior remains the primary way of reducing the spread of this disease. Education about safe sex practices has been strongly supported within the gay community, and research has shown that most gay men report having protected sex most of the time.

There is little research on AIDS in the lesbian community. The few studies that have occurred indicate a small incidence and no evidence for female-to-female transmission. It is presumed that lesbians who contract the disease have either used intravenous drugs or had intercourse with a man. However, research to determine the true risk factors within this population is needed.

Like the lesbian population, little information is available regarding the incidence of AIDS within the transgender community. It is suspected that the rate of AIDS within the population is high based on the few studies available. In a self-reporting study, 25% of respondents indicated they were HIV positive, and a study of those seeking hormone therapy reported that 15% of respondents were HIV positive (Dean, et al., 2000).

Cancer

Although definitive studies are lacking, the information to date indicates that gay men and lesbians are at higher risk for certain cancers. Gay men are at higher risk for Kaposi sarcoma, which is associated with HIV infection, and AIDS-related non-Hodgkin lymphoma. Bisexual and gay men are at increased risk for anal cancer and Hodgkin disease, according to recent research. It has also been noted that survival time for gay men with cancer is less than the population at large. It is speculated that this is due to HIV–AIDS comorbidity and delay in detection and treatment (Dean, et al., 2000).

Lesbians have been found to be at higher risk for breast cancer than heterosexual women due to increased risk factors, including alcohol consumption, obesity, and nulliparity. Lesbians have been found to receive less frequent gynecologic care and breast cancer screening.

Substance Use

Studies of substance use in the LGBT population are varied at best. Some have shown no greater use of alcohol in this population than in the general population. Others have found higher rates of both heavy drinking and abstention in both gay men and lesbians.

Limited data also indicates that lesbians report greater use of cocaine, inhalants, and marijuana than women in the general population. The data for gay men is similar. However, no good study has been undertaken for this population.

Mental Health

As previously noted, declassification of homosexuality as a mental illness occurred in 1973. However, the LGBT population is at increased risk for certain mental health issues as a result of stressors related to antigay societal attitudes and internalization of negative social attitudes. Significant among the problems encountered by this group are mental disorders and distress, substance use, and suicide.

As with other health issues faced by this population, few scientifically significant studies are available in this area. Studies have found higher rates of depression, generalized anxiety disorder, and conduct disorders in the LGBT population. Various studies have identified increased rates of bipolar disorder and affective disorders in the gay male population.

The studies that address suicide in this population are controversial. Studies have indicated an increased rate of suicidal ideation and attempts in gay and bisexual men and lesbians. However, others have found no increased rates of completed suicides in that population.

The American Psychiatric Association's *Diagnostic and Statistical Manual of Mental Disorders (DSM)* contains four diagnoses that may be applicable to transgender individuals. The most common is gender identity disorder. According to the *DSM*, for the diagnosis to apply, other symptoms evidencing distress and functional impairment are necessary. Therefore, being transgender does not itself mean the person has a mental disorder (Dean, et al., 2000).

However, the transgender population is at risk for mental health problems comparable to others who undergo major life changes, minority status, discrimination, and chronic medical conditions. Studies indicate increased rates of depression, substance use, and anxiety disorders. Unfortunately, suicide attempts and completed suicides are more common in the transgender population, and genital mutilation is also reported at significant rates (Dean, et al., 2000).

Aging

Not surprisingly, there is little information about the needs of LGBT elders. Although they are at risk for the health problems that are common to all, it is believed that they encounter specific problems not usually faced by the general population.

Recent surveys have shown that LGBT elders are more likely to live alone than elders in the population at large (Gay & Lesbian Medical Association, 2001). Furthermore, few agencies exist to meet the social service needs of this group, and the availability of long-term care facilities to meet the needs of this group is virtually nonexistent. Finally, due to their age, LGBT elders are less able to deal with the discrimination in the health care system than younger members of the LGBT community.

CONSIDERATIONS FOR HEALTH PROMOTION AND PROGRAM PLANNING FOR LGBT AMERICANS

To provide appropriate care to any patient population necessitates reliable information on which the practitioner can base care decisions. The lack of reliable information regarding the health needs of the LGBT community is a significant hindrance to providing proper care to this group. Improved research is necessary to provide dependable data to guide care.

Like all cultural minorities, the LGBT community experiences barriers to accessing care. The lack of health insurance for themselves and their partners, discrimination in health care services, cultural barriers, and a poor understanding of their health care needs all impact the health of this group. For health promotion to occur, efforts need to be made to address these problems. Cultural competency must be addressed within the provider community as well. Table   2 and Table   3 provide objectives for creating LGBT cultural competence.

TABLE	2	LGBT Cultural Competence Strategies

Use gender-neutral language in forms and practice.

Do not make assumptions about sexuality.

Utilize nonbiased behavior and communication.

Do not use labels; focus on behavior.

Conduct a thorough sexual-risk evaluation.

Be aware of LGBT health risks.

Be knowledgeable about the health needs of the LGBT community.

Source: Gay & Lesbian Medical Association. (2001).

TABLE	3	Recommended Community Standards for Gay, Lesbian, and Transgender Persons

1. Create and promote open communication and a safe and nondiscriminatory workplace.

2. Create comprehensive policies to ensure that services are provided to LGBT clients and their families in a nondiscriminatory manner.

3. Have procedures available for clients to resolve complaints concerning violation of policies.

4. Prepare and implement assessment tools to meet the needs of LGBT clients and their families.

5. Maintain a basic understanding of LGBT issues within the organization.

6. All personnel who provide direct care to LGBT clients shall be competent to identify and address the health issues encountered by LGBT clients and their families and be able to provide appropriate treatment or referrals.

7. The organization shall ensure the confidentiality of client information.

8. Community outreach shall include the LGBT community.

9. The board of directors of the organization should have an LGBT representative.

10. The organization shall provide appropriate and safe care and treatment to all LGBT clients and their families.

Source: Gay & Lesbian Medical Association. (2001).

TABLE	4	Four Steps for Culturally Competent Care

1. Maintain a nonhomophobic attitude.

2. Distinguish sexual behavior from sexual identity.

3. Communicate clearly and sensitively using gender-neutral terms.

4. Be aware of how your attitudes affect your clinical judgment.

Source: Gay & Lesbian Medical Association. (2001).

Health care providers should provide a nonjudgmental environment for LGBT patients and their families so that avoidance of care can be overcome. Harrison and Silenzio suggested four steps for improving cultural sensitivity and increasing equality of treatment and access (Gay & Lesbian Medical Association, 2001) (see Table 4).

INTRODUCTION TO MIGRANT FARMWORKERS

Migrant farmworkers in the United States are the backbone of the farming community. It has been postulated that their work constitutes a new form of slavery to support the United States (Moore, 2004).

HISTORY OF MIGRANT FARMWORKERS IN THE UNITED STATES

Migrant farmworkers are referred to as the "invisible population" (Gonzalez, 2008). Statistics regarding the actual size of this population vary from 3 to 5 million individuals (National Center for Farmworker Health Inc. [NCFH], 2002; Fisher, Marcoux, Miller, Sanchez, & Ramirez Cunningham, 2004; U.S. Department of Homeland Security, 2002). A National Agricultural Workers Survey (NAWS) is conducted every year by the U.S. Department of Labor, and the Current Population Survey (CPS) is updated by the U.S. Bureau of Labor Statistics monthly, yet it is difficult to track trends in this population. Even with these surveys it is difficult to find accurate statistics due to the fact that "52 out of every 100 of all farm workers do not have authorization or any legal status in the U.S." (Gonzalez, 2008). Because many workers and their families are unauthorized, they are reluctant to provide any demographic information about themselves or their community because of the risk of deportation.

MIGRANT FARMWORKERS IN THE UNITED STATES _____

Today, Mexican workers are the largest population of migrant farmworkers in American agriculture. Migrant farmworkers are also from other countries, including Guatemala, Honduras, Puerto Rico, Dominican Republic, Southeast Asia, Philippines, Jamaica, Haiti, and other Caribbean islands. Farmworkers are predominantly Hispanic, and 7 out of 10 farmworkers are foreign born. Of the foreign-born workers, 94% are from Mexico (U.S. Department of Labor, Employment and Training Administration, 2009). Prior to the Mexican workers' emergence, Chinese workers filled the labor pool. Nearly 200,000 Chinese were legally contracted to cultivate California fields until the Chinese Exclusion Act. Thereafter, Japanese workers replaced the Chinese field hands (PBS, 1999).

Mexican immigration began during the 1850s to geographic land regions that were still considered to be part of Mexico (i.e., California). In the 1920s, the Mexican government addressed complaints of abuse with the United States by securing contracts with the United States to try to trace immigration and provide some type of labor protection to their citizens who traveled to the United States for work. The first was the de facto Bracero Program, which allowed workers to bring their families. During World War II, the United States signed another Bracero treaty to legalize immigration for Mexican workers to fill the labor gaps left by soldiers who were participating in the war. Under this program, approximately 4 million Mexican farmworkers came to support the agriculture industry between 1942 and 1964 (PBS, 1999).

Besides the Bracero Program, the United States has entered into more recent trade agreements that directly affect migrant laborers, like the General Agreement on Tariffs and Trade (GATT) and North American Free Trade Agreement (NAFTA). More recently, the Immigration Reform and Control Act has played a role in the legalization and fluctuation of migrant workers and their services.

According to the National Center for Farmworker Health Inc. and the Atlas of Migrant and Seasonal Farmworkers, migrant workers can be found in almost every state. The states with the most concentrated populations heavily rely on agriculture as a part of their state's economy. California leads with the highest population (approximately 1.3 million), with Texas, Florida, Washington, and North Carolina rounding out the top five (NCFH, 2002).

Recent data indicates that almost 75% of farmworkers earned less than $10,000 per year, and three out of five farmworker families lived in poverty. Few farmworkers had assets of any import, and about one-third owned, or were buying, a house or trailer in the United States (U.S. Department of Labor, Employment and Training Administration, 2009).

Given their meager incomes, many households qualify for social services and housing assistance. However, many migrant workers do not apply for those services for fear of deportation.

According to the National Agricultural Workers Survey (NAWS), migrant farmworkers are poorly educated. More than one-third are school dropouts, and of those who attend school, 17% are at a grade level lower than their same-age peers (U.S. Department of Labor, Employment and Training Administration, 2009). The most recent data shows that the approximate median level of education for the population is at the sixth-grade level, and there is only a 50.7% high school graduation rate among migrant teenagers (U.S. Department of Labor, Employment and Training Administration, 2009). High illiteracy rates are a contributing factor to poor education: 20% of the population are completely illiterate; 38% are functionally illiterate; and 27% are marginally illiterate. Poor English proficiency also contributes to poor education levels.

BELIEFS ABOUT CAUSES OF HEALTH AND ILLNESS AMONG MIGRANT FARMWORKERS

Migrant farmworkers, mostly Hispanic, believe that an imbalance between a person and the environment causes physical and mental illness. Emotional, spiritual, social, and physical ailments are often expressed as having too much "hot" or "cold." In general, cold diseases and conditions are characterized by vasoconstriction and low metabolic rate (such as menstrual cramps, pneumonia, and colic). Hot diseases and conditions are characterized by vasodilatation and high metabolic rate (such as pregnancy, hypertension, diabetes, and acid indigestion).

Mal de ojo is known as the "evil eye." It is also thought to cause illness more in women and infants than in men. Evil eye is caused by a person with a "strong eye" (especially green or blue) who looks with admiration or jealousy at another person. Susto is "soul loss" caused by fright. Susto may be acute or chronic and includes a variety of vague complaints. Folk or ethnomedical illnesses are health problems associated with members of a particular group for which the culture provides etiology, diagnosis, prevention, and a regimen of healing. These illnesses also have psychological and/or religious overtones (Leybas-Amedia, Nuno, & Garcia, 2005).

Fatalism or inevitable predetermination is an attitude possessed by many migrant farmworkers. It is a broad concept that encompasses a religious commitment to acceptance of the conditions in one's life. Hispanic migrant farmworkers reject the concept of germ theory. They believe that the cause of disease or illness is spirit and not germs, making them less likely to seek preventive care and treatment (Kelz, 1999).

HEALING TRADITIONS AMONG MIGRANT FARMWORKERS _____

Migrant farmworkers are prone to skin diseases, and they usually treat the diseases themselves. "Latino migrant and seasonal farm workers experience high rates of skin disease that result from their working and living conditions" (Arcury, Vallejos, Feldman, & Quandt, 2006). Working conditions expose them to many toxins that cause various types of skin diseases and irritations. Causes of occupational skin disease among agricultural workers are diverse and include exposure to wind and sun, pesticides, fertilizer, petroleum products, plants, and infectious agents (Arcury, et al., 2006). Ultraviolet rays, allergic reactions, and the use of untested healing methods may contribute to damaged and sensitive skin.

Farmworkers tend to use home remedies, such as household products and herbs, to cure skin symptoms (Arcury, et al., 2006). Plant products are used as remedies to heal certain types of wounds and sores.

BEHAVIORAL RISK FACTORS AND COMMON HEALTH PROBLEMS AMONG MIGRANT FARMWORKERS _____

Many factors impact migrant farmworkers' health. They tend to be geographically isolated and constantly move from place to place, which makes access to care difficult. In addition, a lack of health education contributes to poor knowledge of good health practices.

Health standards for migrant farmworkers are similar to that of third-world countries, even though they work in the United States. Unsanitary working and housing conditions place farmworkers at risk for many health problems. Most farmworkers cannot afford to take time off from work and also risk losing their jobs to attend doctor appointments (NCFH, 2002).

Farmworkers are exposed to many different types of diseases and injuries, many of which are related to the chemicals and machinery they use, including musculoskeletal injuries, respiratory illness, tuberculosis, HIV, and others.

Musculoskeletal injuries are very common in farmworkers. The labor done by farmworkers consists of heavy lifting and constant, quick movements of certain body parts, such as the wrists. Workers are also encouraged to work at a quicker pace to finish early (NCFH, 2002).

Respiratory illnesses, including asthma, occur due to exposure to pesticides, dust, pollen, and molds. Exposure to these pollutants for long periods of time can have long-term effects on the workers (NCFH, 2002).

Tuberculosis is common among migrant farmworkers due to the prevalence of tuberculosis in their home countries. The disease is transmitted to workers in the United States and spreads amongst the population (NCFH, 2002).

AIDS is prevalent in migrant populations and is associated with increased rates of sexually-transmitted diseases and prostitution in labor camps. Wives of the men who travel to the United States for work are at risk for infection transmitted by their husbands (NCFH, 2002).

CONSIDERATIONS FOR HEALTH PROMOTION AND PROGRAM PLANNING FOR MIGRANT FARMWORKERS

Guidelines for dealing with migrant farmworkers include the following:

- Recognize the concern migrant farmworkers have regarding immigration issues and the possibility of deportation.
- Ensure that appropriate translations services are available.
- Remember to include family members in decision making.
- Determine a person's living situation before planning.
- Understand that fear and mistrust exist.

CHAPTER SUMMARY

Lesbians, gay men, bisexuals, and transgender people have faced significant discrimination as a result of their sexual orientation, and discrimination continues today. The LGBT culture tends to hide from society at large as a survival technique.

In this chapter we have discussed the barriers to care and challenges encountered by these people in their interactions with health care services. We found that they are less likely to seek care because of fear of discrimination, and they tend to have higher incidences of certain diseases as a result. Unfortunately, there are few studies to guide our understanding of the health problems this group encounters outside of HIV–AIDS, which has been closely studied. Therefore, for many health issues there is little reliable information to guide practitioners. Finally, we learned that steps need to be taken to improve the cultural competence of health care providers and facilities to ensure equal care for the LGBT community.

Migrant farmworkers account for approximately 3 to 5 million people in the United States. They are mostly Hispanic people who work in almost every state. Poverty, unsettlement, legal issues, low education level, and harsh working conditions are their main challenges. They are at major risk to skin diseases and exposure to the sun and pesticides. AIDS is common among migrant farmworkers due to lack of education, an increase in sexually-transmitted diseases, and prostitution.

REVIEW

1. Describe three roadblocks to accessing health care that are encountered by the LGBT community and migrant farmworkers.
2. Prepare three cultural competence recommendations for a clinic that provides services to migrant farmworkers.
3. Outline what areas should be covered in a staff training session to address the needs of LGBT clients.
4. Describe how discrimination toward migrant farmworkers and LGBT people impacts their health and health care.

CASE STUDY

In 2008, the Human Rights Campaign Foundation Family Project, in conjunction with the Gay and Lesbian Medical Association, conducted a survey of hospitals to determine the health care industry's practices related to LGBT issues. The 23 questions focused on baseline institutional information and LGBT-specific policies.

Some of the findings were as follows (HRC, GLMA, 2007):

- 98% of the respondents reported including sexual orientation in their patient's bill of rights or nondiscrimination policies. Only 66% included gender identity or gender expression in those policies.
- 69% had a written visitation policy to provide LGBT partners the same access as spouses or next of kin.
- 68% had a visitation policy that allowed same-sex parents the same access to their minor children as opposite-sex parents.
- 88% of the respondents had policies that provided for the LGBT partner to be named as the decision maker in a patient's advance directive.
- 64% provided same-sex parents the same decision-making authority for their minor children as that afforded opposite-sex parents.
- 69% had cultural competency training that addressed LGBT patients and their families.
- 84% had policies barring employment discrimination based on sexual orientation, but only 58% included gender identity or expression.

There are several issues to consider about this case:

- Why do you think only 88 out of 1,000 hospitals responded to the survey?
- What does the survey tell us about the health care provided to LGBT patients and their families?
- What is the relationship between the findings regarding employment and the findings about health care?

MODEL PROGRAM

The Mpowerment Project

The Mpowerment Project is a program in San Francisco conducted by the University of California, San Francisco in conjunction with the Diffusion of Effective Behavioral Interventions (DEBI) project. The program was designed to reduce the rate of AIDS transmission among young gay and bisexual men. It is a community-based prevention program that has the goal of reducing risky behavior in men aged 18–29 years.

The guiding principles of the program are as follows:

- Personal and community empowerment
- Diffusion of new behavior through social networks
- Peer influence
- Placing HIV prevention in context with other issues in young men's lives
- Building community
- Utilizing gay-positive approaches to prevention

The program utilizes a group of young men along with a group of volunteers for outreach to the community. They attend popular events and embark on publicity campaigns to promote safe sex practices. A hallmark of the program is meetings where discussions related to safe sex practices are conducted. The goal of the program is to improve health and prevent disease through a peer group within the community.

Source: Mpowerment Project. (2009).

GLOSSARY TERMS

sexual identity   bisexual
gender identity   gay
homosexual   lesbian
transgender

REFERENCES

Arcury, T. A., Vallejos, Q. M., Feldman, S. R., & Quandt, S. A. (2006). Treating skin disease: Self-management behaviors of Latino farmworkers. *Journal of Agromedicine, 11*(2). Retrieved May 17, 2008, from http://cha.wa.gov/english/documents/TreatmentofSkinDiseaseamongLatino-Farmworkers.pdf

Cason, K. L., & Snyder, A. (2004, November). *The health and nutrition of Hispanic migrant and seasonal farm workers.* Retrieved May 18, 2008, from http://www.ruralpa.org/migrant_farm_workers.pdf

Centers for Disease Control and Prevention. (2004). Health disparities experienced by Hispanics—United States. *Morbidity and Mortality Weekly Report, 53*(40), 935–937.

Dean, L., Meyer, I. H., Robinson, K., Sell, R. L., Sember, R., Silenzio, V. M. B., et al. (2000). Lesbian, gay, bisexual and transgender health: Findings and concerns. *Journal of the Gay and Lesbian Medical Association, 4*(3). Retrieved May 28, 2008, from http://glma.org/document/docWindow.cfm?fuseaction=document.viewDocument&documentid=17&documentFormatID=26

Fisher, K. E., Marcoux, E., Miller, L. S., Sanchez, A., & Ramirez Cunningham, E. (2004). Information behaviour of migrant Hispanic farm workers and their families in the Pacific Northwest. *Information Research, 10*(1) paper 199. Retrieved May 20, 2008, from http://informationr.net/ir/10-1/paper199.html

Franzini, L., Ribble, J. C., & Keddie, A. M. (2001, Autumn). Understanding the Hispanic paradox. *Ethnicity and Disease, 11*(3), 496–518.

Gay & Lesbian Medical Association. (2001). *Healthy People 2010 companion document for lesbian, gay, bisexual and transgender (LGBT) health.* Retrieved May 28, 2008, from http://www.glma.org/_data/n.0001/resourceslive/HealthyCompanionDoc3

Gonzalez, E., Jr. (2008, May 27). *Migrant farm workers: Our nation's invisible population.* Retrieved May 23, 2008, from http://www.extension.org/pages/Migrant_Farm_Workers:_Our_Nation's_Invisible_Population

HRC, GLMA release inaugural healthcare equality index. (2007, October 7). *The Advocate.* Retrieved May 20, 2008 from http://www.advocate.com/news_detail_ektid49485.asp

Huang, G. G. (n.d.). *What federal statistics reveal about migrant farm workers: A summary for education. ERIC Digest.* Retrieved May 23, 2008, from www.ericdigests.org/2003-4/migrant-farmworkers.html

Hunt, L. M., Arar, N. H., & Akana, L. L. (2000). Herbs, prayer, and insulin: Use of medical and alternative treatments by a group of Mexican-American diabetes patients. *Journal of Family Practice, 49*(3), 216–223.

Kelz, R. K. (1999). *Conversational Spanish for health professionals: Essential expressions, questions, and directions for medical personnel to facilitate conversation with Spanish-speaking patients and coworkers.* Albany, NY: Delmar.

Kemp, C. (2005, March). *Mexican & Mexican-Americans: Health beliefs & practices.* Retrieved May 20, 2008, from http://bearspace.baylor.edu/Charles_Kemp/www/hispanic_health.htm

Leybas-Amedia, V., Nuno, T., & Garcia, F. (2005). Effect of acculturation and income on Hispanic women's health. *Journal of Health Care for the Poor and Underserved, 16*(4)(Suppl. A). Retrieved May 23, 2008, from http://muse.jhu.edu/journals/journal_of_health_care_for_the_poor_and_underserved/v016/16.4Aleybas-amedia.html

Moore, M. (2004, March 31). *Migrant farmworkers: America's new plantation workers.* Retrieved May 25, 2008, from http://www.foodfirst.org/node/45

Mpowerment Project. (2009). Retrieved January 23, 2009, from http://www.mpowerment.org/

National Center for Farmworker Health Inc. (2002). *Factsheets About Farmworkers*. Retrieved May 23, 2008, from http://www.ncfh.org/?pid=5

O'Hanlan, K., Cabaj, R. B., Schatz, B., Lock, J., & Nemrow, P. (1997). A review of the medical consequences of homophobia with suggestions for resolution. *Journal of the Gay and Lesbian Medical Association, 1*(1), 25–40.

Palerm, J. V. (2006). *Immigrant and migrant farm workers in the Santa Maria Valley, California.* Retrieved May 23, 2008, from http://repositories.cdlib.org/cgi/viewcontent.cgi?article=1005& context=ccs_ucsb

PBS. (1999). *Mexican immigrant labor history*. Retrieved May 24, 2008, from http://www.pbs.org/ kpbs/theborder/history/timeline/17.html

Rangel, I. (2002). *Overview of America's farm workers*. Retrieved May 19, 2008, from http:// www.ncfh.org/?pid=4

US Department of Health and Human Services, Office on Women's Health. (2000). *Lesbian health fact sheet*. Retrieved June 9, 2008, from http://www.womenshealth.gov/pub/faq.cfm

US Department of Homeland Security. (2002). *Fiscal year 2002 yearbook of immigration statistics* (formerly, *Statistical yearbook of the Immigration and Naturalization Service*). Retrieved May 23, 2008, from http://www.dhs.gov/ximgtn/statistics/publications/YrBk02En.shtm

US Department of Labor, Employment and Training Administration. (2009). *The national agricultural workers survey*. Retrieved May 24, 2008, from www.doleta.gov/agworker/report/ch1.cfm

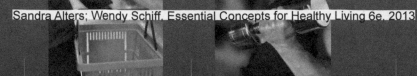

Diversity in Health
Hunting for Supercentenarians

Consumer Health
Choosing a Long-Term Care Facility

Managing Your Health
After the Death of a Loved One

Across the Life Span
Dying and Death

Content removed due to

copyright restrictions

Chapter Overview

The status of aging Americans

Why we age

The effects of aging on health and well-being

The spiritual and emotional aspects of dying

The options for terminal care

The definition of death

How to prepare for death

Student Workbook

Self-Assessment: Preparing for Aging and Death

Changing Health Habits: Can Changing a Health Habit Extend Your Life?

Do You Know?

Who was the oldest person to ever live?

What happens to your body as you age?

How to increase your chances of living a long and healthy life?

Aging, Dying, and Death

On April 15, 2011, Walter Breuning died in Montana. You might be thinking, "So what?" When Walter died of natural causes, he was *114* years of age—the oldest man in the world. Walter's recipe for living more than 100 years included the following recommendations:

- Accept change. "Every change is good."
- Take care of your mind and body.
- Eat two meals a day.
- Work as long as possible.
- Help others.
- Accept death. "You're born to die."[1,2]

Centenarians are people who are older than 100 years of age; people who are at least 110 are *super*centenarians. Why are centenarians able to live such long lives? Lifestyle, environmental, and social factors are known to influence *longevity*, but genetic differences play a major role in determining whether a person lives to be at least 100 years of age.[3]

> "Take care of your mind and body."

Figure   1

Jeanne Calment.

Content removed due to

copyright restrictions

In December 2010, nearly 72,000 Americans were 100 or more years of age.[4] Today in the United States, more people are living to be 100 years old than in past decades. According to the U.S. Census Bureau, more than 600,000 Americans will be centenarians by 2050.[5]

Gerontologists, scientists who study aging, note that individuals who have the genetic potential to live longer than average often eliminate this advantage by adopting unhealthy lifestyles, such as using tobacco and being physically inactive.[6] Therefore, an important key to enjoying a long and healthy life is taking actions now to improve your health and well-being.

For humans, growing old is a natural and universal process. The prospect of aging and dying, however, has troubled people for centuries. Instead of dreading this time of life, many older adult Americans are busy pursuing a variety of enjoyable and rewarding activities. Healthy people do not let the aging process interfere with their active lifestyles.

The Across the Life Span sections of each chapter of this textbook highlight specific health concerns of older adults. This chapter provides more detailed information concerning the aging process, including ways to enjoy good health and a positive sense of well-being while growing old. Additionally, this chapter examines dying and death as well as ways of coping with loss and grief. To determine if you are prepared for aging and death, answer the questions in the assessment activity for this chapter in the Student Workbook section of this text.

Aging

We can define **aging** as the sum of all changes that occur in an organism during its life. The **life span** is the maximum number of years that members of a species can live when conditions are optimal. The life span of an adult mayfly is a few days; the life span of a human is 122 years. In 1997, Jeanne Calment of Marseilles, France, died at the age of 122. According to official records, Ms. Calment lived longer than any other person (**Figure   1**). However, very few people live longer than 105 years. Contrary to popular belief, there are no regions of the world where populations usually live more than 100 years (see the Diversity in Health feature "Hunting for Supercentenarians" that follows).

Medical experts customarily divide the human life span into stages or periods (see Chapter 1, Table 1-7). Most people reach physical maturity or adulthood by the time they are 25 years old, but *adulthood* usually refers to the period spanning 21 through 65 years of age. Older adulthood, or **senescence**, is the stage of life that begins at 65 years of age and ends with death. In this chapter, the terms *older adulthood*, *old*, *aging*, *older adult*, and *elderly* are interchangeable with *senescence*. The ages that define these life stages are arbitrary; there are no obvious physical signs that indicate the precise ages when one passes from young adulthood into middle age or from middle age into senescence.

Diversity in Health

Hunting for Supercentenarians

Despite the high standard of living and excellent quality of medical care in the United States, few Americans live to be 100 years old. According to verifiable records, no one in the United States has lived longer than 120 years. Yet in certain isolated parts of the world, hundreds of people claim to be more than 120 years old (supercentenarians). Do people who live in these places actually live longer than Americans or the rest of the world's population?

In the first half of the twentieth century, reports emerged concerning the extreme longevity of people living in the Hunza area of northern Pakistan, in the village of Vilcabamba in Ecuador, and in the Caucasus region in the eastern European country of Georgia. Scientists visited these regions to question the very old people and determine factors that were associated with their extreme longevity. After interviewing the oldest people in these regions, some experts concluded that living in an isolated and unpolluted rural environment, eating a simple nutritious diet, avoiding the use of alcohol and tobacco, and maintaining an active daily schedule were the keys to superlongevity.

By the 1970s, however, the real story began to unfold concerning the existence of the so-called supercentenarians. As some investigators returned to locate and interview the same old people that they had met previously, their elderly subjects gave ages that did not match. For example, if 5 years had lapsed since the first interview, instead of being 5 years older, the old person reported being 7 or 10 years older. It did not take researchers long to realize that these elderly people typically inflated their ages. How could so many people have been fooled into believing that supercentenarians existed?

It is difficult to verify the ages of very old individuals who live in rural, undeveloped places. During the 1800s, birth records that could document the ages of very elderly persons were not kept, or they were destroyed. In some cases, investigators initially believed the authenticity of an extremely old individual's birth record, but later rejected it after determining that the person shared the name of a long-dead ancestor who was the rightful owner of the document. Even if individuals who claim to be extremely old have their birth records, the documents' value is questionable because birth dates can be altered.

Why would elderly people add years to their actual ages? In many isolated and impoverished places, conditions are not ideal for enjoying a lengthy life. Aged members of these populations know that the longer they live, the more fame, respect, and status they can expect to receive from younger members of the population. Government officials often do little to refute citizens' astounding superlongevity claims because the notoriety attracts a steady stream of curious international visitors whose money supports the local economy.

Scientists who study individuals who claim to be supercentenarians think that their subjects are old, but not that old. They may be older than 80 years of age, but few are older than age 90. Thus, no convincing evidence exists that supports the amazing longevity claims of supercentenarians. Many people, however, persistently believe stories that there are concentrations of extremely old people living in certain regions of the world.

Life Expectancy

Life expectancy is the average number of years that an individual who was born in a particular year can expect to live. In the United States, life expectancies vary according to age, sex, and socioeconomic status. Overall, American females outlive American males by about 5 years.[7] As a result, the older adult population consists of about one-third more women than men. The reasons for these differences are unclear, but hormonal, genetic, and socioeconomic factors are thought to influence life expectancy.

As mentioned in Chapter 1, life expectancies increased dramatically during the twentieth century, especially for people who live in developed countries. In the United States, for example, individuals born in 1900 could expect to live 47 years; individuals born in 2009 can expect to live 78 years.[7] An increase in life expectancy generally occurs when fewer people die during the earlier stages of life rather than in the later ones.

In the first part of the twentieth century, people lived past 65 years of age, but so many younger individuals died from serious injuries, infections, and in childbirth that these statistics lowered overall life expectancy. By the 1950s advances in scientific and medical technology significantly reduced the number of deaths from these conditions. Today, a greater proportion of the American population lives beyond age 65 than in the past.

In 2009, 13% of the U.S. population was 65 years of age and older.[4] Between the mid-1940s and the mid-1960s, the birthrate was unusually high in the United States. As a result, experts estimate that almost 20% of the U.S. population will be 65 years and older by the year 2030.[5] **Figure 2** shows estimates of the number of Americans who are or will be 65 or more years of age in 2020, 2030, and 2040.

Scientists are learning more about the causes of aging and are seeking ways to extend life expectancy. Their efforts have led to the development and testing of new therapies for today's major killers: cancer and cardiovascular disease. Advances in genetic engineering offer ways to prevent and treat inherited disorders that can lead to disability and premature death. Additionally, organ transplantation gives thousands of dying individuals the opportunity to survive by replacing their failing organs with healthy ones. Liv-

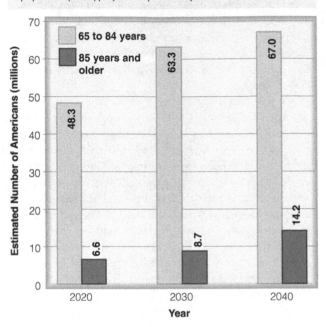

Figure 2

Estimates of the U.S. Population 65 Years of Age and Older in 2020, 2030, and 2040. The number of older adults in the United States is expected to increase significantly in the next 30 years.

Source: U.S. Census Bureau. (n.d.). *U.S. population projections.* Retrieved on on May 29, 2011, from http://www.census.gov/population/www/projections/summarytables.html

ing longer, however, does not necessarily mean living better.

Preserving the quality of life becomes increasingly important as people grow older. By the time Americans reach 65 years of age, chronic illnesses and disabilities often reduce their quality of life. A measurement called "years of healthy life" estimates the negative impact that quality of life can have on life expectancy. A broad goal of *Healthy People 2000* was to increase years of healthy life from 64 years to at least 65 years.[8] Presently, Americans can still expect to live in good health for about 67 years.[9]

The Characteristics of Aged Americans

The majority of Americans older than 65 years of age own their homes or live with family members, and they can handle their financial matters and manage various daily living activities such as bathing, dressing, and cooking. Most older adults suffer from at least one chronic health problem, particularly hypertension, heart disease, arthritis, cancer, and diabetes.[10]

Figure 3

Independent Living. Adding certain features to homes, such as "grab bars" in and next to the shower stall and supportive arms around the toilet, can help older adults with physical disabilities live independently.

Many older adults with mild physical disabilities live independently by making some adaptations to their homes. For example, installing elevated toilets, grab bars, and shower seats makes it easier for people with physical conditions such as arthritis to take care of their personal hygiene (**Figure 3**).

In July 2009, 5.6 million Americans were 85 years or older.[4] This population is increasing so rapidly, experts think about 21 million people will be in this age group by 2050. People who are 85 years old and older, the "oldest of the old," are more likely to be severely disabled and unable to live independently than the "young old" who are 65 to 74 years. In 2009, about 4% of Americans 65 years and older lived in institutional settings, such as extended-care or long-term care facilities ("nursing homes").[10] However, more than 14% of people 85 years or older lived in these places.

A significant number of older adults are independent and financially secure, often because they planned for their retirement needs when they were young. Today, fewer older Americans live in poverty than in the late 1960s, thanks largely to federal programs such as Social Security, Medicaid, and Medicare. Nevertheless, many older Americans must live on lower incomes than when they were younger. In 2009, about 9% of older adults had incomes that were less than the federal government's poverty level.[10] Older adults who are members of minority groups, particularly African Americans and Latinos, are more likely to have lower retirement incomes and live in poverty than are elderly white people.

Although some of their expenses are less because they are no longer working, healthcare costs of retirees are generally higher than those of younger individuals. Almost all older American adults have **Medicare**. Medicare is a federal health insurance program that provides benefits for people 65 years of age and older. The program, however, does not pay for every medical expense. Thus, elderly people must often buy additional health insurance. The cost of health care is not a major barrier to health care for most older adults. Nevertheless, people with low incomes and less education often have difficulty paying for medical expenses not covered by insurance. Without adequate insurance, serious chronic health conditions can drain the financial resources of older adults and their families. Many older adults continue working beyond the usual retirement age to help pay for health insurance and other expenses.

Why Do We Age?

People age at different rates. A person's *chronological age*, as measured in years, may not match his or her *physiologic age*, as measured in functional ability. For example, some 50-year-old people experience the physical changes of aging earlier than average; they look, act, and feel older than others who are the same age. Inheritance accounts for some of this variation because a person's genes determine when certain physiologic events occur.

Genes are hereditary material located on *chromosomes* within a cell's nucleus. Genes provide chemical instructions for the production of vital proteins that are needed for cellular activities. For example, most body cells can divide to form new cells. A cell's genes control the number of times it can divide. After dividing its maximum number of times, the cell dies. Most tissues produce a surplus of cells, so they can afford the death of some cells. As people age, however, the rate of new cell production in tissues normally slows and the number of living cells declines as existing cells die.

Telomeres are structures that form the tips of chromosomes. Telomeres play a major role in the aging process by serving as biological clocks that control the number of times cell division can occur. Each time a normal cell divides, its telomeres shorten. When telomeres reach a certain length, they cannot become shorter and chemical processes that initiate cellular death occur. Theoretically, people who inherit instructions to produce chromosomes with longer telomeres have the genetic potential to live longer than those who inherit instructions to produce shorter telomeres. More research, however, is needed to determine the role of telomere length in the human aging process.

External factors such as environment and lifestyle also influence the aging process. For example, exposure to certain environmental conditions can damage genes. Damaged genes make mistakes in copying and transferring information concerning protein production. Young cells can correct many of these errors, but aging cells are less efficient at correcting such mistakes. When the parts of cells that manufacture proteins receive faulty instructions from the genes, they are unable to produce these compounds. Without an adequate supply of proteins, the affected cells eventually die.

An organ fails if it does not contain enough functioning cells. The systems of the body are interrelated, so when the organs of one system fail, the organs of the other systems soon lose their functional capacities. For example, when a heart that has been weakened by disease cannot pump blood efficiently, the lungs and kidneys are not able to function properly. As a result, other organs fail to perform their jobs, and death occurs.

Radiation, pollution, and some drugs and viruses may damage genes, thereby accelerating the rate of aging and shortening life expectancy. By limiting contact or exposure to these agents, you may be able to lengthen your life expectancy. Furthermore, adopting a lifestyle that includes regular exercise and that avoids smoking can reduce your risk of heart disease, stroke, and cancer. Eating more fruits and vegetables may lower your risk of cancer also. The "Changing Health Habits" feature of this and the other chapters can help you identify and change unhealthy practices (see the Student Workbook section at the end of the book).

The Effects of Aging on Physical Health

People begin to experience a gradual and irreversible decline in the functioning of their bodies when they are about 30 years old. Even healthy people experience this progressive decline as they grow older. Some common signs of aging, such as menopause, delayed sexual responsiveness, graying and thinning hair, loss of height, and *presbyopia*, the inability to see close objects clearly, reflect normal changes associated with growing old. **Table 1** describes some significant physical changes that are associated with normal senescence. As you can see, growing old affects every system of the body.

Aging is an individual process. There is no timetable that specifies at what age people can expect a particular physical change to occur. The rate at which these alterations occur, however, accelerates after 65 years of age. As a result of these normal changes, the aging body is less able to adapt to stress, repair itself, and resist or fight infection. Infections and accidents that were minor health problems when a person was young can become disabling or deadly experiences when a person is old.

Compared to young adults, elderly people are more likely to develop nutritional deficiencies, especially of vitamins D and B_{12}, because aging bodies are less able to absorb or use certain nutrients. The serious health problems that often affect older adults, such as heart disease and hypertension, are associated with lifestyle and are preventable to some extent. Previous chapters discuss cardiovascular disease, hypertension, osteoporosis, and cancer in depth.

Although certain chronic conditions such as arthritis commonly affect elderly people, they are not normal aspects of aging. These ailments may not be life threatening, but they frequently reduce the quality of life.

Age-Related Macular Degeneration In the United States, **macular degeneration** is a leading cause of vision loss for people age 60 and older.[11] The macula is a small region in the eye that enables you to see objects in your central line of vision clearly. As many people age, the light-sensitive cells in the

Table 1

Biological Effects of Normal Aging

System	Normal Changes
Cardiovascular	Heart function remains normal, but the heart muscle thickens; arterial walls thicken; pulse rate declines
Skeletal	Bone loss occurs, which can be abnormal if excessive (osteoporosis)
Nervous	Brain weight decreases, especially in the cerebral cortex; neurotransmitter levels decline, nervous message transmission and muscular responses slow; short-term memory becomes less efficient; visual and hearing ability decreases; the ability to taste bitter and salty foods declines; sleep disturbances, such as taking longer to fall asleep and frequent awakening during the night, often occur
Immune	Immune response against pathogens or developing cancer cells declines
Endocrine	Many hormone levels decline, including insulin (regulates carbohydrate metabolism), aldosterone (regulates sodium metabolism), and thyroid, estrogen, and growth hormones
Digestive	Tooth loss becomes more likely as gums recede; levels of stomach acid drop; intestinal absorption of calcium is less efficient; constipation can occur, often the result of medications or poor diet
Muscular	Muscle mass declines, resulting in less strength; stamina reduction occurs
Reproductive	Menopause occurs in women, resulting in thinning of vaginal lining, less vaginal lubrication, and shrinkage of reproductive organs; breast tissue shrinks; prostate gland enlarges in men; sexual responsiveness slows so that it takes longer for erections to occur; orgasms are shorter and less intense
Urinary	Kidneys become less efficient at filtering wastes from the blood
Skin (integument)	Skin becomes drier and less elastic, resulting in wrinkles; scalp hair growth slows, and its loss increases; hair growth in the nose and ears increases; fingernails often become yellow, develop ridges, and split

macula gradually die, resulting in distorted, blurry, or lost central vision. People with macular degeneration have difficulty reading, driving, and viewing television or a computer monitor. To test your vision for macular degeneration, visit www.amd.org/living-with-amd/resources-and-tools/31-amsler-grid.html.

In about 10% of cases, tiny blood vessels form under the macula and leak fluid and bleed, causing severe vision loss ("wet" or advanced macular degeneration). Medication and laser surgery can stop the bleeding in early stages of wet macular degeneration, but these treatments cannot restore lost vision. There is no effective treatment for the "dry" form of macular degeneration, and this condition can lead to the "wet" form.

Preventing macular degeneration is important. Aging people who smoke and have a family history of macular degeneration have a high risk of developing the condition. Other risk factors include age, obesity, and female sex. Eating a diet that contains plenty of dark green leafy vegetables, such as spinach, collards, and mustard greens, may protect against macular degeneration. For people who have been diagnosed with the disease, zinc and antioxidant supplements may slow the deterioration of the macula. However, these dietary substances can be toxic and should not be taken without consulting a physician.

Cataracts Although the reasons for their occurrence are unclear, **cataracts** are common in people older than 50 years of age. A cataract forms when the normally transparent lens of the eye becomes cloudy and opaque with aging. Clouded lenses scatter light

as it enters the eyes, making it difficult to see images clearly. Symptoms of cataracts include blurry and double vision, sensitivity to bright light, and seeing halos around objects. Without surgery to remove damaged lenses, cataracts can lead to blindness. In many cases, surgeons can replace natural lenses with artificial ones; in others, they remove the damaged lenses and prescribe eyeglasses or contact lenses.

Some medical experts think that exposure to ultraviolet light can cause cataracts. You may be able to reduce your risk of cataracts by wearing sunglasses to shield your eyes, when you are outdoors.

Glaucoma Glaucoma is another ailment that frequently affects the vision of aged people. In this condition, an abnormal amount of fluid accumulates in the eyeball. Over time, the high fluid pressure causes vision loss by permanently damaging the optic nerve, the nerve that transmits visual information to the brain. Eye pain, headache, and loss of peripheral vision are symptoms of glaucoma. Risk factors for developing glaucoma include family history, African ancestry, diabetes, and cardiovascular disease. In most cases, placing medicinal drops into the eyes can control the condition. In severe cases of glaucoma, surgery is necessary to reduce the fluid pressure within the eyeball.

Glaucoma may not produce noticeable symptoms; therefore, early detection is the best way to control the effects of the disorder. A simple, painless screening test is available that can identify the disease before serious damage to the optic nerve occurs. Thus, you can prevent the irreversible effects of glaucoma by having a physician or optometrist perform periodic screenings.

Arthritis Arthritis is a broad group of chronic joint diseases characterized by inflammation, pain, swelling, and loss of mobility ("stiffness") of affected joints. Rheumatoid arthritis, osteoarthritis, "lupus," fibromyalgia, and gout are forms of arthritis. Rheumatoid arthritis and lupus can affect multiple organs and cause a wide variety of symptoms (**Figure 4**).

According to the Centers for Disease Control and Prevention, an estimated 50 million adult Americans suffer from doctor-diagnosed arthritis.[12] Regardless of age, arthritis is the leading cause of disability among Americans.[12] In *osteoarthritis*, the cartilage that protects the ends of bones and keeps them from rubbing together at joints wears away and breaks down. As a result, tiny bits of cartilage or bone float in the fluid that fills the joint and the joint becomes misshapen (**Figure 5**). People often confuse osteoarthritis with osteoporosis, a different condition that affects older adults. Information about osteoporosis is in Chapter 9.

Older adults are more likely to develop osteoarthritis than young persons are.[12] Joints simply wear out as a person ages. Other contributing factors include heredity, overuse, injury, and obesity. Overuse and injury of joints can occur when performing sports or jobs that place excessive stress on joints. Obese older adults have a high risk of developing osteoarthritis because carrying around extra weight stresses joints, especially the knees.

Content removed due to

copyright restrictions

Figure 4

Effects of Arthritis on the Hands. Arthritis damages joint tissue, resulting in deformities and the loss of flexibility.

Figure 5

Effects of Osteoarthritis on Joints. (a) In a healthy joint, such as the knee joint, the ends of bones are encased in smooth cartilage. The bone ends are protected by a joint capsule line with a synovial membrane that produces synovial fluid. The capsule and fluid protect the cartilage, muscles, and connective tissues. (b) This illustration shows a knee joint severely affected by osteoarthritis. Note that the cartilage has worn away. Spurs grow out from the edge of the bone, and synovial fluid within the joint increases. As a result, the joint is difficult to move and it is sore.

Source: National Institute of Arthritis and Musculoskeletal and Skin Diseases. (revised May 2006). OsteoArthritis. Retrieved on July 20, 2007, from http://www.niams.nih.gov/hi/topics/Arthritis/oahandout.pdf.

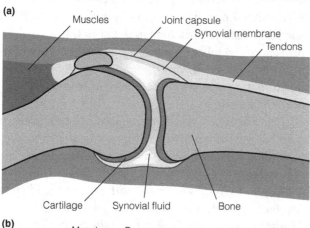

(a)

Muscles • Joint capsule • Synovial membrane • Tendons • Cartilage • Synovial fluid • Bone

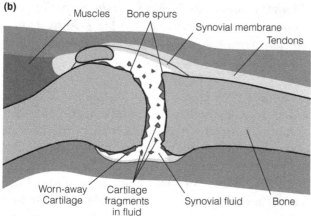

(b)

Muscles • Bone spurs • Synovial membrane • Tendons • Worn-away Cartilage • Cartilage fragments in fluid • Synovial fluid • Bone

Although arthritis is a chronic disease, symptoms tend to come and go. Treatment for osteoarthritis includes medications to relieve inflammation and pain, and exercises to strengthen muscles and improve or maintain joint mobility. Losing weight reduces stress on weight-bearing joints in obese people. In some cases, surgery is necessary to replace damaged joints with artificial implants.

Urinary Incontinence Urinary incontinence, the inability to control the flow of urine from the bladder, is an embarrassing and costly problem for millions of Americans. As people age, the muscles that control bladder emptying weaken, making it easier for urine to leak out when people move, sneeze, cough, or lift heavy things. Additionally, many older adults experience involuntary contractions of their bladders that cause some urine to be eliminated unexpectedly. Medications, infections, strokes, tumors, history of childbirth in women, and enlargement of the prostate gland in men can contribute to urinary incontinence.

The fear of leaking urine accidentally while in public often makes many incontinent people avoid social situations. If family members cannot manage an incontinent elderly relative at home, they often find it necessary to place him or her in an extended-care facility.

Many older adults restrict their fluid intake to reduce their urine production. This practice can lead to dehydration. The majority of individuals who experience urinary incontinence can benefit from treatment, such as behavioral techniques that enable them to be more aware of the bladder's state of fullness. By learning to empty the bladder more frequently, a person may be able to avoid the leakage. People can learn and practice a series of exercises that strengthen the pelvic muscles that control urination. These exercises, called *Kegel* exercises, involve imitating the same muscular movements that individuals make when they voluntarily stop urinating. Incontinent people can also wear absorbent pads and undergarments designed to prevent incidents of urine leakage. Medication and surgery may alleviate incontinence. Embarrassment or concerns about surgery, however, keep many incontinent people from discussing this common problem with personal physicians.

Alzheimer's Disease You cannot find your keys; you forget an appointment; you sometimes call your child by your cat's name. Do you ever have the feeling that you are losing your mind? It may be reassuring to know that everyone has these and other similar annoying experiences from time to time, but many middle-aged Americans worry that instances of forgetfulness are early symptoms of **Alzheimer's disease (AD)**. According to the Alzheimer's Association, the most common early sign of the disease is difficulty recalling newly learned information.[13]

AD is an incurable, progressive, degenerative disease that affects the functioning of the brain. People with AD have abnormal amounts of a protein that forms clumps between cells in the brain. These clumps interfere with brain cells' ability to communicate with each other. Furthermore, tangled bundles of useless protein fibers form within the brain cells, disrupting cell function. As an increasing number of brain cells die, the signs and symptoms of AD become more apparent.

Experts with the Alzheimer's Association estimate that 5.4 million Americans, mostly elderly persons, had AD in 2011.[14] As the baby boom generation ages, 10 million more people will be added to this number. By the year 2050, three times as many Americans will suffer from this dreaded disease.

AD is the most common form of **dementia**, a brain disorder that seriously affects normal *cognitive* (thinking) abilities, such as recalling information and solving problems. Strokes and Parkinson's disease also are major causes of dementia. Common features of AD include memory loss, mental confusion, and loss of control over behavior and body functions. Although AD is incurable, a few medications can be prescribed to slow the decline in cognitive functioning, control certain inappropriate behaviors of patients, and improve patients' moods.

Age and family history are major risk factors for AD. Although the disease is common among older adults, it is not a normal feature of growing old. What are the signs of AD? Is it preventable?

In the early stages of Alzheimer's, affected people may notice lapses in their memories and cognitive abilities. For example, they may have unusual difficulty remembering events that happened recently, learning new information, and using information to make reasonable conclusions. These symptoms typically begin between 40 and 60 years of age. Over time, people with the disease become increasingly forgetful, confused, disoriented, restless, and moody. Communicating becomes difficult as their speech deteriorates; depression is common. These changes are distressing to patients with AD, their family members, and their associates. One woman recalls her affected mother-in-law's gradual loss of cognitive functioning:

The first time I had a feeling that my elderly mother-in-law might have a serious problem with her memory occurred in April when she got lost while driving to our house. We live close to her and she had made the short trip dozens of times. When I told my husband that this was unusual behavior for her and could be a sign of a memory problem, he disagreed and said it was "easy" to make a wrong turn on the way to our house. A few months later, I was driving Mother to a store when she insisted that I should be making a right turn instead of a left one at a familiar intersection in our town. When I told her she was wrong, she became angry and argued with me about the directions to the store. When I finally reached the store, she recognized the place but didn't apologize for her behavior. At Christmas, Mother was very quiet and seemed to be in a fog. My husband and his sister finally recognized that she was "not herself," and they took her to the doctor's for an evaluation. After a series of medical tests to rule out minor strokes and other causes of brain damage, her condition was diagnosed as mild-to-moderate Alzheimer's disease.

Mother now takes two medications that seem to help her memory a little. At this point, she is not supposed to drive and she needs help with housework. She still cooks, but I'm concerned she'll forget that she's making something and she'll start a fire in her kitchen. My husband and his sister are thinking about selling Mother's house and placing her in a special group home for people with this terrible disease. I dread the day when my husband greets his mother and she doesn't recognize him.

As AD progresses, its victims neglect their personal hygiene; their facial expressions become "flat" (emotionless); and they exhibit inappropriate and unpredictable behaviors such as undressing in public and attacking caregivers. In the terminal stages, individuals with this devastating illness require constant care. They are bedridden and unable to talk and eat. Nothing can be done to stop the relentless progression of the disease. After diagnosis, the average person can expect to survive about 8 years. Some people with AD live only 4 years after diagnosis, whereas others are able to live for 20 years with the disease.[14] Death often results from pneumonia and starvation as the degenerating brain is unable to control vital functions such as breathing, swallowing, and digestion. In 2009, about 79,000 Americans died of AD, making it the sixth leading cause of death.[7]

Physicians often diagnose AD when patients cannot answer questions like those listed in **Table 2**.

Table	2
Simple Memory Test for Identifying Dementia	

Ask the person:

1. His or her age
2. His or her date of birth
3. The time to the nearest hour
4. His or her address
5. The current year
6. Where he or she is
7. The names of two people who are pictured in family photos
8. The years of World War II
9. The name of the current president of the United States
10. To count backwards from 100 to 1
11. His or her phone number

Source: Adapted from Wattis, J. (1996). What an old age psychiatrist does. *British Medical Journal, 313*:101–104.

Using aluminum cookware does not increase the risk of Alzheimer's disease.

Until recently, the only way to confirm the diagnosis was by examining the patient's brain after death. Brain imaging techniques such as magnetic resonance imaging (MRI) scans can now detect shrinkage in areas of the cerebral cortex, the thinking part of the brain. Such brain shrinkage is a sign of AD.

The factors that cause AD are unclear. At least two forms of the disorder are inherited. Although genetic testing is available to determine whether relatives of patients with AD have the genes associated with the condition, many people who test positive do not develop the disease. Other forms of AD may be the result of slow-acting brain viruses, brain injury, or exposure to pollutants. At one time, scientists thought that aluminum poisoning caused the disease because higher than normal amounts of this metal are found in the brains of patients who died of AD. Many people are concerned about the safety of using aluminum cookware and the natural presence of this element in drinking water. However, most experts think that the unusual concentration of aluminum in the brains of persons with AD is a result, not a cause, of the disorder. Nevertheless, scientists are investigating whether environmental factors, such as exposure to other minerals, may contribute to AD.

Can Alzheimer's disease be prevented? Lifestyle factors appear to play a role in reducing the risk of AD. Keeping physically active, being involved in a variety of intellectually stimulating activities, and maintaining an extensive social network are associated with a lower risk of AD.[15] Making certain dietary changes may also help. Results of one study indicated that people who eat high amounts of salad dressing, fruit, nuts, fish, tomatoes, cruciferous vegetables (broccoli and cabbage, for example), dark green and leafy vegetables, and low amounts of high-fat milk products, red meat, and butter have lower risk of AD than people who did not eat this dietary pattern.[16] More research is needed to determine whether a particular dietary pattern protects against AD.

Elevated blood cholesterol levels, particularly LDL cholesterol, are associated with increased risk of AD.[17] Results of recent studies, however, do not support taking cholesterol-lowering medications, such as certain *statins*, to reduce the risk of AD.[17,18] Nevertheless, more research is needed to confirm these findings.

Inflammation and the effects of excess oxidation in the body, especially in the brain, may increase the risk of AD.[19] Thus, herbal preparations and substances in foods that have anti-inflammatory and antioxidant activity may protect against AD. *Curcumin*, a chemical with anti-inflammatory and antioxidant activity, may help prevent the disease.[20,21] The spice and food coloring agent turmeric contains curcumin. *EGb 761*, an extract made from leaves of the ginkgo biloba tree, has antioxidant activity. Promoters of dietary supplements that contain ginkgo claim their products can treat memory loss, confusion, depression, and other conditions associated with Alzheimer's disease.[22]

Analyzing Health-Related Information

The following article is an abbreviated version of "Alzheimer's: Few Clues on the Mysteries of Memory" that appeared in *FDA Consumer* magazine. Read the article and evaluate it using the model for analyzing health-related information. The main points of the model are noted on the following page; the model is fully explained in Chapter 1.

Alzheimer's

Few Clues on the Mysteries of Memory

by Audrey T. Hingley

It happened some years ago but the memory is still firmly implanted in my mind. One sunny afternoon I heard the sound of a car pulling into our driveway, peered out of my living room window, and saw one of my father's friends, Sam (not his real name), then in his early 80s. Sam got out of his car and walked just a few steps. I watched as he stood for a few moments, gazing at our house with an expressionless face. Then he silently returned to his car, got in, and drove away, without ever knocking on our door or communicating with us in any way.

I thought the incident puzzling, but it wasn't until months later that I learned the reason for it. Sam had Alzheimer's, a progressive disease in which nerve cells in the brain degenerate and brain substance shrinks.

A widower living alone, Sam clearly was in a dangerous position. Once he was followed home by a police officer, who told his grown children he had found Sam stopped by the side of the road, not able to remember how to get home by himself.

Sam's story is being played out in the lives of up to 4 million Americans who suffer from Alzheimer's disease. The disease plays no favorites, attacking rich and poor, famous and ordinary. Among its most famous sufferers: former President Ronald Reagan.

With an average lifetime cost of care per patient of $174,000, it is the third most expensive disease in America, fol-

lowing only heart disease and cancer. But perhaps even more staggering than the monetary costs are the emotional and psychological costs borne by both patients and their families.

"People are very frightened of the possibilities because they know it represents a loss of one's self," says Steven T. DeKosky, M.D., director of the Alzheimer's Disease Research Center at the University of Pittsburgh and a practicing neurologist. "It's a very frightening prospect to see a loved one who looks the same but doesn't talk or act the same."

"I Have Lost Myself"

Alzheimer's disease, a progressive, degenerative disease attacking the brain and resulting in impaired thinking, behavior and memory, was first described by Alois Alzheimer, M.D., in 1906. German researchers recently found an important set of notes from Alzheimer's journal of the world's first documented case of the disease. The patient exhibited many of the symptoms seen in Alzheimer's patients today. But perhaps most poignant of all is the patient's own description of the disease: "I have lost myself."

In Alzheimer's, nerve cells in the part of the brain responsible for memory and other thought processes degenerate for still-unknown reasons. Some of the most severely affected cells normally use acetylcholine, a brain chemical, to communicate. Tacrine (brand name Cognex, also called THA), the first drug approved by the Food and Drug Administration specifically to treat Alzheimer's disease, works by slowing the breakdown of acetylcholine. This results in relieving some memory impairment.

Tacrine does not cure Alzheimer's or slow the disease's progression. It has only been studied in those with mild to moderate Alzheimer's disease who were otherwise in generally good health. Because tacrine can increase the blood levels of a liver enzyme that can indicate liver damage, regular monitoring is necessary. Other side effects include nausea, vomiting, diarrhea, abdominal pain, skin rash, and indigestion.

Aricept (generic name donepezil hydrochloride, also called E2020), approved by the FDA in 1996, is by far the most used drug for Alzheimer's treatment. Like tacrine, Aricept inhibits the breakdown of acetylcholine but does not cause the kind of increase in liver enzymes that tacrine does. It can also cause diarrhea, vomiting, nausea, fatigue, insomnia, and anorexia, but in most cases, such side effects are mild and decline with continued use of the drug. Again, the drug helps only those patients with mild to moderate symptoms of Alzheimer's and does not stop or slow the disease's progression.

Forgetfulness or Alzheimer's?

While most people understand at least some of the horrifying aspects of Alzheimer's disease, DeKosky says a big challenge is educating people regarding the widely held assumption that people are supposed to have memory impairment as they age.

"There's this huge prejudice where we think people should have severe mental impairment as they get older," he says. Memory loss, disorientation, and confusion are not part of the normal aging process, he explains. They are symptoms of dementia, and the most common form of dementia is Alzheimer's.

"You need to look at the functional consequences of what someone cannot remember," DeKosky says. "If mom forgets where she put her car in the parking lot at the mall, that's not abnormal. But if she walks home from the mall because she forgot she took her car, that's not normal. Memory is the first and worst change, but you will also see social withdrawal and less willingness to interact with others."

The Need for Answers

Although no cure for Alzheimer's is available now, planning and medical/social management can help ease the burden on both patient and family members. Physical exercise, good nutrition, and social activities are important. A calm, structured environment may also help the person to continue functioning.

At some point, however, people with Alzheimer's require 24-hour care. The financing of such care, including diagnosis costs, treatment, and paid care, is estimated to be $100 billion annually, according to the Alzheimer's Association. The federal government covers $4.4 billion and the states another $4.1 billion, with much of the remaining costs borne by patients and their families.

"It's a national imperative to find effective means to diagnose, treat and prevent this disease," says David Banks, R.Ph., a public health specialist in the FDA's Office of Special Health Issues. "When you look at it demographically, the nearly 80 million baby boomers living in the United States . . . now have an average life expectancy of approximately 78 years. One in five Americans could be age 65 or older by 2030, and tens of millions of baby boomers will live into their 80s. The Alzheimer's Association projects that as many as 14 million Americans could have Alzheimer's disease in 2050. When viewed in the context of accelerating Social Security and Medicare costs . . . , the future monetary costs of Alzheimer's disease may be unsustainable. The human costs could be even greater."

Note: Audrey T. Hingley is a freelance writer in Mechanicsville, Virginia.

---

1. Which statements are verifiable facts, and which are unverified statements or value claims?
2. What are the credentials of the person who wrote the article? Does this person have the appropriate background and education in the topic area? What can you do to check the person's credentials?
3. What might be the motives and biases of the person who wrote the article?
4. What is the main point of the article? Which information is relevant to the issue, main point? Which information is irrelevant?
5. Is the source reliable? What evidence supports your conclusion that the source is reliable or unreliable? Does the source of information present the pros and cons of the topic?
6. Does the source of information attack the credibility of conventional scientists or medical authorities?

Based on your analysis, do you think that this article is a reliable source of health-related information? Explain why you think it is or is not. Summarize your reasons for coming to this conclusion.

Although a review of several scientific studies indicated EGb 761 can improve cognitive functioning, the extract's beneficial effects were slight.[23] Results of the Ginkgo Evaluation Memory Study indicate ginkgo had no effect on memory loss or AD.[24]

Vitamins E and C have antioxidant effects. According to results of certain studies, populations that consume vitamin E–rich diets have lower risk of Alzheimer's disease.[25] No such benefit, however, was observed in groups of people taking high amounts of vitamin E, multivitamin, or other vitamin supplements.[24] Researchers continue to investigate the association between dietary sources of antioxidants, such as fruits, vegetables, and vegetable oils, and the risk of Alzheimer's disease. At present, there is no conclusive scientific evidence that supports the effectiveness of any specific dietary supplement in preventing the disease.[24]

Patients with Alzheimer's often live at home until they reach the terminal stage and require the care provided in a skilled nursing care facility. Living with an affected loved one can be emotionally stressful and physically demanding. While caring for a patient with this disease, family members must try to maintain their own health and well-being. To provide assistance, many communities have special "adult day care" centers where persons with AD can spend a few hours during the day before returning to their homes. Not every community offers this service, so if you need help caring for someone with AD, check with your local mental health association or Alzheimer's Association for information about adult day care centers in your area. The following Analyzing Health-Related Information feature involves evaluating excerpts of an article about AD.

The Effects of Aging on Psychological Health

As they approach the end of middle age, most employed people face retirement, and many aging parents have grown children with families who have moved away. If older adults equate retirement from jobs and separation from their families with being old and useless, they may experience serious psychological distress. Additionally, the dramatic reduction of financial resources that often accompanies retirement can mean a serious loss of economic stability.

Older adults often enjoy caring for their grandchildren.

Many older adults began planning for their future financial security while they were young. Therefore, not every older adult dreads the prospect of retiring from job and family responsibilities. Many people approach retirement with a positive outlook and look forward to this time of life. Retired individuals often find pleasure from traveling, volunteering in their communities, caring for their grandchildren, and exploring new interests. Other retirement-age adults choose to continue working, especially if they enjoy what they do and their work is intellectually stimulating and personally fulfilling. Older adults often have a wealth of knowledge and experience that they can share with younger members of society.

Older adults, especially those older than 85 years of age, frequently experience deteriorating health, difficult social circumstances, and poor economic conditions. Deaths of spouses and friends, separations from family, and reductions in financial resources create emotional stress. As a result, elderly persons often suffer depression.

Regardless of one's age, depression is associated with an increased risk of suicide. In the United States, older adults are twice as likely to commit suicide when compared to people who are 10–24 years of age.[26] Divorced or widowed elderly persons are more likely to kill themselves than married older adults are.[27] Additionally, poor health is a risk factor for suicide. Older adults suffering from chronic conditions, particularly mental illness, heart failure, obstructive lung disease, and pain, are more likely to commit suicide than older adults who did not have these conditions.[28]

Like younger people, depressed or isolated aged individuals can benefit from participation in social and physical activities. In addition, antidepressant medications or psychotherapy may be necessary to help them regain and maintain their emotional balance.

The Effects of Aging on Social Health

Although a large segment of the U.S. population is older than 65 years, our society is highly youth-oriented. Not surprisingly, middle-age Americans often worry that aging will mean losing their jobs to younger people, being forced into early retirement, becoming widowed, and suffering from debilitating illnesses. Growing old in America can have serious social impacts on older adults; they may be ignored, neglected, and abused by younger members of the population.

Some people in our society have negative attitudes toward older adults. For example, they stereotype elderly people as poor, sick, useless, and dependent. Additionally, some young adults believe that older adults demand too much from the rest of society. **Ageism** is a bias against older adults. Ageism creates conflict between the generations because the old do not trust the young and vice versa. To combat ageism, people need to recognize that growing old does not always mean having poor health, living in an institution, depending on public support, and being useless.

Older adults represent a valuable social asset that is not well used. Aging parents and grandparents often have experience and wisdom that they can share with younger family members. Additionally, many retirees have a variety of talents and special organizational skills that enable them to serve as consultants, managers, or advisors in business, governmental, or educational settings. Both young and old benefit when each accepts, values, and trusts the other.

Successful Aging

Many people would like to believe that it is possible to prevent aging or delay the process. Restricting caloric intakes without creating nutritional deficiencies may slow the rate of aging.[29] The modern search for a "fountain of youth" has resulted in the promotion of pills, potions, diets, or treatments that are touted as having "anti-aging" or "life-extending" capabilities. Contrary to the claims of advertisers, none of these substances or regimens prevents or slows aging.[30]

Instead of searching for magic formulas to extend your life, you can take various actions while you are young to increase your chances of aging successfully. Although there is no generally agreed upon definition for "successful aging," people who age successfully have good physical functioning.[29] Other characteristics of such healthy older adults include having positive attitudes toward themselves and the future and being connected socially with others.

To increase your chances of aging successfully, evaluate your health status and lifestyle, identify specific unhealthy or risky behaviors, and then work at changing those behaviors. Although modifying all unhealthy behaviors is commendable, certain practices are associated more closely with lengthening one's life span than others are.

Physically active people live longer than people who are sedentary.[31] Engaging in regular exercise throughout your life will help you control your body weight as well as improve your circulation, strengthen your heart, and maintain your muscle and bone mass. People older than 65 years of age who perform regular exercise improve their physical strength and flexibility, features that can enhance their quality of life.[31] Exercise may improve some cognitive abilities of aging adults, such as memory, and delay the onset of Alzheimer's disease.[32] More research, however, is needed to further support these findings. **Table 3** lists some basic recommendations for enhancing your health and quality of life as you age, such as managing stress, maintaining relationships, and developing a positive attitude. The other chapters of this textbook provide more detailed information about these recommendations. It is worth remembering the words of Eubie Blake, a jazz musician who died in 1983 at the age of 100, "If I had known that I was going to live this long, I would have taken better care of myself."

Healthy Living Practices

☐ Planning for your future financial needs while you are still young can help you enjoy your retirement years.

☐ To age successfully, evaluate your present health and lifestyle, identify risky behaviors, and then consider changing those behaviors.

Table 3

Tips for Successful Aging

Taking the following actions now, while you are still young, may help you enjoy a healthier, longer life:

- Maintain a healthy weight and eat a nutritious, low-fat diet that includes plenty of whole grains, fruits, and vegetables.
- Be physically active; exercise daily.
- Do not smoke, drink too much alcohol, or abuse other drugs.
- Manage stress; take time to relax daily.
- Have regular physical examinations.
- Adopt safer sex practices.
- Do not drive while under the influence of alcohol or other drugs; always wear a seat belt in vehicles.
- Protect your skin and eyes from sunlight.
- Obtain enough sleep.
- Be concerned about your safety at home, work, or play.
- Maintain social networks with your family and friends.
- Be flexible; expect changes.
- Develop a positive attitude; have a sense of humor.
- Find opportunities to learn new skills or information.
- Get involved with living while accepting your mortality.

Sources: Adapted from Kerschner, H., & Pegues, J. A. (1998). Productive aging: A quality of life agenda. *Journal of the American Dietetic Association, 98*:1445–1448; and Turner, L. W., Sizer, F. S., Whitney, E. N., & Wilks, B. B. (1992). *Life choices: Health concepts and strategies.* Minneapolis, MN: West Publishing.

Dying

Many Americans, including health professionals, fear dying and death, especially the possibility that dying will be premature and painful. Fearing death makes it difficult to be around someone who is dying. One reason many Americans fear dying and death is that few have had contact with dying persons or dead bodies. Usually an ambulance rushes the critically injured or terminally ill person to a hospital, where he or she is connected to a variety of life-support machines and placed in an intensive care unit (**Figure 6**). Most hospitals permit family members to visit the seriously ill patient for only a few minutes each hour. In other instances, elderly or incurably ill pa-

Figure 6

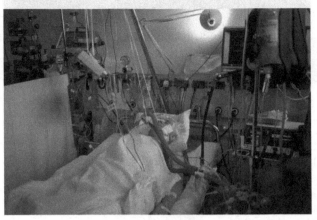

Intensive Care. Treatment of a critically injured or terminally ill person may include being connected to a variety of life-support machines in a hospital's intensive care unit.

tients die in long-term care facilities with few or no family members present. In the United States, dying often becomes a mechanized, isolated, and depersonalized process.

Dying was very different a hundred years ago. In that era, nearly everyone died at home, surrounded by family and friends. Shortly after death, the body was cooled, and it often remained in the home for the funeral ceremony. It was even customary for people to have photographs taken of their deceased loved ones to remember them (**Figure 7**). These practices helped survivors accept dying and death as a part of life.

The Spiritual Aspects of Dying

Some people who have been revived after being unresponsive describe "near-death" experiences and relate them as spiritually uplifting events. They report that they were aware of what was happening before they recovered consciousness. They often recall feeling temporarily disengaged from their bodies and having unusual but peaceful sensations. Accounts of near-death experiences often include some features of the person's spiritual or religious beliefs. People who have been in these situations are often profoundly affected by their experiences, but scientists have no ways of verifying their stories.

People who believe in an afterlife may have less fear of dying and death. Many people believe that a soul exists, which leaves the body after death and goes to heaven or hell. Others believe in reincarnation, com-

Figure 7

Remembrance Photo, Circa 1896. A hundred years ago, nearly everyone died at home, surrounded by their families and friends. It was customary for people to have photographs taken of their deceased loved ones to remember them. This African-American mother is posing with her dead infant.

neered efforts to understand the psychological processes of dying and death.[33] After interviewing more than 200 terminally ill patients, she formulated a five-stage model to describe the emotional responses that people often experience as they face their deaths (**Table 4**).

The first stage of this coping process is denial. People in denial may act shocked after receiving news of their terminal condition. Frequently, they do not believe their physician's prognosis. While in denial, dying individuals may ignore their troublesome symptoms or seek more optimistic outlooks from other physicians. Some dying patients completely lose faith in the value of conventional medical care; some maintain hope of "beating this thing" by using untested alternative treatments.

As the dying begin to accept their situation, they may enter the second stage, anger. In this stage, dying people are provoked easily; they may lash out at loved ones, medical staff, and anything or anybody. They often demand to know "Why me? Why not someone else?" It is important for people who care for or visit dying individuals to expect this reaction and not take such anger personally.

ing back to life as another person or organism after death. Some individuals are not concerned with what happens to them after death. In many instances, cultural and religious backgrounds provide the foundation for a person's feelings about life after death.

The Emotional Aspects of Dying

Although coping with the death of a beloved person is one of life's most difficult experiences, knowing that your own death is near is especially difficult. In the late 1960s, Elisabeth Kübler-Ross, a psychiatrist at the University of Chicago Billings Hospital, pio-

Table 4

Kübler-Ross's Stages of Emotional Responses to Dying

Stage	Typical Responses
Denial	Feels emotionally numb, avoids thinking about his or her condition, ignores the reality of his or her condition
Anger	Lashes out at healthcare providers and loved ones
Bargaining	Makes deals with healthcare providers, loved ones, or God to live long enough to do special things or experience certain events
Depression	Mourns his or her impending death, withdraws socially
Acceptance	Realizes that his or her condition is terminal, gives away cherished items, makes funeral plans

Source: Data from Kübler-Ross, E. (1969). *On death and dying.* New York: Macmillan.

The third emotional stage of dying is bargaining. Incurably ill individuals may make deals with medical staff or God, promising to exchange exceptionally good behavior for a few more years of life or a painless death. In the fourth stage, depression, dying people become increasingly aware that their condition will not improve. Terminally ill individuals mourn for themselves after realizing that they will not live long enough to enjoy experiences such as watching their children mature or playing with their grandchildren.

The final emotional stage of dying is acceptance. Although terminally ill people continue to hope for cures, they accept the possibility that nothing can be done to save them. Friends, family members, and caregivers can help maintain the self-esteem and dignity of the dying by visiting and touching them, as well as by listening to their concerns.

Critics of Kübler-Ross's research charge that she focused on people who were dying prematurely of chronic illnesses and had time to experience each stage. Therefore, her findings may have been different if she had studied people who were dying of acute illnesses or very sick elderly persons. Some people, particularly the elderly, may not experience all five stages of dying. Additionally, aged people who are terminally ill may accept their impending deaths more readily than people who face the prospect of dying while they are still young. The Kübler-Ross model, however, is useful for understanding the complex emotions of dying people.

Dying people are usually under extreme emotional distress. They often feel helpless and hopeless, and they have difficulty relaxing. Treatments such as surgery, chemotherapy, or radiation add to their discomfort. Some terminally ill people fight the prospect of dying; others accept what is happening to them and choose to make the most out of the time they have remaining. In modern societies, death can be the final stage of personal fulfillment if dying people have opportunities to satisfy their social and emotional needs. Thus, some terminally ill people choose to spend more time with their friends and families; others travel far from home.

As the end of life nears, terminally ill people may become more detached from others and the environment. They tend to sleep more often and may lapse in and out of consciousness. When awake or conscious, dying persons may not want to talk as much as they did before reaching this stage. According to Kübler-Ross, dying individuals are almost without feelings; most die without fear.

When you know that a beloved person is dying, you may experience a variety of intense emotions. You may be afraid of enduring the emotional pain of watching a close friend or relative die. You may be angry at the dying person, physicians, or God because you feel they are responsible for the impending death, or they are unable or unwilling to prevent it. You may feel guilty about your feelings toward the dying individual. Recognizing that someone is terminally ill forces us to face the reality that we will someday die.

Family and friends of a dying person typically feel helpless and intensely sad. As a result, they may avoid the person because such feelings are difficult to hide and uncomfortable to bear. This reaction does little to boost the dying person's dignity and sense of well-being. Being avoided makes the dying person feel isolated and rejected at a time when he or she usually has a high need for the compassionate support and comfort of others.

Physicians and family members have become increasingly aware that positive thinking, including hopefulness, can improve the well-being of the dying. Meeting the emotional and spiritual needs of terminally ill persons can help them live better while dying. Many physicians actively seek the participation of their seriously ill patients and their families in decisions concerning treatment. Medical practitioners can enhance the dignity and self-worth of dying patients by discussing the serious nature of their conditions with them, listening carefully to their concerns, and allowing them to make decisions regarding their medical care.

Terminal Care: The Options

The majority of Americans die in hospitals or extended-care facilities such as nursing homes. The goal of hospital-based health care is to provide technologically sophisticated medical care that enables sick people to become well. Because hospital care is costly, elderly patients who are too ill or frail to return home often move into nursing homes. These extended-care facilities offer less comprehensive medical care than hospitals, but they are designed and equipped to manage the long-term care of people recovering from surgery or illness. Not every condition is curable; many chronically ill patients die while residing in these care centers.

Consumer Health

Choosing a Long-Term Care Facility

The most important feature to consider when choosing a residential facility is the quality of medical care that it provides. Before making this decision for a loved one, visit a few facilities, observe the condition of the buildings, its rooms, and residents, and answer the following questions:

1. Is the facility licensed by the state?
2. Is the facility clean, well maintained, and free of objectionable odors?
3. Are staff members friendly, helpful, and respectful to visitors and residents?
4. Are the rooms clean, comfortably furnished, well lit, and cheerful?
5. Do the residents appear to be appropriately dressed, clean, and well groomed? Do they appear to be alert?
6. Are there enough staff members to take care of the number of residents?
7. Are there handrails along the hallways and grab bars in the bathrooms?
8. Does the facility have rehabilitation and exercise areas, a quiet place with reading material, and a chapel?
9. Does the facility have an activities director and scheduled social events that are appropriate for elderly people?
10. Are the dining room and kitchen clean?
11. Are menus nutritious? Do menus indicate that a variety of foods is offered? Can you sample a meal? How are the special dietary needs of patients handled?
12. If you have an opportunity, ask some residents and staff (privately) what they like and dislike about the facility.
13. What are the monthly fees? Can you afford this facility? Does the facility accept Medicaid?
14. Contact your state's Division of Aging to obtain information about the facility's inspection reports.

Before making a final decision, visit the facility at least one additional unscheduled time to make another set of observations.

Source: Adapted from Goldsmith, S. B. (1990). *Choosing a nursing home.* New York: Prentice Hall.

Older adults enjoying a social activity at a long-term care facility.

Choosing to place an aged parent or relative into a nursing home is often an emotionally difficult decision. Family members may have to select an available facility quickly and without researching their options. The Consumer Health feature "Choosing a Long-Term Care Facility" lists some important questions to answer when selecting a residential facility that provides long-term and/or skilled nursing care.

When patients have only a few months to live, their personal physicians may refer them to hospice. **Hospice** is health care specifically designed to give emotional support and pain relief to terminally ill people in the final stage of life (palliative care). This care may be provided in the patient's home or in a hospice center. The primary goal of hospice care is not to save dying patients with aggressive treatments but to relieve their discomfort. Hospice physicians often prescribe powerful medications to keep terminally ill patients as free from pain as possible. Freedom from extreme pain permits the dying person to manage his or her activities more effectively and die with dignity.

Hospice staff receive specialized training to work closely with and to provide emotional and spiritual support to dying patients and their families. Staff encourage patients and their relatives to participate in decision making regarding care. Most terminally ill people and their families can obtain hospice services in their homes from a team of medical professionals. Family members are taught simple medical procedures such as care of surgical wounds or maintenance of feeding tubes. Hospice nurses make home visits to check patients' conditions and are available to answer questions concerning their care. Dying at home allows patients to remain in a comfortable and familiar environment where they can participate in holiday and other family-oriented events.

Some dying patients receive hospice care in clinical settings that have rooms designed to look more like patients' homes than hospitals. The staff encourage patients to decorate their rooms with favorite possessions to foster a homelike environment. Visiting family and friends provide additional social, emotional, and spiritual support and often participate in caring for their ill loved ones. Regardless of whether the terminally ill person dies at home or in a hospice center, hospice staff provide grief counseling services for survivors.

Many nursing homes and hospitals offer hospice services that are covered by health insurance plans. To find such resources in your community, contact local hospitals or check the Yellow Pages under Hospice. Social workers in these facilities can provide information about local support groups for the terminally ill and their families. The National Hospice and Palliative Care Organization can also provide information about hospice programs in your area; this group's toll-free phone number is 1-800-658-8898.

Death

Many people have a difficult time thinking about and discussing death. For example, they may avoid using the term *died*, preferring to use euphemisms such as *passed away*. Whether people believe in an afterlife or not, most are reluctant to handle matters concerning their own dying and death, such as preparing a will or signing an organ donor card.

What Is Death?

Death, the cessation of life, occurs when the heart or lungs stop functioning. When this happens, no oxygen is available for metabolism, and brain cells begin to die. Within 4 to 5 minutes, the dying person loses consciousness. As remaining body cells die, other signs of death become obvious.

When a person dies, the muscles that control voluntary and involuntary movements no longer function. As a result, the body eliminates the contents of the bladder and rectum, and reflexes are absent. *Reflexes* are neuromuscular responses that do not require thinking, such as eye blinking. Gradually, skeletal muscles become rigid, and body temperature cools until it matches that of the environment. Unless the body is chilled or treated with embalming chemicals, it decomposes rapidly. Decomposition occurs because the immune system no longer prevents bacteria and other microorganisms from breaking down the organic material of the body.

The physician who attended the dying patient is usually responsible for certifying that the patient has died. Then, the medical staff informs family members. In most cases, they deliver the body to a funeral home or medical school, according to the deceased person's wishes. If there are any questions or suspicions about the cause of death, the family, physicians, or coroner can request an **autopsy**. During an autopsy, a specially trained physician conducts various medical examinations and tests that usually determine the cause of death.

In 1968, a team of experts at the Harvard Medical School defined death according to four irreversible physical criteria:

- The absence of electrical activity in the brain
- No spontaneous muscular movements, including breathing
- No reflexes
- No responses to the environment

These criteria define what is commonly referred to as *brain death*. The majority of state laws recognize these criteria as the basis for defining death. A legal definition of death is important for criminal cases that involve murder. Defining death is necessary for physicians who need to establish that patients are dead before removing tissues or organs for transplantation.

Since the 1980s, advances in medical technology have made it necessary for medical experts to reconsider the traditional definition of death. By using *cardiopulmonary resuscitation* (CPR), *respirators* (devices that assist breathing), and feeding machines, physicians can often save the lives of certain seriously ill persons and, in some instances, may sustain patients who have virtually no chance of recovering.

Cerebral Death The cerebral cortex of the brain controls thoughts, interprets sensory information, and integrates voluntary muscular activities. An individual who experiences severe damage to his or her cerebral cortex is **comatose**, that is, unresponsive to the environment and in a *coma*. If the damage is irreversible, it is unlikely that the person will regain consciousness. In some comatose patients, the areas of the brain that control and regulate vital activities, including digestion and breathing, continue to function. Although their conditions do not meet the standard criteria for brain death, such individuals have experienced *cerebral death*. With specialized care, a person with a nonfunctioning cerebral cortex can exist in an irreversible coma, a **persistent vegetative state**, for years.

The level of care required to maintain patients in persistent vegetative states is stressful for their families, as well as expensive. Under what circumstances can physicians remove life-sustaining care from a patient in an irreversible coma? The U.S. Supreme Court decision in the Quinlan case provides an answer.

In 1975, Karen Ann Quinlan, a 21-year-old New Jersey woman, was hospitalized in an unconscious state after allegedly consuming a combination of alcohol and tranquilizers. After realizing that she would not recover, Ms. Quinlan's parents requested that the medical staff and hospital administrators allow their daughter to die by disconnecting her respirator. However, the administrators and attending physicians denied the parents' request, noting that the young woman was not dead according to established criteria.

After lower state courts supported the hospital's position, the Quinlans took their daughter's case to the New Jersey Supreme Court. In 1976, this court ruled that because Karen had previously told her mother and some friends that she would not want to live in a persistent vegetative state, her parents had the right to ask physicians to remove her respirator. After being removed gradually from the ventilation device, Karen was able to breathe without the machine's assistance, but she continued to be fed through tubes. The Quinlans moved their comatose daughter to a nursing home, where she died 10 years later.

Since the Quinlan case, several states have passed laws that establish steps for withholding or removing life-sustaining care in similar cases involving the terminally ill. A later section of this chapter describes how you can inform other people in advance about your wishes concerning such medical care.

> **comatose** The condition in which a person is unresponsive to the environment and in a coma.
>
> **persistent vegetative state** The condition in which a person has a nonfunctioning cerebral cortex and is in an irreversible coma.

Euthanasia and the Right to Die

Euthanasia is the practice of allowing permanently comatose or incurably ill persons to die. In cases of active euthanasia, physicians hasten the deaths of dying people by giving them large doses of pain-relieving medications that can completely suppress breathing. Passive euthanasia involves cases in which terminally ill people die because physicians do not provide life-sustaining treatments, or they withdraw such care.

Since the Quinlan case, the courts have decided several right-to-die cases, particularly those involving people who were seriously ill but not dying. Some chronically ill individuals decide that life is not worth living, or that they are tired of living in pain. To hasten death, these people may refuse life-prolonging medical treatment, demand that it be withdrawn, or remove it themselves. In recent years, the courts often have made or upheld decisions that give such seriously ill people the right to die. After physicians discontinued their life support, many of these patients died naturally within a couple of weeks.

In some instances, the seriously ill person is too physically or mentally incapacitated to actively end his or her life. Concerned relatives, friends, or caregivers risk criminal prosecution by helping people commit suicide. Although most physicians strive to preserve life, some assist in the suicides of dying patients by prescribing overdoses of certain drugs. In the 1990s, retired physician Jack Kevorkian focused national attention on the controversial practice of physician-assisted suicide by helping more than 125 people end their lives. In 1999, a judge sentenced Kevorkian to prison for injecting a deadly dose of drugs into a man who was suffering from an incurable deadly disease. Kevorkian spent about 8 years in prison before being paroled. In 2011, Kevorkian died after a brief illness.

Oregon, Montana, and Washington are the only states that allow physicians to prescribe drugs to terminally ill patients so that they can end their lives. Oregon and Washington maintain records concerning the number of deaths attributed to physician-assisted suicide each year. Between 1998 and 2010, 525 Oregonian patients chose to end their lives by taking a prescribed dose of deadly medications.[34]

In 1990, 26-year-old Terri Schiavo's heart failed and the young woman's body entered a persistent vegetative state after a significant number of her brain cells died from the lack of nutrients and oxygen (**Figure** 8). For several years, Terri's parents fought legal battles with her husband over their desire to keep her alive in a long-term care facility by providing nourishment through tube feedings. Terri's husband contended that her life-supporting care should be withdrawn, because before her heart attack, she had indicated to him that she would not want to be kept alive in such a manner if she were incapacitated. By spring of 2005, the parents' legal options were exhausted after courts ruled consistently in Terri's husband's favor. When the comatose woman's feeding tube was removed, the tragic case made headline news in the United States and around the world, rekindling debate over euthanasia. Terri died almost 2 weeks after her feeding tube was withdrawn.

Figure 8

Terri Schiavo. These photographs show Terri before and after a heart attack deprived her brain of oxygen and resulted in a persistent vegetative state.

Content removed due to

copyright restrictions

Preparing for Death

Young adults may see the need to plan for a comfortable retirement, but planning for a good death seems too morbid to consider. A dying person has a good death if he or she maintains a high degree of dignity and experiences little physical and emotional pain during the dying process. Additionally, a good death causes minimal amounts of emotional trauma for the person's survivors.

Not everyone has time to prepare for a good death; death can be premature and unexpected, such as in cases of homicides or fatal accidents. Healthy people, however, can make various legal, financial, emotional, and spiritual preparations for their deaths. Such planning can reduce their survivors' confusion and anxiety.

Advance Directives The Patient Self-Determination Act gives people the right to prepare advance directives that indicate their wishes concerning treatment if they become incapacitated. The act also allows physicians and administrators of certain medical facilities to withhold or remove life-support care from comatose patients who have no hope of regaining consciousness and who would not want to be kept alive in such conditions.

A living will or a durable power of attorney document can specify your wishes concerning your medical care in the event that you become permanently incapacitated. **Figure** 9 shows a sample living will. Not every state honors such documents. For example, your state may exclude the right to have artificial feeding and hydration (water) tubes removed, regardless of your wishes.

Although some states do not sanction living wills, they allow other advance directives such as a durable power of attorney. In this document, you identify a mentally competent individual to serve as a healthcare surrogate or proxy. A healthcare proxy will make decisions concerning your care if you become unable to do so. Additionally, you may indicate which life-

DISTRICT OF COLUMBIA DECLARATION — PAGE 1 OF 2

INSTRUCTIONS

PRINT THE DATE

PRINT YOUR NAME

Declaration made this _____ day of _____.
  (date)   (month, year)

I, _____,
                          (name)

being of sound mind, willfully and voluntarily make known my desires that my dying shall not be artificially prolonged under the circumstances set forth below, do declare:

If at any time I should have an incurable injury, disease or illness certified to be a terminal condition by two physicians who have personally examined me, one of whom shall be my attending physician, and the physicians have determined that my death will occur whether or not life-sustaining procedures are utilized and where the application of life-sustaining procedures would serve only to artificially prolong the dying process, I direct that such procedures be withheld or withdrawn, and that I be permitted to die naturally with only the administration of medication or the performance of any medical procedure deemed necessary to provide me with comfort care or to alleviate pain.

ADD OTHER INSTRUCTIONS, IF ANY, REGARDING YOUR ADVANCE CARE PLANS

THESE INSTRUCTIONS CAN FURTHER ADDRESS YOUR HEALTH CARE PLANS, SUCH AS YOUR WISHES REGARDING HOSPICE TREATMENT, BUT CAN ALSO ADDRESS OTHER ADVANCE PLANNING ISSUES, SUCH AS YOUR BURIAL WISHES

ATTACH ADDITIONAL PAGES IF NEEDED

© 2005 National Hospice and Palliative Care Organization 2011 Revised.

Other directions:

_____
_____
_____
_____
_____
_____
_____
_____
_____
_____
_____

DISTRICT OF COLUMBIA DECLARATION — PAGE 2 OF 2

In the absence of my ability to give directions regarding the use of such life-sustaining procedures, it is my intention that this declaration shall be honored by my family and physician(s) as the final expression of my legal right to refuse medical or surgical treatment and accept the consequences from such refusal.

I understand the full importance of this declaration and I am emotionally and mentally competent to make this declaration.

SIGN AND DATE THE DOCUMENT AND PRINT YOUR ADDRESS

Signed _____ Date_____

Address _____

WITNESSING PROCEDURE

I believe the declarant to be of sound mind. I did not sign the declarant's signature above for or at the direction of the declarant. I am at least eighteen years of age and am not related to the declarant by blood, marriage, or domestic partnership, entitled to any portion of the estate of the declarant according to the laws of intestate succession of the District of Columbia or under any will of the declarant or codicil thereto, or directly financially responsible for declarant's medical care. I am not the declarant's attending physician, an employee of the attending physician, or an employee of the health facility in which the declarant is a patient.

TWO WITNESSES MUST SIGN AND DATE HERE

Witness _____ Date_____

Witness _____ Date_____

© 2005 National Hospice and Palliative Care Organization 2011 Revised.

prolonging medical actions are acceptable or necessary under certain circumstances. The results of surveys indicate that most Americans would want limited care if they became incapacitated. Few Americans, however, have prepared living wills or other advance directives.

Before preparing an advance directive, it is a good idea to discuss your wishes with family and address their concerns. Your physician can probably answer questions that you or your family may have about life-support care. Family members or the person who agrees to serve as your healthcare surrogate and your personal physician will need copies of these documents. It is a good idea to store your copy along with your other important documents in a safety deposit box.

Estate Management In addition to an advance directive, it is important to have a will, a legal document that specifies how you want your property to be distributed after your death. To prepare a formal will, it is a good idea to consult an attorney, preferably one who specializes in estate administration. For the will to be valid, you must be of "sound mind" (aware of your actions) when you write and sign your will, and the document must be signed and witnessed by at least two people.

Most Americans die without having a will. When this happens, probate courts follow state laws concerning the division and distribution of the deceased person's estate. An estate includes the individual's sources of money, such as checking and savings accounts, life insurance policies, and retirement plans. In addition, possessions that can be sold, such as jewelry, real estate, furniture, and collectibles, are part of one's estate. A carefully constructed will can ensure that these assets go to whomever you want, and not to whom the courts choose. Furthermore, a will can eliminate much unhappiness, stress, and confusion among your survivors. If family members feel that provisions stated in your will unfairly distribute the estate, they can contest it in court.

In addition to making a will, it is a good idea to appoint an executor to manage your estate after your death. The executor uses income from the estate to pay your debts and funeral costs. If you have young children, it is important to identify and ask a person who will act as their legal guardian in case they become orphans. Most people choose a guardian who is a close relative or friend to whom they can entrust the care of their children.

In addition to having a will and an executor, you can protect your survivors' assets by having enough health and life insurance to cover your final medical and funeral expenses. The best time to buy life and health insurance is while you are young and healthy.

Organ Donation In dying, people can make a priceless contribution to the living by donating their tissues or organs. Soon after death, a donor's kidneys, liver, skin, heart, and corneas can be removed and transplanted into people whose organs or tissues are failing. Many seriously ill patients who would have died without receiving donated organs are able to live nearly normal lives after having the procedures.

As of May 31, 2011, more than 111,400 people in the United States were on waiting lists to receive organ transplants.[35] Patients are more likely to need kidneys and/or livers than other organs. Unfortunately, the demand for organs is greater than the supply. In 2010, more than 7,100 Americans died while waiting for matching organs to become available for transplantation.[36] Although people may express an interest in having their organs donated when they die, they often do not make their wishes known to others nor do they document them formally. For example, potential donors may fail to inform family members of their decision or sign organ donor cards. In most states, family members can override the deceased person's wishes concerning organ donation.

People can help those who need healthy tissues and organs by completing and signing uniform donor cards like the one shown in **Figure 10**. This card should be kept in a person's wallet. Additionally, people can fill in and sign the organ donor declaration on the back of their driver's license. Additionally, individuals who would like to become organ donors when they die should inform their relatives of their wishes. Although there are no guarantees that

Figure 10

A Uniform Donor Card. By completing and signing a donor card like this one, people can help others who need healthy tissues and organs.
Source: Reprinted with permission from the National Kidney Foundation.

NATIONAL KIDNEY FOUNDATION
Please keep this card in a safe place and inform your family of your wishes to be a donor.

This is to inform you that, should the occasion ever arise, I would like to be an organ and tissue donor. Please see that my wishes are carried out by informing the attending medical personnel that I have indicated my wishes to become a donor. Thank you.

Signature   *Date*

For further information contact:
NATIONAL KIDNEY FOUNDATION
(800) 622-9010 • www.kidney.org

ORGAN AND TISSUE DONOR CARD

Of _____
(print or type name of donor)

In the hope that I may help others, I hereby make this anatomical gift, if medically acceptable, to take effect upon my death. The words and marks below indicate my wishes.

I give: ☐ any needed organs or tissues
☐ only the following organs or tissues

(specify the organ[s], tissue[s])

for the purposes of transplantation, therapy, medical research or education;

☐ my body for anatomical study if needed.

Limitations or special wishes, if any: _____

Signed by the donor and the following two witnesses in the presence of each other:

Signature of Donor   *Date of Birth of Donor*

Date Signed   *City and State*

Witness   *Witness*

This is a legal document under the Anatomical Gift Act or similar laws.

☐ Yes, I have discussed my wishes with my family. For further information consult your physician or

 National Kidney Foundation
30 East 33rd Street, New York, NY 10016

surgeons will be able to transplant a person's tissues after death, it may be reassuring for some people to know that, even after death, they might be able to help others.

Some Final Thoughts on Death

Funeral and memorial services can help friends and family members deal with the loss of a loved one. You can ease some of the emotional and financial burdens of your survivors by planning your funeral arrangements. A funeral can be very costly, and it is often a difficult emotional task for families to make such arrangements when a loved one dies.

Many mortuaries offer prearranged funerals that enable you to specify the kind of funeral you want and the most affordable services. For example, you could choose to have a simple memorial service, your body *cremated* (burned), and your ashes placed in a container and given to your survivors. You can contact mortuaries in your area for more information about making funeral and burial prearrangements.

In addition to making funeral and burial arrangements, you can prepare spiritually for your death.

One spiritual arrangement you can make in preparation for death is to write your own obituary or death notice. Many obituaries include a brief biography. If you prepare these documents, you can give copies of them to your survivors and let them know where to send them. Newspapers, college alumni associations, and professional organizations usually print death notices.

After a beloved person dies, survivors often experience confusion and distress because they cannot locate the deceased person's will and other important documents. To reduce the likelihood that this situation will occur after your death, share copies of these personal papers with your spouse, adult children, the executor, and the individual who has the power of attorney. A safety deposit box is a safe place to store such documents. To help your survivors find these important papers, you can keep a small card in your wallet that lists their location.

Healthy Living Practices

- ☐ If you would like to be an organ donor when you die, complete a uniform donor card or sign the declaration on the back of your driver's license. Inform your relatives of this decision.
- ☐ Preparing a will can help your survivors manage your estate.
- ☐ To convey your wishes concerning treatment in case you become severely disabled and cannot communicate, consider preparing an advance directive.

grief An emotional state that usually occurs after the loss of something or someone special.

mourning The culturally defined way in which survivors resolve the grief surrounding a death.

 Grief

Grief is the emotional state that nearly everyone experiences when they lose something special or someone with whom they enjoyed a close relationship. Losing someone you love is one of the most significant emotional events that can occur during your life. Some of life's losses are predictable, such as the death of beloved grandparents, parents, and spouses. Unexpected or premature losses, such as the death of a child or the sudden death of a spouse, can be emotionally devastating to the surviving parents, spouse, and other family members.

Regardless of the circumstances surrounding a death, resolving the grief that follows the loss of a loved one (*bereavement*) involves regaining emotional balance and stability. **Mourning**, the culturally defined way in which survivors observe bereavement, can be a difficult and lengthy process.

The emotional and physical reactions to the death of a beloved person vary; some people have a more difficult time coping with the loss than others do. People's emotional reactions are usually more severe after unexpected deaths than after anticipated deaths. Typically, the initial responses of survivors are psychological shock, disbelief, and denial. They next enter the acute mourning stage, which is characterized by crying, withdrawal, and other symptoms of depression. In many societies, people in mourning are expected to display their grief, for example, by crying and by wearing somber clothing. After mourning, survivors are often able to accept the death of their loved one, recognize that they have grieved, and regain a sense of emotional balance.

The most intense period of grieving normally lasts about 4 to 6 weeks after the death. It is not uncommon for people to continue mourning for a year or longer after the loss. Some people experience psychological and physical problems if they are unable to resolve their feelings of grief.

Much of the research that examines the impact of grieving on health involves people whose spouses have recently died. Most widowed people experience some signs and symptoms of depression, such

Managing Your Health

After the Death of a Loved One

The "Managing Grief" sections of this box provide some suggestions that may help you cope with the death of a beloved individual. The "Managing Legal, Social, and Financial Concerns" sections provide some actions that you can take to manage various concerns that often arise after the death of a spouse or other beloved person.

Immediate Actions and Concerns

Managing Grief

- Resolve to survive the first few days of the sorrowful event.
- Accept the support and company of clergy, friends, and family.
- Permit yourself to vent your feelings, for example, to cry or to feel anger.

Managing Legal, Social, and Financial Concerns

- Notify your attorney; obtain the deceased person's will and make several photocopies of it.
- Order several copies of the death certificate; the funeral director may do this for you.

Within the First 4 Weeks

Managing Grief

- Acknowledge those who sent food or flowers or who made memorial donations. Consider responding to those who visited or sent cards. This is an emotionally difficult task, but the process may be beneficial in itself.
- Anticipate feelings of grief: the tears, anger, guilt, and blame. Delayed or prolonged absence of grief may lead to negative physical and psychological consequences.
- If troubled by sleeplessness, nightmares, agitation, headaches, and even skin rashes, consult your physician for help to alleviate these conditions.
- Note changes in your appetite.

Managing Legal, Social, and Financial Concerns

- Notify relevant government agencies and other organizations of the death, such as the Social Security Administration, Veterans Administration, and insurance companies.
- Submit insurance claims and apply for refunds and benefits where applicable. Keep records of all response letters from agencies and organizations.
- Notify the deceased person's banks, credit card accounts, custodians of mutual funds and annuities, and accountant of the death.

Within 6 Months

Managing Grief

- Join a grief support group. For information concerning support groups in your area, contact social workers at a local hospital or hospice or your local United Way.
- Adapt to lifestyle changes. You may need to learn how to do unfamiliar chores such as maintaining the house, tracking investments, cooking meals, or paying bills.
- Continue previous activities such as participating in hobbies or clubs if they are satisfying.
- Participate in healthful physical activities such as walking, swimming, or golfing. Join a health spa or similar organization.

Managing Legal, Social, and Financial Concerns

- Share meals with friends and accept the invitations of others to dine out with them.
- Update your will: change beneficiaries, trustees, or executors if necessary.
- Consult your accountant; your tax situation may have changed.

Long-Term

Managing Grief

- Establish your own identity to function independently. Your degree of dependence and attachment to the deceased may determine the time needed for adjustment.
- Establish new relationships; continue existing relationships.
- Consider participating in activities or organizations that help others.

Managing Legal, Social, and Financial Concerns

- Plan for the future. Do not rush into making major changes or decisions.

as sadness, withdrawal, and sleep disorders. With the support of family and friends, however, grieving individuals can often regain their emotional balance within a few months. Survivors may become saddened again over the loss of a spouse, especially on anniversaries, on holidays, and during family reunions. An estimated 10% to 20% of widowed people suffer severe depression that lasts a year or more after their spouses die. The Managing Your Health feature "After the Death of a Loved One" contains some suggestions that can help people endure the first year after the death of a spouse or other beloved individual.

In addition to affecting emotional health, bereavement often influences the physical health of survivors. Most grieving people are emotionally distressed, and such stress often has a negative impact on their immune systems. Individuals who have weakened immune systems are at risk of developing frequent infections and chronic health problems such as cardiovascular disease. Additionally, grieving people may not take good care of themselves; for example, they may not eat nutritious foods or exercise, and some may abuse drugs, including alcohol.

People who undergo an abnormal grieving process may have had a poor relationship with the deceased person. According to Kübler-Ross, grief includes some degree of anger that is directed toward the dead individual. Survivors may hide their anger; others may express it by lashing out at someone else or by grieving for an unusually long period. **Table 5** lists the signs of abnormal grieving. People with these signs may need professional counseling.

Healthy Living Practices

☐ Consider seeking professional counseling if your grief is severe or does not subside over time after the death of a loved one.

Across THE LIFE SPAN

DYING AND DEATH

In the United States, parents often find it difficult to discuss death with their children until someone or something, such as a pet, is dying or has died. Young children have difficulty grasping the concepts of dying and death (**Figure 11**). For example, if a 4-year-old child attends a funeral and views a loved one's body, the youngster may think this person is asleep.

Children as young as 2 years old miss a familiar person who has died, especially if the deceased was a parent. Preschool-aged children, however, do not express grief as older children or adults do. At this age, children typically grieve differently from how adults grieve; they may act unconcerned about the death and become intensely involved in play activities or misbehave.

School-age children are able to understand that dead things do not come back to life, and they respond to the loss much like adults: crying, withdrawing, or being angry. Older children often associate death with being old, particularly if they have experienced the death of a grandparent. Thus, they may have a great deal of difficulty coping when a peer dies.

Adults need to be honest and straightforward when discussing terminal illness and death with children. They should consider the child's ability to understand

Table	5
Grieving Danger Signs	

Professional counseling to handle grief may be necessary if the grieving person:

- Doubts that his or her grieving is normal
- Experiences frequent outbursts of anger
- Finds little or no pleasure in life and has persistent suicidal thoughts
- Is preoccupied with thinking about the deceased loved one, or has hostile or guilty feelings that persist for more than a couple of years
- Experiences significant weight loss, weight gain, or persistent insomnia
- Begins engaging in risky behaviors such as abusing drugs or practicing unsafe sex
- Loses interest in taking care of personal hygiene for more than two weeks

Source: Adapted from Kouri, M. K. (1991). *Keys to dealing with the loss of a loved one.* Hauppauge, NY: Barrons Educational Series.

Figure   11

Children's Responses to End-of-Life Concepts. Young children have difficulty grasping the concepts of dying and death. When faced with the loss of a loved one, preschool children typically grieve differently from how adults grieve.

the meaning of death. Frequently, children begin to understand and accept death when caring people share what is happening with them. Adults need to allow grieving children to express their concerns and feelings about dying and death. Professional counseling may be necessary if the child's responses are excessive, if the young person becomes preoccupied with death, or if the child becomes depressed.

Healthy Living Practices

☐ If your child becomes preoccupied with death or depressed after someone or something has died, professional counseling can help him or her deal with the loss.

CHAPTER REVIEW

go.jblearning.com/alters6e

Summary

Aging is the sum of all changes that occur in an organism over its life span. The human life span is divided into stages. The final stage, senescence, generally refers to the stage of life that begins at 65 years of age.

The overall life expectancy of Americans has increased since 1900. In the United States, a person born in 2009 can expect to live for about 78 years. Life expectancies, however, vary according to age, sex, and socioeconomic status. For example, American females outlive American males by about 5 years.

As of 2009, 13% of the U.S. population was 65 years of age and older. By the year 2030, nearly 20% of Americans will be in this age group. This segment of the American population is increasing at a rapid rate.

Aged people must often live on incomes that are lower than when they were younger. In the United States, older adult members of certain minority groups are more likely to have lower retirement incomes and live in poverty than are white aged persons. With appropriate financial planning, Americans who have adequate incomes when they are young may be able to maintain adequate incomes during their retirement years.

A gradual and irreversible decline in the functioning of the human body begins to occur around 30 years of age. However, people age at different rates. Genetic, environmental, and lifestyle factors influence the rate of aging.

Some of the physical changes associated with the aging process, such as gray hair, presbyopia, and menopause, are normal and inevitable. Other age-related physical changes such as heart disease, cancer, and osteoporosis are not normal and are signs of disease processes. People who modify their lifestyles while they are young may be able to prevent or delay such conditions.

According to Kübler-Ross, the typical emotional responses to dying include denial, anger, bargaining, depression, and acceptance. However, death can be the final stage of personal fulfillment if dying people have opportunities to satisfy their social and emotional needs. Family, friends, and medical care providers can help terminally ill individuals live better while dying by taking steps to enhance their dignity and self-worth.

Death occurs when the heart or lungs cease functioning and cells in the brain do not receive oxygen. The criteria for brain death include no brain waves, no spontaneous muscular movements, no reflexes, and no responses to the environment. A brain-dead person can exist in a persistent coma for years as long as the heart is functioning, nutritional needs are met, and the supply of oxygen to the heart is maintained by the use of a respirator. Euthanasia is the practice of allowing a permanently comatose or an incurably ill person to die.

The Patient Self-Determination Act gives people the right to prepare advance directives, documents that indicate a person's wishes concerning life-support measures if the individual becomes incapable of making such decisions.

Nearly everyone experiences grief with the loss of something special or someone with whom he or she enjoyed a close relationship. Although it is normal to grieve after such a loss, grief can have negative effects on health. To resolve grief, a person accepts the death of a loved one, recognizes that he or she has grieved for this person, and regains a sense of emotional balance. An individual who grieves for a prolonged period may require professional counseling.

Preschool children do not understand the concept of death, yet they still experience distress over the missing loved one. At this age, children may mourn by acting disinterested about the death or by misbehaving. Older children often grieve like adults by crying, withdrawing, and being angry. Grieving youngsters need to express their concerns and feelings about death. Like adults, children may need professional counseling if their emotional responses to death are severe or prolonged.

go.jblearning.com/alters6e

Applying What You Have Learned

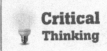

Critical Thinking

1. Develop a will that reflects your wishes concerning the distribution of your assets after death. **Application**
2. Analyze how your present lifestyle may affect your life span. **Analysis**
3. Propose a special program that would prevent ageism by promoting understanding and cooperation between young and old members of your community. **Synthesis**
4. Choose a position concerning the issue of euthanasia. How would you defend your position? **Evaluation**

Key

| **Application**
using information in a new situation. | **Analysis**
breaking down information into component parts. | **Synthesis**
putting together information from different sources. | **Evaluation**
making informed decisions. |

Reflecting on Your Health

Critical Thinking

1. How do you feel about growing old? Are you undergoing the age-related changes that Table 1 describes? Which age-related changes trouble you the most? Are you making any lifestyle changes that will increase your chances of living a long and healthy life? If you answered yes to the previous question, what changes are you making, and how do you think they will affect your longevity?
2. If you suffered severe brain damage in an accident, would you want to be maintained in a persistent vegetative state? Why or why not? If so, for how long would you want to be kept alive? Why?
3. Do you intend to donate your organs if you die in an accident? Why or why not? Have you signed an organ donor card or the back of your driver's license, enabling survivors to donate your organs when you die? If you have not signed an organ donor card on the back of your license, explain why.
4. Have you ever known someone who knew he or she was dying? If so, describe any stages of Kübler-Ross's emotional responses to dying that you observed in that person.
5. If someone you loved has died, how did the grieving process affect your psychological, social, and spiritual health? What did you do to overcome the grief?

References

1. Volz, M. (2011). World's oldest man dies in Montana at 114. *Associated Press*. Retrieved on May 29, 2011, from http://www.foxnews.com/us/2011/04/14/worlds-oldest-man-dies-age-114/
2. Colton, A. (2011, April). Survival skills: World's oldest man. *Men's Journal*, p. 126.
3. Flachsbart, F., et al. (2009). Association with FOXO3A variation with human longevity confirmed in German centenarians. *Proceedings of the National Academy of Sciences, 106*(8):2700–2705.
4. U.S. Census Bureau. (2011, March). Older Americans Month: May 2011. Retrieved on May 29, 2011, from http://www.census.gov/

newsroom/releases/archives/facts_for_features_special_editions/cb11-ff08.html

5. U.S. Census Bureau. (n.d.). *U.S. population projections.* Retrieved on May 29, 2011, from http://www.census.gov/population/www/projections/summarytables.html

6. Kahana, E., et al. (2002). Long-term impact of preventive proactivity on quality of life of the old-old. *Psychosomatic Medicine,* 64(3):382–394.

7. Kochanek, K. D., et al. (2011). Deaths: Preliminary data for 2009. *National Vital Statistics Reports,* 59(4):1–68. Retrieved on May 29, 2011, from http://www.cdc.gov/nchs/data/nvsr/nvsr59/nvsr59_04.pdf

8. U.S. Department of Health and Human Services. (1991). *Healthy People 2000: National health promotion and disease prevention objectives.* Washington, DC: U.S. Government Printing Office.

9. Centers for Disease Control and Prevention. (2010, December). Life expectancy free of chronic condition-induced activity limitations among white and black Americans, 2000–2006. *Vital and Health Statistics, 3*(34). Retrieved on May 29, 2011, from http://www.cdc.gov/nchs/data/series/sr_03/sr03_034.pdf

10. Department of Health and Human Services, Administration on Aging. (2011, February). A profile of older Americans: 2010. Retrieved on May 29, 2011, from http://www.aoa.gov/aoaroot/aging_statistics/Profile/2010/docs/2010profile.pdf

11. U.S. National Library of Medicine, National Eye Institute. (2011, May). Facts about age-related macular degeneration. Retrieved on May 29, 2011, from http://www.nei.nih.gov/health/maculardegen/armd_facts.asp

12. Centers for Disease Control and Prevention, Chronic Disease Prevention and Health Promotion. (2011, February). Arthritis: Meeting the challenge. *At a Glance* Retrieved on May 29, 2011, from http://www.cdc.gov/chronicdisease/resources/publications/aag/pdf/2011/Arthritis-AAG-2011-508.pdf

13. Alzheimer's Association. (2011, May 18). What is Alzheimer's? Retrieved on May 29, 2011, from http://www.alz.org/alzheimers_disease_what_is_alzheimers.asp#basics

14. Alzheimer's Association. (2011). 2011 Alzheimer's disease facts and figures. *Alzheimer's and Dementia, 7*(2):208–244. Retrieved on May 29, 2011, from http://www.alzheimersanddementia.com/article/PIIS1552526011000367/fulltext

15. National Institute on Aging. (2011, January). Looking for the causes of AD. Retrieved on May 30, 2011, from http://www.nia.nih.gov/Alzheimers/Publications/Unraveling/Part3/causes.htm

16. Gu, Y., et al. (2010). Food combination and Alzheimer's disease risk: A protective diet. *Archives of Neurology, 67*(6):699–706.

17. McGuinness, B., & Passmore, P. (2010). Can statins prevent or help treat Alzheimer's disease? *Journal of Alzheimer's Disease, 20*(3):925–933.

18. Ligthart, S. A., et al. (2010). Treatment of cardiovascular risk factors to prevent cognitive decline and dementia: A systematic review. *Vascular Health and Risk Management, 6*:775–785.

19. Lau, F. C., et al. (2007). Nutritional intervention in brain aging: Reducing the effects of inflammation and oxidative stress. *Subcellular Biochemistry, 42*:299–318.

20. Frank, B., & Gupta, S. (2005). A review of antioxidants and Alzheimer's disease. *Annals of Clinical Psychiatry, 17*(4):269–286.

21. Cole, G. M., et al. (2007). Neuroprotective effects of curcumin. *Advances in Experimental Medicine and Biology, 595*:197–212.

22. Evans, J. G., et al. (2004). Evidence-based pharmacotherapy of Alzheimer's disease. *International Journal of Neuropsychopharmacology, 7*(3):351–369.

23. Burns, A., et al. (2006). Clinical practice with anti-dementia drugs: A consensus statement from British Association for Psychopharmacology. *Journal of Psychopharmacology, 20*(6):732–755.

24. Dwyer, J., & Donoghue, M. D. (2010). Is risk of Alzheimer disease a reason to use dietary supplements? *American Journal of Clinical Nutrition, 91*(5):1155–1156.

25. Morris, M. C., et al. (2005). Relation of the tocopherol forms to incident Alzheimer disease and to cognitive change. *American Journal of Clinical Nutrition, 81*(2):508–514.

26. Centers for Disease Control and Prevention. (2009, September). National suicide statistics at a glance: Trends in suicide rates among both sexes, by age group, United States, 1991–2006. Retrieved on May 30, 2011, from http://www.cdc.gov/violenceprevention/suicide/statistics/trends02.html

27. Podgorski, C. A., et al. (2010). Suicide prevention for older adults in residential communities: Implications for policy and practice. *PLoS Medicine, 7*(5):e10000254.

28. Juurlink, D. N., et al. (2004). Medical illness and the risk of suicide in the elderly. *Archives of Internal Medicine, 164*(11):1179–1184.

29. Jeste, D. V., et al. (2010). Successful cognitive and emotional aging. *World Psychiatry, 9*(2):78–84.

30. Perls, T. T. (2010). Antiaging medicine: What should we tell our patients? *Aging Health, 6*(2):149–154.

31. Warburton, D. E., et al. (2006). Health benefits of physical activity: The evidence. *Canadian Medical Association Journal, 174*(6):801–809.

32. Larson, E. B., et al. (2006). Exercise is associated with reduced risk for incident dementia among persons 65 years of age and older. *Annals of Internal Medicine, 144*(2):73–81.

33. Kübler-Ross, E. (1969). *On death and dying.* New York: Macmillan.

34. Oregon Department of Human Services. (2011). *Death with Dignity Act annual reports.* 2010 Summary. Retrieved on May 28, 2011, from http://public.health.oregon.gov/ProviderPartnerResources/EvaluationResearch/DeathwithDignityAct/Documents/year13.pdf

35. United Network for Organ Sharing. (2011, May 31). Data: Waiting list candidates. Retrieved on May 31, 2011, from http://www.unos.org

36. U.S. Department of Health and Human Services, Health Resources and Services Administration, Organ Procurement and Transplant Network. (2011). Death removals by region by year. Retrieved on May 31, 2011, from http://optn.transplant.hrsa.gov/latestData/viewDataReports.asp

Photo Credits

Special Features

Diversity in Health © Mike Flippo/ShutterStock, Inc.; Managing Your Health © Kzenon/ShutterStock, Inc.; Consumer Health © sevenke/ShutterStock, Inc.; Healthy Living Practices © djgis /ShutterStock, Inc.; Across the Life Span © Galina Barskaya /ShutterStock, Inc.

Opener © Larry Beckner/Great Falls Tribune/AP Photos; 1 © Launette/AP Photos; © Martin Puddy/age fotostock; © STILLFX/ShutterStock, Inc.; 4 © Dr. Ken Greet/Visuals Unlimited; © Hamera Technologies/PhotoObjects.net/Thinkstock; © Mel Curtis/Photodisc/Getty Images; © LiquidLibrary; 6 © mauritius images/age fotostock; 7 Courtesy of Library of Congress, Prints and Photographs Division. [Reproduction number LC-DIG-ppmsca-11042]; © Monkey Business Images/Dreamstime.com; 8 © Schindler Family Photo /AP Photos; © David Kay/ShutterStock Inc.; 11 © Cheryl Casey/ShutterStock, Inc.

Closing the Gap: Strategies for Eliminating Health Disparities

The future health of the nation will be determined to a large extent by how effectively we work with communities to reduce and eliminate health disparities between non-minority and minority populations experiencing disproportionate burdens of disease, disability, and premature death.

—Guiding principle for improving minority health
(Office of Minority Health & Health Disparities, 2007)

KEY CONCEPTS _____

- Best practices
- Telemedicine

- Cultural Competence

CHAPTER OBJECTIVES _____

1. List the six priority areas for eliminating health disparities.
2. Describe at least six strategies for reducing or eliminating health disparities.

Throughout this book, we have discussed the fact that the health disparities in the United States are extensive as demonstrated by the differences in the incidence and consequences of diseases and mortality rates. The causes of health disparities are complex, systemic, personal, integrated, and multifactorial, and there are no easy and immediate solutions to reduce or eliminate them. The complexity of the problem should not deter our efforts to work on reducing, and eventually eliminating, these differences in health, because these disparities have a negative impact on the people of our nation and are viewed as morally wrong by many. The problem will continue to be magnified because the changing demographics that are anticipated over the next decade will amplify the problem; hence the importance of addressing disparities in health. Groups who are currently experiencing poorer health status are expected to grow as a proportion of the total U.S. population;

therefore, the future health of America as a whole will be influenced substantially by our success in improving the health of these groups. A national focus on disparities in health status is particularly important as major changes unfold in the way in which health care is delivered and financed (Office of Minority Health & Health Disparities, 2007).

The government has highlighted the need to reduce health disparities, and this focus is reflected in the *Healthy People 2010* objectives. *Healthy People 2010* is designed to achieve two overarching goals: (1) increase quality and years of healthy life; and (2) eliminate health disparities. The second goal of *Healthy People 2010*, to eliminate health disparities, includes differences that occur by gender, race, ethnicity, education, income, disability, geographic location, or sexual orientation. Compelling evidence indicates that race and ethnicity correlate with persistent, and often increasing, health disparities among U.S. populations in all these categories and demands national attention (Office of Minority Health & Health Disparities, 2007).

The U.S. Department of Health and Human Services (HHS) has selected six focus areas in which racial and ethnic minorities experience serious disparities in health access and outcomes:

1. Infant mortality
2. Cancer screening and management
3. Cardiovascular disease
4. Diabetes
5. HIV infection and AIDS
6. Immunizations

These six health areas were selected for emphasis because they reflect areas of disparity that are known to affect multiple racial and ethnic minority groups at all life stages (Office of Minority Health & Health Disparities, 2007). Many other federal agencies and states have developed strategic plans to eliminate health disparities. These plans can be useful to organizations when they are developing their own objectives and interventions.

Eliminating health disparities will require enhanced efforts and changes in research, improving the environments of people who are affected by health disparities, increasing access to health care, improving the quality of care, and making policy and legal changes. These five areas are the spokes of the overarching goal of this chapter, which is to provide information about strategies for reducing health disparities.

STRATEGIES FOR REDUCING OR ELIMINATING HEALTH DISPARITIES ____

A variety of approaches are needed to reduce health disparities. This task requires a systematic, coordinated, and collaborative effort to effectively implement the strategies. The methods necessitate implementation at different ecological levels with community, local, state, and national organizations and politicians at the helm.

Research

Eliminating health disparities will require new knowledge about the determinants of disease, causes of health disparities, effective interventions for prevention and treatment, and innovative ways of working in partnership with health care systems. The advances in knowledge about topics such as genetics and best practices need to be put into action and applied to the health care industry and not just lie in the pages of professional journals.

Best practices (also known as promising practices) of disparity reduction initiatives and programs are being identified and shared. This needs to continue and be magnified. We recommend that government organizations and researchers work to document and publicize those programs and policy changes that have been proven to be effective, but it is just as important to identify programs that do not work! Most of what is published in journals and on Web sites illustrates the successes, but the unsuccessful programs and policies add to the knowledge as well. Knowing what does not work eliminates health care professionals from channeling valuable resources to interventions that have already been shown to not produce positive effects.

There also is a need for data on specific populations. A majority of the data report on broad categories of race and ethnicities, such as Asians and American Indians. In addition, much of the research combines groups, such as Asians with Pacific Islanders and American Indians with Alaska Natives. There is great diversity within these groups, so more specific data is needed to help identify the health problems within the subpopulations and successful strategies for reducing them. Researchers and government agencies are encouraged to collect and report on data for racial and ethnic subgroups instead of the current commonly used broad categories.

In the United States, socioeconomic status has traditionally been measured by education and income. Surveys also should capture information about a range of contextual variables that have been found to be explanatory in health differences, such as social support, social networks, family supports, levels of acculturation, social cohesion, community involvement, perceived financial burdens, discrimination, and differences in the health status of foreign-born versus U.S.-born individuals, which at times also are linked to socioeconomic status.

Improving the Environments of People Affected by Health Disparities

There is little doubt that neighborhood characteristics are an important association with health. Residents of socially and economically deprived communities experience worse health outcomes on average than those living in more prosperous neighborhoods. This is because neighborhoods may influence health through relatively short-term influences on behaviors, attitudes, and health care utilization, thereby affecting health conditions that are more immediate. Neighborhoods also can impact health on a long-term basis through "weathering," whereby the accumulated stress, lower environmental quality, and limited resources of poorer communities experienced over many years negatively impacts the health of residents.

Minorities are more likely to live in poor neighborhoods. These neighborhoods often have poor-performing schools, crime, substandard housing, few health care providers and pharmacies, more alcohol and tobacco advertising, and limited access to grocery stores with healthy food choices. These social determinants of health can accumulate over the course of a life and can be detrimental to physical and emotional health.

Policies have historically led to racial segregation through regulations such as legal restrictions on which racial and ethnic groups may purchase property in certain geographic regions. Policies continue to have an impact on minorities, such as decisions related to regions with a high number of minorities often being targeted for placement of waste sites, for example. Policies are needed to reduce or eliminate environmental inequalities. An example of such a policy is that, in 2004, Senator Hillary Rodham Clinton (D-NY) and Congresswoman Hilda L. Solis (D-CA) announced the introduction of the Environmental Justice Renewal Act. The legislation championed by Senator Clinton and Congresswoman Solis was designed to increase the federal government's efforts in addressing the disproportionate impact of environmental pollution upon racial and ethnic minority and low-income populations. The purpose of the act was to expand existing grant programs and create new grant opportunities to help community-based groups and states address environmental justice, require the U.S. Environmental Protection Agency (EPA) to engage in additional outreach at the community level, and create the position of Environmental Justice Ombudsman to investigate the agency's handling of environmental justice complaints. It also was designed to increase accountability by requiring routine, independent evaluation of the government's actions to reduce and eliminate the disparate impact of environmental pollution upon minority and low-income communities.

Increasing Access to Health Care

More than half of the uninsured people in the United States are racial and ethnic minorities (McDonough, et al., 2004). Our nation needs to make coverage more accessible and equitable. Accessibility is not just related to financial barriers, because there are people who can afford coverage but are denied based on their medical history. Is universal health care coverage the answer? That is a major debate that we will not wrestle with here, but some consider it to be a possible solution.

Access to care also is related to having health care providers within your geographic region. There are imbalances in how the health care workforce is distributed, and this leads to lower access to care in some geographic regions of the United States. Poor neighborhoods tend to have a lower person-to-health care provider ratio than more affluent regions. **Telemedicine**, which offers incentives and competitive salaries to providers who work with low-income regions, and training community members as peer educators and outreach workers are all possible solutions to be explored.

Improving Quality of Care

Improving quality of care is related to training of health care providers, providing equal care, reducing language barriers, and increasing diversity in the workforce. Each of these four areas is discussed in the following paragraphs.

With regard to training health care providers, fostering a culturally-competent health care system that reflects and serves the diversity of America must be a priority for health care reform. States and academic centers that train health care professionals can develop, and some already have, requirements for training in this area. This can assist with providing equal treatment.

The groundbreaking report *Unequal Treatment: Confronting Racial and Ethnic Disparities in Health Care*, released in 2002 by the National Academies' Institute of Medicine (IOM), showed that racial and ethnic minorities receive lower-quality health care than Caucasians, even when insurance status, income, age, and severity of conditions are comparable. The report's first recommendation for reducing these disparities is to increase awareness of the issue among the public, health care providers, insurance companies, and policy makers. It also recommended the standardized collection of data on health care access and utilization by patients' race, ethnicity, socioeconomic status, and, where possible, primary language.

Language barriers can lead to numerous problems, such as damage to the patient and provider relationship, miscommunication with regard to the health problem and treatment approach, medication and correct-dosage mistakes, and legal problems. Health care has a language of its own and can make communication with people with limited English proficiency (LEP) skills even more difficult. Barriers can be reduced by multilingual signage, providing interpretive services, making record of a patient's native language and communication needs, and having documents (i.e., consent forms and educational materials) available in languages that reflect the demographics of the region served.

Diversity in the workforce is another goal. The health care workforce is under-represented by people who are nonwhite, yet people of color are more likely than white physicians to practice in federally-designated underserved areas, to see patients of color, and to accept Medicaid patients. As stated in a Commonwealth Fund report (McDonough, et al., 2004), racial concordance of patient and provider leads to greater participation in care and greater adherence to treatment.

Policy Changes and Laws

Policies and laws that mandate cultural competency training for medical professionals have been shown to be effective. A few of these laws are discussed here.

In 2005, New Jersey became the first state to enact a law, Senate Bill (SB) 144, to address the issue of equity in health care and cultural competency training of physicians. The law requires medical professionals to receive cultural competency training to receive a diploma from medical schools located in the state or to get licensed or relicensed to practice in the state. Each medical school in New Jersey is required to provide this training.

California has taken several steps to ensure cultural competency across the state's health care infrastructure. In 2005, Assembly Bill 1195 required mandatory continuing medical education courses to include cultural and linguistic courses. In the previous session, SB 853 was enacted, which requires commercial health plans to ensure members' access to linguistic services and to report to state regulators steps being taken to improve the cultural competency of their services. Similarly, the state's Medicaid program, Medi-Cal, requires all health plans providing services for Medicaid patients to ensure their linguistic needs are met, including 24-hour access to interpretive services and documents in native languages.

The state of Washington enacted SB 6194 in 2006, which requires all medical education curricula in the state to include multicultural health training and awareness courses. All of these laws strive to establish cultural competence among health care professionals.

CULTURAL COMPETENCE

There is no universally-accepted definition of cultural competency in health care. In general, **cultural competence** is a set of congruent behaviors, attitudes, structures, and policies that come together to work effectively in intercultural situations (National CASA Association, 1995–1996). That set of behaviors can be adopted and practiced by a solitary professional or an entire organization. Cultural competence requires a set of skills by individuals and systems that allows an increased understanding and appreciation of cultural differences as well as the demonstrated skills necessary to work with and serve diverse individuals and groups.

According to the National CASA Association (1995–1996), the culturally competent organization:

- values diversity
- conducts cultural self-assessments
- is conscious of and manages the dynamics of difference
- institutionalizes cultural knowledge
- adapts services to fit the cultural diversity of the community served

Cultural competency entails the willingness and ability of individuals and a system to value the importance of culture in the delivery of services to all segments of the population at all levels of an organization. It includes activities such as policy development and implementation, governance, education, promoting workforce diversity, and the reduction of language barriers.

Becoming culturally competent is an ongoing process. It requires a dedication to growing with a changing society that is becoming more diverse and to serving the individuals and communities with the most culturally appropriate, and hence highest quality care possible.

Improving cultural competency levels should begin with an assessment to determine where an individual and/or organization can improve. It can assist with directing training and education for the workforce, policy development, and other systematic changes. We included an individual and an organizational cultural competency assessment tool in Chapter 2.

CHAPTER SUMMARY

To achieve quality and affordable health care for all, health care reform must include concrete steps to reduce health disparities. Ensuring access to coverage is only part of the answer. Other strategies include reducing barriers to quality health care for people of color by requiring cultural competency training of medical professionals, recruiting a diverse workforce, eliminating language barriers, coordinating public and private programs that target disparities, providing more funding to community health centers, and improving chronic disease management programs by making them more responsive to minorities. Health disparities reflect and perpetuate the inequity and injustice that permeates American society. Eliminating health disparities will help create equal opportunity for all Americans in all sectors of our society.

In this chapter, we discussed a variety of methods for reducing health disparities. These include strategies such as diversifying the health care workforce, changing policies, training health care professionals in the area of cultural competency, and conducting additional research. These changes can help reduce the gap in health among Americans, and this needs to continue to be a priority for our nation, particularly in light of the changing demographics of the United States.

We hope that you have achieved a higher level of cultural competency as you complete the final chapter of this textbook. As we have mentioned, cultural competency is a process, and you still have a lot to learn. You will never learn all there is to know about the numerous cultures, but what is important is that you are aware of the major differences, challenge your assumptions, respect and embrace values and beliefs that are different from your own, and provide the same high standards of care to all humans, regardless of race, ethnicity, gender, sexual preference, or other attribute. We hope that you will go beyond this by advocating for equality and striving to improve health care systems to help close the gaps in the levels of health that exist among certain groups. We leave you with this quote:

Cultural differences should not separate us from each other, but rather cultural diversity brings a collective strength that can benefit all of humanity.

—Robert Alan

REVIEW

1. List the six priority areas for eliminating health disparities.
2. Describe strategies to reduce or eliminate health disparities.
3. Describe what cultural competency is and why it is important.

Confronting Disparities While
Reforming Health Care
A Look at Massachusetts

Health Reform in the States

As health care costs and the number of uninsured rise steadily throughout the nation, the lack of a federal solution to this growing crisis has prompted more and more states to take matters into their own hands. Innovative health reform plans have been popping up across the country, from Maine to California. These reform efforts present a unique opportunity to harness the growing political momentum to fix our health care system and to bring attention to the persistent racial and ethnic disparities that plague the system.

It is a common misconception that efforts to provide universal health care will automatically translate into equitable, quality health coverage for all. This is simply not the case: Access alone will not eliminate health disparities.[1] The issue of health disparities must be specifically addressed within health care reform efforts so that inequities can be eliminated.[2]

In 2006, Massachusetts made national headlines when it passed health reform legislation that extended coverage to nearly all Bay Staters. Health advocates from across the country have looked to Massachusetts as an example of how to successfully enact bold health policy reform. However, Massachusetts can serve as a model for more than its work to expand coverage—recent experience there can also provide guidance in how to address health disparities in the context of health reform.

Massachusetts: A Unique Health Policy History

Massachusetts has a long history of progressive health reform, which has served as a necessary foundation for its most recent expansion.[3] In 1985, the state legislature created the Uncompensated Care Pool, which reimburses hospitals and community health centers (CHCs) that provide free care to eligible low-income uninsured people. That same year, the legislature also established a special commission charged with developing a plan for achieving universal health coverage in Massachusetts. A bill based on the commission's plan was signed into law in 1988, and parts of this legislation are still in place today, including programs that provide coverage for children, pregnant women, uninsured workers, adults with disabilities, and college students.

In 1996, the state undertook a massive reform that reinvented its Medicaid program and created MassHealth, which extended Medicaid coverage to an additional 300,000 residents. That legislation also included expanded coverage for children, limits on the amount of out-of-pocket money seniors were required to pay for prescriptions, as well as assistance for low-wage workers purchasing health insurance.

In 2004, health care advocates in Massachusetts once again saw the opportunity to move forward with new health reforms. Health Care for All (HCFA), a prominent health policy organization in the state, led a diverse coalition of stakeholders in drafting legislation that would expand health coverage to virtually all state residents. The coalition was made up of consumers, patients, community and religious organizations, businesses, labor unions, doctors, hospitals, health plans, and community health centers. It came to be known as the Affordable Care Today (ACT!) Coalition.

ACT! was largely responsible for the passage of the most recent health care reform legislation, commonly known as Chapter 58. Passed in 2006, Chapter 58 was designed to expand health coverage to nearly all Massachusetts residents through several mechanisms, including the creation of the Commonwealth Health Insurance Connector (a program designed to help individuals and small employers purchase affordable insurance more easily), a modest expansion of MassHealth, and an individual mandate.

Racial and Ethnic Health Disparities in Massachusetts

As all of this work to expand health coverage was taking place, momentum was also building around the effort to eliminate health disparities. Soon after the landmark Institute of Medicine report, *Unequal Treatment: Confronting Racial and Ethnic Health Disparities in Health Care*, was released in 2002, Boston Mayor Thomas Menino called for city hospitals and community clinics to develop concrete strategies to reduce racial and ethnic health disparities. Menino later established the Mayor's Task Force to Eliminate Racial and Ethnic Disparities and charged it with developing a set of standards and recommendations to help eliminate health disparities in Boston.

In 2005, Menino declared health disparities to be the city's most pressing health care issue and, drawing on recommendations from the task force, launched The Disparities Project to combat health disparities.[4] The Boston Public Health Commission took the lead and created a "blueprint" that laid out 12 sweeping recommendations designed to eliminate disparities in Boston. Mayor Menino raised more than $1 million to fund implementation of the blueprint recommendations through contracts with local groups that were already working to eliminate racial and ethnic health disparities.[5]

The effort to eliminate disparities was not limited to Boston. At the state level, a Special Legislative Commission on Racial and Ethnic Health Disparities was investigating health disparities and developing recommendations and an action plan for addressing such disparities statewide. HCFA played a leadership role in writing this commission into state statute.

The key political support of Mayor Menino and the array of disparities reduction campaigns helped move health disparities into the public eye. Suddenly, people who had never heard of health disparities were opening *The Boston Globe* to find stories on The Disparities Project. The strong support of the health research community also helped to make health disparities a serious legislative issue. The general public and, perhaps more importantly, state legislators, were hearing about health disparities around the same time that they were hearing about broader health reform efforts. This timing created a political climate that was favorable to the inclusion of provisions that addressed racial and ethnic health disparities in the new health reform legislation.

In addition to Mayor Menino, Governor Deval Patrick, who took office in 2007, has shown a real commitment to eliminating health disparities. Not only did he speak at the state's first ever disparities advocacy event [see page 367], leading officials in his administration have also pledged to work with disparities advocates around developing the state's health disparities agenda.

Chapter 58 Legislation and Health Disparities

The Chapter 58 legislation contains four provisions that address racial and ethnic health disparities:[6]

1. **Section 160** calls for the creation of an ongoing **Health Disparities Council** that is charged with developing recommendations on several minority health issues, including workforce diversity, disparate disease rates among communities of color, and social determinants of health.
2. **Section 16 L. (a)** calls for the creation of a **Health Care Quality and Cost Council**, which will focus on health care quality issues with the goals of lowering costs, improving health care quality, and reducing disparities.
3. **Section 13B** develops standards for **Hospital Performance and Rate Increases**, with a specific stipulation regarding hospital rate increases being based on quality issues such as reducing racial and ethnic health disparities.
4. **Section 110** requires a **Community Health Worker Study** to be conducted by the Public Health Department to determine the effectiveness of community health workers in reducing racial and ethnic health disparities.

The Health Disparities Council mandated by Section 160 convened its first meeting in December 2007. The council established several broad initial goals, such as implementing the recommendations of the State Commission to End Racial and Ethnic Health Disparities, as well as ensuring that implementation of Chapter 58 included a consideration of the unique needs of communities of color. More specifically, the council discussed how to integrate the disparities agenda into larger efforts around improvements in health care quality via the Health Care Quality and Cost Council, which was also established by Chapter 58.

Including these provisions in Chapter 58 was an important and necessary step in beginning to tackle health disparities. However, disparities advocates in Massachusetts recognized that reducing disparities would require more than these provisions: Although these measures created a solid foundation, many advocates working on minority health issues felt it was necessary to build more substantive policy on this foundation.

Expanding Health Disparities Legislation

To build on the disparities provisions in Chapter 58, and to more thoroughly address the host of issues that affect health disparities, a coalition came together to file omnibus legislation whose sole focus was reducing racial and ethnic health disparities. HCFA once again took the lead in bringing the project together, and it was joined by a wide range of individuals, organizations, and institutions, ranging from the Boston Public Health Commission to the local chapter of the Service Employees International Union (SEIU). Others involved in the process included legal associations, research organizations, community health organizations, large health care providers, health policy organizations, as well as multi-issue organizations concerned with equity and justice in health policy. Together, they formed the Disparities Action Network (DAN).[7,8]

The DAN formally convened for the first time in June 2006 with the goal of drafting omnibus disparities legislation for the 2007–2008 state legislative session. Its work was based partly on recommendations put forth by the Special Legislative Commission on Racial and Ethnic Health Disparities. From there, the group determined what it thought was missing from Chapter 58, drawing upon the collective knowledge of its diverse membership to come up with real policy solutions.

The DAN wrote its legislation using a collaborative work group process, meeting several times throughout the summer and fall of 2006 to write and review the legislation before it was filed. First, the coalition held a brainstorming session to determine what should be included in the legislation, which yielded an exhaustive list of policy recommendations and ideas. The final legislation grew from one key premise, which was the need to create a Health Equity Office. The members of the DAN believed

MEMBERS OF THE DISPARITIES ACTION NETWORK (DAN)[9]

- Action for Boston Community Development
- AIDS Action Committee
- Alliance for Community Health
- American Cancer Society
- American Diabetes Association
- American Heart/American Stroke Association
- American Red Cross of Massachusetts Bay
- Association of Haitian Pastors
- Association of Haitian Women
- Berkshire Area Health Education Center
- Boston Center for Community & Justice
- Boston Medical Center Haitian Health Institute
- Boston Public Health Commission
- Boston University Center for Excellence in Women's Health
- Boston Urban Asthma Coalition
- Cambridge Health Alliance
- Caring Health Center
- Center for Community Health Education Research and Service
- Community Catalyst
- Community Change Inc.
- Conference on Boston Teaching Hospitals
- Critical MASS
- Diabetes Association Inc.
- Greater Lawrence Family Health Center
- Haitian Multi-Service Center
- Haitian Nurses Association
- Health Care for All
- International Medical Interpreters Association
- Jewish Alliance for Law and Social Action
- La Alianza Hispana

- Latin American Health Institute
- The Lawyers' Committee for Civil Rights under Law of the Boston Bar Association
- Lowell Community Health Center
- Lynn Health Task Force
- Mass CONECT, Harvard School of Public Health
- Massachusetts Asian and Pacific Islanders for Health
- Massachusetts Association of Community Health Workers
- Massachusetts Breast Cancer Coalition
- Massachusetts General Hospital, Disparities Solutions Center
- Massachusetts Hospital Association
- Massachusetts League of Community Health Centers
- Massachusetts Medical Society
- Massachusetts Public Health Association
- Medical-Legal Partnership for Children
- Multicultural AIDS Coalition
- NAACP Boston
- NARAL Pro-Choice Massachusetts
- ¿Oíste?
- Oral Health Advocacy Task Force
- Physicians for Human Rights
- Planned Parenthood League of Massachusetts
- Project RIGHT
- SEIU 1199
- Tobacco Free Massachusetts
- Vietnamese American Civic Association
- Whittier Street Health Center
- YMCA of Greater Worcester, Central Community Branch
- Youth and Family Enrichment Services

that the abundance of projects, programs, and other efforts to eliminate racial and ethnic health disparities in Massachusetts could be greatly strengthened if they were not so fragmented. A Health Equity Office could serve as a coordinating body for all of the disparities work within the state. Under the guidance of such an office, disparities could be addressed in a systematic, cohesive approach through strategic planning and coordination of efforts on multiple fronts.

These efforts include programs that address both disparities in health and disparities in health care. More specifically, these programs involve developing standards based on best practices from across the state. These standards focus on health literacy, healthy communities initiatives that address environmental and social determinants of health, and workforce diversity (through coordination of existing labor standards). Other programs include support for medical interpreter services, community health workers, wellness education, community-based participatory research, and coordination of racial and ethnic data collection projects across public and private agencies.[10]

The legislation, entitled *An Act Eliminating Racial and Ethnic Health Disparities in the Commonwealth* (H. 2234), was introduced in the Massachusetts legislature on January 9, 2007, by Representative Byron Rushing. In anticipation of the bill's hearing, the DAN formed several committees to build momentum around ending health disparities. This included a grassroots advocacy committee to help bring a community voice to the policy process and to reach out to communities to help them understand more about disparities and why passing this legislation is important. The network also formed lobbying and communications workgroups to educate members of the Joint Committee on Public Health both about the bill and about health disparities in general, as well as to gain more publicity in local media to broadly publicize information on disparities and the DAN legislation.[11]

The bill was heard on May 16, 2007, and it remains in the Public Health Committee. A panel comprised of health care and disparities experts, community members, and the legislative leads for the bill used their testimony as an opportunity to further educate legislators about the importance of addressing health disparities within health reform efforts.

Since that hearing, the DAN has submitted one redraft of the legislation, which made the following minor changes per the recommendation of the committee chair: the grant programs have been consolidated and made less prescriptive by the language; all grant programs have been clearly designated as subject to appropriation; and the Environmental Justice provision has been shortened and simplified.

The redrafted bill was submitted in late November 2007, and it remains in committee. In the meantime, in November 2007, the Patrick administration announced that it would distribute $1 million in grants to agencies throughout Massachusetts to eliminate health disparities, and it released a report that documented widespread disparities in health across the state. Many of the grant recipients were DAN member organizations.

An Act Eliminating Racial and Ethnic Health Disparities in the Commonwealth includes the following provisions:[12]

- **Office of Health Equity**
  The Office of Health Equity will be housed under the State Executive Office of Health and Human Services and will be advised by the Health Disparities Council that was created by Chapter 58. The Office of Health Equity will be responsible for coordinating all disparities elimination efforts in the state. The office will publish annual disparities impact statements, put out annual disparities report cards on regional progress, set evaluation standards, determine reimbursement rates for medical translation services, and manage programmatic provisions of the legislation.

- **Community Agency Grants Program**
  The Office of Health Equity will run a grant program to support efforts by community-based health agencies to eliminate disparities in underserved populations.

- **Data Collection Coordination**
  The Office of Health Equity may choose to publish best standards on data collection. The office will also coordinate the data collection, analysis, and dissemination activities of all parties involved in the collection of data on patient race, ethnicity, and language spoken.

- **Community Health Workers**
  The Office of Health Equity will run a competitive grant program to provide funds to hospitals, community health centers, and nonprofit community organizations to employ community health workers to better the health of the communities in which they live.

- **Community-Based Participatory Research**
  The Office of Health Equity will run a competitive grant program to provide funding for research partnerships between community-based organizations and academic researchers focusing on the elimination of health disparities.

- **Health Literacy**

  The Office of Health Equity will designate and disseminate best practice guidelines for the creation of health-related materials and literature drawing on federal and public health standards. The goal is to make materials widely accessible to patients, including those with limited educational attainment and limited English proficiency.

- **Workforce Development**

  The Office of Health Equity will establish a council to coordinate state, local, and private-sector efforts to establish health care workforce diversity and development.

- **Environmental Justice**

  A statewide community health index will be created to demonstrate which communities suffer from high rates of death and illness based on a weighted set of primary and secondary indicators of health outcomes.

- **Chronic Disease Management**

  A chronic disease management program will be established in the Department of Public Health to begin wellness education of individuals who suffer from chronic disease.

Lessons Learned

The goals and ideas put forth by the DAN are far from unique. There was already an enormous amount of work going on around the elimination of health disparities prior

---

DAN ADVOCACY ACTIVITIES

Legislative Advocacy

The DAN has advocated broadly throughout the legislature, and it has rallied black and Latino caucus members in support of the legislation. In October 2007, the DAN hosted the first ever health disparities advocacy event at the State House. The event drew more than 350 attendees from around the state, many of whom were consumers of color. What's more, representatives from 42 legislative offices came to the event. One highlight of the program was a surprise visit from Governor Patrick, who affirmed his commitment to eliminating health disparities. After the event, DAN members and consumers visited those legislative offices to further educate members of the State House about the bill and about health disparities.

(Continues)

Budget Advocacy

The DAN has begun working on another approach to accomplishing the objectives of the original legislation. Because the bill has remained in committee since early 2007, the DAN has looked to the governor's budget as a vehicle for moving specific pieces of the legislation. In November 2007, the DAN submitted a request to the governor's office to include in his budget funding for many of the programs contained in the bill, such as the creation of an Office of Health Equity that would administer grant programs for community health agencies, community health workers, and community-based participatory research. The budget is expected to be released in late January 2008, and while this approach would provide immediate funding for some much-needed programs, the DAN will also continue to pursue its legislative strategy so that these programs become codified into state law.

WHAT ABOUT THE SOCIAL AND ENVIRONMENTAL DETERMINANTS OF HEALTH?

Racial and ethnic health disparities are not simply the result of disparities in access to quality health care. Rather, they result from complex social, economic, and environmental factors. After the initial brainstorming process, the DAN work group realized that many of the provisions it had discussed were focused on the structural and social determinants of health, as opposed to reforms of the health care system itself. For example, there were several provisions that addressed access to healthy grocers, green space, healthy school lunches, and safe places for children to play within communities of color.

These provisions presented a challenge because the legislation was meant to be a "health care bill," and the group did not want to weaken the bill by spreading its focus too broadly. At the same time, the group did not want to develop a bill that focused solely on health care and ignored the larger environmental determinants of health—such a bill would send the message that policies that improve quality and access in the health care system are all that is needed to eliminate racial and ethnic health disparities.

Although the majority of the legislation was focused on reforms within the health care system, DAN advocates wanted to acknowledge the deeper roots of health disparities. They therefore included a provision that requires the Office of Health Equity to monitor social and environmental effects on health. The Office of Health Equity will be responsible for addressing these effects by engaging other state agencies, such as the housing and transportation authorities, and by generating annual disparities impact statements on the major initiatives of these agencies. The Boston Public Health Commission, a member of the DAN, also filed smaller-scale legislation on environmental equity issues (this legislation is currently on hold), while the DAN made a concerted effort to emphasize the important role of environmental and social justice in the effort to eliminate disparities.

to the convening of the DAN. Yet there is much to learn from the experiences of minority health advocates in Massachusetts as they move forward with their health disparities legislation.

- **Framing the Message and Getting Media Coverage**

  The DAN showed that by harnessing the political and media attention surrounding health care expansions and reforms, it is possible to successfully elevate a disparities policy agenda to the state level. As more and more states begin to develop their own health care expansion legislation, disparities advocates must be ready to seize any political opportunities that can move the issue of health disparities into the public eye. The DAN advocates were successful because they were able to use all of the public attention surrounding health reform in Massachusetts, as well as the media attention garnered by the mayor's Disparities Project, to successfully raise awareness about health disparities and simultaneously put forth a substantive strategy aimed at eliminating those disparities.

  At the same time, the DAN has faced some challenges in framing its message and fully addressing the disparities issue within the context of Chapter 58. For example, some stakeholders believe that the issue of health disparities is only an issue of health access, and they point to health care reform as the key to eliminating all disparities. The DAN continues to work hard to educate those audiences about factors other than access that can lead to health disparities, such as the social determinants of health and unequal treatment.

  Another challenge the DAN faces is garnering media attention that examines the nuances of disparities in health and health care. The group has found that when media outlets do report on health disparities, they tend to focus only on overt discrimination in health care settings, and they have less interest in investigating or reporting on the full breadth of disparities issues, or on possible solutions. Media outlets have also shown a bit of fatigue when it comes to reporting on health care issues, including disparities.

- **Coalition Strategy and Engagement**

  The collaboration among multiple groups coming together to write legislation focused on disparities demonstrated the political power that advocates can wield through collective action. The DAN has been a powerful driving force because it uses the knowledge, skills, resources, and political power that its diverse membership brings to the table. By drawing on these resources and developing a defined agenda, the DAN was well-positioned to raise awareness about health disparities and to move its policy agenda forward.

Advocates need to keep in mind that raising awareness around disparities is only part of the battle. Introducing disparities legislation is not easy, which is why collaboration is so crucial. Minority health advocates must look beyond their traditional partners and seek out diverse partners. For instance, advocates who are working to expand health coverage may not be the same advocates who are trying to eliminate disparities and ensure health equity. However, these issues must go hand in hand: Conversations around expanding access are a natural place to discuss efforts to ensure health care equity and reduce disparities. Each of these individual efforts can be strengthened through collaboration.

The DAN has found it challenging to diversify its membership so that it includes more community-based minority organizations. Many of these groups have prioritized other important issues (such as housing, violence, or education) over disparities, and they have not had the capacity to join the DAN table. Disparities advocates can address some of these hurdles by taking a few practical steps, such as holding meetings outside normal business hours to attract interested volunteers, helping groups make the connection between larger social issues and policy goals and their own organizational goals, as well as recognizing that not all groups can devote staff time to health disparities efforts.

- **Policy and Advocacy**
Another important lesson to be learned from the experiences of the DAN is that policy is a tool that minority health advocates can, and should, use to help eliminate health disparities. Advocates who work on minority health issues often focus on direct service or disease-specific issues in their efforts to reduce disparities in health and health care. Although these efforts are critical, it is important to look beyond these traditional strategies and use policy as a tool to help eliminate health disparities. Health disparities are a systemic problem that calls for systemic answers, and policy can serve as a powerful tool to address inequities. While the political and historical circumstances in Massachusetts were clearly unique factors that allowed the disparities legislation to advance, minority health advocates can still look to the state as a model for legislation in their own states.

Finally, although expansion of health coverage can be a useful vehicle from which to address disparities in health care access and quality, because disparities are rooted in many sources, advocates must not limit their work to health care access. Disparities result from a wide range of factors, including social and cultural circumstances, physical environment, and individual socioeconomic status. With so many factors contributing to health disparities, it is unrealistic to believe that disparities can be eradicated by pursuing narrow policies that focus solely on health care access and delivery systems. To combat the complex ways in which health disparities affect minorities, advocates must explore program and policy solutions that can address the environmental and social determinants of disparities as well.

Health disparities are complex. By looking at success stories like that of the DAN, minority health advocates can develop and strengthen tools that will eliminate racial and ethnic health disparities and, ultimately, lead to health equity.

Endnotes

[1]Kate Meyers, *Racial and Ethnic Health Disparities* (Oakland, CA: Kaiser Permanente Institute for Health Policy, 2007), available online at http://www.kpihp.org/publications/docs/disparities_highlights.pdf.

[2]Jack Geiger, "Race and Health Care—An American Dilemma?", *New England Journal of Medicine* 335 (September 1996): 815–816.

[3]ACT! Affordable Care Today, *Previous Health Care Reform Efforts in MA: A Brief Background* (Boston: Health Care for All, 2006), available online at http://www.hcfama.org/act/reform101.asp.

[4]Boston Public Health Commission, *The Disparities Project: Year One Report* (Boston: Boston Public Health Commission, 2007), available online at http://www.bphc.org/reports/pdfs_222.pdf.

[5]Ibid.

[6]ACT! Affordable Care Today, *Chapter 58 of the Acts of 2006: An Act Providing Access to Affordable, Quality, Accountable Health Care* (Boston: Health Care for All, 2006), available online at http://www.hcfama.org/act/mahealthreformlaw.asp.

[7]Health Care for All, *Disparities Action Network* (Boston: Health Care for All, 2006), available online at http://www.hcfama.org/index.cfm?fuseaction=page.viewPage&pageID=516.

[8]Camille Watson, "Policy and Advocacy Efforts to Eliminate Disparities in Massachusetts," presentation at Universal and Equal: Ensuring Health Equity in Health Reform meeting, March 9, 2007.

[9]Health Care for All, op cit.

[10]Camille Watson, op cit.

[11]Ibid.

[12]Health Care for All, *An Act Eliminating Racial and Ethnic Health Disparities in the Commonwealth: Summary* (Boston: Health Care for All, 2006), available online at http://www.hcfama.org/_uploads/documents/live/Dan%20Summary.pdf.

Source: Families USA. (2008). Reproduced with permission.

GLOSSARY TERMS

best practices   cultural competence
telemedicine

REFERENCES

Families USA. (2008). *Confronting disparities while reforming health care: A look at Massachusetts.* Retrieved October 27, 2008, from http://www.familiesusa.org/assets/pdfs/ma-disparities-case-study.pdf

McDonough, J. E., Gibbs, B. K., Scott-Harris, J. L., Kronebusch, K., Navarro, A. M., & Taylor, K. (2004). A state policy agenda to eliminate racial and ethnic health disparities. The Commonwealth Fund.

National CASA Association. (1995–1996, Fall/Winter). *What is cultural competence? Family Resource Coalition's report.* Retrieved April 20, 2008, from http://www.casanet.org/library/culture/competence.htm

Office of Minority Health & Health Disparities. (2007). *Eliminating racial & ethnic health disparities.* Retrieved April 6, 2008, from http://www.cdc.gov/omhd/About/disparities.htm

Smedley, B. D., Stith, A. Y., & Nelson, A. R. (Eds) (2003). *Unequal treatment: Confronting racial and ethnic disparities in health care.* Washington, DC: The National Academies Press.

PHOTO CREDITS

Chapter Opener

,   © Andresr/ShutterStock, Inc.

Unless otherwise indicated, all photographs and illustrations are under copyright of Jones and Bartlett Publishers, LLC, or have been provided by the author(s).

Index